AMERICAN LITERATURE:
A CRITICAL SURVEY

VOLUME TWO

AMERICAN LITERATURE:
A CRITICAL SURVEY

Thomas Daniel Young
Ronald Edward Fine

Vanderbilt University

AMERICAN BOOK COMPANY

Copyright Acknowledgment

Grateful acknowledgment is made to the following publishers and individuals for permission to reprint material which is in copyright or of which they are the authorized publishers.

FARRAR, STRAUS AND GIROUX, INC.: for selections of T. S. Eliot's poetry from *On Poetry and Poets* as they appear in S. E. Hyman's "Poetry and Criticism: T. S. Eliot."

HARCOURT, BRACE AND WORLD, INC.: for excerpts from the poetry of T. S. Eliot and from his essay, "Tradition and the Individual Talent," quoted in the essays by Stanley Edgar Hyman, William Moynihan and Everett A. Gillis, copyright 1932, 1936, 1950, by Harcourt, Brace & World, Inc.; copyright 1960, 1964, by T. S. Eliot.

HOLT, RINEHART AND WINSTON, INC.: from *Complete Poems of Robert Frost,* and *In the Clearing.* Copyright 1923, 1928, 1947 by Holt, Rinehart and Winston, Inc. Copyright 1936, 1951, © 1956, 1962 by Robert Frost.

RANDOM HOUSE, INC. AND ALFRED A. KNOPF, INC.: for excerpts from William Faulkner's works as they are quoted in the essays by Slatoff and Backman; for excerpts from *The Divine Comedy,* translated by Lawrence Grant White, as they appear in this text. Quotations from The Collected Poems of Wallace Stevens are protected by copyright and have been reprinted by special permission of Alfred A. Knopf, Inc.

MR. ALFRED RICE: for the poem by Ernest Hemingway, "Champs d'Honneur," which appears in the E. M. Halliday article.

CHARLES SCRIBNER'S SONS: Quotations from the works of Ernest Hemingway which appear in this book are protected by copyright and have been reprinted by special permission of Charles Scribner's Sons. Quotations from *The Great Gatsby* by F. Scott Fitzgerald (Copyright 1925 Charles Scribner's Sons; renewal copyright 1953 Frances Scott Fitzgerald Lanahan) are reprinted by special permission of Charles Scribner's Sons.

PREFACE

While we, as English professors, demand that our undergraduate students write literary reports, we seldom actually expose them to the writings of established literary critics. The limitations of the average college library coupled with the inherent problem of selecting representative critiques make it very difficult to put in the hands of the undergraduate those tools from which he would most profit. The essays in this collection present a carefully integrated set of formal critiques of the major figures of American literature in two volumes. The essays are arranged by author and genre—Volume I, from Taylor to Melville, Volume II, from Whitman to Faulkner. Some of them are concerned with the author's basic pattern of thought, some with influences, some with sources and the author's use of these sources. Others treat form at the level of style, sentence by sentence, while still others concentrate upon the larger questions of structure or literary genre. We have included critical perspectives ranging from the general to the microscopic—from discussions of trends such as puritanism and naturalism to closely worked analyses of, for example, Emerson's creative methodology and the color imagery of Emily Dickinson. Our criteria for selection have been excellence and variety. The essays, then, function on two levels—they both inform and serve as models of the variety of contemporary literary criticism.

The footnotes found in the original selections have been retained in their entirety, and in a very few instances, we have supplemented them with additional notes. Our intention is to allow the student the full exercise of his energies and imagination. We hope he will be prompted to utilize these methods in new critical situations.

In addition to offering the student a broad spectrum of critical methodologies, these essays supply considerable information concerning the works, life and times of the figures under discussion. We believe that even the brightest reader will have his critical acumen sharpened and directed by the information and methodology presented.

Brief headnotes introducing each author provide the biographical essentials. In order to aid the student in further study, we have included a guide to methods of research in American literary study, an annotated general bibliography, and selected bibliographies for each author.

We trust that these essays sufficiently indicate the existing variety of critical approaches to American literature.

In every stage in the preparation of these volumes we have been ably assisted by Mary K. Fine, Robert Neill, and Don Harrell. For their many suggestions in the selection of essays—as well as for their help in preparing the bibliographies, securing permissions, typing, and proofreading—we are most grateful.

Thomas Daniel Young
Ronald Edward Fine

CONTENTS

AMERICAN LITERATURE:
A CRITICAL
SURVEY

WALT WHITMAN

1819-1892

Walt Whitman was born into a barely literate farming family on rural Long Island, New York. In 1823 they moved to the growing seaside community of Brooklyn, where Whitman attended public school until he was eleven years old. After this, his only formal education, he held different jobs including apprentice typesetter in 1831 and schoolmaster in various villages on Long Island, 1836-1841. But his interests were turning more toward writing and journalism, and after numerous contributions to New York and Brooklyn publications as writer, reporter, and editor, he achieved, at the precocious age of twenty-seven, the position of editor of the Brooklyn *Daily Eagle* (1846-1848).

During his journalistic period he was actively committed to local and national political concerns, and it was a political issue which forced his resignation from the *Eagle* in 1848. Whitman supported the Free Soil Party, while the owners of the newspaper favored a compromise with southern Democrats. At this point Whitman's American travels began. As a reporter for the New Orleans *Crescent,* he embarked with his younger brother, Jeff, upon an arduous journey across country to Cairo, Illinois, and down the Mississippi to New Orleans. When he returned to Brooklyn a half-year later, his growing sense of involvement with the democratic national destiny, and his concern over the Mexican War and the slavery issue, combined with his aesthetic sensibility. The consequent fusion of these energies was pre-

1

sented to the public on July 4, 1855, with the first printing of *Leaves of Grass*. Although not widely popular, the volume earned the instantaneous praise of Emerson, and soon, the respect of Thoreau, Bronson Alcott, and other important figures in America and in Europe.

Throughout Whitman's life *Leaves of Grass* continued to grow and change; the additions and revisions resulted in nine editions of the poem during Whitman's lifetime.

His heroic service as volunteer nurse in the Civil War left him subject to malaria. The lingering effects of this disease combined with a paralytic stroke to bring him to his death in 1892.

MAIN DRIFTS IN WHITMAN'S POETRY*

FLOYD STOVALL

It is a mistake to suppose, as some do, that Whitman had reached his full stature as a poet in 1855. On the contrary, he was at that time, notwithstanding his thirty-six years, relatively immature. His experiences during the next decade developed his character and his poetic faculties enormously. This development, as it is reflected in *Leaves of Grass,* is both progressive and, in the main, consistent. It falls roughly into three periods, the approximate limits of which are determined by the composition of four major poems, here designated key-poems because they are most characteristic of their respective periods. In this essay I shall attempt to trace this development through Whitman's characteristic ideas and to indicate the main drifts or persistent tendencies according to which these ideas were modified.

I

The first period covers the time approximately from 1855 to 1859, and its key-poem is "Song of Myself." In its amorphous structure

* The conclusions of this essay are based on what I conceive to be the predominant trends of thought in Whitman's poetry. I think of them as a kind of majority report. A minority report might also be made, with other conclusions. I see no hope of reducing Whitman's thought to a system harmonious in every detail. *Leaves of Grass* is like the Bible in this, that its general import is of more significance to the intelligent reader than any particuar text, however emphatic, that may appear to be inconsistent with it.

and in its arrogant tone it exemplifies the dominant principle it incorporates: the love of freedom. Concurrently with the announcement of this principle, Whitman began more noticeably to follow it in his personal conduct. "I wear my hat as I please," he boasts, "indoors or out."[1] He approves what he calls the pioneer's "boundless impatience of restraint,"[2] and declares himself the spokesman of those "whom laws, theories, conventions can never master."[3]

For this assumption of freedom he finds both authority and example in nature. "I see that the elementary laws never apologize," he remarks.[4] He sometimes envies the animals because he attributes their apparent happiness to their freedom from social responsibility.

> They do not lie awake in the dark and weep for their sins,
> They do not make me sick discussing their duty to God
>
> .   .   .   .
>
> Not one is respectable or unhappy over the whole earth.[5]

Nature, he believes, is not only free, but also good. "How perfect is the earth," he exclaims, "and the minutest thing upon it!"[6] He imagines that man might be similarly perfect if he were similarly free, and resolves therefore to throw away man-made standards and habits and to live according to nature:

> I harbor for good or bad, I permit to speak at every hazard,
> Nature without check with original energy.[7]

Since all natural things are equally good, the body is for him as much an object of reverence as the soul, and every part and function of the body shares in this holiness. "Not an inch," he says, "nor a

---

[1] "Song of Myself" (1855), p. 40. All references are to Emory Holloway's Inclusive Edition of *Leaves of Grass* (New York, 1925). The date in parentheses, except when otherwise specified, is the date of first publication as given by Holloway.

[2] "Song of the Broad-Axe" (1856), p. 157.

[3] "By Blue Ontario's Shore" (1856), p. 297.

[4] "Song of Myself," p. 40.

[5] *Ibid.*, p. 50. Original reading, "industrious" for "unhappy," p. 570.

[6] "To Think of Time" (1855), p. 368.

[7] "Song of Myself," p. 24.

particle of an inch is vile, and none shall be less familiar than the rest."[8] For him, therefore, sex and the entire process of generation were suitable and necessary subjects for poetry. By segregating his sex poems, however, and publishing them under the separate title of *Children of Adam,*[9] he ascribed to sex a special importance that is hardly normal in nature. This overemphasis was due, I think, not mainly to what Professor Bliss Perry calls Whitman's "endeavor to express the spirit in terms of the flesh,"[10] but rather to his effort to find in the cloisters of the spirit a sanctuary for the flesh after it has sinned against some moral law that persists in the conscience long after the mind has repudiated it. When the flesh offends the spirit, the mind seeks to make peace by asserting the identity of body and soul, as Whitman did in these poems.[11] It may be that his theory of the sanctity of sex was a consequence of previous sexual indulgence. When the period of indulgence was definitely passed, the theory, being no longer useful as a defense of conduct, became dormant except as it was recalled to justify the early poems.

That the sexual frankness of *Children of Adam* was not intended merely to illustrate a theory but expressed the inherent sensuality of Whitman's nature is apparent from the fact that sensual ideas and images unconnected with sex appear frequently in his verse, and in the most unexpected places. "I believe in the flesh and the appetites," he avers.[12] His images often seem inappropriate, as in these lines describing an attractive personality:

> Toward the fluid and attaching character exudes the sweat
>   of the love of young and old,
>
> .   .   .   .
>
> Toward it heaves the shuddering longing ache of contact.[13]

Some lines are nothing short of disgusting; for example,

> The scent of these arm-pits aroma finer than prayer.[14]

[8] *Ibid.,* p. 26.
[9] Though these poems were not given this group title until 1860, they properly belong to the first period; several were published in 1855 and 1856.
[10] *Walt Whitman: His Life and Work,* p. 80.
[11] "I Sing the Body Electric" (1855), p. 79.
[12] "Song of Myself," p. 44.
[13] "Song of the Open Road" (1856), p. 128.
[14] "Song of Myself," p. 45.

In a description of the dawn otherwise free of association with sex, we find the following figure of speech:

> Something I cannot see puts upward libidinous prongs,
> Seas of bright juice suffuse heaven.[15]

Not only was Whitman a sensualist, but he was also at this period of his life primarily a materialist. It is true that he proclaims himself the poet of the soul as well as the poet of the body,[16] and asserts that the spiritual is equally true with the material,[17] yet the tone and subject matter of his poetry do not bear out these statements. In theory he was the poet of the soul, but in fact he was as yet the poet of the body almost exclusively. The supernatural he held of no account;[18] and though he said, "I know I am deathless,"[19] he also said that immortality was no more wonderful than eyesight or any other fact in nature,[20] thus indicating the materialistic basis of his conception of immortality. He was, in fact, as nearly pure pantheist as anything else. Identity, as he conceived it, pertains to the body only:

> I too had been struck from the float forever held in solution,
> I too had receiv'd identity by my body,
> That I was I knew was of my body, and what I should be I
>   knew I should be of my body.[21]

Nothing remains of this identity after death except what is absorbed in nature. Thus he writes at the close of the "Song of Myself":

> I bequeath myself to the dirt to grow from the grass I love,
> If you want me again look for me under your boot-soles.[22]

Since everything in nature is perfect in its time and place, Whitman accepted his own world as the best possible world under the circumstances. "I will show," he declares, "that there is no imper-

---

[15] "Song of Myself," p. 46.
[16] *Ibid.,* p. 41.
[17] "With Antecedents" (1860), p. 204.
[18] "Song of Myself," p. 64.
[19] *Ibid.,* p. 40.
[20] "Who Learns My Lesson Complete" (1855), p. 330.
[21] "Crossing Brooklyn Ferry" (1856), p. 136.
[22] "Song of Myself," p. 76.

fection in the present, and can be none in the future."[23] If the world were reduced again to its primordial condition, it would "surely bring up again where we now stand, and surely go as much farther."[24] The human race shares the same blessing of irrepressible progress.[25] This view of the world is closer to the eighteenth-century conception of progress than to the evolutionism of Darwin; for having outgrown the past, Whitman seems to think he can dispense with it and forget it. He examines his inheritance, admires it, then dismisses it to stand in his own place in the present.[26]

For one holding such a philosophy it was easy to be an egotist, and to think himself potentially if not actually superior to his antecedents. Thus he writes,

> I sat studying at the feet of the great masters,
> Now if eligible O that the great masters might return and
> study me.[27]

Again he writes, "I am an acme of things accomplish'd, and I an encloser of things to be."[28] Though his "I" is here typical or generic, it is not always so, as when he writes, "I bathe and admire myself,"[29] or "I dote on myself,"[30] or "I find no sweeter fat than sticks to my own bones."[31] And he confesses, "I know perfectly well my own egotism."[32] In 1858, while preparing for a lecture, he wrote in his notebook: "Washington made free the body of America, for that was first in order. . . . Now comes one who will make free the American soul."[33] Thus he charms more by his honesty than by his modesty.

Whitman was not only an egotist himself, but he would establish a democracy of egotists, himself their poet. "I will effuse egotism . . . I will be the bard of personality," he announces.[34] But

[23] "Starting from Paumanok" (1860), p. 18.
[24] "Song of Myself," p. 70.
[25] *Ibid.*, p. 71.
[26] "Starting from Paumanok," p. 14.
[27] *Ibid.*, p. 14.
[28] "Song of Myself," p. 68.
[29] *Ibid.*, p. 26.
[30] *Ibid.*, p. 45.
[31] *Ibid.*, p. 40.
[32] *Ibid.*, p. 66.
[33] Clifton J. Furness, *Walt Whitman's Workshop*, p. 35.
[34] "Starting from Paumanok," p. 18.

he also proclaims with convincing vehemence, "By God! I will accept nothing which all cannot have their counterpart of on the same terms."[35] This principle of equality was of major importance in Whitman's teaching, but it is hard to see how he could reconcile it with the principle of egotism, or individuality.[36] His desire for equality extended to the offices of government, and he expected to see the day "when qualified mechanics and young men will reach Congress and other official stations, sent in their working costumes, fresh from their benches and tools, and returning to them again with dignity."[37] In his journalistic years before *Leaves of Grass* he had been an active Democrat and states' rights advocate,[38] as well as an equalitarian, and later he became a staunch Lincoln unionist; we may assume, therefore, that his ideas of equalitarianism and individualism were philosophical rather than political.

The effect of this poetry of the first period of *Leaves of Grass* is to exalt the individual man and his physical nature, the poet himself standing as the type. This individual possesses some admirable traits, but is lacking in all those qualities which derive chiefly from social cultivation and self-restraint. He is a splendid animal, but little more. Obviously, then, Whitman had not yet given full expression to his personality. Years afterwards, in the Preface to the edition of 1872, Whitman said that from the beginning of *Leaves of Grass* the religious purpose underlay all others; yet I am of the opinion that if he had such a purpose in 1855 it must have been still only a theory without the support of natural feeling, and hence incapable of affecting his poetry deeply at that time. I can find no slightest trace of a religious purpose in these early poems, unless the joyous and sensuous love of life may be called religious.

II

In the second period of Whitman's poetical development, extending from 1859 to 1865, his barbaric yawp is silenced, and in its place are heard the softer song of love and the melancholy chant of death.

[35] "Song of Myself," p. 44.

[36] In "A Backward Glance o'er Travel'd Roads" (1888) Whitman said he had stressed individuality as a counterpoise to the leveling tendency of democracy. See Holloway's *Leaves of Grass*, p. 532.

[37] Quoted by Furness in *Walt Whitman's Workshop*, p. 81, from a manuscript dated 1856.

[38] See *ibid.*, p. 225.

These themes, illustrated in the key-poems, "Out of the Cradle Endlessly Rocking" and "When Lilacs Last in the Dooryard Bloom'd," which mark the beginning and conclusion respectively of the period, give to it a predominantly elegiac tone. The change from the joyous to the pensive mood, while not completed and confirmed until he had learned to forget himself in the army hospitals at Washington, had its origin probably in some more intimate experience that reached a crisis in 1859. "Out of the Cradle Endlessly Rocking," first published near the close of that year, has all the characteristics of a lament for the loss, by death or permanent separation, of a beloved companion and mistress. It is the first and only true love poem that Whitman ever wrote; this fact in itself gives it special significance. It is, moreover, his first poem that is tragic in tone and that is concerned seriously with death. It is difficult to account for this sudden change in mood except on the supposition of such an emotional upheaval as might be caused by the loss of a lover.

Some justification of this supposition is to be found in Whitman's numerous allusions, both in his poetry and in conversations reported by Horace Traubel, to a serious love entanglement with a woman of the South. On one occasion he told Traubel that he had "sacred, precious memories" of friends in the South;[39] and at another time he spoke of "the one big factor, entanglement (I may almost say tragedy) of my life about which I have not so far talked freely with you."[40] We here see that though Whitman professed to have been intimate with more than one woman he remembers only one as a "big factor" in his life. The word "tragedy" is significant. He promised over and over to tell Traubel this big secret, but never did. So far as this poem is concerned, it does not matter whether or not Whitman had a normal sexual life; it may be, as many believe, that he was "romancing" in his famous letter to Symonds about his six children. Nevertheless he could have felt the agony of a bereaved lover, even as Poe felt it, and out of that agony produced a poem.[41]

[39] Horace Traubel, *Walt Whitman in Camden*, III, 43.
[40] *Ibid.*, II, 543.
[41] Emory Holloway thinks the poem was inspired by the death, shortly before the poem was composed, of a woman whom he loved. See *Walt Whitman: An Interpretation in Narrative*, p. 164.

Clara Barrus, in her recent book *Whitman and Burroughs: Comrades*, seems to think Whitman's story of six children a pathological fabrication (p. 337). Yet

Whether the experience that gave rise to it was real or imaginary, the poem unquestionably reveals a definite modification in the style and subject matter of *Leaves of Grass*. It has an intensity of feeling, a beauty of phrase and rhythm, and a definiteness of structure almost entirely lacking in Whitman's earlier work. In the experience here related he first discovered the true nature and meaning of the songs he should sing. The mocking bird is the symbol of the genius or daemon (spelled *demon* by Whitman) of the poet's soul.

> Demon or bird! (said the boy's soul,)
> Is it indeed toward your mate you sing? or is it really to me?
> For I, that was a child, my tongue's use sleeping, now I have
>   heard you,
> Now in a moment I know what I am for, I awake,
> And already a thousand singers, a thousand songs, clearer,
>   louder and more sorrowful than yours,
> A thousand warbling echoes have started to life within me,
>   never to die.

The child of the poem is perhaps symbolic of the immaturity of the poet of the first *Leaves*. The awakening here described certainly does not refer to his real childhood. Nor do I believe it refers to the original conception of *Leaves of Grass*, for the songs that the bird taught him were all sorrowful, whereas the first *Leaves* were joyous.

The songs are sorrowful because they spring from "unsatisfied love" which "the messenger there arous'd, the fire, the sweet hell within, the unknown want, the destiny of me." How shall this untold want be satisfied, the fire of unfulfilled love be quenched? Surely there is some solution, some solace for this pain, some hope that he can weave into his song. He looks to the sea, symbolic of the mystery of eternity, and pleads for a clue, a key-word, that will help him in his perplexity.

> Whereto answering, the sea
> Delaying not, hurrying not,

---

in a footnote (p. 338) she quotes from a letter from Whitman to Bucke, May 23, 1891, in which he said: "I have two deceased children (young man and woman—illegitimate of course) that I much desired to bury here with me—but have abandoned the plan on account of angry litigation and fuss generally, and disinterment from down South."

Whisper'd me through the night, and very plainly before
daybreak,
Lisp'd to me the low and delicious word death,
And again death, death, death, death,
Hissing melodious, neither like the bird nor like my arous'd
child's heart,
But edging near as privately for me rustling at my feet,
Creeping thence steadily up to my ears and laving me softly
all over,
Death, death, death, death, death.

Death is the consoler, the clue to man's destiny, because it is the
divine complement of human imperfection, through which love is
made complete and immortal. The poignant emotions associated
with this revelation awakened Whitman's latent æsthetic sense, and
he turned away from his former poetry of theory and animal sensation and began to chant the sorrowful songs that now started to
live within him, of which "Out of the Cradle Endlessly Rocking"
was the first.

As a consequence of this awakening there came a change in
Whitman's view of life and nature. The self receded, and the community loomed larger in his view than before. He began to perceive
that the individual cannot escape the law of the group that "all
must have reference to the ensemble of the world."[42] But he attains
this view only after passing through a period of spiritual upheaval
and profound dejection. He who in 1855 was an untamed egotist,
joyous and sensual, has become humble, melancholy, and perplexed.

O baffled, balk'd, bent to the very earth,
Oppress'd with myself that I have dared to open my mouth,
Aware now that amid all that blab whose echoes recoil upon me
I have not once had the least idea who or what I am,
But that before all my arrogant poems the real Me stands yet
untouch'd, untold, altogether unreach'd,
Withdrawn far, mocking me with mock-congratulatory signs and
bows,
With peals of distant ironical laughter at every word I have
written,
Pointing in silence to these songs, and then to the stand beneath.[43]

[42] "Laws for Creations" (1860), p. 324.
[43] "As I Ebb'd with the Ocean of Life" (1860), pp. 216–217.

11

He who was so free, so proud, so wholesome now sees himself (as in a mirror) a slave, diseased, and mentally abased. "Such a result," he cries, "so soon—and from such a beginning!"[44] His optimism is gone; the perfectionist sees the ills of the world—sorrow, pain, cruelty—but he has no remedy:

> All these—all the meanness and agony without end I sitting look
>   out upon,
> See, hear, and am silent.[45]

Having perceived the inadequacy of love and the imperfection of life without the fulfilment of dealth, he began to feel as a reality what at first he had conceived only as a theory; namely, that he was to be the poet of death and the soul as well as of life and the body.

> Give me your tone therefore O death, that I may accord with it,
> Give me yourself, for I see that you belong to me now above all,
>   and are folded inseparably together, you love and death are.[46]

He understands now better than ever the value of companionship, and considers himself especially qualified to be the poet of the love of comrades. "For who but I," he says, "should understand lovers and all their sorrow and joy?"[47] He recognizes two degrees of love. One, a kind of benevolence, which he bestows upon all without condition, he symbolizes by gifts of lilac, pine, moss, laurel, and other herbs and flowers; the other is special, a jealous love which he reserves for those who love as he himself is capable of loving, and its symbol is the calamus root.[48] The peculiar expression of this special love in the *Calamus* poems, which were probably begun in the latter part of 1859,[49] has led some readers of Whitman to suspect him of sexual abnormality; yet it seems to me possible to explain the distinction here referred to without reference to such abnormality. The calamus root was for his intimate friends, the companions of his body, whom he loved with a sense of possession, and of whom

[44] "A Hand-Mirror" (1860), pp. 228–229.
[45] "I Sit and Look Out" (1860), p. 232.
[46] "Scented Herbage of My Breast" (1860), pp. 96–97.
[47] "These I Singing in Spring" (1860), p. 99.
[48] *Ibid.*, pp. 99–100.
[49] See "In Paths Untrodden," p. 95.

he demanded an equally exclusive love; the other symbolic herbs were for the friends whom he reached or hoped to reach through his poems, including the whole world if possible, and who therefore could not all return his affection in kind.

He dreamed of arousing America to engage with him in a crusade to establish throughout the world the institution of the love of comrades as he proclaimed it.[50] Politically, he imagines the world of the future as a democratic hegemony with America in the leading rôle, "a new race dominating previous ones."[51] His enthusiastic support of the North during the Civil War, in spite of some Southern sympathies and ties, was doubtless due to his belief that a victory for the North would advance his own plan to revolutionize society through the love of comrades. To him the North represented the new America, while the South represented the forces of the past. But above all, like Lincoln, he hoped that the union might be maintained.

His benevolent spirit naturally led him to the hospitals instead of the army camp. This move is to be construed as a sign of strength, not of weakness; a weaker man would have become hard and bitter in self-defense against the harrowing scenes he witnessed, but Whitman became more gentle than ever. In fact, as I have already suggested, his hospital experience only completed the emotional development that had commenced in 1859 and that culminated in the full expansion of one of the tenderest and deepest natures ever recorded in the literature of the world. For the second time he is made acquainted with death; this time he is not prostrated as one who suffers an unexpected personal loss, but softened and purified in mind and spirit by the power of sympathy. In the generous service of those who had no means of making an equal return he discovered in himself at last a love which transcended even the love of comrades because it was the love of man. In this situation he found it difficult to play the part of war poet:

> Arous'd and angry, I'd thought to beat the alarum, and urge
> relentless war,

[50] "States," published in 1860, later rejected, though most of its original lines are retained in other poems. See Holloway's *Leaves*, p. 402.
[51] "Starting from Paumanok," p. 22.

> But soon my fingers fail'd me, my face droop'd and I resign'd
> myself,
> To sit by the wounded and soothe them, or silently watch the
> dead.[52]

Though not less firmly convinced than before of the justness of the Northern cause, he finds it difficult to maintain his enthusiasm, for these wounded and dead of whom he writes were both Northern and Southern soldiers, and he had attended them impartially. At the end of the war he comes forth spiritually enriched though saddened. Nothing could be less arrogant or more tender than this brief poem called "Reconciliation":

> Word over all, beautiful as the sky,
> Beautiful that war and all its deeds of carnage must in time be
> utterly lost,
> That the hands of the sisters Death and Night incessantly softly
> wash again, and ever again, this soil'd world;
> For my enemy is dead, a man divine as myself is dead,
> I look where he lies white-faced and still in the coffin—
> I draw near,
> Bend down and touch lightly with my lips the white face in
> the coffin.[53]

As the beginning of the second period of Whitman's poetic development was marked by the composition of the key-poem, "Out of the Cradle Endlessly Rocking," an elegy commemorating the death of one personally beloved, so its close was distinguished by the writing of another key-poem, "When Lilacs Last in the Dooryard Bloom'd," an elegy also, though not merely personal, but representative of a nation's grief at the loss of its friend and hero, Lincoln. Both poems are remarkable for a perfection of form which the poet achieved in no other work. I do not mean that the lines are regular, for they are not; but each poem is an artistic whole, finely proportioned in structure and unified in thought and feeling. Undoubtedly they were struck off under great emotional and imaginative excitement, and I believe that it was this extraordinary excitement and not any meticulous craftsman's labor that accounted for their artistic superiority.

[52] "The Wound-Dresser" (1865), p. 261.
[53] P. 271.

But Whitman could not have written this elegy if he had not previously gone through the various experiences reflected in the poems of this period—poems of friendship, sympathy, suffering, and death in many moods; poems of enthusiasm and pride and partisan fury; poems, at last, of melancholy victory and tender reconciliation. For in Lincoln, somehow, he personified the otherwise incompatible ideals of individualism, democracy, and unionism; and in the poem written in his memory he fused the three great themes of the poetry of this period: love, death, and nationalism. Yet he keeps the tone of the poem personal, avoids the grandiose in style, and throws over all an atmosphere mingled of fresh fields and the solemn and mystic night.

Here as in "Out of the Cradle Endlessly Rocking" a bird is the symbol of the poet's soul, only in this case it is a hermit thrush instead of a mocking bird. Two other symbols are used: the star, standing for Lincoln, and the lilac, standing for enduring love. Though Whitman calls Lincoln "my departing comrade," it is clear that the love here symbolized by the lilac is different from that elsewhere symbolized by the calamus-root. He was not personally acquainted with the President, but he uses the language of friendship because for the moment he is the representative of the bereaved millions who had loved Lincoln as an ideal "big brother," which is the democratic fashion of hero-worship. This broadening of the sentiment of love from a purely personal to a national scope was the result chiefly, though not altogether, of the war and its attendant circumstances. The idea of death, too, is more fully developed in this poem than in the earlier elegy, where it is named as the key to man's "unknown want," but not elucidated. In the Lincoln poem Whitman explicitly states that death is greater than life and joy and love because it brings freedom, comfort, and certainty to the harassed soul, delivering it from the difficulties it faces in the "fathomless universe." In a vision he beholds those who have died, and they are fully at rest.

In structure his poem is much like the conventional elegy, consisting of the two main divisions, the lament for the dead and the consolation. But the manner in which the thrush, which is to sing the consolatory carol of death, is introduced at the beginning and twice thereafter mentioned, yet held in reserve until the end of the section of lamentation, is unlike the conventional elegy and superior to it, because it gives to the poem a greater effect of unity and intensity. Technically speaking, the poem is not without flaw, for it contains some absurd jingles and some flat commonplaces; but, taken as a whole, it is artistically perhaps the finest of Whitman's poems.

III

In the third period of Whitman's development, the period from 1866 to his death, all the principal ideas introduced into *Leaves of Grass* in the second period were retained and expanded. Poems in praise of death led to the making of poems on immortality, which became the dominant theme of this last period. Love, already national in scope, now reached out to include the entire world. The poet grew more conservative, but remained fundamentally a democrat; and from a nationalist he tended more and more to look towards an eventual union of all the nations of the world in politics as well as in commerce and culture. In the poems on death there is an important change in the point of view. Before, he had written as one who mourns the death of a friend, but now he records the thoughts and feelings that arise from the anticipation of his own death.

Though he is now never so terribly depressed as he had been after his first great sorrow and disillusionment in 1859, he is keenly aware of the perpetual struggle by which alone one may hope to release his higher impulses from the lower. In the early *Leaves* he had declared the good and evil of human nature equally acceptable, but now he desires the triumph of the good and pins his faith upon it.

You degradations, you tussle with passions and appetites

.   .   .   .

Ah think not you finally triumph, my real self has yet to come forth,
It shall yet march forth o'ermastering, till all lies beneath me.[54]

The ego of former years, though not dead, is now reduced to the

[54] "Ah Poverties, Wincings, and Sulky Retreats" (1865–6), p. 398.

16

conservative virtue of self-reliance, by which he defends the soul against a world of uncertain values:

> When shows break up what but One's-Self is sure?[55]

Sometimes, too, his religious nature breaks through old reserves of theory and produces a poem, like "The Singer in the Prison,"[56] that for its reverence and tenderness is almost a paradox in *Leaves of Grass*. He is more than ever convinced that his soul's restlessness, "the untold want," can be satisfied only through death;[57] that life, in fact, is the tillage and death the harvest according,[58] the only true life coming after death;[59] and that death is after all but a sleep in camp breaking the forward march of the spirit.[60] He now requires of man an idealism which shall assist him in seeking the good and avoiding the evil, since only the best, the ideal, the divine is worthy of being called God.[61] The body pertains merely to the life of sensation, which can never fulfill the desires of the idealist, for life's mystery baffles him and its struggles beat down his hope.[62]

He is impressed with the evanescence of human life:

> To-day gives place, and fades—the cities, farms, factories fade;
> A muffled sonorous sound, a wailing word is borne through
>   the air for a moment
> Then blank and gone and still, and utterly lost.[63]

Life has meaning only when viewed as a part of God's plan, and the individual has value only as he partakes of the divine character and function. Of his own particular case Whitman writes:

> My three-score years of life summ'd up, and more, and past,
> By any grand ideal tried, intentionless, the whole a nothing,
> And haply yet some drop within God's scheme's ensemble—
>   some wave, or part of wave,
> Like one of yours, ye multitudinous ocean.[64]

---

[55] "Quicksand Years" (1865), p. 374.
[56] "The Singer in the Prison" (1869), p. 316.
[57] "The Untold Want" (1871), p. 415.
[58] "As I Watch'd the Ploughman Ploughing" (1871), p. 378.
[59] "Pensive and Faltering" (1868), p. 378.
[60] "Camps of Green" (1865), p. 414.
[61] "Gods" (1870), p. 229.
[62] "Life" (1888), p. 433.
[63] "Yonnondio" (1887), p. 433.
[64] "By that Long Scan of Waves" (1885), p. 427.

He had thought to solve the problem of life and death by giving them a place in nature, but now he knows they are never solved—

> By each successive age insoluble, pass'd on,
> To ours to-day—and we pass on the same.[65]

Through all the changes of nature nothing is lost or in vain, for all things move imperceptibly through infinite cycles of growth and decay to some ultimate goal, certain yet undiscerned.[66] With all his dreams and his enterprise man cannot hasten this process much, but it is reassuring to Whitman to reflect

> That coursing on, whate'er men's speculations,
> Amid the changing schools, theologies, philosophies,
> And the bawling presentations new and old,
> The round earth's silent vital laws, facts, modes continue.[67]

It is clear that law had now become a more important word than freedom in his philosophy of life. Only the soul dares to be free; it points the way to perfection, but the body, which must abide by the laws that govern the progress of this world, lags behind. Thus death is for the soul a joyful release, frequently compared by Whitman to the launching of a ship for a long-awaited voyage to some wonderful unknown land.

Thus we see that Whitman in old age turned even more definitely to thoughts of the spiritual side of life than poets ordinarily do in old age. It is the more remarkable because of his early materialism. All the forms of the material world, grand as they are, at last seem to him as nothing without the soul, which is more vast, multiform, and puzzling than they.[68] Even his great pride in America is not proof against this change. America's "proudest material civilization," he writes, "must remain in vain" until it attains also a "moral wealth and civilization."[69] She lacks also what he calls the greatest gift of all—the gift of "beauty, health, completion."[70] He

---

[65] "Life and Death" (1888), p. 435.
[66] See "Continuities" (1888), p. 432, and " 'Going Somewhere' " (1887), p. 433.
[67] "The Calming Thought of All" (1888), p. 435.
[68] "Grand is the Seen" (1891), p. 457.
[69] "Thou Mother with Thy Equal Brood" (1872), p. 382.
[70] "With All Thy Gifts" (1876), p. 335.

foresees the day when his beloved land shall have all these—the moral and æsthetic as well as the material accomplishments, all in perfect proportion—but that time is not yet.

As Whitman grew older, his interests and attachments expanded until they became fairly international in scope. This expansion is reflected in his poetry. He wrote a sympathetic and encouraging poem to France in the midst of her tragic ordeal of 1871,[71] and two years later addressed a poem to Spain welcoming her among the nations exalting the flag of liberty.[72] When Brazil abandoned the monarchical for the republican form of government, Whitman, speaking for the United States, greeted her with congratulatory verses.[73] Nor was his interest restricted to movements towards democracy, but extended even to the most conservative nations, as indicated by his admiration for Frederick William, Emperor of Germany, on whose death he wrote a brief poem "mourning a good old man—a faithful shepherd, patriot."[74]

He perceived that America had much to learn from the elder nations, which, in the pride of her youth, she was in danger of forgetting. Thus in 1871 he wrote:

Not to repel or destroy so much as accept, fuse, rehabilitate,
To obey as well as command, to follow more than to lead,
These also are the lessons of our New World;
While how little the New after all, how much the Old, Old
    World![75]

In "Proud Music of the Storm" he records a dream in which he hears, blended in the music of the blast, the songs of all lands and times, which he understands to be for his instruction in the writing of poems "bridging the way from Life to Death."[76] Here he clearly recognizes his obligation to write poetry that shall pertain not to America alone, but to all the world.

"Passage to India" is very likely one of those "poems bridging the

[71] "O Star of France" (1871), p. 331.
[72] "Spain, 1873–1874," p. 400.
[73] "A Christmas Greeting" (1889), p. 450.
[74] "The Dead Emperor" (1888), p. 450.
[75] "Song of the Exposition" (1871), p. 166.
[76] See pp. 337–342. Composed, according to Holloway, in 1868. First published in 1871.

way from Life to Death" that had been "vaguely wafted" to him in his dream.[77] The poem was inspired, however, by two material achievements: the opening of the Suez Canal and the completion of the Union Pacific Railroad. These two improvements made India and the Orient commercially accessible to Europe and America as they had never been before.

This is the key-poem of Whitman's third and last period. Since it did not appear at the beginning of that period, but rather sums up and fuses most of the themes of his later poetry, I have reserved it for final analysis. Though inferior in form to the two elegies, perhaps, it is in my opinion the most profound and characteristic work of his life.

"Passage to India" has a three-fold meaning, physical, intellectual, and spiritual. In the first place, it celebrates the physical union of the nations of the earth. Life began, the poet presumes, somewhere in Asia, possibly in India itself. Thence man spread eastward and westward until the two movements came together in America, and so completed the circle of the earth. The American nation, therefore, may expect to become the greatest in the world, being the culmination of a long process of political and economic evolution:

> Lands found and nations born, thou born America,
> For purpose vast, man's long probation fill'd,
> Thou rondure of the world at last accomplish'd.

From this physical union of East and West there should follow eventually an intellectual union. Indeed, such a union is essential to the fulfilment of the vast purpose he assigns to America,

> For what is the present after all but a growth out of the past?

In the development of the ideal man the marvels of modern science will do much, but not all. The Western mind must also hold commerce with the mind of the East, and returning to the place of its origin, recover what has been lost in its long progress; it must return

> To reason's early paradise,
> Back, back to wisdom's birth, to innocent intuitions,
> Again with fair creation.

[77] See pp. 343–351. Composed, according to Holloway, in 1868. First published in 1871.

20

But even more than for the body and the mind, India has food for the soul of man, and it too must return "to the realms of budding bibles," to the "teeming spiritual darkness" in search of an answer to its eternal questions: *"Wherefore unsatisfied soul? and Whither O mocking life?"* After the world shall have been thus unified, the true poet shall arrive, "the true son of God shall come singing his songs." Then indeed,

> All these hearts as of fretted children shall be sooth'd,
> . . . . . the secret shall be told,

. . . . .

> The whole earth, this cold, impassive, voiceless earth, shall be
>   completely justified,
> Trinitas divine shall be gloriously accomplish'd and compacted
>   by the true son of God, the poet,
> (He shall indeed pass the straits and conquer the mountains,
> He shall double the cape of Good Hope to some purpose,)
> Nature and Man shall be disjoin'd and diffused no more,
> The true son of God shall absolutely fuse them.

Man's long search for an all-water passage to India is made to typify the soul's long and baffled search for truth and for God, and the discoverer is the type of the poet who plumbs the depths of the spiritual universe. For the soul, then, this voyage is a passage to more than India—

> Passage to you, your shores, ye aged fierce enigmas!
> Passage to you, to mastership of you, ye strangling problems!
> You, strew'd with the wrecks of skeletons, that, living,
>   never reach'd you.

And as the body and mind return for completion to the place of their origin, to India and the East, so the soul must return for completion to the place of its origin in God.

> Reckoning ahead O soul, when thou, the time achiev'd,
> The seas all cross'd weather'd the capes, the voyage done,
> Surrounded, copest, frontest God, yieldest, the aim attain'd,
> As fill'd with friendship, love complete, the Elder Brother found,
> The Younger melts in fondness in his arms.

21

This is a far cry from the egotism, sensuality, and materialism of "Song of Myself." And yet there is nothing in "Passage to India" that is not consistent with the basic character and promise of that earlier poem. One emphasizes the spiritual side of man's nature, the other the material. There has been no radical change, but only development through experience. In *Leaves of Grass*, as Whitman often explained, he attempted to express his own personality. Necessarily, then, the character of his poems altered with the alteration in his personality under the stress of circumstance. Hence it would be a mistake to judge his achievement by the early poems only, when he was spiritually and emotionally immature, or by the poems of his old age, after his poetic faculty had passed the summit of its power, which, in my opinion, is reached in "Passage to India." Rather should we estimate his value by his best work, which was mostly completed within the decade from 1859 to 1869.

In concluding this essay I repeat that I attempt to indicate only the main drifts in Whitman's thought and feeling as they are revealed in *Leaves of Grass*. These main drifts covered most of the interests of human life and thought in the America of the nineteenth century. Some of the more important of them may be summarized as follows: (1) in politics, the drift from individualism to nationalism, with strong tendencies toward internationalism; (2) in general philosophy, the drift from love of freedom towards love of law; and (3) in religion, the drift from materialistic pantheism towards a highly spiritualized idealism. The direction of his development is also apparent in the changing themes that dominate his poetry from time to time. In the first period of the *Leaves* he was moved to poetic activity almost exclusively by his interest in life, especially life as sensation and spectacle. In the second period he was moved chiefly by the thought of death, and in the third period by the hope of immortality. The extent of his progress is clearly shown in his changing view of love as it is illustrated in the four key-poems of *Leaves of Grass*. Of these, the "Song of Myself" celebrates man's self-love and arrogant pride in the possession of all life's material blessings, whereas the other three are concerned with unselfish love as manifested in some relation to death. "Out of the Cradle Endlessly Rocking" describes how death by intensifying makes pure the love of man for woman; "When Lilacs Last in the Dooryard Bloom'd" shows how death may exalt and consecrate the love of man for his fellowman; and "Passage to India" reveals how in death the love of man for God is consummated and brought to fruition. These key-poems therefore mark the progress of a special personality, incorrectly supposed by Whitman to be typical, from youth to old age, and from love of self to love of God.

Editor's Note: "Main Drifts in Whitman's Poetry" is reprinted, with permission of Floyd Stovall and the Duke University Press, from *American Literature*, IV (1932), pp. 3–22.

Before his retirement in July, 1967, Professor Stovall was Edgar Allan Poe Professor of English at the University of Virginia. His numerous publications include *Walt Whitman* (American Writers Series, American Book Co.), *Eight American Authors: A Review of Research and Criticism, American Idealism,* and (editor of) *The Poems of Edgar Allan Poe.*

THE FUNDAMENTAL
METRICAL PRINCIPLE
IN WHITMAN'S POETRY

SCULLEY BRADLEY

"The world," wrote John Burroughs,[1] "always has trouble with its primary men, or with the men who have any primary gifts. . . . The idols of an age are nearly always secondary men: they break no new ground. . . . The primary men disturb us. . . ." According to this standard Whitman's claim to primary rank as an artist is established by seventy-five years of controversy among critics of his verse. Even to this day no general agreement has been reached concerning the exact nature and effect of Whitman's experiments in verse.

Whitman himself realized what a problem his work presented to the critic. "I will certainly elude you," he predicted. He shared with other great artists the instinct to avoid defining himself, knowing that a work of art is indefinable and illimitable in effect. To his notebook he confided the resolve to write "for the five or six grand poets, and the masters of artists. I waste no ink, nor my throat, on the ever-deploying armies of professors, authors, lawyers, teachers and what not. Of them we expect that they be very learned, and nothing more."

Yet the work of the "ever-deploying army" has been ceaseless, and it has contributed to a strengthening of the poet's reputation and to a deeper understanding of his meaning. It would seem that we are now within measurable distance of a satisfactory rationale of Whitman's verse. The general recognition of a fundamental metrical form in his verse will enormously increase the value of Whitman to his readers.

We can at once discard many of the theories advanced in the past

---

[1] *Whitman* (Boston, 1904), pp. 22–23.

and still maintained by certain critics: that he was an artist "by a sort of divine accident" and "equally pleased with himself when . . . he was not an artist or poet at all . . .;[2] that he wrote Ossianic or "prose-poetry";[3] that his line is a sort of "ruined blank-verse";[4] that he substituted for vocalic accent the "pitch-glides of prose";[5] and that he merely wrote in balanced logical units.[6] That the last two theories are in the direction of the truth we shall see. It seems also clear that the many critics who have found the basis for Whitman's verse in oratory[7] or in Hebrew poetry as translated in the English Bible[8] have suggested fundamental principles.

Yet as a rule these writers have confined themselves either to generalizations or to a study of Whitman's obvious use of logical balance and parallelism. No explanation of the rhythmical regularity in his verse, except that accompanied by logical recurrence, has been attempted. Yet it must be clear to any sensitive reader of *Leaves of Grass* that the principle of regularity is operative even when it is not induced by return or repetition of a phrase. Almost no attention has been given to the insistent question: what is the fundamental principle of rhythm or meter which Whitman substituted for syllable-counting in his lines; by what means is this rhythm indicated; how general was his practice of it? I believe it can be shown that the poet employed without deviation the same principle throughout, and that this is the most primitive and persistent characteristic of English poetic rhythm, rather than a new development from prose rhythms.

This view is based upon a fundamental consideration concerning

[2] John Bailey, *Walt Whitman* (London, 1926), p. 83.

[3] Bliss Perry, *Walt Whitman* (Boston, 1906), pp. 84–86.

[4] *Ibid.*, p. 82.

[5] Fred N. Scott, "A Note on Whitman's Rhythm," *J. E. G. P.*, VII, 134–153 (1908).

[6] Basil De Selincourt, *Walt Whitman: A Critical Study* (London, 1914), pp. 96-97.

[7] See George R. Carpenter, *Walt Whitman* (New York, 1909), pp. 42–43; Thomas B. Harned, "Walt Whitman and Oratory," *Complete Writings* (10 vols., New York, 1902), *Prose IV; H. B. Binns, A Life of Walt Whitman* (London, 1905), p. 98; Clifton J. Furness, *Walt Whitman's Workshop* (Cambridge, Mass., 1928), p. 27; Jean Catel, *Rhythme et langage dans l'édition des "Leaves of Grass," 1855* (Montpellier, 1930).

[8] See Perry, *op. cit.*, pp. 86 and 96; De Selincourt, *op. cit., passim;* A. N. Wiley, "Reiterative Devices in *Leaves of Grass*," *American Literature*, I, 161–170 (May, 1929); Gay W. Allen, *American Prosody* (New York, 1935), "Walt Whitman."

rhythm and meter. It is universally accepted that all speech, whether prose or poetry, has rhythm; that the emotional and imaginative speech of poetry tends toward regularity; and that meter is a highly regulated, patterned or predictable rhythmic recurrence. What has divided the prosodists and frequently puzzled the poets, is the question, *What recurs?* What is the essential rhythmic index of our poetry? Are we to think of a patterned recurrence of long and short syllables as the foundation of meter, or is it rather the regulation of a principal stress or beat, occurring at regular intervals of time? Every historian and critic of English poetry is aware of the enormous importance of this fundamental problem. On the surface, the question appears very simple, yet it has been the cause of continuous disagreement among critics and prosodists.

The beginning of the confusion in the case of Whitman, may be traceable to the poet's practice, so natural to a revolutionist, in over-estimating the completeness of his revolt. One would think, from certain of his statements, that he had embraced artistic anarchy and lawlessness. "Many trouble themselves about conforming to laws. A great poet is followed by laws—they conform to him."[9] To a generation bred on the idea that conventional, syllabic meter was the absolute outward sign of the inward grace of poetry, Whitman's determined stand against the usual meters, which he likened to "lulling piano-tunes,"[10] his reiterated intention "to let nature speak without check, with original energy," seemed an artistic indecency. Most of his readers—indeed, even most of the critics—were too little acquainted with the true nature and history of English rhythm to recognize, beneath the disguise of innovation, the rugged face of a well-known English ancient.

Again and again Whitman explained his substitute for what he considered arbitrary meter, and affirmed that his rhythmical device was closer to nature. "The truest and greatest poetry, (*while subtly and necessarily always rhythmic,* and distinguishable easily enough) can never again, in the English language, be expressed in arbitrary metre," he declared in *Collect*. He had made a personal memorandum recalling that he had learned the trick of his rhythm by "spouting" Homer and Shakespeare to the waves of the sea.[11] In an

[9] *Complete Writings* (1902), VI, 39.
[10] "To a Certain Civilian," *Leaves of Grass* (Incl. ed.), p. 272.
[11] Furness, *op. cit.*, p. 28.

unpublished preface, quoted by Bliss Perry,[12] occurs the statement that his lines are apparently "lawless at first perusal, although on closer examination a certain regularity appears, like the recurrence of lesser and larger waves on the sea-shore, rolling in without intermission, and fitfully rising and falling."[13] Burroughs,[14] in his artist's rapport with the spirit of nature, saw that Whitman's rejection of "the old forms," as he called them, was "only equivalent to the abandonment of vestments, sacraments and rituals in religion, and relying solely on the spontaneous motions of the spirit," and Trent[15] pointed out that the rhythm of Whitman's verses was unlike either prose rhythm in general or the rhythm of Whitman's prose in particular. Yet the old error, that Whitman's rhythm is derived from prose, persisted, and is shown in Bliss Perry's completely mistaken analysis.[16] The most entirely satisfactory clue to his prosody was given in the very beginning by the poet himself, in the Preface to the 1855 edition of *Leaves of Grass:* "The rhyme and uniformity of perfect poems show the free growth of metrical laws and bud from them as unerringly and loosely as lilacs or roses on a bush, and take shapes as compact as the shapes of chestnuts and oranges and melons and pears, and shed the perfume impalpable to form."[17]

The poet was not expressing a completely new and original ideal, although he acted upon it perhaps more fully than any previous artist had done. The same principle had been inherent in much of the theory which actuated the earlier romantic movement. Coleridge might have been speaking directly for Whitman in his lecture on "Shakespeare, a Poet Generally" when, in praise of Shakespeare's freedom of form, he made his distinction between "mechanic" and "organic" form. The latter was the mark of truly original greatness. "The form is mechanic," he wrote, "when on any given material we impress a pre-determined form, not necessarily arising out of the properties of the material;—as when to a mass of wet clay we give

[12] *Op. cit.,* p. 207.

[13] An extension of this illustration occurs in Horace Traubel, *With Walt Whitman in Camden,* I, 414–415.

[14] "Walt Whitman and His Art," *Poet Lore,* VI, 64 (Feb., 1894).

[15] W. P. Trent, *A History of American Literature* (New York, 1903), p. 494.

[16] *Op. cit.,* pp. 81–96, *passim.*

[17] See, for a similar statement, *In Re Walt Whitman,* ed. Traubel, Bucke and Harned (Philadelphia, 1893), p. 16.

whatever shape we wish it to retain when hardened. The organic form, on the other hand, is innate; it shapes, as it develops, itself from within, and the fulness of its development is one and the same with the perfection of its outward form. Such as the life is, such is the form. Nature, the prime genial artist, inexhaustible in diverse powers, is equally inexhaustible in forms;—each exterior is the physiognomy of the being within—its true image reflected and thrown out from the concave mirror;—and even such is the appropriate excellence of her chosen poet. . . ." This seems to express completely the ideal which Whitman practiced so steadily to perfect in the form of his verse.

That the organic theory of composition had influenced Whitman[18] profoundly is shown by a study of the rhythm of his individual lines. Perhaps even more strikingly it is demonstrated by an analysis of the longer sections of composition which he substituted for more conventional and traditional stanzas. Although he nowhere speaks of his artistic devices as being "organic," he continuously refers to them as being based upon nature itself. It seems clear that the critical principle, originating in the rise of romanticism in Germany, had somehow reached Whitman. It is unlikely that he had derived it directly from such German critics as Herder, Schelling, or Goethe, although his notes refer to the reading of works of Goethe and Friedrich Schlegel. However, the organic theory had such a wide currency in romanticism that the quest for an immediate source is not perhaps necessary. To seek no further, Whitman must have become well aware of this critical attitude in the work of Emerson, Carlyle, and Coleridge, with which he was familiar.

To achieve this impalpable subtlety of form, this rhythmic shape of nature, required endless rewriting and revision, both in manuscript and between successive editions. Every close student of Whitman's manuscripts and of the variorum readings has perceived the poet's increasing sensitiveness to a rhythmical principle. That this principle was rooted in the very nature of English speech, and had been employed in English poetry, especially in popular poetry, con-

---

[18] Since this article was written, Mr. Fred W. Lorch has published an article, "Thoreau and the Organic Principle in Poetry," *PMLA*, LIII, 286–302 (March, 1938), in which is given an interesting account of the manner in which identical influences operated in the case of Thoreau.

tinuously since the Old English period, is the fact that seems to have escaped critical attention.

It has been pointed out that so much emphasis has been laid upon the classical ancestry of our English prosody that criticism has frequently lost sight of the earlier and very strong Germanic and Old English ancestry. The classical system employed a rhythm based on the inherent quantity, long or short, contained in the syllables of words. But the English language largely lacked from the beginning, and subsequently lost entirely, the fixed quantities which rendered the classical system rational. Old English poetry did not, and could not, regulate itself by counting syllables. Quantity was felt as the duration of time elapsing between stresses, and this elapsed time was a relatively fixed interval throughout the entire extent of any composition. Between stresses the number of unstressed syllables was variable. Such a verse as the following, in which the number of syllables between principal stresses varies from one to four, is not unusual:

Ic þaet hogode þa ic on holm gestah[19]

What is not generally recognized is that the prosodic principles represented by that line have survived throughout the history of our poetry. The amount of freedom in respect to syllabic regularity in the poetry of various periods of English poetry bears direct relationship to the strength or weakness of classicism at the time. From the beginning of the romantic movement onward, freedom in respect to syllabic regularity has increased, partly as a result of the influence of the popular ballad, in which the Old English tendency persisted strongly.[20] Walt Whitman's verse merely marked an extreme instance of the general evolution. Unfortunately for the reception of *Leaves of Grass,* most critics and prosodists have been of the classical school. Even so clear an exposition as that of T. S. Omond[21] of the freedom in English meter resulting from the compromise between

---

[19] *Beowulf,* l. 632.

[20] An interesting analysis of this influence of ballad meters on modern technique of verse is made in George R. Stewart, Jr., *Modern Metrical Technique as Illustrated by Ballad Meter (1700–1922)* (New York, 1922).

[21] *A Study of Metre* (London, repub. 1920).

the Old English and the classical prosody, has been lost sight of by recent writers.

In connection with this entire question it is interesting first to observe that Whitman obviously intended his lines to be read aloud; that he wrote for the ear and not for the eye. This, of course, should be true of all poetry. Yet one observes in English poetry through the ages that the more "popular" it is, or the more closely connected with an oral tradition, the more prevalent is the tendency to discard the counting of syllables and to regulate rhythm by the interval of elapsed time between stresses—what Mr. Omond conveniently calls the "period." The first evidence of Whitman's determination to appeal to the ear rather than to the eye, lies in his discarding the verse or line whose length was arbitrarily fixed by predetermined metrical pattern and writing in the unit of the logical clause or sentence. He realized, as Mr. Erskine pointed out,[22] that English readers in oral reading had in large measure ceased to observe line-ends or terminal caesurae in verse unless they represented logical pauses. In his desire to be as natural as possible, therefore, Whitman usually constructed his lines as logical units. It is obvious, however, that the rhythm of such lines is clearly self-conscious, and that, both in respect to rhythm and to length, these verses generally conform to the organic principle as expressed by Coleridge—"such as the life is, such is the form."

Perhaps the connection of such a line with the long tradition of English nonsyllabic, or "periodic," rhythm will be made clearer by the following lines, listed in chronological order, and chosen almost at random from an anthology of standard authors:

Metudes miltse þeah þe he modcearig

Wanderer, 1.2.

Were beth they that biforen us weren

Ubi Sunt, anon. c. 1350.

O father, father, draw your dam!

There's either a mermaid or a milk-white swan!

Binnorie, old ballad.

[22] John Erskine, "A Note on Walt Whitman's Prosody," *Studies in Philology,* XX, 336–344 (July, 1923).

⏑　´⏑　⏑　´　　⏑　´⏑　´
If hosen and shoon thou gavest nane
　⏑　´　⏑　⏑　´　⏑　⏑　´　´
The whinnies shall prick thee to the bare bane

> "A Lyke-wake Dirge,"
> *anon. c.* 1475.

　⏑　⏑´　⏑　⏑´　´
Come away, come away death,
⏑　⏑　´　´　⏑　´⏑　⏑　´
And in sad cypress let me be laid.

> Shakespeare, 1599.

　´　　´　⏑　´
Toll for the brave,
⏑　　´　　⏑　´　⏑
The brave that are no more,

> Cowper, 1782.

´　⏑　´　⏑　⏑　⏑　´⏑
This—all this—was in the olden
　´　´　⏑´
Time long ago.

> Poe,
> "The Haunted Palace," 1839.

´⏑　　´　⏑　⏑　´　⏑　´　⏑⏑　´⏑　´⏑　　⏑　´
I must down to the seas again, to the lonely sea and the sky,
⏑　´⏑´　⏑⏑　´　´　⏑⏑　´⏑　´　⏑　´
And all I ask is a tall ship and a star to steer her by.

> Masefield, c. 1901.

It is obvious that such lines as these are not made by counting so many syllables to a foot. And although Whitman's lines are also marked by other devices, such as parallelism, which these examples do not manifest, they are none the less rhythmically based on the same principle of periodicity. Once the period or interval in such a line has been established, the words beat their own time for the verse and establish not only the pattern, but the logical and emotional subtleties which the poet intended. This is an important consideration, for the poet can convey his complete meaning only by his rhythm, which it is therefore necessary for the reader to apprehend exactly.

In his feeling for naturalness of rhythm Whitman also developed another principle already inherent from early times in English poetry and speech. It becomes apparent to the attentive reader of Whitman, especially when reading aloud, that in a great many cases the stress does not fall sharply on a single vowel, but is distributed along the word, or a pair of words, or even a short phrase. This is

31

the familiar phenomenon of the hovering accent, and the reader will find it illustrated above in the second line from the ballad "Binnorie," where the accentual impulse "glides" over the entire adjective "milk-white." Mr. Fred N. Scott called attention to this characteristic in Whitman years ago,[23] but he erroneously supposed that what he calls the "pitch-glide" of prose was the only source for such a practice, when as a matter of fact the phenomenon is inherent in the nature of our English speech, whether prose or verse.

It is difficult to read *Leaves of Grass* without the employment of the hovering accent; it is interesting to note how a sense of naturalness and colloquial ease immediately results when this phenomenon of our speech is allowed to function. A typical example is found in the four-stress couplet:[24]

Which of the young men does she like the best?

Ah the homeliest of them is beautiful to her.

If one reads that second line without the "glide," and with strong vocalic accent on the words "them" and "her" the quality and emotional sense are changed, and the line, indeed, becomes jocose instead of pathetic.

Examples could be multiplied to show that Whitman wrote invariably, at his best, in this nonsyllabic meter. Perhaps the proposition is one which each reader will have to test for himself. The present writer can only say that he has found it to be true, in repeated readings of *Leaves of Grass,* except in the very small number of lines in which the conventional syllabic meter appears to survive, perhaps accidentally. A few verses, selected because they manifest such a variety of metrical patterns, will illustrate the general characteristics of Whitman's rhythm:

To behold the day-break!

The little light fades the immense and diaphanous shadows,

[23] Scott, *op. cit.*

[24] "Song of Myself," Sec. II, ll. 6–7, Inclusive ed., p. 32.

The air tastes good to my palate.

Dazzling and tremendous how quick the sunrise would kill me,
If I could not now and always send sunrise out of me.

I am he who tauntingly compels men, women, nations,
Crying, leap from your seats and contend for your lives!

Whispers of heavenly death murmur'd I hear,
Labial gossip of night, sibilant chorals,
Footsteps gently ascending, mystical breezes wafted soft and
low. . . .

It is a fact, of course, that the reading of Whitman's lines, or of any meter not based on syllable-counting, requires a greater degree of participation on the part of the reader than does the reading of syllabic verse. That fact did not trouble the poet—on the contrary, such participation by the reader was precisely what he wished to achieve. Once the conception is established of the rhythm as a succession of equal time-intervals marked *either* by vocalic stress or by hovering accent, the reading becomes a natural and simple process. For example, De Selincourt, whose work has much to recommend it, failed[25] to grasp the basic rhythmic principle. He scans the following pair of lines[26] as of six and four stresses. Actually, they constitute a pair in seven stresses, a favorite length with Whitman; and each line is divided by a caesura into two sections of three and four stresses respectively:

A child said *what is the grass?* fetching it to me
with full hands;

[25] *Op. cit.*, see, e.g., p. 71.
[26] "Song of Myself," Sec. 6, Inclusive ed., p. 28.

33

How could I answer the child? I do not know what it is

any more than he.

The passage above when scanned by periods reveals a highly developed meter. Each line of a couplet of seven-stress verse is broken by medial caesura at precisely the same point, after the third stress. The rhythmic equivalence between the two lines is striking, and it is not caused by either logical recurrence or the iteration of identical phrases. This purely rhythmic patterning is quite as characteristic of Whitman's writing as the logical balance. It has not apparently been studied by previous writers, some of whom have given valuable data regarding the reiterative parallelism of Whitman's logic. De Selincourt noted the logical balance in 1914.[27] N. A. Wiley[28] later made an exhaustive study of 10,500 lines of *Leaves of Grass* to discover that some form of logical reiteration such as epanaphora (initial) or epanalepsis (within the line) occurred in more than 40 per cent of the lines. Such studies have demonstrated the logical parallelism of Whitman and have established an inescapable consideration in the comprehension of Whitman's poetics, but it is insufficient to stop there, with De Selincourt's[29] summary: "The identity of the lines in metrical poetry is an identity of pattern. The identity of the lines in *Leaves of Grass* is an identity of substance." For in the majority of the lines of Whitman, which are not brought into equivalence by repetition of substance and phrases, there is still the equivalence of a rhythm regulated by a periodicity of stress so uniformly measured as to constitute a true "meter." It is a device capable of infinite subtlety, and we must understand it fully in order to appreciate the extent of the poet's craftsmanship.

The organic principle, so powerfully operative in Whitman's poetic line, is even more fundamental to his conception of the longer units—the stanzas and odic sections which are so readily perceptible to the eye. It is true that large portions of his poetry, generally those in which the material itself is of a more pedestrian quality, seem to have an organization no more complex than the

[27] *Op. cit.,* pp. 96–97.
[28] "Reiterative Devices in *Leaves of Grass*," *American Literature,* I, 161–170 (May, 1929).
[29] *Op. cit.,* p. 97.

line-balance, which has already been briefly illustrated. In such passages there frequently is no attempt to build beyond the limits of the single line; or at most, two or three successive lines will be bound together by an arrangement of component rhythmic groups. But where Whitman's material takes wings, and his imagination begins really to soar, we find much larger units, which impress the reader with their organic quality and manifest an obvious unity of form which even the casual reader feels without analysis. These passages rise from the text and take palpable forms with sharp outlines, and substantial, purposeful patterns. The poet has discarded end rime, but obviously he has substituted a more subtle device for controlling his utterance to the shape of his intention. This characteristic is so pronounced and so clearly associated with the greatest of the poet's passages, that numerous attempts have been made to define it. The consensus of opinion has been that such passages are devised on the principle of logical parallelism, borrowed from the English Bible. It becomes apparent on closer examination that this assumption will not satisfactorily explain these longer flights. In the light of the rhythmic principle just discussed, one finds that the organized rhythmic recurrence is even more fundamental and more universally applied than logical parallelism, not only in the single line, but in longer passages as well.

I do not presume to reject the hypothesis that Whitman, to whom the English Bible was as native as the air of Long Island, frequently employed, in the construction of his larger units, a parallelism and balance of ideas possibly derived from Hebrew poetry. This theory is all the more convincing when one reflects that the English translators employed precisely the same sort of rhythm—periodic instead of syllabic—to which I have drawn attention. Yet more remarkable still is the rhythmical balance through which the poet achieved pattern in stanzas, both long and short, and frequently gave to entire poems a beautiful homogeneity and integrity of construction, even when logical parallelism is reduced to a minimum, or absent altogether.

To understand this clearly it is perhaps necessary to recall the sort of logical construction, similar to that of Bible poetry, which previous writers have illustrated. Perhaps the most careful study is that of Mr. Gay W. Allen in his *American Prosody*.[30] It will be

[30] New York, 1935, "Walt Whitman," chap. viii. See also the same writer's "Biblical Analogies for Walt Whitman's Prosody," *Revue Anglo-Américaine*, X, 490–507 (Aug., 1933).

noticed immediately that his conception of Whitman's prosody is based entirely upon logical recurrence—parallelism of thought expressed in parallel construction, and a phonetic recurrence caused solely by repetition of phrases.

Mr. Allen has given valuable attention to Whitman's extensive use of the "envelope," a stanzaic device of biblical prosody in which "the initial line states an idea or a proposition, succeeding lines state parallel thoughts regarding the first line, and the final line states a concluding thought." Frequently the first and last lines are identical, as in "Tears," or equivalent, as in "Quicksand Years." But Mr. Allen, because of his failure to note that the essential rhythm of Whitman's line is caused by something even more fundamental than logical parallelism or phonetic reiteration, does not indicate the amazing subtleties of rhythmic balance to be found in such poems. I could take as examples several scores of poems, but I have selected "Tears"[31] for illustration. To the left of each line I have indicated the number of its stresses. It will be seen that the poem, while a remarkably unified organic whole, contains three logical divisions, of five, three, and five lines, respectively, and that each division has its own organic design within the larger pattern:

3 Tears! tears! tears!

3 In the night, in solitude, tears,

5 On the white shore dripping, dripping, sucked in by the sand,

5 Tears, not a star shining, all dark and desolate,

3 Moist tears from the eyes of a muffled head.

5 O who is that ghost? that form in the dark, with tears?

6 What shapeless lump is that, bent, crouched there on the sand?

5 Streaming tears, sobbing tears, throes, choked with wild cries;

6 O storm, embodied, rising, careering with swift steps along the beach!

[31] Inclusive ed., p. 218.

6 O wild and dismal night storm, with wind—O belching and
   desperate!

8 O shade so sedate and decorous by day, with calm countenance
   and regulated pace,

7 But away at night as you fly, none looking—O then the un-
   loosened ocean

3 Of tears! tears! tears!

I hope it is clear that this poem is like a large wave or breaker
with three crests. The shape of the entire poem may be interpreted
as pyramidal, beginning with a three-stress line, rising to two pin-
nacles of six and eight stresses, and subsiding again to three stresses
in the last line. Similarly, the rhythmic shape of each of the constituent "crests" is pyramidal. The first section of five lines, in which
the rain in the night is likened to tears, announces the pyramid in
the swell and fall through lines of 3, 3, 5, 5, and 3 stress; in the
second, in which the spirit of the world broods over the night, the
initial impulse is paralleled more grandly in the succession of 5, 6
and 5 stress; in the final section, in which the identity of an individual weeper merges with the cosmic woe of nature itself, the full
rhythmic diapason is unloosed in the great cloudhead, or crest, of
6, 6, 8, 7 and 3 stresses. The artistic integrity of this poem should be
clear to anyone who analyzes it rhythmically. When we find similar
technical perfection in poem after poem, we must conclude that it
is the result of consistent artistic purpose. Sometimes the artist's
reach exceeds his grasp, but the great poetic craftsman is always
discernible, groping for the ideal organic expression of his thought.

It should be emphasized that such rhythmic "frames" appear
continually, whether in connection with the "envelope" form or
not; and that similar devices are employed both for the complete
organic outline of the short lyric and as stanzaic structures within
the body of longer poems. Such shorter lyrics are "A Noiseless,
Patient Spider," "Lo, Victress on the Peaks," "A Sight in Camp in
the Daybreak Gray and Dim," "Prayer of Columbus," and many
others, but no two of them are alike in form. One lyric form which
does appear over and over in many variations is presumably based

on the logical construction of the Italian sonnet, having the bipartite arrangement into a forward and backward movement of thought with clearly marked division. "By Broad Potomac's Shore"[32] is a beautiful example of this, divided into sections of seven and five lines, respectively. The analysis by rhythmic line-lengths reveals the same sort of construction as that observed in "Tears" although perhaps less dramatic. Each section of the poem is again pyramidal, ascending to an extended impulse in the middle. Strongly marked medial caesurae accentuate the balance of phrase units in parallel patterns of three, four, and five stresses:

5 By broad Potomac's shore, again old tongue

5 (Still uttering, still ejaculating, canst never cease this babble?)

9 Again old heart so gay, again to you, your sense, the full flush
    spring returning,

9 Again the freshness and the odors, again Virginia's
    summer sky, pellucid blue and silver,

4 Again the forenoon purple of the hills,

6 Again the deathless grass, so noiseless soft and green,

4 Again the blood-red roses blooming.

5 Perfume this book of mine O blood-red roses!

5 Lave subtly with your waters every line Potomac!

8 Give me of you O spring, before I close, to put between its
    pages!

6 O forenoon purple of the hills, before I close, of you!

3 O deathless grass, of you!

A complete analysis of the wide variety of formal devices employed in Whitman's stanzas should no doubt be made. The present

---

[32] *Ibid.*, p. 400.

intention is merely to establish the principle that the balance of his lines in longer units is so striking as to indicate conscious effort. Perhaps it will be sufficient at this point to illustrate several of the patterns which recur most frequently in shorter lyrics. Besides those already analyzed—the balanced stanza of "Tears," and the sonnet-like poem as found in "By Broad Potomac's Shores," there are several other prevailing forms. A single stanza based on the pyramid form is the device most frequently employed in every period of Whitman's writing. In the familiar "Quicksand Years,"[33] for example, we find the simple pyramid, in a poem of six lines. The fourth line is the longest, of nine stresses, the others lead up to and away from it in a pattern of 5-8-8-9-8-5 stresses. Reiterative logic appears in only one instance in this poem. Many interesting variants of the pyramid poem occur. The following, "Lo, Victress on the Peaks,"[34] is typical:

2 Lo, Victress on the peaks,

5 Where thou with mighty brow regarding the world,

5 (The world O Libertad, that vainly conspired against thee,)

6 Out of its countless beleaguering toils, after thwarting them
 all,

4 Dominant, with the dazzling sun around thee,

9 Flauntest now unharmed in immortal soundness and bloom—
 lo, in these hours supreme,

8 No poem proud, I chanting bring to thee, nor mastery's
 rapturous verse,

5 But a cluster containing night's darkness and blood-dripping
 wounds,

2 And psalms of the dead.

In this poem, the four-stress line, the fifth in a nine-line poem, is

---

[33] *Ibid.*, p. 374.
[34] *Ibid.*, p. 273.

both formally and logically the middle of the poem. There are four lines before and four after it. The preceding lines increase in stress-length in stages of 2-5-5 and 6 stresses. The succeeding four lines decrease in length through the stages of 9-8-5 and 2 stresses, the last line of the poem being of the same length as the first. Logically considered, this shorter medial line, "Dominant, with the dazzling sun around thee," marks a moment of emphatic and leisurely reflection, and serves to divide the material roughly into two parts; the first, dealing with the power and victory of the nation; and the concluding four lines, dealing with the nature of the poet's song. Certainly there is a remarkable consistency between the shape of the idea and the shape of the poem.

Another characteristic variation of the pyramid is seen in the tender lyric "Reconciliation,"[35] one of the best known of Whitman's utterances:

4 Word over all, beautiful as the sky,

8 Beautiful that war and all its deeds of carnage must in time
be utterly lost,

12 That the hands of the sisters Death and Night incessantly
softly wash again and ever again this soiled world;

6 For my enemy is dead, a man divine as myself is dead,

6 I look where he lies white-faced and still in the coffin—
I draw near,

6 Bend down and touch lightly with my lips the white face in
the coffin.

In this poem of six lines, the first three, ending in a logical climax, develop the idea of the ultimate banishment of war from the earth. In each of the three lines the emotional intensity increases while the line-lengths mount from four stresses to eight, and twelve respectively. The last three lines, given to quiet, reflective reaction,

[35] *Ibid.*, p. 271.

are all in six stresses. Again we are struck by the appropriateness of the form for the ideas expressed.

The pyramid also appears as Whitman's favorite stanza pattern in extended composition. In a poem of several stanzas the lines of each stanza will be arranged in the conventional pyramidal order, yet no two of the stanzas will have lines of exactly the same length. The remarkable poem, "A Noiseless Patient Spider,"[36] illustrates this form. That the stanza pattern is not a mere convention, however, that the poem is truly organic in the fact that each line takes its length inevitably from the nature of its idea, will be clear to the critical observer:

3 A noiseless patient spider,

5 I marked where on a little promontory it stood isolated,

5 Marked how to explore the vacant vast surrounding,

6 It launched forth filament, filament, filament out of itself,

5 Ever unreeling them, ever tirelessly speeding them.

3 And you O my soul where you stand,

5 Surrounded, detached, in measureless oceans of space,

7 Ceaselessly musing, venturing, throwing, seeking the spheres
    to connect them,

6 Till the bridge you will need be formed, till the ductile anchor
    hold,

6 Till the gossamer thread you fling catch somewhere, O my soul.

As in the case of all Whitman's greatest poems there are other elements in this lyric, besides its rhythmic organization, which evoke respect for his craftsmanship. For example, since earlier mention has been made of the poet's use of logical repetition in similar words, we may note the effects of this device in the last two lines of this poem. Here the two verses, printed as six-stress lines, are in effect broken down into distichs of three stresses by the reiteration

---

[36] *Ibid.*, p. 375.

of the phrases beginning in each case with the words "till the," aided by medial caesurae. Thus the rhythm of three stresses, with which each stanza opens, is subtly returned, with delicate variations, at the very end of the poem, and the circle is completed.

The principles illustrated in these shorter lyrics are found to be operative also in the longer poems. In many poems of medium length, like "Out of the Cradle Endlessly Rocking," "When Lilacs Last in the Dooryard Bloom'd," or the "Prayer of Columbus," there is an obvious, conscious shaping of the entire poem as a unified rhythmic organism, into which the shorter stanzas fall in their inevitable places, always simple, always consistent with the harmony of the whole, yet rich with that variety which comes from the perfect appropriateness of each formal component for the thought that it conveys.

In the longest poems, even, such as "Song of Myself," "Thou Mother with thy Equal Brood," and others, in which the material is usually divided into logical sections of varying lengths depending upon the amount of material to be presented, the balance and return of rhythmic patterns are continuously present and obviously controlled with great skill. Sometimes the form is a very simple arrangement of balanced couplets or reiterative parallelism. At other times a succession of such simple lines will suddenly give way to a passage of very complex rhythmical counter-point. For example, in Section 21 of "Song of Myself," the familiar line, "I am he that walks with the tender and growing night," announces a passage in which subtle patterns are embroidered upon each other in a manner comparable to that of great symphonic music:

5 I am he that walks with the tender and growing night,

5 I call to the earth and sea half-held by the night.

7 Press close bare-bosom'd night—press close magnetic nourishing night!

5 Night of south winds—night of the large few stars!

5 Sill nodding night—mad naked summer night.

4 Smile O voluptuous cool-breath'd earth!

4 Earth of the slumbering and liquid trees!

6 Earth of departed sunset—earth of the mountains misty-topt!

6 Earth of the vitreous pour of the full moon just tinged with

blue!

6 Earth of shine and dark mottling the tide of the river!

7 Earth of the limpid gray of clouds brighter and clearer for my
sake!

6 Far-swooping elbow'd earth—rich apple-blossom'd earth!

3 Smile, for your lover comes.

7 Prodigal, you have given me love—therefore I to you give love!

3 O unspeakable passionate love.

This beautiful passage stands out from Section 21, which it concludes, as a logical unit with organic structure. Its four logical
divisions are carefully balanced as to form. The first and last divisions, each a pair of lines, are logically similar in expressing an initial and final relationship between the poet and the earth. The two
internal sections, of three and eight lines, respectively, are likewise
similar in material, since each is composed of vocative and descriptive expressions concerning the earth. The rhythmic rise and fall of
the lines in the several sections are accomplished by subtle variations of the same pattern, which three times swells to the length of
seven stresses and then subsides sharply. The opening is in a couplet of five stresses. The next section bursts at once into a passionate
line of seven stresses and then falls away into two lines of five
stresses divided into parallel sections by caesurae. The third section,
in eight lines, rises more slowly to its climax in the seven-stress line,
through a succession of lines in 4-4-6-6 and 6 stresses. From the
seven-stress line the falling away is more sharp than before, through
two lines of six and three stresses respectively. The fact that this
six-stress line is broken into two phases of three stresses each by
strong medial caesura sets up an iteration of three beats, which perhaps renders more telling and dramatic the sudden ending of the
passage in the next couplet, with marked decline from a seven-

stress to a three-stress line. Of course it is obvious that these rhythmic characteristics are also aided and emphasized by the logical repetitions in parallel construction.

Occasionally the entire section will be thus organically composed. Section 2 of the "Song of Myself," the magnificent parable of the twenty-ninth bather, is a good example of this:

4 Twenty-eight young men bathe by the shore,

4 Twenty-eight young men and all so friendly;

6 Twenty-eight years of womanly life and all so lonesome.

4 She owns the fine house by the rise of the bank,

6 She hides handsome and richly dressed aft the blinds of the
    window.

4 Which of the young men does she like the best?

4 Ah the homeliest of them is beautiful to her.

4 Where are you off to, lady? for I see you,

6 You splash in the water there, yet stay stock still in your room.

5 Dancing and laughing along the beach came the twenty-ninth
    bather,

5 The rest did not see her, but she saw them and loved them.

6 The beards of the young men glistened with wet, it ran from
    their long hair,

4 Little streams passed all over their bodies.

4 An unseen hand also passed over their bodies,

4 It descended tremblingly from their temples and ribs.

10 The young men float on their backs, their white bellies bulge

to the sun, they do not ask who seizes fast to them,

7 They do not know who puffs and declines with pendant and

bending arch,

4 They do not think whom they souse with spray.

Of the eight sections in this poem, the first and last alone are tercets —the remainder are couplets. The fourth couplet, however, is peculiar: it conveys the climax of the action and is the only one in five stresses. The other couplets are balanced on each side of this climactic couplet; the complete pattern being:

4,4,6—4,6—4,4—4,6—5,5—6,4—4,4—10,7,4

It is apparent that the couplets and tercet before the five stress couplet have the longer line last, and those after this central climax have the shorter line last—another use of the pyramid. The couplet in five stresses, in which the woman consummates her rebellion by running to join the young men in their ocean of life, is clearly set apart by the dissimilarity of its line-length; and the other two isometric couplets, each in four stresses, are carefully balanced in the third position before and after the central five-stressed couplet. Finally, an unmistakable conclusion is given the final tercet by the extraordinary swell of the first two lines into ten and seven feet, respectively. Surely the organic principle is convincingly demonstrated in this remarkable passage. Many others, in all portions of the longer works, are obviously constructed on the same principle.

It would be foolhardy to declare, since we have no direct evidence, that Whitman had rationalized the formal tendencies which I have illustrated, and that he had organized them into a prosody which he consciously followed. It has been said that he avoided, for wise reasons, the concrete declaration of his specific practices. Yet if such formal perfection as I have shown came merely by the exercise of artistic instinct during years of revision and rewriting, then surely that instinct was the mark of a profound artistic genius. In summary there are a few generalizations which it seems important to make. The first is that, whether instinctively or consciously, the poet achieved the aspiration revealed in his prefaces: to shape his words to the exact surface and movement of the spirit in nature or

45

in truth. By 1876 he knew that he had succeeded, when he wrote in the Preface of that year, "My form has strictly grown from my purports and facts, and is the analogy of them." Next it must be noted that the poet did not completely reject any device of the older poetry. He made consistent use of assonance, alliteration, stanza, refrain, return, and even occasional rime.[37] His revolution centered on three things: a new emphasis, to the point of organic use, upon ancient repetitive devices, like epanaphora and epanalepsis; the construction of stanzas and larger units on the basis of rhythmic balance and parallelism; his conscious rejection of syllabic meter in favor of that more ancient and native English meter based on the rhythmic "period" between the stresses.

All of this would have had little point but for the genius by which he was able to transmute his special sense of rhythm into phrases which, as Symonds said,[38] "should exactly suit the matter or the emotion to be expressed. The countless clear and perfect phrases he invented . . . are hung, like golden medals of consummate workmanship . . . in rich clusters over every poem he produced. And, what he aimed at above all, these phrases are redolent of the very spirit of the emotions they suggest, communicate the breadth and largeness of the natural things they indicate, embody the essence of realities in living words which palpitate and burn forever."

Editor's Note: "The Fundamental Metrical Principle in Whitman's Poetry" is reprinted, with the permission of Sculley Bradley and the Duke University Press, from *American Literature,* X (1939), pp. 437–459. This essay is protected by copyright and cannot be reprinted without the consent of the author.

A Professor Emeritus of the English Department of the University of Pennsylvania, Philadelphia, Professor Bradley's extensive contributions to American studies include contributions to *Literary History of the United States* and co-editorship of *The Collected Writings of Walt Whitman,* 12 vols., in progress. He recently published *Reader's Comprehensive Edition of Whitman's Leaves of Grass,* and *A Textual Variorum of Leaves of Grass* is in progress.

[37] See Lois Ware, "Poetic Conventions in *Leaves of Grass,*" *Studies in Philology,* XXVI, 47–57, *passim* (Jan., 1929).

[38] J. A. Symonds, *Walt Whitman: A Study* (London, 1893), p. 150.

THE STRUCTURE OF WALT WHITMAN'S
"SONG OF MYSELF"

CARL F. STRAUCH

Goethe said that a distinguishing mark of the great poet is his ability to build. Architectonics is the word he used. This ability a minor poet does not have; Edgar Allan Poe, for example, can write an exquisite song like "To One in Paradise," but he cannot create a fairly long poem and give it that articulation, that symmetry, that final shaping which elicit our admiration and praise. The difference is brought out never so well as when we set side by side a magnificent success like *Samson Agonistes* and a failure, however glorious in some reaches, like *Endymion*. The one has the finality of solid structure; the other throws up brilliant skyrockets of phrase and image, pyrotechnics that pale into the empyrean. Critics of the Romantic persuasion have not sufficiently remarked the aesthetic pleasure derived from the recognition of structure. They have been too much occupied with the verbal felicity and the glowing aura of short poems like the best of Keats and Shelley. Critics of the Romantic persuasion have been too easily satisfied with long poems that are brilliant failures. They have not demanded structure; and since they have not demanded structure, they have not particularly looked for it.

Baudelaire said that a writer of verse did not deserve the name of poet until, growing in power and clarity, he knew exactly what he was about. The great long poems of the world, whatever the differences otherwise, have this at least in common: they have something to say, and that something is said with clarity, power, and conviction because the poet, whether Sophocles or Milton, Racine or Whitman, brought to the poem a talent for organizing ideas into well-shaped and coherent masses.

"It stands to reason," says one critic, "that Whitman gave much thought to the planning and organizing of his poems."[1] Not enough attention, however, has been paid to the architectonics of Whitman's poems. It is, of course, a commonplace of criticism that "When Lilacs Last in the Dooryard Bloom'd" is the high-water mark of American poetry; and certainly the estimate of this poem is due to more than the exquisite phrasing of powerful emotion. But people have gone to *Leaves of Grass,* as they should, of course, for novel ideas vigorously expressed rather than for an encounter with magnificent structure. Whitman has been a seer, a prophet; he has called people to a new religion.

> It was an experience to hear an elderly man—looking a venerable seer—with absolute abandonment tell how *Leaves of Grass* had meant for him spiritual enlightenment, a new power in life, new joys in a new existence on a plane higher than he had ever hoped to reach. All this with the accompanying physical exaltation expressed by dilated pupils and intensity of utterance that were embarrassing to uninitiated friends. This incident illustrates the type of influence exercised by Whitman on his disciples—a cult of a type such as no other literary man of our generation has been the object. . . .[2]

That Walt Whitman could inspire such loyalty, such faith, was well —was, in fact, marvelous.

But of three methods of approach to the poet, one, it seems to me, offers for the moment the richest returns. Many critics of varying degrees of either hostility or sympathy have dealt with the religion of Whitman. Other students, feeling that his ideas have been sufficiently reviewed, have occupied themselves with certain problems of his life. As this investigation, highly important and certainly interesting, comes to a successful end or degenerates into futile scholarship, it may be both profitable and zestful to shift our attention to the significance of Whitman as an artist—as a creator, for example, of such an admirable long poem as "Song of Myself." Out of the study of the structure of such a poem may arise a new realization of the greatness of this greatest American poet.

[1] Killis Campbell, "The Evolution of Whitman as Artist," *American Literature,* VI, (November, 1934), 256.

[2] Sir William Osler writing about Dr. Bucke in Harvey Cushing's *The Life of Sir William Osler* (Oxford: Clarendon Press, 1925), I, 266.

In submitting "Song of Myself" to analysis, I am at present not particularly interested in various readings, changes, or improvements. The study of these is valuable in estimating any poet; Tennyson, for example, shows us his growth in taste and power by his rejections and improvements, and Whitman's revisions are almost always for the better. But while I recognize the value of such a study, I do not think we need now consider any more than "Song of Myself" as it appears in any good edition of *Leaves of Grass*.[3]

Two other matters must be briefly mentioned before the analysis proceeds. First, I am not at all concerned in this scrutiny of a great philosophic poem with ideas except in their relation to form. There can, consequently, be no discussion of them. Second, and I am aware that mention of this is probably superfluous, there need be no apology to the lovers of Whitman for a piece of schoolroom pedantry. A proper analysis always enhances the richness and the appeal of a work of art.

As a matter of convenience let me immediately put down the results of analysis. There are five large divisions in the poem.

1. Paragraphs 1–18, the Self; mystical interpenetration of the Self with all life and experience
2. Paragraphs 19–25, definition of the Self; identification with the degraded, and transfiguration of it; final merit of Self withheld; silence; end of first half
3. Paragraphs 26–38, life flowing in upon the Self; then evolutionary interpenetration of life
4. Paragraphs 39–41, the Superman
5. Paragraphs 42–52, larger questions of life—religion, faith, God, death; immortality and happiness mystically affirmed

This synopsis will serve as a guide throughout the more elaborate analysis which now proceeds.

To begin, in the first paragraph[4] Whitman announces three important themes: the Self, the identification of Self with others, and "Nature without check with original energy." Transitions in this poem, as in others by Whitman, are clear; the last line of one paragraph frequently suggests the theme, either by way of contrast or

---

[3] Dr. Triggs has given variorum readings in *Leaves of Grass* (ed. Emory Holloway [Doubleday, Doran, 1931]). For convenience' sake all references will be made to this edition.

[4] I shall call the numbered sections of "Song of Myself" paragraphs.

by way of continuation, of the next paragraph. So here. In paragraph two the Self declares its independence of "civilization," which is represented by "houses and rooms." The poet then indulges in a catalogue of the scattered and diverse phenomena of nature and the ecstasies of the Self in nature.

". . . . the song of me rising from bed and meeting the sun." The paragraph concludes with an invitation to others to have this firsthand primary relationship with the universe. We are assured in paragraph three that we are being invited to something worth our attention. The world is still good and productive.

"Clean and sweet is my soul, and clean and sweet is all that is not my soul." Whitman is satisfied; he dances, laughs, and sings. This third paragraph may be characterized as the abundance of nature and the poet's satisfaction with nature. The section ends with the parable of the loving bedfellow and the "baskets cover'd with white towels."

The fourth paragraph introduces a theme of hesitation. The major theme, which has been announced, may be too startling; in its dismissal of the temporal it may be too shocking for most readers. After all, Whitman would ruthlessly tear us out of our social context, friends, dinners, clothes, authors, and the like; so that for a moment he hesitates and balances on the periphery of his ideas, stormy, husky, and brawling, certainly not polite and well mannered. For Whitman our social context is a "game."

Paragraph five shows a marked advance; now the picture of companionship in nature is more vivid than in paragraph two, and here also there is a more emphatic declaration of the basis of the universe than in three. Here Whitman says that "a Kelson of the creation is love." The music of the poem has grown into a larger and nobler mood of acceptance. The symbol of the grass, as the most universal and common and even meanest phenomenon, is employed in paragraph six and leads to the themes of pantheism and immortality. Toward the close of this paragraph Whitman speaks of dying as "different from what any one supposed, and luckier." This theme floods over into paragraph seven, which, like four, marks an important transition. Here the poet emphasizes his universal quality by stating that he passes "death with the dying and birth with the new-wash'd babe." More emphatically than in paragraph three, the universal Self finds all things good; all are "as immortal and fathomless" as he himself. There is here a tentative beginning of the vast catalogue which gets under way in eight and storms through to eighteen, abating only in nineteen with a few iridescent drops. This catalogue is the procession of his mystical interpenetration of all life. "I am there," he says, "I saw the marriage," "I behold the picturesque giant." In paragraph eleven there is the marvelous picture of the twenty-eight young men bathing and of the young woman who "owns the fine house by the rise of the bank." This mystical interpenetration of the universe floods over into paragraph nineteen, a very important transition, in which the impetuosity of the previous paragraphs has largely abated. Whitman is a master of change of pace; here the music is slower; there are fewer instruments.

> This hour I tell things in confidence,
> I might not tell everybody, but will tell you.[5]

So far in this poem there has been only declaration of the Self, nature, love, immortality, and closely allied themes; there has been only invitation to ecstasy; Whitman has audaciously omitted definition or analysis. Now, however, the rhythm, the movement of the music have ceased their tantivy. "Who goes there?" he asks in paragraph twenty. He describes himself. He is "hankering, gross, mystical, nude"; he is a great ego, a representative ego, an ego no prouder than Nature itself—

> I see that the elementary laws never apologize,
> (I reckon I behave no prouder than the level I plant
>   my house by, after all.)[6]

In paragraph twenty-one there is a clear presentation of what Whitman includes under the name of Self: (a) body, (b) soul, (c) good, (d) evil, (e) man, (f) woman. The conclusion of this paragraph is among the most lyrical passages Whitman ever wrote; and the crowning touch to this ecstasy is love.

> Prodigal, you have given me love—therefore I to
>   you give love!
> O unspeakable passionate love.

This lyrical rush surges over into the twenty-second paragraph, in

---

[5] *Leaves of Grass*, p. 39.
[6] *Ibid.*, p. 40.

which, after an apostrophe to the sea, Whitman comes to grips with the meaning of what he has been so variously trying to say. "I moisten the roots of all that has grown," says Whitman, and as the poet of balance he accepts both good and evil. It is because he moistens the roots of all that has grown that Whitman is able to call himself "a kosmos."[7] All students of Whitman know how this audacious term aroused disgust or tickled easily tickled risibilities in various quarters when *Leaves of Grass* was reviewed. But Whitman certainly had a right to the word. Its occurrence is well timed, for it comes immediately after the long catalogue of mystical interpenetration and constitutes another definition of the Self. The word could not have been very well understood had it occurred earlier in the poem; but there was no reason for delaying its use beyond this point or for not employing it at all; it fits admirably into the scheme of the poem in the position it occupies. So well calculated is the artistic and philosophic justness of the word that the cavil of earlier critics must be set down as stupid; today there is no reason for denying to Whitman the highest attributes of the conscious artist, all of whose effects, or certainly the most important of them, are precisely calculated. For, of course, I have no intention of claiming that Whitman is careful of all detail; he is not. But an analysis of "Song of Myself" reveals in him an artist who is conscious of the movement and direction of his ideas, an artist who goes from climax to climax like a god striding mountain peaks.

In linking the word "kosmos" with the clause "I moisten the roots of all that has grown," I have anticipated somewhat. In paragraph twenty-three Whitman accepts reality, materialism, and science. But these, the poet says, are not his dwelling; he but enters them to an area of his dwelling. Then, after opening the twenty-fourth paragraph with the word "kosmos," he gives in a third catalogue his ethical interpenetration of life. Now we have not mere *presence* at a scene, as in the previous interpenetration of life, but a *transfiguration* of life, for Whitman is now assuming the burden of all evil:

> Through me forbidden voices,
> Voices of sexes and lusts, voices veil'd and I remove the veil,
> Voices indecent by me clarified and transfigur'd.[8]

[7] *Ibid.*, p. 43.
[8] *Ibid.*, p. 44.

If Walt Whitman is to "moisten the roots of all that has grown" he must accept all life; accordingly he must identify himself with the manifestations and phenomena that are somewhat less pleasant than the fire of roses or the rush of lovers' kisses. It is interesting to note, however, what some have missed, that he accepts these phenomena "only to lift them up." This interpenetration is highly ethical. It is ethical because life as Whitman conceives it is ethical. He could not accept these phenomena on their own level, because he stands always in a primary relation to the universe, which in its goodness acts as a challenge to him.

> Dazzling and tremendous how quick the sun-rise would kill me,
> If I could not now and always send sun-rise out of me.[9]

But the final merit of the Self cannot be spoken. There is always a mystery; a hush on his lips. In silence the first great half of the poem ends, all instruments mute, the mystical Being quiescent, passive, not storming out upon the world, not identifying itself with all the varied life-forms, but ready to receive into itself the magic flow of life.

The second half of the poem begins with twenty-six. Here instead of expression we have impression—phenomena flowing in. Now that the great and expressing Self is passive, bathing in a flood of impressions, these phenomena are puzzling.

> . . . . I lose my breath,
> Steep'd amid honey'd morphine, my windpipe throttled in
> fakes of death,
> At length let up again to feel the puzzle of puzzles,
> And that we call Being.[10]

In twenty-seven and twenty-eight Whitman records his sensitive reaction to this puzzle, this experience of other existences; and in twenty-nine there is record of the returns, in spite of aches, of this experience—"rich showering rain, and recompense richer afterward." The conclusion at which he arrives as a result of this experience is that "all truths wait in all things." This is preparation for the fifth catalogue, which begins in thirty-one and goes through thirty-eight. This catalogue is different from the other two great and most important catalogues. In eight to eighteen we have mystical interpene-

[9] *Ibid.*, p. 46.
[10] *Ibid.*, p. 48. Paragraph twenty-six is the fourth catalogue.

tration as mere *presence* at a scene; twenty-four gives us an *ethical* interpenetration ending in transfiguration; in the present catalogue we have *evolutionary* interpenetration. For the character of this catalogue we had been prepared in thirty, in which Whitman says, "I believe the soggy clods shall become lovers and lamps." This is interpenetration under space and time, announced in thirty-three, and the range is greater and the identification closer than in eight to eighteen. He is "stucco'd with quadrupeds and birds all over"; he "could turn and live with animals"; he walked "the old hills of Judea with the beautiful gentle God"; he is "the hounded slave." Those who are interested in such a study as this article is pursuing have undoubtedly noticed the close identification of the poet with his subjects. The contrast of this catalogue to that from eight to eighteen is interesting:

8–18	31–38
I lift the gauze	I find I incorporate gneiss
I witness the corpse	I am the man, I suffer'd, I was there
I am there, I help	All these I feel or am
I hunt	I am the hounded slave
I saw the marriage	I am the mash'd fireman
I heard his motions (a runaway slave)	I am an old artillerist
I had him sit next to me at table	Askers embody themselves in me
I behold the picturesque giant	

I think we have assured ourselves that there has been a profound movement from the objective to the subjective. And since the mystical experience in this last catalogue is encompassing and universal under space and time, Walt Whitman justifies the use at the beginning of thirty-nine of the term "the friendly and flowing savage." This phrase is as accurately and as consciously employed as was the word "kosmos." The phrase is pivotal; it not only refers to the immediately preceding evolutionary interpenetration but it also shoots forward into the announcement of the Superman, which is given us in forty and forty-one in the sixth catalogue, another mystical interpenetration of life, this time that of the man of power who can "dilate you with tremendous breath," and "buoy you up." Here is the Superman flowing through life.

> I seize the descending man and raise him with resistless will,
> O despairer, here is my neck,
> By God, you shall not go down! hang your whole weight upon me.[11]

[11] *Ibid.*, p. 63.

The Superman brushes aside the old gods, for god is in all. The growth in the poem can be noted by contrasting the questions asked in paragraph twenty to those asked now in forty-two: "What is a man anyhow? what am I? what are you?" (par. 20). "And what is reason? and what is love? and what is life?" (par. 42). Between these two sets of questions is packed a tremendous experience of life. The more universal questions of forty-two indicate the character of the close of the poem, the flight upward and onward into the Unknown. In paragraph forty-three Whitman tells us his faith is all faiths; and there is a final grand utterance of optimism. From forty-four to the end the poet launches all men and women forward with him into the Unknown. There is the doctrine of progress, from "the huge first Nothing" to "my robust soul."[12] Life promulgates life, he says in forty-five, and all creation ends in God. Eternity is the theme of forty-six; each must have the experience for himself. Whitman is the teacher of athletes, those who will have the experience for themselves. In paragraph forty-seven, which is the seventh catalogue, he tells us that nature and those living naturally understand him. In forty-eight there is appropriate emphasis on the universal presence of God; in the remainder of the poem Whitman goes beyond death and announces eternal life and happiness as central. The poem concludes with the emphasis on the ego, "I stop somewhere waiting for you."

For a recapitulation, let me refer the reader to the synopsis with which I have introduced the analysis.

I do not by any means labor under the delusion that this scrutiny of "Song of Myself" establishes for the first time the fact that Whitman was a conscious artist, careful of the design and direction of his ideas. But such an analysis as has here been prosecuted helps to show how very much Whitman was in command of his materials, how orderly was his march from climax to climax, how effectually he secured the unimpeded progress forward and upward in his ideas by well-placed transitional passages and even single words which gather into themselves the whole meaning of large sections of the poem. That he was not the most meticulous and refined artist is rather obvious; and I should acquiesce in Mr. Santayana's judgment that there is an "absence of any principle of selection,"[13] if that

[12] *Ibid.*, pp. 68–69.
[13] George Santayana, *Interpretations of Poetry and Religion* (New York: Scribner, 1900), p. 181.

stricture were limited to the catalogues, the materials for which are gathered without the selective principle the absence of which Mr. Santayana feels. But this judgment carries with it a wholesale indictment to which in defense of Whitman one may be permitted to reply that Mr. Santayana was overwhelmed by the abundance of a poet who had taken all life for his theme and from it had made a wide but representative selection after his own manner. Overwhelmed by this abundance and perhaps fatigued and bored by the rich catalogues, Mr. Santayana entirely missed the magnificent and consciously directed structure of such a poem as "Song of Myself"; otherwise he could not have delivered himself of the opinion that there is in Whitman's poetry an abundance of detail without organization.[14] The obvious inaccuracy of such a judgment is undoubtedly the result of an impatience with a poetry that appeared chaotic, and the consequent failure to examine any one poem to discover either a presence or an absence of organization. That "Song of Myself" is an artistically organized poem, this analysis, I think, has sufficiently demonstrated.

But I have no argument with an essay that was written many years ago and which people will condemn or praise as their sympathies toward either Santayana or Whitman move them. One can only deplore the inaccuracy of one of our greatest critics; for it is obvious that in spite of occasional indifference to relatively unimportant details, Whitman is one of the great artists in poetry.

Editor's Note: "The Structure of Whitman's 'Song of Myself' " is reprinted, with the permission of Carl F. Strauch and the National Council of Teachers of English, from *English Journal,* College Edition, XXVII (1938), 597–607.

A Professor of English at Lehigh University, Professor Strauch has published numerous articles on Hardy, Whitman, Thoreau, Hawthorne, Melville, and especially Emerson. He has edited symposia on American literary figures in the *Emerson Society Quarterly.* He is preparing a study of Emerson's poetry as well as an edition of his poems, which is to be a volume in the *Collected Works* sponsored by the Center for Editions of American Authors.

[14] *Ibid.,* p. 180.

WHITMAN'S "LILACS"
AND THE TRADITION OF
PASTORAL ELEGY

RICHARD P. ADAMS

Whitman liked to picture himself as an innocent, primitive genius whose "barbaric yawp" was prompted by nature, not culture, and whose originality was ignorant of precedents and uncontaminated by book learning. But modern scholars and critics have shown that he and his art are not so simple as they pretend to be. They are products of a well-advanced artistic and literary development. My purpose is to examine one of his best poems, "When Lilacs Last in the Dooryard Bloom'd," in relation to one of the oldest, most highly respected literary traditions in our civilization—that of pastoral elegy. Everyone knows that "Lilacs" is an elegy, and several writers have compared it in a general way to others, such as "Lycidas," "Adonais," and Emerson's "Threnody."[1] George Meyer of Newcomb College has pointed out the relation of "Lilacs" to pastoral elegy in class lectures, and doubtless others have noticed the same relation in various ways. But no one to my knowledge has made a systematic study of it.

This circumstance, which is rather surprising when we think of it, may be a fair indication of the success with which Whitman covered his cultural tracks. But, by my count, out of seventeen devices commonly used in pastoral elegies from Bion to Arnold,[2] seven appear in "Lilacs." They are the announcement that the speaker's

[1] H. S. Canby, *Walt Whitman* (Boston, 1943), p. 240; James Thomson, *Walt Whitman* (London, 1910), p. 36; and G. W. Allen, *The Solitary Singer* (New York, 1955), p. 341.

[2] See G. Norlin, "The Conventions of Pastoral Elegy," *AJP*, XXXII (1911), 296–312, and C. G. Osgood's note in *The Works of Edmund Spenser*, ed. E. Greenlaw et al. (*The Minor Poems*, Baltimore, 1943), I, 399.

friend or alter ego is dead and is to be mourned; the sympathetic mourning of nature, with the use of the so-called pathetic fallacy; the placing of flowers on the bier; a notice of the irony of nature's revival of life in the spring, when the dead man must remain dead; the funeral procession with other mourners; the eulogy of the dead man; and the resolution of the poem in some formula of comfort or reconciliation.

The other ten, omitted from "Lilacs," are the dramatic framework; the formula "Where were ye. nymphs?"; the inquiry of friends concerning the cause of the speaker's grief; the account of when and how the man died; Echo's lament; the dead man's biography; the pastoral setting; the use of archaisms; the reference to Aphrodite, Urania, or Clio as the dead man's mother or lover; and the account of the dying speech and death.

From Whitman's point of view these ten omissions can be reduced to only two. The first is an avoidance of the literally pastoral element together with all reference to classical mythology. The second is the elimination of any personal reference to the speaker or the dead man that would tend to keep the poem from being about the death of all men. Neither omission damages the fundamental structure or meaning of the traditional elegy, and neither requires to be explained on grounds of ignorance. The first can be accounted to Whitman's bias in favor of the modern over the ancient, and the second to his carefulness never to celebrate the individual at the expense of the general.

Any theory that depended on an assumption of Whitman's ignorance of the conventions of pastoral elegy would be suspect from the start. He must have known "Lycidas," which embodies nearly all of them.[3] He also knew Shelley and referred to him more than once as one of the greatest of English poets.[4] He claimed that he was not well acquainted with Shelley's works,[5] but he admitted on at least one occasion that he was intensely interested in Shelley and Byron as persons if not as poets.[6] He may have minimized his familiarity with Shelley, in somewhat the same way as he did his early knowl-

---

[3] See J. H. Hanford, "The Pastoral Elegy and Milton's Lycidas," *PMLA*, XXV (1910), 409–446.

[4] See, e.g., *The Complete Writings of Walt Whitman*, ed. H. L. Traubel et al. (New York, 1902), VI, 289, and VII, 23.

[5] H. L. Traubel, *With Walt Whitman in Camden*, II (New York, 1908), 345.

[6] Ibid., IV (Philadelphia, 1953), 452.

edge of Emerson, because he had borrowed more heavily from both writers than he wanted to admit in view of his claims to complete originality. This possibility seems especially strong in connection with the 1855 Preface to *Leaves of Grass,* which has a good deal in common with Shelley's "A Defence of Poetry."[7] Whitman was interested enough to clip the "Hymn to Intellectual Beauty" out of an anthology and "To a Skylark" out of some book, probably before 1855.[8] A priori, it seems unlikely that he would not have read "Adonais" by 1865; and there, as in "Lycidas," he would have found almost all the conventions of pastoral elegy as they appear in the older tradition.[9]

Moreover, there are some remarkably specific resemblances in thought and imagery between "Lilacs" and some of the pastoral elegies, notably "Adonais." According to E. R. Wasserman's recent study, the dominant symbols of "Adonais" are light, which is embodied in a star and which represents life, and moisture, which appears as a mist or cloud and which represents death.[10] Whitman associates a star with the living Lincoln and a cloud with Lincoln's death. The star is the same in both poems, Venus, the evening—and also the morning—star. Venus may be the "day-star" of "Lycidas"; it is certainly the "Hesper-Phosphor" which is Tennyson's final symbol of immortality in "In Memoriam." Its meaning is indicated in the epigraph to "Adonais," an aphorism from Plato which Shelley translated,

> Thou wert the morning star among the living,
>   Ere thy fair light had fled;—
> Now, having died, thou art, as Hesperus, giving
>   New splendour to the dead.   (Barnard, p. 386)

These uses of Venus are in harmony with the oldest associations of pastoral elegy. Venus, as the lover of Adonis in Bion's Lament and in the fertility myth that Bion had in mind, represents the principle of life as well as of love and of the rebirth of nature in the spring.

[7] See Allen, p. 156.

[8] Allen, p. 127; *Complete Writings,* X, 82 (also p. 67 for another clipping on Shelley).

[9] See notes in *Shelley: Selected Poems . . . ,* ed. Ellsworth Barnard (New York, 1944), pp. 386–416.

[10] *"Adonais:* Progressive Revelation as a Poetic Mode," *ELH* XXI (Dec. 1954) , 282, 292.

Whitman may not have been fully aware of these associations, but he knew that the evening star was Venus and that it was also the morning star, and he must have known the story of Venus and Adonis. Milton, Shelley, and Tennyson were so keenly aware of the classical references that even if Whitman did nothing more than borrow their terms he might be said to have incorporated the ancient fertility myth in his poem.

Whitman's thrush in "Lilacs" has a close resemblance to some of Shelley's birds. In "Adonais" "Thy spirit's sister, the lorn nightingale" associates Keats with the bird which in his own great ode is a prime symbol of immortality. In "A Defence of Poetry" Shelley remarks that "A poet is a nightingale who sits in darkness and sings to cheer its own solitude with sweet sounds; his auditors are as men entranced by the melody of an unseen musician, who feel that they are moved and softened, yet know not whence or why." And in the poem Whitman clipped and saved, "To a Skylark," the bird is said to be

> Like a poet hidden
>   In the light of thought,
> Singing hymns unbidden,
>   Till the world is wrought
> To sympathy with hopes and fears it heeded not . . .

Whitman liked to imagine himself, in similar terms, as a singer hidden and alone. He says in "Starting from Paumanok," "Solitary, singing in the West, I strike up for a New World." Addressing the bird in "Out of the Cradle," he says, "O you singer solitary, singing by yourself, projecting me./O solitary me listening, never more shall I cease perpetuating you . . ." The thrush in "Lilacs" is introduced in the same situation:

> In the swamp in secluded recesses,
> A shy and hidden bird is warbling a song,
> Solitary the thrush,
> The hermit withdrawn to himself, avoiding the settlements,
> Sings by himself a song.

In "Adonais" the nightingale is parallel to Echo, who is " a shadow of all sounds," hidden in the mountains, and who "will no more reply to . . . amorous birds," a passage which Shelley borrowed from the Lament for Bion attributed to Moschus. Whitman makes no use of the classical nymph Echo in "Lilacs," but he does speak of "the tallying chant, the echo arous'd in my soul" by the bird's song, which is the substance of his poem.

"Lilacs" is very close to "Adonais" in the use both poets make of the irony of death and the thought or memory of death in the spring. The classical source is again the Lament for Bion: "Ah me, when the mallows wither in the garden, and the green parsley, and the curled tendrils of the anise, on a later day they live again, and spring in another year; but we men, we, the great and mighty, or wise, when once we have died, in hollow earth we sleep, gone down into silence; a right long, and endless, and unawakening sleep."[11] Shelley emphasizes this irony in "Adonais," where he says, "Ah, woe is me! Winter is come and gone,/But grief returns with the revolving year"; and again,

> Nought we know, dies. Shall that alone which knows
> Be as a sword consumed before the sheath
> By sightless lightning?

That is, shall there be conservation of matter and energy, but not of human life? The date of Lincoln's death, 15 April, made a similar emphasis easy and natural in "Lilacs." The lilacs were actually blooming then in Brooklyn, and Whitman remarked later, "By one of those caprices that enter and give tinge to events without being at all a part of them, I find myself always reminded of the great tragedy of that day by the sight and odor of these blossoms. It never fails."[12]
His use of lilacs in the poem is not capricious, but functional:

> Ever-returning spring, trinity sure to me you bring,
> Lilac blooming perennial and drooping star in the west,
> And thought of him I love.

The handling of the irony of death and the memory of death in the spring is not explicit; Whitman lets the juxtaposition of images

[11] *Theocritus, Bion and Moschus,* tr. A. Lang (London, 1932), p 201.
[12] *Complete Writings,* V, 246 (Whitman's lecture on the death of Lincoln, first given in New York, 14 April 1879).

demonstrate it emotionally, or aesthetically, and makes no logical statement about it. But it is the same irony that Shelley found in the Lament for Bion and used in "Adonais."

The reference of lilacs in Whitman's poem is broader than their meaning as representing the rebirth of life in the spring, important as that is. They are also associated more generally, as flowers usually are in the tradition of pastoral elegy, with love. The "heart-shaped leaves" are mentioned three times, and "the perfume strong I love" is related to the leaves before the word "perfume" occurs, twice, in the phrases "what shall my perfume be for the grave of him I love?" and "I'll perfume the grave of him I love." Then the star and "the lilac with mastering odor" hold the speaker back from the attraction of the bird's song until he is joined by "the knowledge of death" and "the thought of death," after which he listens to the song and realizes its meaning and is reconciled. All the major symbols are related in terms of love: the song is of sorrowing love for the dead man, the star is Venus and Venus is the goddess of love, and the lilac is the heart-shaped reminder exuding the mastering odor of love. At the end, as "retrievements out of the night," we are given "Lilac and star and bird twined with the chant of my soul, / There in the fragrant pines and the cedars dusk and dim." So the associated symbols of love remain in the soul of the singer, in the darkness of death, among the "fragrant" trees.

Shelley also systematically relates his major symbols to the theme of love. His Urania seems to be not only the goddess of astronomy, or the Muse of spiritual poetry, but the Uranian Aphrodite as well, the goddess of spiritual love (Barnard, p. 394). Keats is compared, in an apparent echo from "Lamia," to "a pale flower by some sad maiden cherished, / And fed with true-love tears, instead of dew." Even the cloud that seems to connote death in "Adonais" as in "Lilacs" is treated as one of Keats's personified Dreams, who, weeping for love of him, melts away. And "the lorn nightingale / Mourns not her mate with such melodious pain" as loving friends mourn Keats—a treatment that may cause us to wonder if Whitman borrowed from "Adonais" for "Out of the Cradle" as well as for "Lilacs."

These parallels indicate only part of the whole relation of "Lilacs" to the tradition of pastoral elegy. The rest involves some questions of metaphysical meaning and aesthetic value that are much more important than any particular resemblances of wording or imagery. The basic requirement imposed on any elegist, what-

ever his place in the tradition, is to effect some kind of reconciliation between men's desire for immortality and their knowledge that
death is inevitable. The pattern by which this requirement is met
is remarkably stable throughout the history of the genre: first, the
fact is given that the speaker's friend is dead; second, various other
friends mourn with the speaker, and he realizes that death must
come to all, including himself; third and last, he is comforted,
usually by some assurance or at least suggestion that his friend is
immortal in spite of death. The speaker's emotion runs from dis-
may and sorrow to despair, and thence to hope and often rejoicing.

But the formulas, particularly that of the final consolation, have
changed at various points in the course of the tradition. In the
fertility cults, comfort was found in the faith that the demigod
would be reborn or revived, that the goddess of fertility would rejoice, and that the earth would be replenished in the spring. In the
classical elegies, there is usually some indication that the speaker's
friend will be given a comparable kind of immortality. Christian
elegies nearly always reinforce this pattern with references to the
Crucifixion and the Resurrection, holding out the hope of immortality and heaven to all men. In "Lycidas" both formulas are used:
the dead man simultaneously becomes an angel in a Christian
heaven and a pagan "genius of the shore." Romantic poets tend to
modify the formula still further and in an even more radical
fashion.

"Adonais" may be said to contain very nearly the whole process
and history of this changing tradition. It begins with an almost
literal incorporation of the classical point of view, as well as the
classical conventions, and then it works almost completely away
from both. Most critics have considered this shift a fault, believing
that Shelley leaves an unresolved inconsistency, or even a contradiction of views. But Wasserman persuasively argues that the structure
of "Adonais" is progressive, in that it presents two inadequate ways
of understanding death and immortality before arriving at the satisfactory one with which it concludes.[13] It may be said in the present
context that Shelley uses the old formulas only to reject them, or,
more precisely, that he aims to transcend the tradition of pastoral
elegy in modern romantic terms. "Adonais" works from the classical
mode and imagery into a romantic statement of the meaning of life,
death, and immortality.

---

[13] Passim; most clearly summarized on p. 295.

This development involves, among other changes, a shift of emphasis away from the allegorical method used in both pagan and Christian elegies, and tends to erase the distinction carefully made by humanist poets between mind and matter, or between the human individual and the universe. Romantic poets emphasize instead the relations, affinities, and sympathies they find or imagine between the individual and the environment, both natural and social. In their organic picture of the universe they see the particular organism, such as the human mind or personality, taking its place as one of many functional elements that make up the unified whole. The life of an individual is one aspect of the life of the universe, and it is included in, rather than set apart from, its environment. Accordingly, birth is often regarded as the emergence of an individuality from the greater life of the universe, and death as a reabsorption of that individuality into the living whole. Life is eternal, whether the individual is or not, and the individual life is one among many particular manifestations of the living universal principle. A romantic elegist can hardly avoid expressing some attitude, opinion, or feeling about this doctrine.

Wordsworth, for example, in the Immortality Ode (although that poem is not formally an elegy) appears to reason that, because we feel our relation to nature more keenly when we are young than when we are old, we must have had a purer relation before birth than afterward to the principle of life that pervades the universe; therefore we may expect to return to the prenatal relation after we die. Shelley, in "Adonais," says that Keats has been assimilated, "made one with Nature," by "the one Spirit's plastic stress" which gives all things their shape and beauty. This Coleridgean use of the word "plastic" indicates that Shelley has in mind the organic metaphor of the romantics, rather than the Platonic archetype, as the structural principle in terms of which Keats's spirit is assimilated to the spirit of nature. The same formula seems to underlie the imagery by means of which Arnold suggests, in "Thyrsis," that because the elm tree remains to assure him of the Scholar-Gypsy's continued life and quest for knowledge, he knows that his friend Clough also lives after death in the same eternal search. Tennyson tries emotionally to reject the formula at one point:

> That each, who seems a separate whole,
> Should move his rounds, and fusing all

> The skirts of self again, should fall
> Remerging in the general Soul,
>
> Is faith as vague as all unsweet . . .

But the final resolution of "In Memoriam" is an acceptance of the idea that the speaker's love is "vaster passion" than before, because his friend's soul in death is "mix'd with God and Nature." In the end "we close with all we loved, / And all we flow from, soul in soul." Emerson, with his usual optimism, finds no difficulty; the "deep Heart" comforts him in "Threnody" by saying that

> When frail Nature can no more,
> Then the Spirit strikes the hour:
> My servant Death, with solving rite,
> Pours finite into infinite.

For Emerson, death is not the end of life but a change that enables life to continue by freeing it from the restrictions of the particular form it happens to take on earth.

Whitman's belief is more complex than Emerson's, but it is equally in the romantic tradition. His plainest expression of it is perhaps the statement in "Crossing Brooklyn Ferry":

> I too had been struck from the float forever held in solution,
> I too had receiv'd identity by my body,
> That I was I knew was of my body, and what I should be I
>   knew I should be of my body.

Whitman is saying, if I understand him correctly, that identity is determined by the organic structure of the material body, which is the soul, which is the form life takes in any individual at any time. Life is eternal, and we are therefore in some sense immortal. As Whitman also says, in "Song of Myself," "All goes onward and outward, nothing collapses, / And to die is different from what any one supposed, and luckier." In "Passage to India" he calls on his soul to "Sail forth—steer for the deep waters only," fearlessly into the seas of death, for "are they not all the seas of God?" Everything to Whitman is life, and all life is divine, and there is nothing to fear from any change, even death. His contemplation of the grass in "Song of Myself" leads him to believe that "there is really no death, / And if ever there was it led forward life, and does not wait at the end to arrest it . . ." In the Preface to the 1876 edition, he reaffirms this conviction, "estimating Death, not at all as the cessation, but as somehow what I feel it must be, the entrance upon by far the greatest part of existence, and something that Life is at least as much for, as it is for itself."

There is no explicit statement in "Lilacs" of Whitman's faith in immortality, but the imagery is consistent with his ideas expressed elsewhere. When the speaker of the elegy has faced and realized the fact of death, as given in the song of the thrush, he finds some comfort in the thought that it is not the dead who suffer but the living. Death is the end of suffering; therefore the song of the thrush and "the tallying song" of the speaker's soul are described as "Victorious song, death's outlet song," and the realization of death is not fearful but reassuring. The very sorrow that the speaker feels and the song expresses is one kind of suffering from which the dead man is free. At the same time the sorrow and the song are both contributions to the remembrance of "the sweetest, wisest soul of all my days and lands," which is a kind of immortality. By a somewhat paradoxical train of logic, the speaker celebrates and rejoices, not by giving up or forgetting his sorrow but by revaluing it. He does not deny the reality of death, does not say, as most elegists do in one way or another, "He is not dead." Rather he says, "He is dead—therefore I rejoice."

The final worth of Whitman's elegy lies more than that of most elegies, I would suggest, in the song itself:

> Song of the bleeding throat,
> Death's outlet song of life, (for well dear brother I know
> If thou wast not granted to sing thou would'st surely die.)

The song, as an expression or "outlet" of feeling, is to some extent a substitute for death in its relief of suffering. But more than that, and more important to us as readers, it is valuable first as a lasting monument to the dead man and our feeling of love and sorrow for him, and second as a beautiful object in its own right, quite aside from any reference to its occasion. The transmutation of experience into art is a mystery that we might not want to explain if we could, but it is a reality we all recognize. In "Lilacs" Whitman made out of death and sorrow and suffering one of the greatest works of literary art thus far produced in America, and by so doing he made himself immortal.

Editor's Note: "Whitman's 'Lilacs' and the Tradition of Pastoral Elegy" by Richard P. Adams is reprinted by permission of the Modern Language Association from *PMLA*, LXXII (1957), 479–487.

Professor Adams is University Chairman of English at Tulane University. He has published numerous essays, primarily on nineteenth and twentieth century American literary figures. He translated, in collaboration with the author, Roger Asselineau, *The Evolution of Walt Whitman*, Vol. I.

EMILY DICKINSON

1830-1886

Emily Dickinson's father, Edward, was a prosperous lawyer and statesman, a member of the state legislature, and once a United States Congressman. His patrician influence set the mood of her home in Amherst, where she spent most of her life, with only occasional trips to Boston and one to Philadelphia and Washington, D. C. She attended Amherst Academy and Mount Holyoke Female Seminary, and until her early twenties, carried on the typically active life of a young New England girl devoted to her family and friends. It is difficult to draw with confidence, out of what little available biographical information we have, what exactly prompted her into a reclusive spinsterhood devoted largely to her family and the writing of great poetry. Two frustrated loves are often suspected, the first a young law apprentice of her father's named Ben Newton, who was living with her family in 1848. Her letters reveal a close relationship between the two, but he left in 1850 and died of tuberculosis in 1853. In 1854 she met the Reverend Charles Wadsworth in Philadelphia, and a devoted friendship resulted but was abbreviated by Wadsworth's acceptance of a call to a church in San Francisco.

Early literary stimulation included her own religious doubts, the generally intellectual atmosphere of her home (e.g., among the literary people to be entertained at the Dickinson home was Ralph Waldo Emerson, a visiting lecturer, in 1857), her friendship with Helen Hunt Jackson, and the advice of Thomas Wentworth Higginson (1823-1911), a literary man to whom she wrote in 1862. After Emily Dickinson's death, Higginson assisted Mrs. Mabel Loomis Todd, another friend of the family, in bringing out the first edition of Miss Dickinson's poems. Only seven of her poems had been published during her lifetime. A definitive edition of her poetry was edited by Thomas H. Johnson in 1955.

EMILY DICKINSON'S
PALETTE

REBECCA PATTERSON

Writing to Emily Dickinson in late December 1873, Thomas Wentworth Higginson made a pointed allusion to one of his Christmas presents, a water color sketch of field lilies in yellow and scarlet. These were not her favorite colors, he said, and perhaps not his own favorites either, but he thought they both should try to cultivate "these ruddy hues of life." Did she remember Julia Ward Howe's poem "I stake my life upon the red"?

A few weeks earlier, during a lecture trip to Amherst, he had called briefly at the Dickinson house and had received an impression of abnormality so strong as to give him irritated concern. He now recommended a tonic of color with what must seem peculiar confidence in its quasi-magic effect upon emotional and physical health. That he knew nothing about her real tastes and attitudes is made clear by the table of color incidence on pages 72-73, which reveals as the most striking characteristic of her color system this very insistence upon red and its different shades, including a purple that she sometimes identified with blood. The way to know her would have been to read her poetry, but her supposed critic saw very few of her poems, and these were increasingly occasional, often no more than a pair of lines or a stanza, with little indication of her absorbing interest in color. Yet the symbolic and emotional values she attached to any particular hue, and indeed her whole use of color, are aspects of her work that invite attention.

Even a casual reading of her work makes a kaleidoscopic impression on the mind of the reader. Letters as well as poems give evidence of a marked responsiveness to color and of a synesthesia, perhaps playful, which led the poet to talk of hearing or tasting or feeling color. After the passing of a circus she remarked that she had "tasted life" and could still "feel the red" in her mind although

71

Table of Color Incidence in Dickinson's Work

Poems (1858–86)

	Letters: 1850–56 %	No.	1858 %	No.	1859 %	No.	1860 %	No.	1861 %	No.	1862 %	No.	1863 %	No.	1864 %	No.
red	12.0	(18)	43.5	(10)	21.0	(12)	25.0	(10)	13.3	(6)	25.8	(34)	10.2	(6)	26.5	(9)
yellow	20.0	(30)	13.0	(3)	16.0	(9)	7.5	(3)	22.2	(10)	24.0	(32)	25.4	(15)	17.6	(6)
green	15.0	(22)	17.5	(4)	7.0	(4)	5.0	(2)	4.4	(2)	7.6	(10)	5.0	(3)	2.9	(1)
blue	15.5	(23)	0.0	(0)	10.5	(6)	17.5	(7)	4.4	(2)	8.3	(11)	13.6	(8)	2.9	(1)
purple	2.7	(4)	4.3	(1)	22.8	(13)	12.5	(5)	24.4	(11)	7.6	(10)	18.7	(11)	8.8	(3)
brown	6.8	(10)	13.0	(3)	1.7	(1)	10.0	(4)	4.4	(2)	6.0	(8)	1.7	(1)	8.8	(3)
black	9.5	(14)	0.0	(0)	3.5	(2)	7.5	(3)	4.4	(2)	3.0	(4)	3.4	(2)	5.9	(2)
gray-white	18.0	(27)	8.7	(2)	17.5	(10)	15.0	(6)	22.2	(10)	17.6	(23)	22.0	(13)	26.5	(9)
Total color words				23		57		40		45		132		59		34
Total lines				653		1166		836		1236		5420		1751		1698
Lines per color word				28.4		20.5		20.9		27.4		41.0		29.7		49.9

	1865 %	No.	1866 No.	1867–68 No.	1869–74 %	No.	1875–79 %	No.	1880–86 %	No.	No date %	No.
red	25.0	(4)	(0)	(0)	32.0	(8)	21.7	(10)	34.8	(8)	22.7	(5)
yellow	25.0	(4)	(1)	(0)	24.0	(6)	10.9	(5)	4.3	(1)	31.8	(7)
green	6.3	(1)	(0)	(0)	12.0	(3)	8.7	(4)	17.4	(4)	0.0	(0)
blue	6.3	(1)	(0)	(0)	4.0	(1)	15.2	(7)	0.0	(0)	4.5	(1)
purple	18.7	(3)	(2)	(0)	12.0	(3)	4.3	(2)	21.7	(5)	18.2	(4)
brown	0.0	(0)	(1)	(0)	0.0	(0)	17.4	(8)	4.3	(1)	0.0	(0)
black	0.0	(0)	(0)	(0)	0.0	(0)	6.5	(3)	8.7	(2)	4.5	(1)
gray-white	18.7	(3)	(1)	(0)	16.0	(4)	15.2	(7)	8.7	(2)	18.2	(4)
Total color words		16	5	0		25		46		23		22
Total lines		678	304	272		1957		1242		1270		1054
Lines per color word		42.4	61.0	0		78.0		27.0		55.2		48.0

	Dickinson Totals %	Dickinson Totals No.	E. Browning: Aurora Leigh	R. Browning: Men and Women	Emerson: Early Poems	Keats: Nar. Poems and Odes	Shakespeare: 6 plays; Sonnets	Shakespeare: Non-Dramatic
red..........	23.0	(122)	14.4	17.7	17.0	11.3	16.5	21.0
yellow.......	19.3	(102)	8.2	16.8	12.0	17.3	19.3	14.8
green........	7.2	(38)	12.4	5.0	11.0	13.7	9.6	6.0
blue.........	8.5	(45)	11.3	12.6	11.0	9.6	1.0	2.5
purple.......	13.9	(73)	2.8	0.0	9.0	4.0	2.4	2.0
brown........	6.0	(32)	4.8	3.7	5.0	1.9	4.0	1.0
black........	3.9	(21)	9.9	13.6	7.0	4.3	19.3	14.0
gray-white...	17.8	(94)	36.6	29.0	26.0	36.0	27.0	37.7
variegated...	0.0	(0)	0.0	1.4	2.0	1.4	1.0	0.0
Total color words...	527		255	214	100	415	290	284
Total lines......	19537		10938	5029	3900	5900	18425	6895
Lines per color word....	37.0		42.9	23.5	39.0	14.2	63.5	24.3

the drums were "out (L318).* Or she might say that the world, "usually so red," took on a "russet tinge" when her sister was unwell (L207). Days were "Topaz" (L212), hills took off "purple frocks" (L226), the sky put on "new Red Gowns—and a Purple Bonnet" (L315). In her poems she wrote that the "Tint" she could not take, the "Color too remote," was always the best (627), and that "Blaze" could never be adequately represented by "Cochineal" or noon by "Mazarin" (581). She spoke of artists, tint, easel (110), of paints, brush, picture, canvas (451), of Autumn's pencil (163), of famous painters like Domenichino, Titian, Guido, or Van Dyck (chosen for their well-sounding names, it would seem, since all were treated as frustrated landscape artists). God too is an artist who produced, "drew," Emily Dickinson (155). Late in life she acknowledged the gift of a painting with the remark, "To the Bugle every color is Red" (L985).

Some of these examples suggest a decorative and even precious use of language and are plainly the result of self-conscious deliberation. Higginson's letter is a useful reminder that her interest in color was by no means unprecedented or isolated. One of the marks of Romantic style was a deliberate cultivation of color, and Romantic theorists devoted chapters of mystic speculation to its influence on the soul. A belated Romantic herself, Emily Dickinson knew that a poet handled color words as a painter handled colors, and when she decided to become a poet she set about acquiring a serviceable selection of color words as one more element in the vocabulary appropriate to her craft.

Scarcely a dozen examples can be culled from the twenty-eight letters surviving between her childhood and her twentieth year, and half of these occur in stereotyped expressions from which the sense of color has all but vanished, like golden opportunity, silver cord, golden bowl, golden harps, or golden chain of friends. The remaining color words are also conventional and lack emotional tone. She referred to her brother Austin's yellow hen, joked about her golden tresses, alluded to the sere and yellow leaf, waxed enthusiastic over the blue eyes and rich brown hair of a teacher, feared to get a black mark, walked in green fields beside pleasant streams,

---

* The number references, preceded by the letter "L," used here and throughout this article, refer to the three-volume *Letters* of Emily Dickinson, edited by Thomas H. Johnson and Thodora Ward, published by the Harvard University Press, 1958. See *Bibliographical Note*, p. 103.

and found bloodroot and yellow violets. This is all that can be discovered in the long, effusive letters of her adolescence, but of course the list appears scanty only in comparison with later years and is doubtless normal for the intelligent, prose-centered adolescent that Emily Dickinson then was. No scrap of poetry survived from these years, and no friend remembered any poems or any interest in poetry.

In January 1850 the sun flew in splendor and glory out of its purple nest, and a young poet was born (L31). The same letter had other, less striking evidence (little snakes are *green,* the friend wears a quiet *black* gown) that the new poet was striving to envisage a universe of color. Not scientifically or naturalistically, however. Emily Dickinson shared the Romantic antipathy to science and was so little the close observer that she would write, "Nature rarer uses yellow than another hue." What she was trying to do, and for the first time, was to see her world in the emotional tone of its colors. It is a way of seeing that has nothing to do with noble-metal stereotypes or with simple color identifiers like the yellow that distinguishes one hen from another.

Why January 1850? No answer can be given other than the suggestion that if she were at the flash point, as appears likely, then the ignition may have come from a gift volume of Emerson's poems, acknowledged in that month, with a color system rather closer to her own than that of any other poet who would influence her. The greens, blues, browns, and blacks of her 1850-56 letters agree fairly well with those of Emerson's early poems. But she would always use fewer gray to white shades and far more yellow, or rather gold, and eventually her red shades would be as much in excess of his as they now came short. As for purple, a color word of almost monotonous occurrence in Emerson, particularly in descriptions of the sky, Emily Dickinson used her first two within a few weeks after receiving his poems and two more in a letter to Austin in October 1851. Purple then vanished from her color vocabulary until it returned with more than Emersonian force about 1859.

Shortly after January 1850 she wrote her first surviving poem and betrayed a mysterious excitement connected with some secret ambition. During the next several years the evidence multiplied that she was striving to become a poet, and concurrently her vocabulary became more and more colorful. In fall 1851 she described an unusual display of northern lights—a beautiful crimson sky and rays of gold pink shooting out of a sunlike center—and in other phrases of this letter demonstrated her lively new delight in verbal splashes of color. There were rustling brown leaves, rosy and golden peaches, and her brother's "birthright of purple grapes." Recurring to the purple of the grapes, the poet fancied that not even kingly robes were "a tint more royal" (L53). A few days later she told her brother that duty was black and brown, but the dying day was golden, a bird sang high up in a crimson tree, and a thousand little painters were busy tingeing the countryside (L57). A week later she was writing to him of his favorite brown bread, of green jackets, crimson leaves, blue hills, and earth's silver hairs (L58). Still more literary was a reference to the "blue mantillas" of the hills (L63).

The color notation was liveliest in 1851, 1852, and spring 1853, when the poet presumably worked hardest at her new craft; it then abated somewhat more rapidly than the number of her letters. No letters at all have survived between spring 1856 and spring 1858, and probably few were written. Years later the poet would allude to a period of depression in her middle twenties when she found herself unable to write poetry, and the decline in letters and the more precipitate decline in color words support her statement.

When she broke silence again, about mid-1858, she at first seemed little changed from the girl of the early 1850s. The poems in her 1858 handwriting have the look of poems written in earlier years, particularly those in one 1858 packet (editorially numbered 82), which is richest in color words and contains a poem known to have been written as early as spring 1853; but the notion that any considerable number of her lost poems survived in the later handwriting weakens upon examination of color incidence. The color distribution of 1858 and afterwards differs significantly from that of 1850-56. Beginning in her late twenties, the reds and purples markedly increased, the blacks and the cool colors declined—with some temporary oscillation of the color blue. These colors are heavily weighted emotionally, and their appearance or nonappearance is significant.

The most important development of 1858 is her emergence from the profound discouragement of her middle twenties. Lyric poets are so rarely made at twenty-eight, the odds against her would have been all but overwhelming. Almost certainly the discovery of a new poet model inspired her to resume the writing of poetry about mid-1858. In the early 1860s she would write idolatrous poems to Elizabeth Browning, whom she would revere all her life. Perhaps she had some acquaintance with Mrs. Browning's earlier work, but it was the reading of *Aurora Leigh,* a versified novel about the early discouragements and eventual triumph of a woman poet, which proved decisive. If Aurora Leigh could become a great poet and establish the worth of woman as artist, why not Emily Dickinson? The most important discovery for the color system was the symbolic possibilities of the heavenly city of Revelation as exploited by Mrs. Browning. A running series of allusions throughout *Aurora Leigh* culminates in these lines:

'Jasper first,' I said
'And second, sapphire; third, chalcedony;
The rest in order, . . . last, an amethyst.'

In the next several years Mrs. Browning's disciple would use most of the heavenly jewels as color words. After mid-1858, but not before, letters and poems alike would be studded with such borrowings or with allusions to the promises of Revelation.

Emily Dickinson's own copy of *Aurora Leigh* is dated 1859, but she must have read a borrowed copy in late summer or early fall 1858, perhaps one belonging to her sister-in-law, Sue Dickinson. A letter of late September to Sue quoted phrases from Chapter 7 of Revelation. A letter of early November to another friend alluded to the "bright chirographies of the 'Lamb's Book'" (Revelation 21:27), and the stars of an 1858 poem (24)** swing there "cups of Chrysolite" (Revelation 21:20). In October the poet and her young cousin, Louise Norcross, talked excitedly of achieving fame as writers. Apparently much was stirring in late 1858 that would be manifested in the stronger poems and enlarged vocabulary of 1859.

The reds, though never again so dominant as in 1858, remained high in 1859 and afterwards. The strong reemergence of blue and purple would seem to have significance also, for these colors were associated in her mind with freedom, status, successful love, and happiness. Finally, her 1859 color vocabulary was charged with a series of important new words, among them four color words

** The number references, used here and throughout this article, refer to the three-volume *Poems* of Emily Dickinson, edited by Thomas H. Johnson, published by the Harvard University Press, 1955. See *Bibliographical Note,* p. 103.

borrowed from the jeweled foundations of the New Jerusalem—jasper, emerald, topaz, and amethyst. Other color words making a first appearance were azure, amber, cochineal, damask, alban and snow as synonyms for white, and Tyrian as a synonym for purple. Except for cochineal and alban, she would have found all these color words in *Aurora Leigh* or in Revelation, Browning's *Men and Women,* and the poems of Keats, to which, if she had not already read them, Mrs. Browning's poem now strongly directed her. In 1862 she would tell Higginson that Keats, Revelation, and the two Brownings were her poets, but of course she knew thoroughly the early poems of Emerson and the work of Shakespeare and of Milton, where she would also have found most of these color words.

In 1860 appeared two more borrowings from the New Jerusalem, beryl and sapphire, plus ruby, russet, ebon, and dun. In 1861 the words rouge, daffodil, and bronze made their unique appearance among her color words. In 1862 she tried out such professional artist's colors as mazarine and gamboge and in a poem of the next year the color umber. Garnet, coral, Parian (a belated borrowing from Emerson, it would seem), argent, tawny, and livid are among the 1862 additions. Perhaps in the autumn of that year she experimented with blood as a color word, for she wrote that the "hue" of autumn "is Blood" (656), and about the same time she described a sunset of "solid Blood" (658). Phosphor or phosphorus, an apparent borrowing from Keats' *Lamia,* is doubtfully a color word. In an 1862 poem it is associated with fire (422), and in a poem of the next year with the color red (689), but it may mean, as in Keats, a light rather than a color, to which Emily Dickinson has clearly added the notion of heat. The 1863 innovations were a hazel to describe her eyes, a rather startling iodine of a rich violet shade, and a blonde that became one of her death colors. Iodine figured in four poems of the 1863-64 period, then vanished. Blonde, which had the same frequency in 1863-64, reappeared twenty years later in a new poem or perhaps in an old poem copied into 1884 handwriting.

As the table of color incidence shows, she reached the peak of her production in 1862. The next two years, though high in comparison with any year other than 1862, witness a marked decline, and in 1865 and 1866 the drop is abrupt, with the color words declining still more precipitately. No color words appeared at all in the few

1867-68 poems, and the letters of those years were scanty and equally colorless. It was clearly a period of lessened vitality reminiscent of a similar period ten years earlier. The evidence suggests that from this depression the poet never really emerged.

More important than statistics of incidence are the uses to which she put her colors, the meanings which she attached to them. About half are used, more or less naturalistically, to describe sunrises, sunsets, flowers, birds, the coming of spring, a summer's day, or the like. Purple ships toss on daffodil seas (265); sunset washes the banks of a yellow sea, and purple ships nightly strew opal bales over the landing (266). The sun rises in ribbons, hills untie their bonnets, steeples swim in amethyst, and at night little yellow girls and boys climb purple stiles and are led away by a gray dominie (318). The morning sky hurries into ruby trousers (204); the feminine day, undressing, pulls off gold garters, a petticoat of purple plain, and dimities fresh as the newest star (716). These are set pieces in a maidenly rococo, of which the chief effort appears to be to ring some change on the figure of a natural object wearing or putting on or taking off clothes. Apart from these decorative uses, her colors have a significance which can be most readily examined in the individual color.

Green

For many people, including poets, green is the color of hope, new life, or, at worst, unripe judgment or jealousy. Keats calls it "exuberant green" and uses it with exuberance. For Emily Dickinson green is, quite simply, the "color of the grave" (411). Even where the grave is not immediately apparent, it is usually lurking in the neighborhood of the color word. The maids who keep their "Seraphic May" on a "remoter green," a "mystic green," are dancing and singing in the kingdom of death (24). If children are playing on still another "green," we learn next moment that "New Weary" are sleeping below (99). The green hills of Yorkshire are associated with Charlotte Bronte's death (148); the death of Aunt Norcross is "in the Green" of the year (995). Blasted by lightning or fire, Nature's "Green People" struggle on with fainter vitality even if "they do not die" (314).

Apparent exceptions are three jewel greens taken from the New Jerusalem, beryl, chrysoprase, and chrysolite; but though they are correctly associated with objects naturally green, their color is not so conspicuous a value as their poetic names, and all of them together achieve no more than eight or nine mentions in the poetry. Clearly an exception is emerald, a recognizable color word in popular use, which appears at least ten times in the poems. For Emily Dickinson emerald becomes almost the "exuberant green" of Keats. An untidy housewife of a sunset litters the east with "Duds of Emerald" (219), the pine bough is an "Emerald Nest" (161), the wild rose is trimmed or belted with emerald (138), and the wings of the triumphant hummingbird are resonant with emerald (1463). But this word too is always ready to slip into the macabre. During the ominous "Green Chill" of a storm the poet bars windows and doors against an "Emerald Ghost" (1593), and the "Emerald Seams" of graveyard grass enclose a "narrow spot" (1183). In a late letter death becomes the "emerald recess" (L952).

It was not always so. In early 1850 she writes of attractive little green snakes (L31), and a few weeks later of a wholly figurative "green grove," with branches coming and going, which for some reason is pleasurably exciting to her (L35). This letter may reflect the excitement of her first surviving poem, a long, absurd, half-humorously erotic valentine in which everything is in love with something else—sun and moon, bee and flower, night and day, earth and sky, wind and branches. The recipient is urged to climb a tree boldly, and seizing one of the six maidens perched on the tree, carry her off to the "greenwood" and build a bower for her. Among the six maidens in the tree are the poet herself and a new and admired friend, Susan Gilbert, her future sister-in-law. Elsewhere she repeatedly associates the color green with Sue. In a letter of spring 1852 she plans to send her absent friend some of the new green grass growing beside the doorstep where they "used to sit, and have long fancies" (L85). She imagines herself going through the "green lane" to meet Sue (L94) or Sue tripping on the "green grass" toward her (L96). A painful disagreement between them leaves the poet feeling cold as a stone and silent as a block that had once been a "warm and green" tree with birds dancing in its branches (L172). In January 1855 she remembers that their love for each other began "on the step at the front door, and under the Evergreens" (L177). A few weeks later the knowledge that Sue is coming "makes the grass spring" in her heart (L178). In April 1856, shortly before the marriage of Sue and Austin, the poet writes less happily to her cousin John Graves, who in April 1854 slept at the Dickinson house to protect her and Sue during the absence of the other Dickinsons. That earlier April, she says, "got to Heaven *first,*" where she hopes to meet it again at God's right hand. In a context that reeks of death she tries to describe the present April but can only stress the transiency of a world of crumbling "evergreens—and *other* crumbling things" (L184).

Reference to the table of color incidence shows greens in abundance during 1850-56, and analysis indicates that these greens *are* colors of hope and life. Never again would they be so abundant or so hopeful in letters or poems (the total for the letters during the rest of her life is a mere nine greens or 5.6 per cent). It is surely no accident that the greens decline so markedly in later years and that the remaining greens so hover about the graveyard. These are signs of waning hope and of frustrated life. Such a frustration, turning the mind inward toward death, may account for one of the two early instances of a graveyard green. Writing to Abiah Root on 31 December 1850, she says she will make a pilgrimage next spring to the grave of her former school principal, "when the grass is growing green." She will bring birds and flowers and insects to honor this grave (L39). But she cannot keep her mind on her dead schoolmaster, who seems to be largely a pretext for the plangent melancholy of this letter. There is some evidence that at this time she thought herself neglected by Sue.

The idea of tending a grave returns powerfully in an 1862 poem which begs the beloved, when dying, to send for the poet. Afterwards the poet will insure that the "Jealous Grass" grow greenest and fondest over the beloved dead (648). When her own turn comes she will journey toward her lover dressed in the "Sod Gown" (665).

Blue

The ambivalence that bisects the poetry of Emily Dickinson is nowhere more obvious yet subtle, more complex yet simple, than in the color word blue. It is one of her personal colors, perhaps because it went well with her reddish-brown hair. In an early letter she tries to decide whether to wear her fawn-colored or her blue dress for the important ceremony of welcoming Susan Gilbert home from Baltimore, and she chooses the blue (L96). A few years later she herself is the little "Heart's Ease" or pansy that, like heaven, will never change her blue (176). But blue is also the color of the beloved. In an early letter the poet imagines herself paddling down the "blue Susquehanna" to meet a friend; in an 1860 poem she *becomes* the stream and begs to be absorbed into the "Blue Sea" of another person (162). As early as fall 1851 blue is associated with the hills seen from her bedroom window, acquiring their attributes of distance, mystery, unapproachableness. These hills are feminine, for they wear "blue mantillas" and hence become protective, maternal deities (722)—an identification that seems natural enough but may have been assisted by these lines from *Aurora Leigh:*

> And now I come, my Italy,
> My own hills! are you 'ware of me, my hills,
> How I burn toward you? do you feel to-night
> The urgency and yearning of my soul,
> As sleeping mothers feel the sucking babe
> And smile? (V, 1266-71).

Whether azure, mazarine, sapphire, or plain blue, the color is most often and naturally associated with the sky. If the poet is happy, blue connotes warmth, freedom, boundlessness, unlimited power. If unhappy, then it is the color of death or of the cold, frightening, yet alluring veil between this world and the next. Writing to Austin on a "glorious afternoon" of March 1852, she says the sky is "blue and warm," and the sunshine makes gold look dim; it is a day made for "Susie" and them (L80). The first blue awarded to Sue herself, however, is associated with water rather than sky. The poet regrets that she has no "sweet sunset to gild" the pages for Sue, "nor any bay so blue" (L77). A few weeks later she begs Sue to put the enclosed violets under her pillow and dream of "blue-skies, and home" (L94). In late February 1853 Sue has become "all my blue sky" and "sweetest sunshine" straying far from the poet and cruelly refusing to answer letters. A few days later another unhappy letter tries to explain what Sue means in the color system. Sue sketches her pictures for her, and it is "their sweet colorings," not this dim reality, that the poet longs for. When her friend is gone she cannot feel peaceful; she needs "more vail" between her and the staring world (L107).

The engagement formed between Sue and Austin a few days later necessarily and permanently altered the relationship between the two young women, and Emily Dickinson somewhat unhappily adjusted to the change. Writing to her brother shortly afterwards, she describes Sue reading a letter from him and looking up now and then at the "blue, blue home beyond" (L118). These are certainly Emily Dickinson's words, whether Sue's or not. She writes less often to her brother, explaining that she is afraid of sounding "rather bluer" than he would like (L123). Shortly afterwards things still "look blue," and she is not even sure Austin wants to hear from her (L128).

Next summer produced a violent rupture between the two young women. Apparently forgetting that Sue is to be her sister-in-law, the poet tells her their friendship is ended. She adds bitterly that she will "simply murmur *gone*" while her boat goes down and the billow dies "into the boundless blue" (L173). Of course she cannot remain in this absurd posture, and the passage of a few weeks finds her begging for letters and describing a fair day, "very still and blue," and a crimson sunset (L176).

The letter to John Graves in April 1856 makes an early association between blue and Italy. After writing of crumbling evergreens and "*other* crumbling things," the poet says the skies that day are "fairer far than Italy" and "in blue eye" look down on her (L184). Of course she knew and loved the Italy of "Ik Marvel" and other writers of her youth, but the association would be strengthened by the reading of Hillard's *Six Months in Italy* and Mrs. Browning's *Aurora Leigh*, whose heroine longs for "the white walls, the blue hills, my Italy" (I,232).

Blue is absent from her 1858 poems but appears in a rough draft letter to an unknown "Dear Master." Her friend is ill. He has not written for so long that she thought him dead and seems surprised to learn that he is not. She has sent him flowers and wishes she could paint a picture for him. "Each Sabbath on the Sea" (obviously life's troubled main) has her counting the Sabbaths till they "meet on shore" (obviously the life beyond), and she wonders whether the hills there will be as "blue" as reported by sailors. The letter has a curiously unreal, manufactured sound, as if to a ghost or a figment of the imagination; it is unlike anything she ever wrote to any one else. Her expectation that they will meet again only in death suggests that he is already dead, if he ever existed at all outside her fantasy. The blue hills where they are to meet belong to the region beyond the ocean of life. Blue is a death color here.

The other-worldly blue reappears in an 1859 poem (78). Here the "blue havens," a reminiscence of Psalm 107:29-30, lead by the hand the "wandering Sails" that have been gathered in from the storms. An 1860 poem has the outward look of death, but the exile of this poem, "haunted by native lands" and "blue, beloved air," may be secretly dreaming of a quite earthly paradise (167). For the characteristic mood of these 1859-60 "blue" poems is ecstatic happiness, or as one poem puts it, they have an "Azure . . . Transcending extasy" (122). Indian summer is a wonderful "blue and gold mistake" (130). "Breadths of supple blue" and "withes of supple blue" appear in another 1859 poem which lightheartedly rephrases the great questions of Job (128). In 1860 the poet reels happily from "inns of Molten Blue" (214), the poet-river longs to be absorbed into the other's "Blue Sea" (162), the little "Heart's Ease" (an obvious pun) clings to her blue (176). Those "Sapphire Fellows," the skies, are constantly spilling their secret to the hills, who overflow to the orchards, and so on (191). Even the mood of an 1861 poem, which offers to exchange "Straits of Blue" and other valuables for one hour of her beloved's face, is less desperate than that of other 1861 poems.

By 1862 the mood is changing. The blue buzz of the fly that comes between her dying eye and the lighted window is not ecstatic. Its stumbling uncertainty, which projects the stumbling, failing mind, is the eeriest element in the poem, unless it be the cold blue that portends death (465). Less successful but still interesting is a drowning poem in which the billows toss her up like a ball and make "Blue faces" in her face (598). An 1863 poem remembers icicles prickling "blue and cool" on her soul the day she foresaw the loss of her happiness (768). In still another 1863 poem the love, hope, or happiness is a little brig overtaken by blast and sunk in a storm. The poet adds that "Ocean's Heart" is "too smooth—too Blue" to break for this little boat. The ocean appears to be the lover's indifference. An 1864 poem describes the heart as measuring in "Blue Monotony" like the sea until it is overtaken by the hurricane of suffering (928). Here it may be difficult to determine which condition is preferable. Monotony is rarely attractive, however, and Emily Dickinson appears to prefer storm, even though painful.

It is obvious that these blues are unpleasant; they are cold, forbidding, totally opposite to the ecstatic *molten* blues of 1859-60. Other blues of the 1862-65 period are not so readily assigned. An

1865 poem observes that nature is prodigal of "Blue" (1045). Although analogies are drawn between wild nature and human behavior, the color here has no other reference than the blue of skies, seas, flowers, or distant hills. On the other hand, an early 1863 poem, which declares that "Blue is Blue" throughout the world, is not talking about nature's blue at all. Although not precisely an invitation to suicide, the poem seems to urge the other person ("Seek—Friend") to risk flight into the next world for the blue that is unavailable in this.

A curious poem of 1862 assigns the color blue to the brain, not in the commonplace sense of melancholy but rather in the sense of the infinity, hence the omnipotence, that is symbolically associated with the blueness of sky and sea. The brain, says the poet, is wider than the sky, deeper than the sea, "just the weight of God" (632). If brain and sea are held "Blue to Blue," the brain will absorb the sea just as a sponge absorbs a bucket of water. The poet is saying, as she has repeatedly said elsewhere in different ways, that her brain has the quality of the infinite. The psychologist calls it omnipotence of thought or magical thinking. It is strictly an infantile or primitive way of feeling about oneself, although by no means absent from the unconscious of the civilized adult. Undoubtedly the curious power of Emily Dickinson's work derives in part from its successful embodiment of infantile fantasy.

In an early 1863 poem the moon's blue dimities refer to the blue sky, but the moon itself appears to be identified with a beloved lost friend, and the blue may also symbolize an unattainability like that of the sky (737). This is clearly the meaning in an 1862 poem, where the moon has "vaulted" so far above the poet that the latter cannot follow the moon's "superior Road" or its "advantage—Blue" (629). Another 1862 poem begins in the recollection of a childish fear that the blue sky might fall on her, but in the last stanza it is precisely the distance, the unattainability, of this blue that seems to worry her. She wants "Heaven" to "tumble—Blue" on her (600). Still another 1862 "blue" poem must be doubtfully interpreted. To races that have never seen the light, she says, can you represent "Blaze" in "Cochineal," "Noon" in "Mazarin" (581)? She is questioning the adequacy of all symbols, to be sure, but she is seldom merely didactic. When she generalizes—a habit that grew upon her two years later—she generalizes on her own recent experience. Noon is a frequent symbol for love, as are blazes and reds of all descriptions. To those who have never known love, can even the intensest blue properly symbolize it?

The remaining blues of 1862-65 are clearly associated with the lost beloved. In an 1863 poem the poet remembers painfully a time when the "Heavens below" obscured the one above with a "ruddier Blue" (756). Her first editor changed the phrase to "ruddier hue," missing entirely the symbolism of the paradisal blue of happiness suffused with the warmth of life's blood. In another 1863 poem the lovers are imagined to be still united by a noon blue that unwinds from east to west until it covers them both like a warm blue blanket (710). An 1862 poem combines the symbols of paradisal blue and a warm, alluring Italy; the lost beloved, or perhaps the remembered happiness of their love, becomes the longed for "Blue Peninsula" (405). It is noteworthy that the poet has been at pains to warm every one of these blues. They are reminiscences of the molten blues of 1859-60.

Only one poem mentioning the word blue can be dated with any certainty between 1865 and summer 1877. Written about 1872, it tells of her liking for March, always a favorite month, and rather oddly ascribes to March a "British Sky" in which "Blue Birds" are exercising (1213). But 1877 is the *annus mirabilis,* for blue birds as well as the last year in which she originated any "blue" poems. In August 1877 she sent to Higginson a poem describing a blue bird as first to come in March, last to adhere at summer's end, and a model of "Integrity" (1395). The same letter also carried an exuberant description of nature in her "Opal Apron" (variant: "Bluest Apron") mixing fresh air (1397). About the same time she must have worked at the draft of another blue bird poem which she finished some years later. In its 1877 form it begins by asking who would care about a blue bird's tune when all that it sung for had been "undone" (1530). About the same time she copied off the last lines of the 1872 blue bird poem on a scrap of paper where she also confided that she no longer "Yearns . . . for that Peninsula" (the full text of the 1877 "Peninsula" poem, describing the sweeping away of her soul by an "inundation" (1425), is preserved on other paper). The following March, it would seem, she rewrote the whole 1872 blue bird poem and sent it to her sister-in-law. About the same time she rewrote an early 1862 poem concerning two lost butterflies, introducing the unusable word "Peninsula" into her confused draft (533). Such a thickening of peninsulas and blue birds, unique in her poetry, makes 1877 (and the two or three months immediately following) an interesting though puzzling year. It is also, proportionately, the richest color year in her poetry, with an average of one color word to every 18.3 lines. According to the last of her 1877 "blue" poems, the "parched Corolla" of the gentian is dried azure, the beatification of Nature's juices (1424). Later than others flowers, it comes to assist "an aged Year" and is a symbol of "Fidelity," in which, incidentally, it resembles the blue bird. This "dried azure" would seem to be the final reduction of her molten blue.

Yellow

Yellow is Emily Dickinson's workaday word, used seventeen times simply to describe the sunlight. It is not surrounded by an aura of value like gold or golden, does not share with amber the sense of something delicate, precious, shining, and is not attended by any of the sacrificial quality that seemingly attaches to gilt or gilded (topaz, which occurs twice, and saffron, daffodil, and gamboge, once each, are exotics of no great importance). Yellow can be humorously used, as in the sun's yellow play (496), the yellow boys and girls climbing the purple stile of evening (318), the daffodil's yellow bonnet (134) or yellow gown (348), the yellow knee on which the poet as awkward little bird falls adoringly (941). Other uses of the word yellow, suggesting that it is sometimes too bright, too painfully stimulating, recall the fact that the poet spent many months in Boston during 1864 and 1865 for treatment of her eyes. There does not seem to have been any organic defect; the affliction was apparently nervous, but it may have left her over-sensitive to bright light. On the other hand, it would seem that she anticipated her eye trouble some years before it happened.

In an anguished poem written about spring 1861, the poet describes the loss of love as "Blindness" (236). A year later she recalls the happy time before she got her "eye put out" (327). In another 1863 poem she is looking into the "face" of a cannon, whose "Yellow eye" glares death into her eye (590). About this time occurs one of her early references to lightning: it plays, sings, "alarms us"—and has "Yellow feet" (630). The following year the poet herself becomes a "Loaded Gun" and lays "Yellow Eye" and "emphatic

Thumb" on her "Master's" foes (754). About 1864, the year of her first eye treatment, comes a graveyard poem which adjures the sun not to "interrupt this Ground" with any "yellow noise" (829); synesthesia converts intrusive light to intrusive sound. Of the same period is a poem describing how the lightning "showed a Yellow Head" and a "livid Toe" (824). A revision makes the lightning more cruelly terrifying: "Yellow Head" becomes "Yellow Beak" and "Toe" becomes "Claw." About 1870 the lightning is described as a "Yellow Fork," the "awful Cutlery" of the sky (1173). A few months later the sun takes down his "Yellow Whip" and drives the fog away (1190). Finally, an undated poem places the "yellow lightning" in a context of volcanic cloud and mangled limbs (1694). No other shade and indeed no other hue has precisely these connotations of fear, violence, and cruelty.

Gilt or gilded appears to be associated with pain or with the effort to conceal pain. The earliest instance is an 1861 poem about a "clock" that has stopped, its "Gilded pointers" indicating a "cool —concernless No" to any one who importunes it now (287). An 1862 poem describes a lip "gilded" with a smile to hide its pain (353). Another 1862 poem, which affirms that heaven has a hell to "signalize" itself, says every sign in front of heaven is "Gilt with Sacrifice" (459). The "Gilded Hands" of another clock seem tormented with anticipation of a joy that proves shortlived (635). The last of these poems, written apparently in 1863, describes the torture of a balloon, a "Gilded Creature" that tries desperately to fly but rips apart on a tree and falls into the ocean (700).

The yellows of all shades are too brilliant to be suitable graveyard colors, the yellow sun being specifically asked to stay away. The honorific gold or golden can be and is applied to the world beyond the grave, but rarely and with no great conviction. On her return from Baltimore, Susan Gilbert is to shun the golden wings of angels and people beckoning from clouds. Looking toward the "golden gateway beneath the western trees" (the direction from which Sue will actually come to the Dickinson house on Pleasant Street), the poet seems to make some half-conscious association between the golden west and the next world (L96). A few months later the association is explicitly made. Once more looking toward the west, the poet calls it the "golden West" and speaks of the "silent Eternity, for ever folded there," which will presently open its arms and gather Sue and her in (L103). Writing in January

1856 to Mrs. Holland, she imagines herself a rather unusual mill-wheel translated to the new stream of heaven where her "belts and bands" will appropriately be of gold (L213). In the poetry two rather perfunctory uses of golden suggest the next world. The "more golden light" of an 1854 poem sent to Susan Gilbert appears to be the light of heaven (5). The "golden floor" of another poem is that of the heavenly city (117). Finally, the "Yellower Climes" toward which the birds precede the poet may allude to the next world where alone she hopes to be with her lover (250).

Amber and gold or golden, the shades most in esteem for their preciousness, are those applied to love, the beloved, or some particularly admired friend. The lost "guinea golden" of an 1858 poem (23) may be Susan Gilbert or, less probably, some other young friend who is being urged to answer letters; the poem looks early and is recorded in Packet 82, where some of the vanished 1850-56 poems may have been preserved. In an 1859 poem the poet is a peripatetic "Daisy" following the "golden walk" of the sun-lover toward the latter's home in the amethyst West (106). An 1861 poem recalls this happier time as a straying "beyond the Amber line"— that is, a straying into the sun-drenched West of love, whose "purple Moat" she now tries in vain to climb (262). Sun, amber, and purple are once more united in an 1863 poem. Rare among her poems, it has a title, "Purple," which the poem tells us is the "color of a Queen" and, with "Amber," of a "Sun at setting" (776). An 1862 poem, describing the haze of pain through which a former delight is now seen, says it makes the latter pictorial like the amber haze surrounding a mountain, which, when approached, flits and becomes—"the Skies" (572). The shifting of the amber to the skies may be an involved way of alluding to the possibility of regaining the lost delight in heaven. In a poem already mentioned, when "Blue is Blue" and "Amber—Amber," it would seem that amber also symbolizes the love that must be sought in the world beyond (703).

Although gold or amber is connected with the sun-lover, it is equally the color of the moon as beloved. An 1862 poem associates the two by comparison. Just as the moon controls the sea with "Amber Hands," so does the lover's "Amber Hand" control the poet (429). A poem of the same year explicitly identifies the lover with the moon, which throughout its period of waning continues the "Golden Same" until it is cut away by "slashing Clouds" (504).

Another 1862 poem, already referred to, has the moon sliding away, "independent, Amber," like a guillotined head or a "Stemless Flower," then vaulting so far above the poet that the latter can no longer follow its "advantage—Blue" (629). The implicit longing for the unattainable moon hints at an association between moon and beloved. A poem of early 1863 appears to identify the moon with some particular person. Only a "Chin of Gold" a few nights ago, the moon now turns a "perfect Face" on the world below. If the "Lips of Amber" should ever part, what a smile the moon would bestow upon the poet, who longs for the privilege of being even the "remotest star" taking its way past the moon's "Palace Door" (737).

The lamp of an 1861 poem that still "burns golden" after its oil is gone signifies the continuance of her love after the other's love has been withdrawn (233). For this unoriginal metaphor she need look no further than *Paradise Lost,* where Love lights "His constant Lamp" (IV, 763-64). A curious poem sent to Samuel Bowles in late 1861 is more obscure. The subject is love, or rather the loss of love, and the "Eagle's Golden Breakfast" which *"dazzles"* her seems to be some kind of love satisfaction. But Emily Dickinson is not an eagle. She is explicitly a robin, whose little mouth is better suited to cherries or crumbs. She is so far from desiring the "Eagle's Golden Breakfast" that in a revised version she says it "strangles" small-mouthed creatures like her (690). A few weeks later she sent to Bowles another curious poem describing some unconsummated love relation. She says she has *not* had the swoon that ensues when "Garnet" is held to "Garnet" and "Gold—to Gold" (1072). Superficially there is not much resemblance between an "Eagle's Golden Breakfast" and a swoon that comes with the union of garnet reds and golds; in the reconciling universe of symbols they may nevertheless be the same. According to one brave theory, however, the second of these demonic poems expresses a longing for a double ring ceremony!

Another 1862 poem recalls the period of happiness when she dealt words of "Gold" to everyone; now the "Wilderness" has rolled back along her "Golden lines" (430). Still another 1862 poem laments her failure to dive for the pearl rightly hers. Now the jewel she thought too precious for a "Vest of Amber" is borne on the "Dusky Breast" of a "Swarthy fellow," a "Negro" indifferent to his good fortune (452). But in a poem of the same period she is fearlessly diving for her jewel and hopeful that her next dive may be the "golden touch" that obtains it (427). Saturated with Shakespeare as she was, it is possible that she recalled these lines:

> For Orpheus' lute was strung with poet's sinews,
> Whose golden touch could soften steel and stones . . .
>   (*Two Gentlemen of Verona*, III, ii, 78–79)

Her poetry is precisely what she would use in any attempt to win back an estranged friend. That a person is intended would seem to explain the tender, caressing references to the jewel, which is addressed as "You." In another 1862 poem she is waiting for death, when her lover will take her home in an "Equipage of Amber" (603). A disillusioned poem of 1864 sums up her history as "Finding . . . loss . . . Expedition for the 'Golden Fleece' . . . No Discovery . . . no Crew . . . no Golden Fleece," and poet-Jason doubtless sham, too (870).

In conclusion, a poem of 1866, taking a mournful farewell of a "Retreating" person, states that a "Perished Sun" is doubly more endearing than all the "Golden presence" (1083). It is reminiscent of the earlier poems linking some important person with the sun, especially with the setting sun. Although the other person is most probably alive, the tone is elegiac and final, as for the apotheosis of the golden beloved. There are no later poems linking any shade of yellow with any cherished person.

Purple

Purple, amethyst, Tyrian, violet, lilac, and iodine are freely interchangeable throughout the poetry, perhaps because the color word, without ever losing a sense of deep rich color, is far more important as symbol than as epithet. This also appears true with respect to the poets who influenced her. Milton's Love not only lights his constant lamp, he waves his "purple wings," and Keats' Psyche and Cupid sleep in each other's arms on a couch of "budded Tyrian." Though not rich in color words, Shakespeare makes occasional telling use of purple. The "purple pride" on the loved friend's soft cheek has been "grossly dy'd" in "my love veins" (Sonnet 99), and the "little Western flower" from which Oberon distills his love potion is "purple with love's wound" (MND, II, i, 166-67).

Emerson, whose extravagant use of purple approaches that of Emily Dickinson, calls love's illusions "bandages of purple light" ("To Rhea"). For the most part, Elizabeth Browning used her purples descriptively, but she gave amethyst a prominence that caught the eye of her disciple. It occupies the most important position in *Aurora Leigh,* being the absolute last word and uttered with meaningful emphasis. Moreover, in the thirty-eighth of the *Sonnets from the Portuguese* Mrs. Browning compared her lover's first gallant hand-kiss to a "ring of amethyst," adding that the eventual kiss on the lips "was folded down/In perfect, purple state."

When Emily Dickinson turned to her dictionary (and the attentive student of the 1847 Webster's soon gets the slightly uncanny feeling that he is reading over her shoulder), she discovered that "AMETHYST, in *heraldry,* signifies a purple color. It is the same, in a nobleman's escutcheon, as *purpure* in a gentleman's, and *mercury* in that of a sovereign prince." This last item, incidentally, may explain why the sun, retiring into a cloud, "sulked in mercury" on a "scarlet log" (1693). For iodine as a color word she had no poetic predecessor—nor any successor; but having discovered it, she learned from her dictionary that "its vapor is a beautiful violet," and that the name originated in the Greek word for violet (she read etymologies). Under the definition of purple she found that it was a much-admired color worn by Roman emperors and hence signified imperial government. In poetry it might be "red or livid; dyed with blood." Purple of mollusca, she read, is "secreted by certain shellfish . . . and is supposed to be the substance of the famous Tyrian dye." That Emily Dickinson avidly collected color words, studied definitions, and tried out new specimens should be fairly obvious. She knew something about the theory of colors, too. In a love poem she writes that the love of the other is a "Prism" (prismatic color?) "Excelling Violet" (611).

To these associations of love, happiness, dignity, imperial state, she added that of death, perhaps because it was to her the most important of all state occasions. She may also have known that the pall thrown over coffin or tomb in ceremonious funerals might be purple velvet instead of black. An early poem describing the funeral ceremony says this is a "purple," a "Crown," that no one can evade (98). In another poem the "Modest Clay," the erstwhile "Democrat," now lies in a state "Full royal" and "purple" (171). A poem in late handwriting describes death as a brook which must be leaped to secure the "Flower Hesperian" or "Purple Flower"

(1558), perhaps a recollection of Shakespeare's "little Western flower . . . purple with love's wound." According to these poems, death levels upward, and the humblest, most impotent denizen of earth (herself perhaps) may achieve dignity in death—and possibly the satisfaction of desire in the world beyond.

As a color word for flowers purple is infrequently used. The clover blossom is a "Purple Democrat"—an intended oxymoron (380), and the lilacs sway with "Purple load" (342). The most important instance is the "Purple Creature," the gentian of an 1862 poem, which, after the humiliating failure of its summer-long effort to be a rose, is brought to "Tyrian" perfection by the approach of frost (442). The gentian of this poem is a personal symbol, referring either to her belated love affair or to the dramatic efflorescence of her poetry under the sharp stimulus of personal tragedy.

In two poems purple signifies blood—the "purple brook" in the breast (122) and the "purple" in her vein, every drop of which she would give in order to live over one particularly happy hour (663). The "purple Host" of another poem doubtless has blood as one of its connotations, for it gives and sustains wounds on the field of battle; but it is also triumphant and victorious, attaining the supreme value that purple appears to symbolize in a number of poems. In one such poem she offers to buy an hour of her lover's face with "Purple" from "Peru," itself another symbol of supreme value because of the wealth wrung from it by the conquistadores (247). This meaning is made explicit in an 1859 poem which equates supreme personal happiness with setting foot on the "purple territories" of "Pizarro's shore" (73). The "purple line" of another poem (137) around which the butterflies of St. Domingo are cruising may be nothing more than the deep violet of a summer day; on the other hand, this may be one of many instances where metaphor appears to hesitate on the border of symbol. Elsewhere the butterfly is a symbol for the beloved, and St. Domingo is one of several place-names symbolizing the south of erotic happiness and freedom. In brief, butterflies may be butterflies here, the "purple line" the noonday summer sky, and St. Domingo only a playful way of suggesting summer warmth, yet Emily Dickinson could not write this poem without being aware of the possibilities of symbolism. This "purple line" is very close in feeling to Pizarro's "purple territories" and to the "amber line" or her "golden lines" which explicitly signify former happiness.

Purple is a favorite sunrise and sunset color and is associated with

hills, the four cardinal points, sun, noon, autumn, spring, and peculiarly associated with the month of March. Most of these poems
give the reader an uneasy feeling that he is reading about something more or other than sunrise, sunset, or the season of the year.
This ambiguity is the subject of one poem, which states that purple
is "fashionable twice"—at this season of the year and in that inner
season when the soul knows itself an emperor (980). Since the
supreme value in poem after poem is simply love, presumably to be
an emperor is to be loved; as she wrote to a friend in August 1859,
she would "rather *be* loved than to be called a king in earth, or a
lord in Heaven" (L185). When she writes that on the "Purple
Programme" of the East every dawn is the first one, she is describing the lover's sense of miraculous uniqueness, but this interpretation would be guess work if she had not made it herself in the
opening stanza (839). In another poem she deliberately spells out
her metaphors: the beloved's absence is night, the beloved's presence is dawn, and this presence, in another metaphor, is the "purple
on the hight" that is called morning (1739). In short, the beloved
can be and, as the poems witness, frequently is represented by
purple, hill, and morning.

Since the beloved's departure ushers in the night, the beloved is
just as often, indeed more often, represented by the setting sun and
its purple. In a poem already mentioned, the poet, now an
"Eastern Exile," tries vainly to climb the "purple Moat" that once
led her over the "amber line" into the sun-drenched West of love
(262). In a poem discussed under "Blue," the "East" keeps her
"Purple Troth" with the "Hill," and at night the North signals to
the separated lovers by blazing in iodine—displaying violet auroral
light (710).

In her dry school books Aurora Leigh learned "by how many
feet Mount Chimborazo outsoars Teneriffe" (I, 409-10). This piece
of information proved not at all dry to Emily Dickinson, who made
Chimborazo the peak of love that she could not climb (453). In
another poem she addresses Teneriffe as a "Receding" or "Retreating" mountain for which the "Purples of Ages" halt or pause.
Clad in its icy mail, granite of thigh and steely of thew, Teneriffe
is most unresponsive to the poet, who is "kneeling" and "pleading"
(666). Such emotion appears in excess for a mountain, and as a
matter of fact the poet addressed a copy to her sister-in-law, Sue
Dickinson. This raises the question of Sue's identification with the

purple mountain. In a poem already mentioned, purple is described as the color of a queen and of the setting sun, and it will be remembered that Sue was very early associated with the west. Despite an occasional "grandfather" mountain, it is probably true also that the various hills are commonly, though perhaps unconsciously, thought of as feminine. Not only are they the "strong madonnas" of one poem (722), not only are they forever undressing or donning mantillas, shawls, bonnets, gowns, they are simply felt through and through as women, as in Elizabeth Browning's very clear analogy with nursing mothers.

But if purple was Sue's color, then curiously it was never associated with her in the early letters. Although sparing in the use of purple up to the beginning of 1859, Emily Dickinson did use the color twice in a letter to Austin and once each to two other friends, but at no time does purple or any related shade appear in the early letters to Sue—or in the 1858 poems, written largely under Sue's influence, with one marked exception. This poem, which uses purple to symbolize an astonishing new happiness, is itself so puzzling as to suggest the possibility that it may have been added to the packet a few weeks later, say in January 1859 (323). Admittedly blue, which was associated with Sue in the letters of the early 1850s, disappeared entirely from the 1858 poems, only to reappear strongly in 1859 and 1860. But the relations between the sisters-in-law were strained and unhappy during 1858, and the absence of blue, which the poet most commonly associates with happiness, is explicable. No plausible improvement in their relations, however, can account for the excitement and intoxication of this returning tide of blue and this surge of purple in 1859.

About March 1859 Emily Dickinson sent a poem across the lawn to her sister-in-law. It may be concerned with flowers, less probably with Sue herself, or it may be a comment on, or a tribute to, some new friend whose recent departure resembles the evening stealing "Purple and Cochineal" after the day (60). In a love poem of the same period, which Sue did *not* see, the Daisy (always a personal symbol for the poet) steals after the "Sun" toward the "parting West," the "Amethyst" (106). Another poem written a few months later seems to be talking about the heaven above but may well be longing for the heaven below. She is a watcher hanging on that moment when the East will open the "Amethyst" lid and let the "morning" go (121). This is the year in which she dreams of the "purple territories" of Pizarro and of the butterflies from St. Domingo cruising the "purple line." In troubled 1861 the price of "purples" has risen as high as death (234). She strives in vain to climb the "purple Moat" and would give Peruvian "Purple" for an hour of her beloved's face, but the unattainable "Heaven" (the quotation marks are hers) merely decoys her with its "teazing Purples" (239). If not in this life, then perhaps in the next, and so she thinks of herself as dropping her life into a "purple well" so plummetless that it will not return before eternity (271). More realistically, perhaps, she says she has lost a gem from her fingers and now has only an "Amethyst remembrance" (245). After 1861 the purples are less frequently, or at least less obviously, concerned with a real person and a real situation. In 1862, it is true, the love of the other person is described as a prism superior to violet, and the poet very directly says she would give the "purple" in her veins to live over some happy hour; and in 1863 she kneels to purple Teneriffe, keeps purple troth with the hill, and defines purple as the color of a queen and of a setting sun. Purple shares in the general dimming of her palette after 1865. Curiously, following the death of her fiancé, it seemed to be returning to favor, and in no unhappy sense, when her own death cut her off.

Red

Although the reds of the 1850-56 letters are less important than the yellows or even the greens and blues, Emily Dickinson was already using crimson, red, rosy, ruddy, scarlet, and pink. In 1858 she added carmine; in 1859, cochineal, vermilion, and damask; in 1860, ruby; in 1861, rouge; in 1862, garnet, coral, and blood. The other additions are a doubtful hyacinth in 1864 and a possible cardinal red in 1882. The importance of red is due to its association with vitality, with blood, with the heart and other vital organs. Whether it is also of special importance to a woman, as a recent study of Emily Dickinson has implied, is questionable. It can be seen that Elizabeth Browning uses rather less red than her husband or Emerson or Shakespeare. Indeed if the plays are eliminated and only the non-dramatic poetry is considered, Shakespeare's reds average twenty-one per cent, or very nearly the same as Emily Dickinson's.

Not surprisingly, red is well-nigh absent from the graveyard. The earliest poem which in anyway associates the two makes a strong point of the fact that no "ruddy fires" appear on the hearth of this curious "Inn," the grave (115). But after the poet became concerned for the early demise of the person with whom she wished to spend eternity, the grave turned ruddy. She says she can see the other person better in the dark and through the lapse of years and best of all in the grave. Its "little Panels" are "ruddy with the Light" (the lamp of love) which the poet had been holding high all these years (611).

The symbolic red usually indicates a quality or a state rather than a person, but there is some evidence that cochineal points toward a particular individual. A poem already discussed, written about March 1859, describes a "Martial" person, or flower, who has withdrawn in a "Chapeau of fire" and has gone westward in "Purple and Cochineal" like the evenings (60). Four years later the poet chooses for her "Knitting" a "Cochineal" that "resembles Thee" and a "Dusker" border that represents her dimmer self (748). In a poem sent to a cousin in late July 1862, however, she identifies herself with an enclosed flower, whose "Depths of Ruby" the other is invited to sip like a hummingbird (334). She may also be the collective "Flowers" that waste their "Scarlet Freight" in lonely isolation (404).

Red is Emily Dickinson's color. Outwardly she may wear the white of martyred renunciation, but inwardly she is red, scarlet, carmine, vermilion, whether in ecstatic happiness or in the violence of loss and suffering—until after 1865, when the vitality drains away and the white so gains upon the red that the latter pales to pink. The earliest of these associations occurs in a poem written about summer 1859. If this is "fading" or "sleep" (her own quotation marks), then she wants immediately to "fade" or sleep. If it is "dying" (her own quotation marks), then she wants to be buried "in such a shroud of red" (120). The occasion is a happy one, however else it may be interpreted. In an 1860 poem the "Rose" capers on the cheeks of two unidentified lovers (208). In an 1862 poem about her lost happiness, she remembers that she once "told it—Red" in the color of her cheek (430). Very early in this year or very late in 1861 comes the apparently rueful admission that the lovers never held fiery garnet to garnet nor gold to gold (1072). In early 1862 she tends her flowers in memory of her "Bright Absentee" and muses sadly that she "had as lief" they bore no more "Crimson"

(339). Another 1862 poem, which appears to recall a declaration of love, tells of the "Carmine" tingling to her fingertips (470). Of the same period is the poem demanding whether "Blaze" can be shown in "Cochineal" (581). In another poem of the same packet "Life" is a "Wine" to be measured out "Naked of Flask" and "Cask"; it is to be "Bare Rhine." Her meaning is a life stripped of all non-life, but the stress on nakedness and bareness is felt at the literal level also. Finally she demands which "Ruby" is hers (583). Of very nearly the same date appears to be the poem identifying herself with a flower and begging the other to sip from its "Ruby" depths.

In early 1863 she spells out her symbol in terms of opposites. The "Zeroes" of her unloved life taught her that there must be a "Phosphorus." "Playing Glaciers" as a "Boy," she learned to want the "Fire." "Paralysis" was her dumb primer to "Vitality," and the "White" of deprivation and asceticism convinced her that "Red— must be" (689). Later in the same year she remembers the "ruddier Blue" of that one-time "Heaven below" (756). Elsewhere she recalls the "Cunning Reds" of love's dawn that broke in on her egg-life and freed her briefly from her shell, which she must now "resume" (728). In an 1862 poem she is rejected by "Morning" and condemned to "Midnight"; she asks whether she cannot at least look toward the "Red" East (425).

By 1864 the "crumb" that once satisfied the little robin is the "crumb of Blood" that momentarily "eased" the tiger (872). Another poem gives a more detailed account of her love experience. At some time in the past there bloomed a "Single Noon" (a frequent symbol for love's zenith) with a flower "distinct and Red." As in many another poem, she believes that she did not properly value it at the time. Too late she learns that this was the one and only flower intended for her (978). The flower with which the beloved is identified is commonly the rose, and in these poems the red color may be presumed.

Red is life, vitality, erotic ecstasy. It is also the color of suffering, and this meaning attaches to it early, perhaps initially to describe the pain of temporary separations. A poem that appears to belong to spring 1860 says wounded deer leap highest and cheeks are reddest where they sting (165). This is no more than an anticipation of real pain. The difference is apparent when one turns to a poem written a year later, perhaps about April 1861. Here no attempt has been made to polish metaphors or achieve a neat finish, and

more than half the words are underlined. In an anguish of abase-
ment the poet describes herself as her lover's little spaniel whose
life is leaking "red" (236). Of the several spaniels that she encountered in her reading about this time, one that she undoubtedly
has in mind here is Helena's. To the stony-hearted beloved, Helena
cries:

> I am your spaniel; . . .
> The more you beat me, I will fawn on you.
> Use me but as your spaniel—spurn me, strike me,
> Neglect me, lose me; only give me leave
> (Unworthy as I am) to follow you.
> *(Midsummer Night's Dream,* II, i, 203–07)

A poem written later in 1861 suggests that if one could only
foresee the end of pain, if the depth of the bleeding and the "drops
of vital scarlet" were limited, then it would be bearable (269).
Another 1861 poem says she will keep singing. Like the robins,
though more slowly, she too will journey southward with her "Redbreast" and her "Rhymes" (250). The "Redbreast" is a play upon
the robin's common name and the emotional wound she has
suffered. A poem written in late 1861 and sent with autumn leaves
to a visitor in her brother's house makes unique use of "rouge."
There is no explanation other than that the recipient had a fair
command of French and may have liked to display it. The poem
says that the red of the leaves cannot mean "Summer" (her own
quotation marks and hence a symbol), for Summer—with the slight
dash that often suggests a catch of the breath—"got through." It is
too early for "Spring" (her own quotation marks and therefore
another symbol), and besides she must first cross "that long town of
White." Nor can it be "Dying"; it is "too Rouge" and the *"Dead
shall go in White"* (a reminiscence both of the white robes of the
martyred dead in Revelation and of Aurora Leigh, who observed
angrily that she would rather take her part "With God's Dead, who
afford to walk in white," II, 102). Since the leaves point neither to
the vanished summer of love nor to the resurrection of love after
the long white town of the grave (and they are "too rouge" for the
intermediate stage of dying), their redness would seem to symbolize
not love but suffering (221). It is a queer, puzzling poem; but in
October 1861, according to a hint given T. W. Higginson next

spring and by the evidence of other letters and poems, Emily Dickinson was almost out of her mind with fear and suffering.

In an 1862 poem she says she has chosen the "Scarlet way" of suffering and renunciation (527). A poem in the same packet, however, calls her renunciation the "White election." By this white election and by the "Sign in the Scarlet prison" (the scarlet prison being presumably her suffering self), she hopes to reclaim her lost happiness. Still another 1862 poem suggests that the symbolic white is the incandescence of the suffering red. In this white blaze the "impatient Ores" are refined until they become the "Designated Light" itself and quit the human forge (365). This theme of purification by suffering occurs in a number of her poems.

As early as spring 1860 she began to associate her inner turmoil with a volcano. Happiness is a delectable vineyard that she holds on uncertain lease in the shadow of some danger symbolized by a volcano overwhelming a Pompeii (175). By early 1861, according to one of the so-called "Master" letters (L233), the cataclysm has occurred. As her tension increased, so did the violence of her metaphors. A confused poem of 1862 says the ordinary person lives a peat life of steady, subdued warmth; hers has the heat and violence of "Popocatepetl" or "Etna's Scarlets" (422). In another 1862 poem the "peat" lives become "natures this side Naples" and denizens of the cold "North." These passionless innocents "cannot detect," let alone understand, her "Solemn—Torrid—Symbol," the "still Volcano" of suffering that has opened the "hissing Corals" of its lips and destroyed her "Cities" (601). About 1869 she wrote, or more probably rewrote, a poem making the only other use of the "Garnet," the "Naples," and the "Etna" of these 1862 poems. A one-stanza volcano poem, it is probably a redaction of a longer poem contemporaneous with the earlier volcano poems. Naples, she says, fears a basking and purring "Etna" [sic] even more than one that "shows her Garnet Tooth" (1146). Although the poem has no manifest personal application, it would be a mistake not to expect one. An undated poem about a volcano (in a transcript made by Sue Dickinson) resembles these earlier ones and probably belongs with them. Her volcano, she observes, is now overgrown with grass and looks a "meditative spot," but the fire is rocking "red" below (677).

The last poem in what might be called her "red" period is one of the saddest. She has sung birdlike from her heart, dipped her beak in it to help out her song, offered up her death as her only wealth. If the tune drips too much or seems too "Red," she begs her erstwhile lover to forgive the "Cochineal," accept the "Vermilion," suspend "Liturgies" and "Chorals" while she repeats that lover's "Hallowed name" (1059). This poem was written about 1865.

The most curious aspect of her color system after 1865 is the dulling and fading of her palette. Prior to that time she employed an unusually high proportion of vivid colors—saturated reds, sky blues, rich golds, imperial purples. The browns, though treated mostly as warm, comfortable colors, are few in number; and the achromatic whites, grays, and blacks, which make up forty to fifty per cent of the colors employed by other poets, amount to little more than twenty per cent of Emily Dickinson's. There is a disturbing impression of intense, restless color in a period of raging creativity and of powerful emotional tensions. Little wonder that the image of an erupting volcano or of a blazing fire recurs and recurs.

By 1865 the fire is virtually extinguished. "Ashes" now indicate the "Fire" that was, and the poet begs respect for this "Grayest pile" in memory of what it symbolizes (1063). No reds appear in the 1866 poems, and no colors at all in the 1867-68 poems. During 1869-70 there are a few "red" poems, some or all of which may have originated in the earlier period. The Naples-Etna-Garnet poem (1146), it was suggested, belongs by its imagery to the period around 1862, and a poem in 1870 handwriting recalls the love affair with surprising immediacy and in the vocabulary of the early 1860s (1171). It is a curious fact, however, that a worksheet draft originating perhaps late in 1868 describes a temporary reheating of the fire, suggesting that she has received a visit or perhaps a letter from the disturbing friend of the earlier period. Such a blowing upon the "smouldering embers" (1132) might initiate new poetry on the old theme or incite her to review and tinker with the older poetry. But even if these particular "red" poems originated in 1869-70, they modify only slightly the impression of diminished vitality, almost of bloodlessness, which distressed Higginson in late 1873.

Higginson was unpleasantly struck by her pallor and by the white garments that she now wore habitually. His friend Helen Hunt Jackson made a similar visit in late 1876 and had a similar reaction. An apologetic letter shows that she berated the poet for living out of the sunlight and told her she looked ill ("so white and mothlike"). If Mrs. Jackson or Higginson had had any real acquaintance with her poetry, they would doubtless have found symptomatic the curious bleaching of her once vital red. Whether a conscious and deliberate act or no, the symbolic white appears to have invaded the red and lightened it to pink. In the early letters, for example, the color word pink occurs just once—in contrast to seventeen reds, crimsons, and the like. The letters of 1858-66 employ four pinks (all of them names or descriptions of particular flowers) as against seventeen assorted reds; and the poems of that period exhibit a mere three pinks as opposed to the overwhelming vividness of eighty-eight reds, scarlets, crimsons, cochineals, carmines, vermilions, and the like. But in the 1870s the reds begin to fade into pinks, and the various browns multiply. In some poems of the mid-seventies, as her variants show, she can be seen hesitating between a pink and a red, as if no longer sure of her preference. Perhaps conscious of declining vitality, she begs her heart to put up its "Hoary work" and take a "Rosy Chair" (1310). (Rose or rosy, incidentally, is treated as a fairly deep color—in one poem as an autumn color.) In the letters of 1869-86 there are now a dozen pinks to fourteen of the more vivid red shades, and in the poems of the same period the proportion is nine pinks to thirteen assorted reds.

It is not alone the employment of the word pink; the context in which it occurs becomes oddly symbolic. Shame is a "shawl of Pink" and even the "tint divine" (1412). The general flesh becomes "that Pink stranger" (1527), and, in an 1881 poem apparently recalling some more or less decorous struggle with her fiancé, their particular flesh becomes the "Pink Redoubt" (1529). One wonders whether an undated dream poem describing a pink worm, lank and warm, that turns into a terrifying snake "ringed with power," might not have been written at this prevailingly pink date (1670). The dripping of February eaves, she writes, "makes our thinking Pink" (L450). Hearts are now pink (L654, L845), Cupid drives a "Pink Coupe" (L723), and in the final weeks of her life she writes that the idea of her stirring about is rather like the arbutus, "a pink and russet hope" (L1034). The words are curiously descriptive of the impression made by her colors during the last decade or so of her life.

Although creativity and color alike seem diminished to a uniformly low ebb after 1865, a more careful inspection discovers occasional puzzling ripples. A temporary increase in color around

1869-70, it was suggested, may be due to the reappearance of the person who caused the original disturbance. There is another such increase in the middle seventies, apparently tied to a fire poem of 1876, or 1877, which describes the reappearance of the "Witch" and the uncovering of supposedly dead embers by the hand that once "fondled them" (1383). But after reaching its absolute peak in 1877, the color incidence once more tumbles abruptly. A small increase in 1879 may conceivably reflect the excitement of being sought by the widowed Judge Otis Lord, but if so, it was short-lived. There is a peculiar flatness and lack of color in the poetry written during their engagement. After his death, surprisingly, the old brilliant colors, the old symbols, made a last flickering appearance in letters and poems. And then she too died, having locked up her life in transparent image and symbol. As was said of another pale maiden,

> . . . in faith, 'twas strange, 'twas passing strange;
> 'Twas pitiful, 'twas wondrous pitiful.

BIBLIOGRAPHICAL NOTE

The editions consulted are the three-volume *Poems* of Emily Dickinson, edited by Thomas H. Johnson, 1955, and the three-volume *Letters,* edited by Thomas H. Johnson and Theodora Ward, 1958, both published by the Harvard University Press. The poets and the works chosen for comparison are those known to have particularly influenced her. The six Shakespeare plays are *Romeo and Juliet, Midsummer Night's Dream, Twelfth Night, Othello, Macbeth, Anthony and Cleopatra.* The statistics are intended to be suggestive only—to show the ways in which Emily Dickinson resembled other poets rather than the ways in which she differed.

The Use of Color in Literature by Sigmund Skard (Philadelphia: The American Philosophical Society, 1946) is a helpful bibliography of color studies up to 1940. *The Poetry of Robert Browning* by S. A. Brooke (London, 1911), *Nature in American Poetry* by Norman Foerster (New York, 1923), and *Shakespeare's Imagery and What It Tells Us* by Caroline Spurgeon (Cambridge, 1935) may be consulted for the use of color by Browning, Emerson, and Shakespeare, respectively. The present writer has found no color study, however, that is at all comparable to her study of Emily Dickinson, perhaps because no other poet has used color words with such deliberate symbolic intent. For further analysis of the influence of Elizabeth Browning, reference is made to this writer's "Elizabeth Browning and Emily Dickinson," *The Educational Leader,* XX (July, 1956), 21-48.

Editor's Note: "Emily Dickinson's Palette" is reprinted, by permission of Rebecca Patterson and *The Midwest Quarterly,* from *The Midwest Quarterly,* V, 4 (1964), pp. 271–291, and VI, 1 (1964), pp. 97–117.

Rebecca Patterson is Professor of English at Kansas State College at Pittsburg and Editor-in-chief of *The Midwest Quarterly.* She has published essays on Whitman and Emily Dickinson.

ROBERT FROST

1874-1963

Despite the fact that Frost was born in San Francisco, he derived from an old New England family. When he was eleven, his father died and his mother took him to Lawrence, Massachusetts. Frost graduated from Lawrence High School, and after a few weeks at Dartmouth College he left and held a series of temporary jobs as mill-worker, teacher, and reporter. He married Elinor White, who had previously shared with him the title of valedictorian of their high school class. Another attempt to adjust to formal education—this time at Harvard in 1897—ended after two years, and in 1900 he moved to a farm in Derry, New Hampshire, bought by his grandfather. The income from farming was insufficient, and Frost turned to teaching in order to support his growing family. During these years, Frost's poetic career was frustrated. In a desperate choice bravely encouraged by his wife, Frost sold the farm and the family moved to England in 1912; here Frost could concentrate more fully upon writing. While he was in England, Frost was asquainted with Pound, Yeats, Amy Lowell, and others of the modern movement, but he was more congenial with Georgians such as Rupert Brooke and Edward Thomas. In 1913 Frost's first book of poems, *A Boy's Will,* was published, followed by *North of Boston* in 1914. Both were favorably received.

After his two published successes, Frost returned to the United States and resumed his farming and teaching, with increasing emphasis upon the teaching, and, of course, more time devoted to writing. He taught at Amherst College, the University of Michigan, the University of Vermont, and the Bread Loaf School of English, which he founded. During his lifetime he achieved an appreciation and fame extremely rare among poets. His later books of verse include *Mountain Interval* (1916), *New Hampshire* (1924), *West-Running Brook* (1928), *A Further Range* (1936), *A Witness Tree* (1942), *A Masque of Reason* (1945), *Steeple Bush* (1947), *A Masque of Mercy* (1947), and *In the Clearing* (1962).

ROBERT FROST

AND THE

EDGE OF THE

CLEARING

JAMES M. COX

When Robert Frost nears a university campus in this country there is a bustle of interest and activity extending beyond the confining borders of the English department. A curious observer is struck by the realization that Frost's approaching appearance is no mere item on the college calendar but an event which makes its presence felt in the area of public relations. Even the distant administrative machinery can be heard to stir in anticipation of Frost's arrival, and when the hour comes round for Frost himself to take the stage a member of officialdom above and beyond the orbit of mere liberal arts is likely to perform the rites of introduction as the Frost cycle begins over again. It has been a cycle repeated in one place or another for almost thirty years, expanding with the passage of time as Frost has established himself securely in the position which Mark Twain created in the closing years of the last century—the position of American literary man as public entertainer. Frost brings to his rôle the grave face, the regional turn of phrase, the pithy generalization, and the salty experience which Twain before him brought to his listeners. He is the homespun farmer who assures his audiences that he was made in America before the advent of the assembly line, and he presides over his following with what is at once casual ease and lonely austerity.

Because the popularity surrounding Frost the public figure and hovering about his poetry has become the halo under which admirers enshrine his work, to many serious critics bent on assessing the value of the poetry this halo becomes a sinister mist clouding the genuine achievement. Malcolm Cowley, for example, has raised a dissenting voice against the foggy approval; and even Randall Jarrell, who has written some of the most sensitive appraisals of Frost's poetry, inclines to dissociate the real or "other" Frost from the brassy New England character who parades before his audiences as what Jarrell calls "The Only Genuine Robert Frost in Captivity."

Yet Frost's success as a public figure, rather than being a calculated addition to his poetic career, is a natural extension of it, and one way to approach his poetry is to see that the character who moves in the poems anticipates the one who occupies the platform. They are in all essentials the same character—a dramatization of the farmer poet come out of his New England landscape bringing with him the poems he plays a rôle in. To observe this insistent regional stance is to realize that Frost has done, and is still doing, for American poetry what Faulkner has more recently accomplished in American fiction. They both have made their worlds in the image of their particular regions, and, moving within these self-contained and self-made microcosms, they have given their provincial centers universal significance. But while Faulkner has concerned himself with establishing the legendary Yoknapatawpha county and its mythical components, Frost has, from the very first poem of "A Boy's Will," been engaged in creating the myth of Robert Frost, The Only Genuine Robert Frost in Captivity. It is a myth with a hero and a drama.

The hero is the New England farmer who wears the mask, or better, the anti-mask of the traditional poet. But it is not a literal mask concealing the poet who lurks behind it; rather, it is a mode of being which releases the poetic personality in the person of a character who lives and moves. Whatever duality we may wish to ascribe between mask and man is actually present in the mask itself, for the mask—or character—of Frost is finally more real than any hypothetical Frost we may envision behind the scenes. The very life of the character depends upon his creator's ability to project his whole personality into the image he assumes. Frost is, for his audience, a "character" simply because he represents both in language and outlook a vastly familiar figure to them, a kind of traditional stage Yankee full of gnomic wisdom and prankish humor, carrying his history in his head and venturing cryptic comment upon all experience in a sufficiently provincial manner to remind them of a preconceived caricature.

It is Frost's ability to *be* a farmer poet which distinguishes him most sharply from Wordsworth, with whom he is often compared. Wordsworth played the part of the Poet concerned with common man, but Frost has persistently cast himself in the rôle of the common man concerned with poetry. Such a strategy, while it cuts him off from the philosophically autobiographical poetry which Wordsworth built toward, opens up avenues of irony, wit, comedy, and dramatic narrative largely closed to Wordsworth. For the poetic ego, held in objectivity by the anti-mask which both releases and contains it, is exposed to a control and ironic self-awareness foreign to the serious and subjective Wordsworth, who, although he felt keenly the joy of experience, rarely descended to humor.

Thus, instead of direct revelation through autobiography and confession, Frost has from the start pursued the more indirect but equally effective mode of dramatizing and characterizing himself. Even the lyrics of "A Boy's Will" lean toward narrative and monologue, and the peculiar Frost idiom, so integral a part of the Frost character who eventually emerges, is evident in remarkable maturity in such early poems as "Into My Own," "Mowing," "A Tuft of Flowers," and "In Hardwood Groves." The dramatic monologues and dialogues of "North of Boston," which have impressed many critics as a wide departure from Frost's lyric vein, constitute a full discovery and perfection of that idiom. Moreover, Frost himself emerges prominently as a member of the volume's *dramatis personae,* playing an important rôle in nine of the sixteen poems. As a matter of fact, "Mending Wall," the first poem in the volume, marks the full-dress entrance of the farmer poet. Possessed of all the characteristics by which we have come to know him, this figure is full of sly observations as he assumes a slightly comic poise with eye asquint—already poetry is "his kind of fooling." He goes to great length to disarm his audience with colloquial familiarity and whimsical parentheses. Then, after an agile imaginative leap in the grand style, he returns to earth as if he feared being caught off guard.

This cautious refusal to declaim too far or too soon, while it may leave too much unsaid or enclose the issue in a blurred dual vision which accepts both sides, is often one of Frost's most effective modes of self awareness. Thus, when Yvor Winters, in his discussion of "The Road Not Taken," holds Frost responsible for refusing to make clear the kind of choice represented by the two roads which "diverged in a yellow wood," he misses the comic criticism the speaker is directing against himself. As Professor Ben W. Griffith has rightly observed, Frost is indulging in a bemused self-portrayal. When he made the choice, he made it not profoundly but tentatively and uncertainly; he was even incapable of distinguishing which road *was* the least traveled—"And both that morning equally lay/In leaves no step had trodden black"—but he envisions the day when he shall sighingly, and rather heavily, tell of his decision to take the road "less traveled by," the road that has made "all the difference." The poem, in addition to demolishing the cliché of life's crossroads, is a vision of as well as a warning against the wise old farmer poet whose retrospective summary of his past may attribute a wisdom to former actions which was never there.

Beyond this playfully ironic self portrayal so characteristic of Frost, there is also the tragic self-awareness which enabled him to create the great dramatic monologues. In such poems as "The Fear," "Home Burial," and "A Servant to Servants," for example, sensitive wives are so caught between the lonely natural world and the rigid proverbs of their husbands that, locked in an unutterable loneliness, they disintegrate into hysteria or slump into depression. Those husbands bear enough similarity to the figure of the farmer poet to indicate how much Frost realizes, for all his willingness to exploit the poetic possibilities of aphorism—how blind and hard a proverb quoter can be.

If Frost needs self-awareness to protect himself from the Yankee wisdom in which he specializes, he also needs it to confront the world he moves in, that lonely and desolate world where the Frost drama is staged. Despite his literal realism, Frost has never been a mere reflector of his chosen New England locale; rather, he has managed to create the illusion of making the world he describes, and in his hands the region north of Boston becomes a self-sustaining yet surprisingly inclusive microcosm with the character of Frost himself at its center. Even the eccentricities of crabbed New England speech and attitude have poetic validity because, more than being details to characterize and individuate a geographical province, they belong to the central character and constitute his authentic signature upon the world he makes and owns. The entire region beneath his vision becomes his property, an extension of himself, and Frost's ability to project his character into his provincial world has given his poetry the double thrust it so often possesses—a thrust outward into the wild nature in which he persistently finds himself, and a thrust inward to the darker regions of the self.

Like his great New England antecedents, Emerson and Thoreau, he casts his own shadow upon the landscape he surveys. Skeptical in his cast of mind, Frost inclines away from their tendency to abstract doctrine, but he retains much of the method and many of the attitudes they left behind them, nor is it surprising that "Walden" is one of his favorite books. Thoreau's strategy was to move round and round the pond, keeping his eye alertly upon that self-contained body of water until, in the final chapter of his microcosmic odyssey, he had possessed it. His progress was parabolic in the mathematical sense, for his walking arc was midway between the pond, the focus, and the set of principles which formed the directrix of his journey. The more Thoreau discovered about the pond, the more he plotted a central index to life, since the pond was both mirror for man and eye of God in which the traveler could take a final measure of himself. In sounding it he sounded himself, and Thoreau fulfilled his dual rôle of explorer and surveyor by at once discovering and charting a course to sustain him through all modes of existence.

Frost has also been intent on possessing his world, but he started with no given center, no sure assumptions, and no assurance that there would be assumptions. His work has been no experiment to test himself, but the venture of a lifetime. His first poem in "A Boy's Will," significantly entitled "Into My Own," expressed a wish that the deep woods confronting him, instead of being a mere mask of darkness, stretched endlessly out toward the edge of doom. Doubling his subjunctive, Frost wished that he could lose himself in the infinite depths of such a forest, but extended a subdued invitation to those who loved him to follow his footsteps into the trackless wood. Although Frost's title of this first volume of poetry came from Longfellow's memorable refrain, "A boy's will is the wind's will," he was already advancing into the areas where Longfellow had refused to go. For in "My Lost Youth," Longfellow, after quite brilliantly returning into the Portland of his memory toward the secret regions of his boyhood, had paused at the threshold of Deering's Woods as if confronting a secret terror and, content to excuse himself with a pious admonition—"There are things of which I may not speak"—, he retreated back into nostalgia. Taking and retaining the boy's will to explore, Frost has forced a clearing in the woods which Longfellow declined to enter, and his career has been in many ways a realization of his earliest wish.

The clearing he has wrought is his own, and he works constantly at its edge, laying claim to the marginal world between the wild and the tame. The figure of the clearing, while it obviously does not appear in every poem, suggests the quality of experience which Frost has been intent upon possessing, and in "The Last Mowing," one of his most delicate lyrics, the dimensions as well as the drama of his world appear in sharp focus:

> There's a place called Far-away Meadow
> We never shall mow in again,
> Or such is the talk at the farmhouse:
> The meadow is finished with men.
> Then now is the chance for the flowers
> That can't stand mowers and plowers.
> It must be now, though, in season
> Before the not mowing brings trees on,
> Before trees, seeing the opening,
> March into a shadowy claim.
> The trees are all I'm afraid of,
> That flowers can't bloom in the shade of;
> It's no more men I'm afraid of;
> The meadow is done with the tame.
> The place for the moment is ours
> For you, oh tumultuous flowers,
> To go to waste and go wild in,
> All shapes and colors of flowers,
> I needn't call you by name.

Remaining in the moving margin where resurgent nature returns upon abandoned meadowland, Frost attempts to wrest the moment of beauty elapsing where order dissolves into chaos. He is no more afraid of the threatening woods than at another time he has been afraid of the men who cleared the field, for the wild flowers perish before both forces. In the face of the oncoming woods, Frost discovers a moment of joy in the midst of his tender elegy, since in that forgotten territory he can perform a solitary celebration for the beauty which remains.

Seeing the nature of his task, one can understand why he contended in "The Constant Symbol" that every poem is "an epitome of the great predicament; a figure of the will braving alien entanglements." Indeed, the woods, always ready to encroach upon his tenuous margin, suggest the alien entanglements against which Frost pits his will, and the drama he sees the poet playing recalls Emerson's insistence that a man must be self-reliant, "obeying the Almighty Effort and advancing on Chaos and the dark." But even as he accepts the antagonists of the Emersonian drama, Frost, lacking Emerson's evangelical temperament, recognizes a larger chaos and sees the drama of existence as man's willingness to risk himself before the spell of the dark woods. For him self-reliance becomes self-possession, and the victory lies not in the march forward into the wilderness but in the freedom he feels while patroling the boundary of consciousness. He accepts with almost joy the entanglements because he knows that the material of the unwrought poem inheres in that wilderness. Thus in "Pertinax" he advocates holding on:

> Let Chaos storm!
> Let cloud shapes swarm!
> I wait for form.

And in "The Figure a Poem Makes," he is even more emphatic: "All I would keep for myself is the freedom of my material—the condition of body and mind to summons aptly now and then from the vast chaos I have lived through."

Cryptic though his prose is, it is his own guarded commentary upon his work, offering essential insights into his poetic terrain. When Frost says that chaos lies behind him, he points up the temporal dimension of his world. Unlike Emerson, he is deeply concerned with his past—not the past of organized tradition so much as the disorganized past he himself has strewn behind. The literal facts of his New England world afford a scenic analogy against which the Frost character performs his act, for the woods he works in are no virgin wilderness but second-growth timber come back to claim abandoned human landscape. The black cottage, the belilaced cellar hole "slowly closing like a dent in dough," the overgrown path, the old barn at the bottom of the fogs remain forsakenly within his rural scenes as the surviving witnesses of lost encounters with the forest. In repossessing them, Frost is turning back upon himself to reclaim the fragments of his personal past—fragments which apparently meant nothing when they were current but which come to constitute the primary medium of exchange in the economy of reorganization.

Frugal as Frost's economy is, its aim is no easy security, for his clearing is as hard to hold as it is to win. In addition to the remnants of abandoned farms, there are also the living victims who linger in stunned confusion along the border—the woman in "A Servant to Servants" for example, whose mind is as hemmed in as the lake she gazes out upon; or the old man of "An Old Man's Winter Night," trapped in a house where "all out of doors looked darkly in at him"; or the witch of Coös, who, living with her mentally arrested son, finds her imaginative release in rehearsing for a stranger her half-forged, half-pathetic ghost story. Above all, there is the poet himself, who feels the terror of loneliness. Caught alone in the woods beneath the onset of winter's first snow, he feels the full threat of alien forces, and, although he knows that "all the precedent" is on his side and that spring *will* come again, he stumbles,

> looking up and round,
> As one who overtaken by the end
> Gives up his errand, and lets death descend
> Upon him where he is, with nothing done
> To evil, no important triumph won,
> More than if life had never been begun.

In these moments of terror, the outer threat of nature, with its ominous woods, its appalling snow, its rustling leaves hissing along the ground, gives rise to the deepest inner fears. The entire landscape becomes a haunting reflection of psychic desolation. If Frost can contemplate the infinity of space with a certain equanimity it is not because he feels more secure than Pascal but because, as he says,

> I have it in me so much nearer home
> To scare myself with my own desert places.

Confronting these desert places of his landscape, Frost needs all the restraint at his command, for the dark woods possess a magnetic attraction drawing him spellbound into them. The trees, whose branches reach out toward him and whose leaves insistently whisper an invitation, are, as Frost has written, the "vague dream heads" come out of the ground to beckon him to succumb to the mystery of their depths. Frost finds his power of resistance and control in the measured language of poetry—he even speaks of the poem as a "momentary stay against confusion." And he loves the metered line, choosing to leave free verse to Carl Sandburg on the ground that he, Frost, "would as soon write free verse as play tennis with the net down."

The haunting rhythms of "Stopping by Woods on a Snowy Evening" express the powerful fascination the woods have upon the lonely traveler, who, in the face of a long journey, descending night, and falling snow, pauses in the gathering gloom of the "darkest evening of the year," transfixed by the compelling invitation of the forest:

> Whose woods these are I think I know.
> His house is in the village though;
> He will not see me stopping here
> To watch his woods fill up with snow.
>
> My little horse must think it queer
> To stop without a farmhouse near
> Between the woods and frozen lake
> The darkest evening of the year.
>
> He gives his harness bells a shake
> To ask if there is some mistake.
> The only other sound's the sweep
> Of easy wind and downy flake.
>
> The woods are lovely, dark and deep,
> But I have promises to keep,
> And miles to go before I sleep,
> And miles to go before I sleep.

The poem is *about* the spell of the woods—the traveler's own woods, we want to say, but they are alien enough and belong to someone else enough for him to sense the trespass of his intent gaze into them at the same time he recognizes their sway over him. His heightened awareness projects his concern for himself back to the representatives of civilization, the unseen owner of the woods and the horse in harness. Thus, the indifferent animal becomes, in his master's alerted imagination, the guardian who sounds the alarm which rings above the whispered invitation.

The poem *is* the counter-spell against the invitation, the act by which the traveler regains dominion of his will. The intricately interlocked rhyme scheme (*aaba, bbcb, ccdc, dddd*) and the strict iambic tetrameter, while they imitate and suggest the hypnotic power of the forest, also form the basis of a protective charm against that power. The logic of the rhyme scheme, in which the divergent third line of one stanza becomes the organizing principle of the next, is an expression of the growing control and determination described in the syntax. Thus, the first line of the last quatrain finally *names* the nature of the spell and also provides the term which is answered in rhyme by the poet's decision to refuse the invitation.

Seen in this light, the poem reveals what Frost means when he says that "every poem written regular is a symbol small or great of the way the will has to pitch into the commitments deeper and deeper to a rounded conclusion. . . ." He sees the form as both instrument and embodiment of the will braving the alien entanglements of experience—the commitments—for it must organize and at the same time contain its material. The poem in its totality is the image of the will in action, and the poet's spirit and courage convert words into deeds. The words are the given, and "We make them do," he says, and continues: "Form in language is such a disjected lot of old broken pieces it seems almost non-existent as the spirit till the two embrace in the sky." In the completed poem both form and spirit have encountered not "in rivalry but in creation." The creation is not a forging of a new world, but the discovery and grasp of a world at once familiar and strange. The act of writing is, to return to the statement I have quoted earlier, a plunge into the vast chaos the poet has lived through and a bringing into the full range of consciousness as much of that half-known life as possible. That is the meaning of self-possession.

And Frost, like the Paul Bunyan in "Paul's Wife," is a terrible possessor; indeed, the action of that poem recapitulates Frost's own process of creation. In the pith of an unsound saw log abandoned in disgust by the practical sawyer, Paul discovered the material which, after he had delicately carved it out and carefully dipped it in the waters of a mountain lake, emerged into consciousness to become the fabled wife whom he protected from the brute tribute to beauty offered by the curious lumbermen:

> Owning a wife with him meant owning her.
> She wasn't anybody else's business,
> Either to praise her, or so much as name her,
> And he'd thank people not to think of her.
> Murphy's idea was that a man like Paul
> Wouldn't be spoken to about a wife
> In any way the world knew how to speak.

Frost too has gone back into the desolation of a world abandoned to seize his own particular kind of beauty.

Of course, he has shared it with the world, but he clings fiercely to his poems as his private property, and even the titles of his several volumes describe the progress of his endeavor to lay claim to his world. From "A Boy's Will" he went on to define his province, "North of Boston," and in "Mountain Interval," "New Hampshire," and "West Running Brook," he established enough landmarks within the region to open what he calls "A Further Range." In "A Witness Tree," the tree, once a part of the wilder woods, bears the wound he has given it as a witness of his ownership, and Frost himself assumes the rôle of landowner, leading his reader along the boundaries of his property. Finally, in "Steeple Bush," the hard-back flowering at the edge of the clearing stands as the precious item he holds against the ever-returning woods. The property he reclaims from the ruins of time he insistently refuses to relinquish:

> I could give all to Time except—except
> What I myself have held. But why declare
> The things forbidden that while the Customs slept
> I have crossed to safety with? For I am there
> And what I would not part with I have kept.

Frost's long career of returning into his own to enlarge his province has been a continual thrust of both will and memory, and he quite logically defines the initial delight of making a poem as the "surprise of remembering something I didn't know I knew." If there are times when his poetry fails, as in the editorializing poems which have been increasing in ratio until they fairly dot "Steeple Bush," he fails because he is remembering something he knew all the time, and his poetry hardens into provincial cynicism. Although critics have lamented this departure from the earlier lyric and dramatic vein, Frost's penchant for bald statement followed as necessarily from his earlier poem as self-assurance follows self-possession. Moreover, out of this almost brash assurance comes "Directive," surely one of Frost's highest achievements.

Here the poet is not the listener or the narrator, but the confident guide leading his reader back into a "time made simple by the loss of detail," to discover among the ruins of a vacant farm the broken goblet the guide has hidden under a cedar tree against the day of his return. The broken goblet, originally cast aside by the adults as a mere toy for the children's playhouse and again abandoned when everyone departed, becomes the all important detail which the poet has seized to save from the ruins of the past. It is for Frost an image of the charmed grail itself, a talisman not carried like a spear of grass but stored away in a secret niche and displayed only to the right persons who, following the poet along the intricate pathways toward the heart of his property, are lost enough to find themselves. Possessing this charm, they can, by drinking with him from the waters of the brook which once supplied water for the farmhouse, "be whole again beyond confusion."

Yet Frost maintains a sharp comic detachment from the central association he exploits, the allusion to the grail quest. His poem is not a recapitulation or variation of the legend but a masque, a performance staged for his audience's benefit by the knowing god who owns the salvaged grail. His whimsy—he "only has at heart our getting lost" and he has hidden the goblet "so the wrong ones can't find it"—is actually an aspect of his comic delicacy as he leads his followers through the "serial ordeal" of being watched from "forty cellar holes," and on to the "height of the adventure" which is the height of ground where two village cultures "faded into each other." The chapel perilous is the field "no bigger than a harness gall" marked by a collapsing cellar hole where once a farmhouse stood, and the grail turns out to be the broken goblet stolen from the children's playhouse.

These are the discrepancies which Frost almost mockingly exploits as he conducts the journey, but they are also the miraculous details which authoritatively affirm the reality of this search as opposed to the legendary quest. The guide's command comes from knowing every detail of his private ground, details which were hard to come by but which are securely his own. Even the resurgent woods receive a brashly tender notice as they pass beneath the guide's vision:

> As for the woods' excitement over you
> That sends light rustle rushes to their leaves,
> Charge that to upstart inexperience.
> Where were they all not twenty years ago?
> They think too much of having shaded out
> A few old pecker-fretted apple trees.

In his way an audacious brag, the guide yet makes good on all his claims—and well he might, for "Directive" rehearses the course Frost has pursued as a poet and is thus a survey of the ground he has possessed. But it also points toward what is to come, toward the masques and beyond to his latest poem, "Kitty Hawk," in which, while commemorating the Wright brothers' famous flight, he seizes the chance to celebrate his own first flight into poetry with his sacred muse—an event which considerably anticipated the first propeller-driven flight.

Finally, "Directive" is a performance by the same "character" who so often commands the central stage as lecturer and whose public performances imitate to a remarkable degree the structure of his poems. For Frost's primal subject is always poetry and the poet—*his* poetry and himself the poet. Beginning in conversational manner, he utters a summary remark about the state of the world, the nature of woman, or the status of science. This aptly stated phrase constitutes the ostensible subject for the evening, and, although he returns to it periodically, his digressions move in ever widening arcs until the initial theme reveals itself as but an association leading toward what is Frost's most private and most public possession—his poems. Even in this introductory movement, Frost is already retreating from his audience toward himself, and the conversational idiom functions as an invitation, never as an appeal.

When he reaches the poems he is to "say," as he puts it, Frost has gained a presence of remote loneliness. His manner of "saying" them is neither recitative, declamatory, nor bardic; rather he seems to be remembering each poem as he moves through it, and even when he forgets his way he usually chooses to find himself without benefit of text. There is a manifest anticipation both in speaker and audience as the remembering proceeds, a kind of wonder and suspense as the tenuous thread of the poem is pursued; and when the end is grasped there is a distinct sense of discovery *and* relief. The disparaging remarks which may be, and have been, leveled at Frost's mode of delivery—at his flatness of voice, his frequent pauses, and his halting delivery—are dwarfed by the essential victory achieved on every poem. And much of his success as a reader of his poems stems from his ability to convey this sense of achievement and repossession.

To know Frost's poems and then to watch his mind close tenderly about them is to see again that they are his triumphs in form wrought out of the chaos he has lived through. They are for him the living emblems—the charms which must be *said*—that, like the broken goblet, he has reclaimed from his abandoned experience and ours. Thus, when Frost, speaking for himself and his muse in "Kitty Hawk," says

> This we're certain of,
> All we do and try
> All we really love
> Is to signify . . .

he is celebrating in poetic language the labor of a lifetime.

Editor's Note: "Robert Frost and the Edge of the Clearing" is reprinted, by permission of James M. Cox and *The Virginia Quarterly Review,* from *The Virginia Quarterly Review,* XXXIII (1957), pp. 378–394.

James M. Cox is Professor of English at Dartmouth College and is the author of *Mark Twain: The Fate of Humor.*

THOMAS STEARNS ELIOT

1888-1965

T. S. Eliot was born in St. Louis and educated at Harvard, where he absorbed the influence of Irving Babbitt and George Santayana. After his graduation in 1910 he studied philosophy at the Sorbonne, where he heard the lectures of Henri Bergson. From 1911 to 1914 he studied Indic philology, Sanskrit, and philosophy at Harvard, and went to Germany on a study fellowship. He returned to Merton College, Oxford for continued philosophical studies in 1915. The dramatic beginning of his poetic career was marked by the publication of "The Love Song of J. Alfred Prufrock" in *Poetry* (1915). His first volumes of verse, *Prufrock and Other Observations* (1917) and *Poems* (1920), were followed by *The Waste Land* in 1922. "The Hollow Men" (1925) and *Ash Wednesday* (1930) demonstrate Eliot's increased commitment to an Anglo-Catholic religious point of view. Significantly, in 1927 he became a British subject and a member of the Anglican Church. His later poetic masterpieces are the *Four Quartets,* which he collected in 1943. Eliot's poetic dramas also deserve attention, notably *The Rock* (1934), *Murder in the Cathedral* (1935), *The Family Reunion* (1939), *The Cocktail Party* (1950), *The Confidential Clerk* (1954), and *The Elder Statesman* (1958).

The revolution in sensibility for which Eliot is largely responsible was effected to a considerable degree through

121

his influential literary criticism. His important criticism includes *The Sacred Wood* (1920), *Homage to John Dryden* (1924), *Shakespeare and the Stoicism of Seneca* (1927), *The Use of Poetry and the Use of Criticism* (1933), *After Strange Gods* (1934), *The Music of Poetry* (1942), *The Three Voices of Poetry* (1953), *The Frontiers of Criticism* (1956), and *On Poetry and Poets* (1957).

Collected Poems, 1909–1962 was published in 1963. Eliot died in London on January 4, 1965.

POETRY AND CRITICISM:
T. S. ELIOT

STANLEY EDGAR HYMAN

[Mr. Hyman's book, *Poetry and Criticism: Four Revolutions in Literary Taste,* asserts that "revolutions in criticism follow after revolutions in poetry, sometimes long after, codifying and consolidating them." Hyman illustrates a dialectic in which new poetry of genius becomes a *"challenge"* to the established *"standard"* and its *"poetics,"* and produces new critical principles which are its *"sanction."* The *standard* and *poetics* referred to in the opening sentence of the Eliot section are Milton's *Paradise Lost* and the principles forwarded in Matthew Arnold's "The Study of Poetry."]

A good example of the CHALLENGE to this standard and poetics comes in 1918 with the publication of "Sweeney Among the Nightingales" by the thirty-year-old Thomas Stearns Eliot. It is a sequence of ten iambic tetrameter quatrains, each rhymed on the second and fourth lines. We know nothing of the poem's occasion. It is a complex and opaque work, not readily paraphrased. Suffice to say that it tells of Sweeney, an earthy character who appears in several other Eliot poems, threatened by violence in some sort of dive, and like Pope's "Rape of the Lock" and Wordsworth's "Resolution and Independence," establishes wider significances for its relatively trivial events.

We should first note that after all the elevation of Arnold's slogans, Eliot's poem is defiantly low. The scene appears to be a bar frequented by prostitutes, and public behavior there is somewhat indecorous. We are introduced to the protagonist in the first stanza:

Apeneck Sweeney spreads his knees
Letting his arms hang down to laugh,
The zebra stripes along his jaw
Swelling to maculate giraffe.

The next character enters in the third stanza without much concern
for appearances:

The person in the Spanish cape
Tries to sit on Sweeney's knees

Slips and pulls the table cloth
Overturns a coffee-cup,
Reorganized upon the floor
She yawns and draws a stocking up;

The poem's second conspirator appears after the waiter brings in
exotic fruit:

Rachel *née* Rabinovitch
Tears at the grapes with murderous paws;

The remaining characters, if not as active, are just as low.

We know something of Sweeney from Eliot's other poems. In
"Sweeney Erect" we see him shaving naked in a brothel, undisturbed by a girl's shrieking. In "Mr. Eliot's Sunday Morning Service," while others are in church, he shifts from ham to ham in his
bath. In the unfinished *Sweeney Agonistes,* he lectures a whore
named Doris about life and death, concluding with an anecdote
about a man he knew who murdered a girl and kept her corpse in
a gallon of lysol in the tub, as the result of which he became something of a philosopher. Critics have differed considerably about the
sources of Sweeney, with Eliot's encouragement. Eliot told F. O.
Matthiessen that he modelled Sweeney on a man he first saw in a
bar in South Boston. He told Nevill Coghill many years later that
he pictured Sweeney as a retired professional pugilist who keeps a
pub. Conrad Aiken, who knew Eliot well fifty years ago, has written
that Sweeney may be modelled on a retired fighter who gave Eliot
boxing lessons in South Boston when he was a graduate student in
philosophy at Harvard.

Whatever the source of Sweeney, his nature is fairly clear. He is the type of the physical or sensual man. The poem's simple action is a suggestion of conspiracy. We are told of Rachel in the seventh stanza:

> She and the lady in the cape
> Are suspect, thought to be in league;
> Therefore the man with heavy eyes
> Declines the gambit, shows fatigue,

The heavy-eyed man, described merely as "The silent man in mocha brown" or "The silent vertebrate in brown," may be the object of the conspiracy, and appears to think he is, since he departs abruptly in the next stanza, but the larger framework of the poem suggests that it is Sweeney's death that is plotted, and the man in brown may be declining the chance to be a conspirator. There is some possibility that the whole poem after the second stanza is Sweeney's dream, since it is all one enormous sentence introduced by the line:

> And Sweeney guards the hornèd gate.

which might be the Gate of Horn in the *Odyssey* and the *Aeneid* through which true dreams come. Whether the action is dream or real, however, it is distinguished by its sordidity and the sub-humanity of the characters: Sweeney is ape, zebra and giraffe, the lap-sitter is "the person in the Spanish cape," Brown is a vertebrate, Rachel tears her food like an animal. Unlike Bianca in Elizabeth Barrett Browning's "Bianca among the Nightingales," Sweeney is a brute among the brutes.

The analogues of the action, however, are considerably less brutish. The last six lines of the poem make it clear that past and present meet in the timeless concurrence of so much of Eliot's poetry, and the singing of the nightingales joins the plot against Sweeney with several famous deeds of violence:

> The nightingales are singing near
> The Convent of the Sacred Heart,
>
> And sang within the bloody wood
> When Agamemnon cried aloud,
> And let their liquid siftings fall
> To stain the stiff dishonoured shroud.

The poem's epigraph is a Greek line from the *Agamemnon* of Aeschylus, Agamemnon's terrible cry as Clytemnestra hacks at him:

Alas, I have been struck deep a deadly wound.

The epigraph and the poem's ending in combination suggest strongly that Sweeney is to be killed, that he is in fact a type of Agamemnon, apeneck and gross, sinful and arrogant in his sin, and that we are at the "purpose" stage of tragedy. The "bloody wood" in which the nightingales sang is, Grover Smith says in *T. S. Eliot's Poetry and Plays,* the grove of the Furies in Sophocles' *Oedipus at Colonus,* but it seems much more strongly Sir James Frazer's golden-bough grove in which the sacrifice of the vegetation spirit in various human embodiments goes on eternally.

In an earlier printing, the poem had for its epigraph, not the line from Aeschylus, but a quotation from the anonymous *Raigne of King Edward the Third:*

Why should I speak of the nightingale? The nightingale sings of adulterous wrong.

The reference is to the myth of Philomela from Ovid's *Metamorphoses.* Her brother-in-law King Tereus raped her and cut out her tongue to conceal the crime, and the gods transformed her into a nightingale. Eliot used the story as a motif in *The Waste Land* three years later:

Above the antique mantel was displayed
As though a window gave upon the sylvan scene
The change of Philomel, by the barbarous king
So rudely forced; yet there the nightingale
Filled all the desert with inviolable voice
And still she cried, and still the world pursues,
"Jug Jug" to dirty ears.

"Sylvan scene," incidentally, is from Book Four of *Paradise Lost,* Satan's entry into Eden, and Eliot thus makes Philomela and Tereus one more telling of the story of Proserpina gathered by gloomy Dis, *Eliot's* equivalent for Satan's victory over Eve. "Sweeney Among the Nightingales" thus ends with mutilated Philomela singing "with inviolable voice" while Agamemnon lies butchered, and the sacrificial victims in the bloody wood Sweeney is entering begin to pile up.

Nor are those all. The great god Dionysus himself, endlessly dismembered by his band of maenads and endlessly resurrected, appears in stanza five with his attribute the grapes. It is he who is torn apart when Rachel tears the grapes with murderous paws, and the purple juice shed is his blood. Her murderous animal madness is the sign of his entering into her, she eats him to become him, and Dionysus is thus a divine mystery, both slayer and slain. We are then told that the man with heavy eyes:

> Leaves the room and reappears
> Outside the window, leaning in,
> Branches of wistaria
> Circumscribe a golden grin;

He is now the resurrected Dionysus, framed in the purple blood of wistaria, grinning and golden like the Stranger in *The Bacchae*. Half hidden behind him is yet another slain god, Jesus. The poem continues:

> The host with someone indistinct
> Converses at the door apart,

> The nightingales are singing near
> The Convent of the Sacred Heart,

The nightingales now are the nuns singing the Sacred Heart of Jesus and his Passion, Jesus like Dionysus the god sacrificed to the god. The "someone indistinct" with whom the host converses is the indistinct additional figure of *The Waste Land,* "wrapt in a brown mantle, hooded," who is the risen Christ at Emmaus. The man in brown, like Philomela, has been considerably tranformed. "The host" himself, in a bold pun, is the sacramental wafer of Communion, and "converses" is the "turns-into" of "conversion," another transformation or metamorphosis. The poem, Donald Stauffer says finely in *The Nature of Poetry,* is a "narrative of betrayal by the brute lust of the world." While Sweeney laughs in a South Boston joint, Eve is corrupted by Satan, Persephone is gathered by Hades, Philomela is raped by Tereus, Agamemnon is slain by Clytemnestra, Dionysus is torn apart by maenads and resurrected, Jesus is betrayed by Judas, crucified, and risen.

127

The poem then has its seriousness, if low rather than high seriousness. Eliot has Milton in mind not only in *The Waste Land's* "sylvan scene," but in the very Miltonic "maculate," in the first stanza of "Sweeney Among the Nightingales," restoring "immaculate" to its Latin root-meaning of *physically* unspotted. The second and third stanzas set the action against the Miltonic epic setting of geography and cosmology:

> The circles of the stormy moon
> Slide westward toward the River Plate,
> Death and the Raven drift above
> And Sweeney guards the hornèd gate.
>
> Gloomy Orion and the Dog
> Are veiled; and hushed the shrunken seas;

The "shrunken seas" may even be Arnold's shrunken seas of Faith in "Dover Beach." The poem's last line, "To stain the stiff dishonoured shroud," is borrowed from a line in "Ichabod," John Greenleaf Whittier's bitter poem against Daniel Webster, "To stain the dim dishonored brow." Betrayal goes on in New England too, if lesser betrayal. The poem's organization is associative, lyric, and thematic, building up its figures in layers of significance. But its action is a firm sequence of strong verbs, most of them monosyllabic: Sweeney spreads, guards; Miss Cape tries, slips, pulls, overturns, yawns, draws; Brown sprawls, withdraws, declines, leaves, reappears; Rachel tears; the nightingales sang and Agamemnon cried.

One of the things the poem is about is art. The title "Sweeney Among the Nightingales," in this aspect, is a conceit for the poet and his low subject. The inviolable voice of Philomela that tells her woes after her tongue has been cut out (in the myth, she weaves her story into a piece of embroidery) is art: embroidery, Ovid's poetry, Aeschylus singing the death of Agamemnon, Eliot singing the conspiracy against Sweeney. At the end of the poem, the liquid siftings of the nightingales that fall on Agamemnon's corpse are the pure notes of immortal song. But they are also bird droppings, spotting the dishonoured shroud, making it maculate instead of immaculate. Another of the things the poem is about is excrement. The lovely song of the nightingale is " 'Jug Jug' to dirty ears," and if the sacramental drinking of Dionysus in the grape or eating of Christ in the wafer is high spiritual experience at one end of the process, it is excrement at the other. Eliot's poem is the voice of the modern revolution, insisting against Arnold that poetry must deal with the most sordid details of experience as well as the noblest, and embodying both in Sweeney. Eliot told Matthiessen, in a characteristic statement, "that all he consciously set out to create in 'Sweeney Among the Nightingales' was a sense of foreboding." This may very well be true, but its truth is the cryptic ironic truth of the Delphic oracle. Eliot was not doing an ominous saloon scene, but offering us the deepest forebodings of the human spirit: that man is only a nasty animal; that the dead may not rise; that God's death may be, as Yeats said, "but a play"; that art is merely the child's fouling of his crib.

The sanction for "Sweeney Among the Nightingales" is Eliot's essay "Tradition and the Individual Talent," published the next year, 1919, and collected in a volume, *The Sacred Wood*, in 1920. "Tradition and the Individual Talent" discusses the relationship of a modern poet to his predecessors, the nature of the poetic process, and the aims of poetry and the poet. In it Eliot never mentions "Sweeney Among the Nightingales," nor any of his poems, nor even the fact that he is a poet. The essay is nevertheless a powerful manifesto for his own individual talent. *The Sacred Wood*, Matthiessen writes in *The Achievement of T. S. Eliot*, immediately placed the author "in the main line of poet-critics that runs from Ben Jonson and Dryden through Samuel Johnson, Coleridge, and Arnold," the line of "craftsmen talking of what they knew at first hand." Eliot was performing his friend Ezra Pound's highest function of criticism, formulating the principles his poetry demonstrates. Many years later, in "The Music of Poetry" in 1942, Eliot admitted this. He wrote:

> But I believe that the critical writings of poets, of which in the past there have been some very distinguished examples, owe a great deal of their interest to the fact that the poet, at the back of his mind, if not as his ostensible purpose, is always trying to defend the kind of poetry he is writing, or to formulate the kind that he wants to write.

The key word in "Tradition and the Individual Talent" is "tradition." Eliot begins by saying that it is used mostly as censure or archaeology, that we tend to dwell on differences, to praise a poet for "those aspects of his work in which he least resembles anyone else." Eliot would have us praise a poet as "traditional" and value his resemblances to earlier poetry, but not for simple copying. He writes:

> Tradition is a matter of much wider significance. It cannot be inherited, and if you want it you must obtain it by great labour.

We may be reminded of Arnold's remark in "Milton":

> But excellence is not common and abundant; on the contrary, as the Greek poet long ago said, excellence dwells among rocks hardly accessible, and a man must almost wear his heart out before he can reach her.

A man need not necessarily wear his heart out obtaining tradition, but he must at least ignore his immediate predecessors. Eliot writes, again following Arnold:

> Yet if the only form of tradition, of handing down, consisted in following the ways of the immediate generation before us in a blind or timid adherence to its successes, 'tradition' should positively be discouraged.

In a later essay, "Baudelaire in Our Time," this became the doctrine that tradition skips a generation, and that a poet has more in common with his grandfather's literary generation than with his father's.

In "Tradition and the Individual Talent," Eliot explains that the poet's tradition must be selective but that it cannot be whimsical. He writes:

> To proceed to a more intelligible exposition of the relation of the poet to the past: he can neither take the past as a lump, an indiscriminate bolus, nor can he form himself wholly on one or two private admirations, nor can he form himself wholly upon one preferred period.

Eliot adds:

> The poet must be very conscious of the main current, which
> does not at all flow invariably through the most distinguished
> reputations.

Obtaining a tradition requires a special ability. Eliot writes:

> It involves, in the first place, the historical sense, which we may
> call nearly indispensable to anyone who would continue to be
> a poet beyond his twenty-fifth year; and the historical sense
> involves a perception, not only of the pastness of the past, but
> of its presence; the historical sense compels a man to write not
> merely with his own generation in his bones, but with a feeling
> that the whole of the literature of Europe from Homer and
> within it the whole of the literature of his own country has a
> simultaneous existence and composes a simultaneous order.
> This historical sense, which is a sense of the timeless as well
> as of the temporal and of the timeless and of the temporal
> together, is what makes a writer traditional. And it is at the
> same time what makes a writer most acutely conscious of his
> place in time, of his own contemporaneity.

In this mystic timelessness and simultaneity, we can see the sanction
for "Sweeney Among the Nightingales," just as the poem in turn
helps us to understand what the essay means. Put more dramatically:

> The existing monuments form an ideal order among them-
> selves, which is modified by the introduction of the new (the
> really new) work of art among them.

When he wrote that the historical sense is a requisite for the poet
over twenty-five, Eliot was thirty-one. In the introduction to the
book, he quoted Arnold's remark that the Romantic poets of the
first quarter of the nineteenth century "did not know enough," and
his clear resolve is not to share that fate.

The poets mentioned in "Tradition and the Individual Talent"
are a curious small group: Homer, Aeschylus, Dante, Shakespeare,
Tourneur, and Keats. It is not meant to be an inclusive list, and
other essays in the book make it clear that the Elizabethan and

Jacobean dramatists and the French symbolists share Eliot's esteem. The name of Milton is a marked omission. For years, Pound had been fulminating against Milton: Milton "shows a complete ignorance of the things of the spirit"; "Milton is the most unpleasant of English poets"; "Milton is the worst sort of poison," "the worst possible food for a growing poet"; and so on. Eliot did not publish on Milton until 1936, "A Note on the Verse of John Milton," and then to explain that Milton was an unsatisfactory human being and a bad influence, concluding: "He may still be considered as having done damage to the English language from which it has not wholly recovered." When Eliot ate some of his words in "The Music of Poetry" in 1942 and a second essay on Milton in 1947 (all of these are reprinted in *On Poetry and Poets*), he conceded that he had blamed Milton for too much that was inevitable in the history of culture, and that if Milton made blank verse impossible for the drama, "we may also believe that dramatic blank verse had exhausted its resources, and had no future in any event." The point of all of this is that Milton had no place in 1918 in *Eliot's* poetic tradition, that another kind of poetry had to be written.

Eliot's account of the poetic process in "Tradition and the Individual Talent" centers in the image of the catalyst, "the action which takes place when a bit of finely filiated platinum is introduced into a chamber containing oxygen and sulphur dioxide." Eliot writes:

> When the two gases previously mentioned are mixed in the presence of a filament of platinum, they form sulphurous acid. This combination takes place only if the platinum is present; nevertheless the newly formed acid contains no trace of platinum, and the platinum itself is apparently unaffected; has remained inert, neutral, and unchanged. The mind of the poet is the shred of platinum.

We cannot doubt that the catalyst analogy is aimed at Arnold's touchstones. A touchstone is a flintlike stone used to test the purity of gold and silver. By replacing Arnold's primitive image with an up-to-date scientific one, by transferring the operation from the reading process to the writing process (the poet's mind being platinum, more precious than gold and silver), and by nastily imaging the poem as sulphurous acid, Eliot is producing an ironic counterstatement.

The formal theory that follows from the catalyst analogy, as "high seriousness" followed from the touchstone, is what Eliot calls "this Impersonal theory of poetry." Eliot got it from Pound, who got it ultimately from Poe. "The more perfect the artist," he writes, "the more completely separate in him will be the man who suffers and the mind which creates." Eliot adds: "The poet has, not a 'personality' to express, but a particular medium." Thus:

> Poetry is not a turning loose of emotion, but an escape from
> emotion; it is not the expression of personality, but an escape
> from personality. But, of course, only those who have person-
> ality and emotions know what it means to want to escape from
> these things.

He concludes: "The emotion of art is impersonal." In the essay "Hamlet and His Problems" written the same year, Eliot amplified the Impersonal theory with the doctrine, built on Wordsworth's formula, of the "objective correlative":

> a set of objects, a situation, a chain of events which shall be
> the formula of the *particular* emotion; such that when the
>
> external facts, which must terminate in sensory experience, are
> given, the emotion is immediately evoked.

The ingredients of poetry are the poet's emotions and feelings, with a somewhat shadowy distinction between them, and it will evoke emotions and feelings in the reader, but as the link between those two experiences it is not itself emotional or feeling. In his essay "Dante" in 1929, Eliot repudiates his earlier prejudice "that poetry not only must be found *through* suffering but can find its material only *in* suffering," which found expression in such statements as the one in "Shakespeare and the Stoicism of Seneca":

> Shakespeare, too, was occupied with the struggle—which alone
> constitutes life for a poet—to transmute his personal and pri-
> vate agonies into something rich and strange, something uni-
> versal and impersonal.

Emotions and feelings are thus visibly suffering and agonies, but the poem is to be an artifact to produce them without displaying

133

them. Poetry is "a fusion of elements," and a great variety of combinations is possible. The nightingales will sing for Sweeney too.

Finally, the aim of poetry is delight, as it was for earlier critics. Eliot writes:

> if we seek not Blue-book knowledge but the enjoyment of poetry, and ask for a poem, we shall seldom find it.

Eliot goes directly after Arnold's "high seriousness," tagging it as the Longinean criterion it is. He writes:

> If you compare several representative passages of the greatest poetry you see how great is the variety of types of combination, and also how completely any semi-ethical criterion of 'sublimity' misses the mark. For it is not the 'greatness,' the intensity, of the emotions, the components, but the intensity of the artistic process, the pressure, so to speak, under which the fusion takes place, that counts.

Here, finally, is what will allow the "low seriousness" of "Sweeney Among the Nightingales" to be great poetry, the intensity of the fusion. Eliot has attacked Arnold for not being "altogether the detached critic" but having his own poetry in mind when he wrote, and we are reminded of Wyndham Lewis' statement in *Men Without Art* that Eliot always describes himself in accusing Arnold. The last sentence of "Tradition and the Individual Talent" is a manifesto for the new poet:

> And he is not likely to know what is to be done unless he lives in what is not merely the present, but the present moment of the past, unless he is conscious, not of what is dead, but of what is already living.

In his later account of the poet-critic in "The Music of Poetry," Eliot wrote:

> Especially when he is young, and actively engaged in battling for the kind of poetry which he practises, he sees the poetry of the past in relation to his own: and his gratitude to those dead poets from whom he has learned, as well as his indifference to

those whose aims have been alien to his own, may be exaggerated. He is not so much a judge as an advocate. His knowledge even is likely to be partial: for his studies will have led him to concentrate on certain authors to the neglect of others. When he theorizes about poetic creation, he is likely to be generalizing one type of experience; when he ventures into aesthetics, he is likely to be less, rather than more competent than the philosopher; and he may do best merely to report, for the information of the philosopher, the data of his own introspection. What he writes about poetry, in short, must be assessed in relation to the poetry he writes.

It is the man of fifty-four looking back on the man of thirty-one, who found in the tradition of the past, as Eliot wrote in "Yeats," "the kind of poetry that is in him to write." The young Eliot thus created the taste by which he was to be enjoyed, and "Tradition and the Individual Talent" made it possible for "Sweeney Among the Nightingales," and poems like it before and after, to survive in the world of Milton and the mighty dead without conceding an inch. That is the true relation between poetry and criticism, a marriage based on mutual need, and as marriages go it has been an unusually fruitful and happy one over the centuries.

Editor's Note: "Poetry and Criticism: T. S. Eliot" is reprinted by permission of Stanley Edgar Hyman from Hyman's *Poetry and Criticism: Four Revolutions in Literary Taste,* New York, 1961, pp. 159–178.

Winner of the National Institute of Arts and Letters award for criticism, 1967, Mr. Hyman's literary career includes: editorial staff, *The New Republic,* 1940; staff writer for *The New Yorker* since 1940; author, *The Armed Vision, Poetry and Criticism, The Tangled Bank, Nathanael West, The Promised End, Flannery O'Conner,* and *Standards;* editor, *The Critical Performance, Darwin for Today,* Kenneth Burke's *Perspectives by Incongruity* and *Terms for Order, Selected Essays of William Troy,* and *The Magic of Shirley Jackson;* book column, *The New Leader,* 1961-65. His present academic affiliation is with Bennington College.

THE GOAL OF
THE QUEST IN
THE WASTE LAND

WILLIAM T. MOYNIHAN

Aside from a few shocked reactions which have seen *The Waste Land* as a disorganized potpourri of fragments and parodies, critics have found an increasing degree of unity in the poem. Successively critics have pointed out patterns of comparison and contrast (sordid contemporary versus ideal classic mainly), an organization based on a "music of ideas" or on psychoanalytic states, and most comprehensive of all, the grail-quest pattern. Each succeeding interpretation, inevitably taking something from the preceding—even when in disagreement—has added to our understanding of this obscurely allusive poem.[1] I would like to push one step further what seems to be a tendency to find more and more formal unity. Assuming the general notion of a quest pattern—that is, of someone in search of something and a movement in the direction of that object—I would like to try to identify who that someone is, what is the direction of his search, and what is the object of his quest.

A fundamental difficulty in determining all these things, but

[1] Examples of these attitudes are: Yvor Winters, *The Anatomy of Nonsense* (Norfolk, Conn., 1943), pp. 120–167; Cleanth Brooks, *Modern Poetry and the Tradition* (Chapel Hill, 1939), pp. 136–172; Kimon Friar and John Brinnin, *Modern Poetry: American and British* (New York, 1951), pp. 472–497; I. A. Richards, *Principles of Literary Criticism* (New York, 1934), pp 289–295; Elizabeth Drew, *T. S. Eliot: The Design of His Poetry* (New York, 1949), pp. 58–90; Genevieve W. Foster, "The Archetypal Imagery of T. S. Eliot," *PMLA*, 60 (1945), 567–585; George Williamson, *A Reader's Guide to T. S. Eliot* (New York, 1953), pp. 118–154; Grover C. Smith, *T. S. Eliot's Poetry and Plays* (Chicago, 1956), pp. 72–98.

especially in determining the character of the quester, is the multiplicity of "voices" in *The Waste Land*. It is very difficult to know who is speaking, to whom, and in what context. Theoretically, what we have is a mixture of modes such as Stephen Dedalus describes in his account of a poem moving from lyric to dramatic, from the poet speaking to himself (or being overheard) to the complete removal of the poet's voice in favor of actors. Eliot expresses a variation of the same theory when he says the lyric and epic voices are seldom if ever heard separately.[2] In practical terms what we have is the creation of character through radically different modes of representation—although perhaps the term *character* is not the right one. For Eliot creates, through the multiplicity of modes and personages, more of an everyman, a concrete universal, than a poetic character. Whether or not it is precise to call the composite sensibility that exists behind the words of the poem a quester is perhaps questionable also. But to conceive of groups and voices as parts of a single searching protagonist, and other groups of voices as his antagonists seems to convey even more formal unity to the poem than previous criticism has granted.

The clearest indication that Eliot had a notion of a central protagonist, or better, a central voice, lies in his footnote to Tiresias:

> Tiresias, although a mere spectator and not indeed a 'character,' is yet the most important personage in the poem, uniting all the rest. Just as the one-eyed merchant, seller of currants, melts into the Phoenician Sailor, and the latter is not wholly distinct from Ferdinand Prince of Naples, so all the women are one woman, and the two sexes meet in Tiresias. What Tiresias *sees,* in fact, is the substance of the poem.

This footnote cannot be neglected and we shall return to it shortly in another connection. I think F. R. Leavis right when he says this note "provides the clue to *The Waste Land.*"[3]

Thematically, the notion of a central personage is clearly conveyed also. For one of the major accomplishments of the poem lies in making the "lyric," "narrative," and "dramatic" voices hang together by thematic links. The voice describing cruel April, the voices of the ladies of Part II and the voice speaking "Shantih

[2] *On Poetry and Poets* (New York, 1957), p. 108.
[3] *New Bearings in English Poetry* (London, 1950), p. 94.

shantih shantih"—all appear as speeches and descriptions in the *Odyssey* might be lost if that poem were compressed to a thousand lines. Further, a common sensibility–sad, serious, learned, and frightened–provides the sense of a single observer, if not of related actors. Regardless of whether the voice is a lyric memory of childhood or a narrative of the crucifixion, whether it is a dramatization of love in a formal garden or sex on the typist's sofa, a narrative of Cleopatra or of an obscure assignation in 1920, historical or contemporary, indulgent or penitential–all the principal voices convey a sense of loss. They conveyed a sense of lost time, of lost friends, innocence, religion, love, certitude, knowledge, virtue, excellence, romance, the loss of life itself. And that which was lost is that which the protagonist seeks. He seeks it through changing seasons, countries, through the juxtaposition of historical references through various attempts at finding love, knowledge, self-control and belief.

The extremes of the quest are outlined in apocalyptic and demonic symbolism.[4] The losses referred to above signify the demonic world which the protagonist seeks to escape. Specifically, this world is represented by images of mutability, entrapment and circularity: by seasons, time of day, by the desert, rats, bats, city, and the wheel. Water, and the journey by water, signify the natural through which one reaches (or fails to reach) the apocalyptic world of union with that which was lost, or more likely of union with that which replaces the lost. Fire, light (white), heights and thunder signify the supernatural, the world the quester longs for. The progress of the protagonist is indicated most clearly perhaps by his companions, or tutors. At one extreme is Madame Sosostris who speaks with a bad cold; at the other is the Lord of Creation who speaks through the thunder.

It is in this regard that we may give full credence to Eliot's own regret "at having sent so many enquirers off on a wild goose chase after Tarot cards and the Holy Grail."[5] For, despite the importance of both these themes, the cards are used as a variation of the traditional prophetic device, and, more important, the grail quest is but one of three overlapping quest patterns: the classical, the mythical (which includes the grail), and the mystical. And, in so much as the goal of the quest is essentially a spiritual one, the final inter-

---

[4] See Northrop Frye, *Anatomy of Criticism* (Princeton, 1957), pp. 141–151.
[5] *On Poetry and Poets*, p. 122.

pretation of the images must be more than psychological or epical. The subsuming quest is the mystical.

That there is a general epical movement in *The Waste Land* may be seen from its correspondences with traditional epics. Both for reasons of clarity and of sufficiency I will illustrate these correspondences from *The Odyssey,* although I believe there are structural similarities with other epical works such as the *Aeneid* or *The Faerie Queene,* Book I. The likenesses I am talking about here are not to be found, fundamentally, in a treatment of plot or even of similar events. There are hints of this, certainly, but the real correspondence lies in the parallel human situation where literary characters—seemingly as far separated as conceivable—achieve a curiously parallel resolution through a somewhat similar process.[6]

The "hero" of *The Waste Land,* like the hero of the *Odyssey,* is a man of many guises, and a man who encounters various people and obstacles on his journey. Like Odysseus, the hero (or poet, or speaker, as you will) of *The Waste Land* is a "Noman," an Every-man, an Adam. Homer's hero has lost Penelope and struggles toward home; Eliot's "hero" has lost something far less obvious than a wife (although love is part of his loss) and his goal likewise is far less clear. In one there is a motif of seduction and tedious wander-ing. In the other, the androgynous Tiresias "melts into" the dis-enchanted husband, an absent soldier, the consort of Mr. Eugenides, a Fisher King, a Christ-figure, one who walks with the risen Savior, one who hears God speak, and one who, at poem's end, sits fishing still seeking for a solution. The masculine Odysseus wanders on his quest as the faithful husband, the absent soldier, the companion of women, a Fisher King (he too has received the mysterious wound on the leg [Book 19 and 21][7] which Miss Weston discusses, and his land and he himself were wasted during his wandering). At the end of the *Odyssey* the hero has not completed his quest; he must shoulder his oar and wander still until he has made peace with Poseidon. In *The Waste Land* the protagonist sits with his fishing

---

[6] See Edmund Keeley, "T. S. Eliot and the Poetry of George Seferis," *Comparative Lit.,* VIII (Summer, 1956), 216: "What Eliot attempts to do with the Fisher King, the Phoenician sailor, and Ferdinand Prince of Naples, Seferis attempts with Ulysses, Elpenor, and Orestes."

[7] References to *The Odyssey* are from W. H. D. Rouse's translation (Mentor, N. Y., 1957).

pole knowing that even if he sets his land in order, like Odysseus, his quest too must continue. Though difficult to pin down, the various voices of *The Waste Land* do have a cohesive quality, and this cohesiveness suggests some characteristics of a protagonist who moves in a predictable literary, psychological, and spiritual direction. I would now like to investigate the direction of this movement and the direction of the *quest* in more detail.

The title of Part I, "The Burial of the Dead," suggests quest and rebirth. The connection of burial with the beginning of a journey is evidently as old as mankind. W. F. Jackson Knight says the ritual pattern of initiation itself appears to have begun as a burial rite.[8] St. Paul and Christian rituals (the latter a source for the title) developed the idea of passage in Christian terms, and a quest which begins with such emphasis on burial inevitably suggests a quest for divine life—even if the quester himself is not aware of his goal.

April is perennial image of rebirth, and the speaker of the opening lines evidently feels April is cruel because it reminds him of something he does not possess. It stirs his desire for rebirth, reminds him of once common beliefs in rebirth, and does no more for him.

Eliot deals further with this concept in *The Family Reunion*. Harry, in the speech beginning, "I have spent many years in useless travel," asks: "Is the cold spring/Is the spring not an evil time, that excites us with lying voices?" What excites us is the rebirth, and what is evil is the uncertainty of our own rebirth. Mary tells Harry that in the painful stirring of nature under the snow there is a kind of joy:

> But joy is a kind of pain
> I believe the moment of birth
> Is when we have knowledge of death.

The Waste Land opens *in medias res,* and the protagonist, like Harry, recalls a lifetime of "useless travel" and feels spring is an evil time. There is no Mary in *The Waste Land* to succinctly answer the dilemma of life and death; there is only the enigma of life-in-death and death-in-life. Juxtaposed to nature's endless cycle (the breeding, mixing, stirring, covering, feeding) are the images of personal, purposeless, sterile actions.

[8] *Cumaean Gates* (Oxford, 1936), pp. 1–2.

Lines 8-18 of Part I convey a sense of movement and frustration through the active verbs, through images of passage and through discontinuity. Three different images of passage are present. First we find the colonnade, from which the speaker went on to the Hofgarten and "talked for an hour." Then there is the incident on the sled going down the mountain, and the idea of going south in the winter. Finally, the whole suggests the passage of time since the incidents are not only brief in themselves, but also memories of things past.

The discontinuity is in the narrative itself. The speaker skips from incident to incident in the past and closes with the *non sequitur,* "I read, much of the night, and go south in the winter." The discontinuity of thought conveys restlessness, disillusionment, the desire for escape. Although Marie was afraid on the sled, she remembers that "one feels free" in the mountains. But she has made no effort to return there. She only reads "much of the night" (suggesting sleeplessness) and flees from winter, the time of fear and suffering, but also of freedom. As children the people of the wasteland had a sense of freedom and lived in the mountains, but as adults they travel much and have only a sense of being trapped. This sense of entrapment leads to the desert imagery and the "dry cicada."

The second section of Part I (lines 19-42) defines the precise nature of the quest, or at least gives as precise a picture as any in the poem. The protagonist, it is vaguely inferred, has lost something—a sense of freedom, of innocence, of belief perhaps. Is there anything which holds fast—"What are the roots that clutch,"—the speaker asks. The answer is no, there is nothing to rely on, "only the dead tree gives no shelter"—but strangely there is some relief, the shadow of the rock. A tree is traditionally the symbol of life. Now, whether we take "the dead tree" to be meaningless Christianity, the tree of knowledge, or the tree of life, it is equally dead, and life is an existential hell for the protagonist. The dried tubers of the first section are analogous to the roots that clutch in this section, and will be re-echoed in the leaves that clutch the bank of the river in Part III. They seem to represent the irrepressible tenacity of life even in the wasteland. The epithet, "Son of man," always used in Christian tradition in reference to the Messiah, or prototype of the Messiah, introduces definite Christ overtones, as does the red rock (which we shall see more of shortly). Here the shadow of

the rock is the only hope for the wasteland quester. It is an invitation filled with fear because it is an invitation to love and, as the
fragment from *Tristan und Isolde* reminds us, to a love that is not
necessarily achieved.

While I agree essentially with Unger's treatment of Eliot's rose
garden symbolism, there is another very important level of meaning
that should be emphasized concerning the Hyacinth garden. For,
to judge from Miss Evelyn Underhill's accounts, the terms Eliot
uses to describe this garden experience are those one would use to
describe a mystical vision.[9]

> I could not
> Speak, and my eyes failed, I was neither
> Living nor dead, and I knew nothing,
> Looking into the heart of light, the silence.

In other words, perhaps the speaker did not so much undergo "an
experience of love" (Brooks) as an experience of God, which, looking back is a world lost, looking forward, a world to be gained.
(This interpretation is close to the kind of reading Eliot made of
Dante's relation with Beatrice in the *Vita Nuova*. "The final cause
is the attraction towards God . . . . the love of man and woman [or
for that matter of man and man] is only explained and made
reasonable by the higher love . . .")[10]

The alchemists of the 16th century were trying to express much
the same concepts and experiences which Eliot tries to express in his
poem, and there are curiously parallel uses of imagery which cast
some light on ambiguous points of *The Waste Land*. "Alchemical
terms were increasingly used to express a mystical rather than a
practical experience—they were considered hieroglyphics for the
soul's search and for ultimate union with God. The philosopher's
stone is Christ, the union of the male and female principles *is* the
union of the soul with God, and so on."[11]

In this regard, the *lapis philosophorum,* which was often red, is a
concept which may shed additional light on the red rock of lines
25 and 26. In a wasteland where there is no relief the poet says to
come with him under the shadow of the red rock.

[9] *Mysticism* (Meridian, N.Y., 1955), Chapter VII and VIII.
[10] *Selected Essays*, pp. 234–235.
[11] Liselotte Dieckmann, "Renaissance Hieroglyphics," *CP*, IX (Fall, 1957) 316.

Throughout literature the rock is the symbol of the starting place of new life. It is not life itself (on the contrary, the stone is a symbol of the death impulse), but the *prima materia* out of which life will come. Northrop Frye summarizes the case for the elemental symbolism of rock when he says "life seems, in some way we cannot fathom, to form itself out of dead matter. As the rock is the image of dead matter, all new life struggles out of a rock, and relapses back into it at death."[12] Christ rises from his hewn tomb and rolls away the stone. The king (new life) is marked by pulling the sword from the stone (the Yasilikays Chamber,[13] Arthur, Theseus). [Prometheus and Samson (confined life) are in the shadows of rocks.] The hero of the wasteland will show us "fear in a handful of dust." Personal creation, the formation of man from "the dust of the earth," and the redemptive intercession of the divine lapis cast a burden of initiative upon these sojourning in the wasteland.

Alchemical symbols also apply to the garden episode. The Hyacinth girl and the light are analogous to the "whiteness, the state of Luna, or Silver, the 'chaste and Immaculate Queen,' [which] is the equivalent of the Illuminative Way. . . ."[14] The final secret of alchemic mysticism is the union of the white and the red "from which comes forth the Magnum Opus: deified or spiritual man."[15] The final goal of *The Waste Land* quester is the attainment of the union he envisioned in the garden, or the attainment of a union for which the rose garden is a metaphor.

The first section of Part I shows the protagonist in the midst of the mystic quest. The second section describes the immediate scene—the desert—and recapitulates the specific nature of the quest. Section three now outlines the steps the remainder of the journey will follow.

In the *Odyssey* Circe (whom Levy and Jackson Knight link with the Sibyl of Cumae, referred to by Eliot in his epigraph) sends Odysseus to Hades to consult Tiresias about the journey to Ithaca. In Hades Tiresias recounts what shall befall Odysseus on his voyage. Then Odysseus talks to many others among the dead. The action recounted in lines 43-59 and 60-76 is analogous to this part of the *Odyssey*. I do not think this should be stressed, but it is suggestive.

---

[12] *Fearful Symmetry: A Study of William Blake* (Princeton, 1947), p. 225.

[13] G. R. Levy, *The Sword from the Rock* (London, 1953).

[14] Underhill, *Mysticism*, p. 146.

[15] *Mysticism*, p. 146.

For example, Odysseus (in Book XIV) relates, in one of his tales, how he made an escape after the death of Phoenician sailors, one "a very subtle Phoenician, one of those subverters who have wrought such havoc in the world." The female monsters Scylla and Charybdis have an echo in the Lady of the Rocks; the one-eyed merchant is reminiscent of Polyphemus;[16] "Fear death by water" is an appropriate admonition recalling Tiresias' prophecy that death shall come to Odysseus from the sea (Book XI); and "crowds of people, walking round in a ring," though immediately recalling the *Inferno*, also has overtones of Homer's Hades: "all this crowd gathered about the pit from every side. . ." (Book XI).

The card of the drowned Phoenician Sailor belongs to the protagonist because he too must make a water journey. It symbolizes the "sea-change," that alchemical process analogous to the mystical way whereby we achieve the transformation of a baser nature into gold. There is the possibility that the pearls, in this context, may suggest "the pearl of great price," in addition to the obvious Shakespeare echo.

Prime concerns of both Aeneas and Odysseus in their journeys to the nether world are famous clairvoyants and recently killed companions. Aeneas must bury his helmsman, Palinarus, and Odysseus promises to hold funeral services for Elpenor, one of his oarsmen. Burial meant that the dead would be enabled to reach the land of their final destination,[17] the other world. The corpse planted in the garden implies a similar concern.

There is no distinction in Part I between hell and contemporary life, or to put it more specifically, between Hades and London. The Hades through which the protagonist passes is a state of mind embracing various times and various lives in a present moment. As Eliot's notes suggest, it is the place of those "who lived without blame, and without praise," typified by the man "who from cowardice made the great refusal."[18] Eliot's reference to the *Inferno* follows the expression "unreal city." The subsequent lines of this opening section develop some of the unrealities of the world through which the protagonist now moves. It is a world of the living dead, where time passes with a dead sound, where Stetson (a

[16] Smith, *T. S. Eliot's Poetry and Plays*, pp. 82, 85. Cf. also Smith's "The Fortuneteller in Eliot's *Waste Land*," *AL*, XXV (Jan., 1954), 491.

[17] Knight, *Cumaean Gates*, pp. 3–10.

[18] Dante, *Divine Comedy* (Mod. Lib. Ed.), pp. 22-23.

modern man) is a survivor of Mylae, but still carries out the rituals of the ancient world now without purpose or meaning.

One thing in the final section of "The Burial of the Dead" which tends to be overlooked is the satirical tone. I take it that the protagonist comes to look upon his world as dead and that it is this world of the living-dead that he seeks to escape. This satiric note does not spring unexpectedly, nor does it disappear from the poem after this. It begins with the bad cold of Madame Sosostris and "the Lady of the Rocks," and is maintained throughout the epic-waste-land parallels. After Part I the satire predominates in "A Game of Chess" and recurs in "the Virgin Queen" of Part III. The purpose of all the satiric touches is to criticize, ever so involutedly, modern society.

In the Stetson episode, the reader even is drawn into the general pattern of disparagement. As already noted, the Dante allusion of the opening lines of the final section suggests that those flowing over London Bridge are to be associated with the inhabitants of the Inferno; those who "never wakened to any part either good or evil." Among these is Stetson and, if one is to judge from the similar modes of address, Stetson and the reader are associated in the mind of the speaker of the poem. I take it that Eliot's specific object of satire in this final section is not only the persistence of fertility rituals into contemporary times, but their meaninglessness in the modern world. All of our rituals are as meaningless as wearing hats—even Stetson hats, and we have nothing to replace them. Regardless of any source in the Osiris myth, "to plant a corpse" is Hollywood slang, the word "sprout" is humorous in a macabre sense, and as Eliot reads lines 74-75 his slow deliberate cadence picks up to the tempo of a punch line. The satire seems almost inescapable when we realize that "Or with his nails he'll dig it up again!" not only echoes Webster, but is also an expression of Trimalchio in *The Satyricon*. Giving directions for the arrangement of his monument at his grave, Trimalchio asks that "At the feet of my effigy you have my little bitch put . . ."[19] referring to his wife. Then, after an argument with his wife, he says to her: "All right! I'll make you long yet to dig me up again with your fingernails."[20] At this point in *The Waste Land* death, one termination of the

---

[19] Petronius, *The Satyricon*, Trans., Oscar Wilde (N.Y., 1927), p. 163.
[20] *The Satyricon*, p. 172.

quest, appears to offer neither the possibility of cyclic regeneration nor even of an undisturbed quietus.

II

"A Game of Chess" describes two aspects of the quest which are clearly evident in the *Odyssey:* the temptress preventing the fulfillment of the voyage, and the beleaguered wife who suffers while the quester remains far distant. The Belladonna (a Calypso) "like Virgil's Dido is a temptress, a Circe or Deussa who has trapped the quester in her toils. . . ."[21] Lil is the severely tried woman, who, unlike Penelope, falters and fails. Both of these themes are closely related to the central mystical experience of the Hyacinth garden and reflect the struggle to achieve that ideal, the Illuminative way, the union of the red and white—the fertile union (marriage) of male and female. The task of the Fisher King is to restore health to the wasteland, of Odysseus—to be reunited with his wife and restore order to his kingdom, of the protagonist of *The Waste Land,* to achieve a meaning for existence in the midst of seduction, the disintegration of marriage, madness and despair.

The protagonist, caught in the perfumes of the belladonna, is trapped. Instead of achieving his goal, he is moribund. The cyclic tones of the opening lines of the poem are suggested here by reference to the wheel, Karma, circularity: the perfumes stir the air, "stirring the pattern on the coffered ceiling," the sea-wood is fed, and "if it rains, a closed car." The dormant, inactive, unfertile state is linked with sexual violence (the Philomel reference) and with infidelity.

In the midst of this spiritual dead-end (expressed in *demonic* imagery: "I think we are in rats alley/Where dead men lost their bones."), the haunting image of change persists: "I remember/ Those are pearls that were his eyes."

The second section of Part II presents another aspect of the dilemma (a Scylla and Charybdis dilemma). It makes little difference who is identified as the hero in these episodes. The problem, the situation, is the same. And here, again, it seems well to mention, Eliot effectively uses satire to round off the picture:

> What you get married for if you don't want children?
> HURRY UP PLEASE ITS TIME

[21] Smith, *T. S. Eliot's Poetry and Plays,* p. 83.

> Well, that Sunday Albert was home, they had a hot gammon,
> And they asked me in to dinner, to get the beauty
>   of it hot—

Lil's friend's conversation has made it abundantly clear that her question does not reflect her convictions. Mad Ophelia's lines closing the section catch the essence of the tension, the emotional crack-up, the hostile and ironic world.

"The Fire Sermon" presents further obstacles and entrapments on several levels. Infidelities and sterility surround and practically overwhelm the wanderer. The wheel continues to turn, the seasons pass, but winter predominates. The demonic rat creeps past the protagonist who is

>   fishing in the dull canal
> On a winter evening round behind the gashouse

The dull canal and the gashouse give little hope of fish. And, above all, we must remember the significance of what the Fisher King is angling for. Miss Weston tells us: "There is thus little reason to doubt that, if we regard the Fish as a Divine Life symbol, of immemorial antiquity, we shall not go very far astray."[22]

The hero strives for life in a world "burning" with infidelity and unproductive unions. The union of the soul with God, of the bride with its divine bridegroom is commonly symbolized as a fruitful and blissful union, whereas in Parts II and III we are presented with a series of unfruitful, sterile unions. There is no desert imagery in this central portion except the one reference to Philomel in the desert. Here we are near the river of hell, the Thames in this poem.

The "Unreal City" repeats the motif of the last section of Part I, and Mr. Eugenides, a salesman of the mystery cult, is to be linked with Stetson, and, in terms of the epic, with the cannibalistic Polyphemus. And certainly, if, as Brooks suggests, his invitation is homosexual, the imagery is fantastically comprehensive. A double parodic relationship is implied: one between cannibalism and the Eucharist, another between homosexuality and fruitful marriage.[23] The merchant on the "spiritual" level parallels the presence of a Cyclops

---

[22] Jessie L. Weston, *From Ritual to Romance* (Anchor, N.Y., 1957), p. 127.
[23] Frye, *Anatomy of Criticism*, pp. 147–149.

147

on the physical, the absence of fruitful union the absence of frutiful communion. Mr. Eugenides "meets with" Phlebas and the latter's death concludes the demonic parody. The appearance of the third one on the road to Emmaus episode promises (ever so vaguely and tentatively) fruitful union.

The crowd that went over London Bridge in the morning comes back at the "violet hour." At this point, almost the exact center of the poem, Tiresias appears, and certain aspects of the nature of the "hero" become a bit clearer. Tiresias, the blind man who has vision, emphasizes the predicament of the inhabitants of the waste-land. He symbolizes the blind, yet knowing, human soul. From this central figure radiate all the other figures of the poem, and in his androgynous personality the different characters meet, forging an ironic central figure. His foresuffering and foreknowledge are very similar to the Christian tradition of Christ having foresuffered and foreknown all the sins of subsequent generations. It cannot be an accident that Tiresias, like the typist, awaits the expected guest, or that the clerk leaves figuratively blind: "And gropes his way finding the stairs unlit. . ." Further, like Christ, who daily sat in the temple, Tiresias sat below the wall. It may, or may not, be coincidental that "the Builders of Thebes came from Phoenicia,"[24] but Tiresias catches characteristics of the one-eyed merchant—the Phoenician sailor—as surely as his prophetic nature connects him with Madame Sosostris and his blindness with the wounded Fisher King and other sexually marred and spiritually blind inhabitants of *The Waste Land.*

I think it is misleading to regard the fishermen who lounge at noon as symbols of fertility.[25] They, like the other inhabitants of the city of man, are spiritually dead. They have lost something—perhaps even their jobs—that they "lounge at noon" indicates this. Here, as we have seen previously, the cry of "city city" is a desolate one (O Jerusalem), and associated with primitive worship. The name of the church, "Magnus Martyr," echoes the Phrygian cult of *Magna Mater,* and the pleasant whining of the music is an obvious

[24] Levy, p. 94.

[25] Most commentators have regarded the fishermen as symbolic of a fertility lacking to the rest of the inhabitants of *The Waste Land,* e.g., Elizabeth Drew, *T. S. Eliot: The Design of His Poetry,* p. 81. Eliot's note on line 221 is also of interest: "This may not appear as exact as Sappho's lines, but I had in mind the "longshore" or "dory" fisherman, who returns at *nightfall.*" (Italics mine.)

overture to the songs of the temptresses that follow, and, certainly, no place for the mystic voyager to halt. As Smith says, "The river nymphs suggest . . . the sirens of the *Odyssey*, and in this capacity they are evil powers who lure the quester from his way. . . ."[26]

"The collocation" of Buddha's Fire Sermon and St. Augustine's coming to Carthage, is, as Eliot tells us in his notes, "not an accident." The purgative fires precede the protagonist's arrival at a point from which he may act. That point in *The Waste Land* is asceticism, the death of self, of the "old man." It is only at the conclusion of Part III that we come to understand the meaning of the Fire Sermon. It is by being plucked out, by the burning, that the protagonist, the "central sensibility," can be joined to the Divine fire (fire being an archetype for the heavenly or divine, as well as the means of purification).

Concerning Part IV we must ask ourselves: If the protagonist must be purged by flame, what is the reason for the water symbolism? (In Part III the protagonist knows he must be purged only as Odysseus knows he must return to Ithaca and slay the suitors.) Primarily, Part IV indicates change. Death and the passage of time are the two basic enemies of the quester. The death of Phlebas restates the "fear in a handful of dust," a fact all men should consider. Some men do not complete their quest, do not find what has been lost. They enter again the cycle, the whirl pool. A man overtaken by death in the pursuit of business serves as a reminder and incentive to the protagonist. Further, "Death by Water" brings us back to "The Burial of the Dead." The hero has reached the point from which his quest may be completed. The quester has arrived at the Grail castle, Odysseus has lost his companions and has arrived home to deal with the suitors, Christ has died and may now harrow hell, Adam has digested the apple and faces the task of planting a new garden.

Part V begins "After"—after the agony and crucifixion, after the death of Christ, and suggests the speaker of the poem must follow much the same road. Before he can leave the wasteland he must contest with demons in the desert—the customary place of spiritual growth. Evelyn Underhill, quoting from the biography of Antoinette Bourignan, writes: "When shall I be perfectly thine, O my God? and she thought He still answered her, *When thou shalt no*

---

[26] Smith, *T. S. Eliot's Poetry and Plays*, p. 89.

longer possess anything, and shalt die to thyself. And when shall I do that, Lord? He answered, *In the Desert.*"[27]

"What the Thunder Said" summarizes and restates the thematic material of the poem in religious terms. The opening section of Part V explains somewhat the opening of the poem, *i.e.,* after the agony in the garden, "April is the cruellest month." (Significantly, Eliot makes garden plural, emphasizing the universality of the experience, the extension of the original "agony in the garden" to many gardens; the garden of Gethsemane and the Hyacinth garden are joined.) The scene of Part V repeats the earlier scene. We have left the colonnade for the "Dead mountain mouth of carious teeth that cannot spit." This "nightmare sense of constriction in a cave"[28] provides a more evident rebirth image. We have returned to the mountains of the first lines of the poem. The cicada recalls the grasshopper, the dry rock, the "stony rubbish." Most important, for the first time we are shown a relationship which is not wholly tainted or disintegrating: "When I count there are only you and I together." The protagonist and the girl who carries the flower of the slain god of Part I are reflected in the disciples walking toward Emmaus with the risen Christ. The sandy road of the previous lines has become the white road.

But the imagery portends death not birth. The city of man must crumble. The whole world of the protagonist crumbles; the Belladonna of Part III appears, as do the bats, the "reminiscent bells," and the singing voices. But the quester is in the mountains where men traditionally approach God. Here, as Jung quotes from Abul Kasim, the essence of life is found—"in the mountain where . . . everything is upside down."[29] In the Chapel Perilous—not in the "splendour of Ionian white and gold"—the protagonist realizes what he has betrayed. In the echo of the cock crow comes the damp gust and the lightning (recalling the wet hair and the heart of light of the Hyacinth garden). And then the protagonist hears the voice of God.

We are back at the beginning, both of the period of trial for the protagonist and for the whole world, back to the cradle of religious consciousness.

[27] Underhill, *Mysticism*, p. 213.
[28] Drew, p. 84.
[29] G. G. Jung, *Psychology and Alchemy* (N.Y., 1953), p. 413.

There seems to be some analogy between the commands of Prajapati and various religious triads. The commands strangely echo the counsels of poverty, chastity and obedience, "which best serve the self in its journey towards union with the absolute,"[30] or the triad of "faith," "hope," and "charity." The similarity between Christian and Oriental concepts is implied in the responses of the protagonist. Under *Datta* he recalls the only giving of himself has been sexual:

> The awful daring of a moment's surrender
> Which an age of prudence can never retract.

After *Dayadhvam* he confesses the restricting pride of a Coriolanus. And after *Damyata* appears the forceful image of the boat and the helmsman—an image of paternal direction of the spirit, or of obedience.

The allusive movement of the multiple quest, repeatedly described by cultural, historical and literary references, obscures somewhat the progression I have been trying to describe. A bald recapitulation of the action may be useful.

The voice which speaks to us in the "Burial of the Dead" introduces a protagonist, an everyman, in the midst of a quest for restoration of lost innocence, love, faith and hope. The quest is a coming to awareness, and the degrees of awareness establish a relationship between the five parts. The first section of Part I conveys the quest in terms of the seasons and common life. The second section states the religious nature of the search with the focal image being the Hyacinth garden episode. The third section outlines the remaining quest by the traditional prophecy device. The fourth describes the locale of the search, which is here and now, everywhere and every time, in the fallen world. "A Game of Chess" gives two views of the struggling protagonist. "The Fire Sermon" flashes a montage of sensuality, lust and indifference—enemies of the quest—culminating in the arrival at a point of awareness, the awareness of the necessity for asceticism. The dead Phoenician depicts the inevitability of physical death. This part also expresses the necessity for spiritual change or death in order to achieve the condition of Part V where the Voice of the Thunder may be heard. In

---

[30] Underhill, p. 205.

Part V, where the grail pattern is most explicit, instead of the vision there is the voice of the Lord of Creation and the final awareness on the part of the protagonist as to the nature of his aimless wandering and the necessity for further effort.

I believe there is more of a positive note in the final eleven lines than most commentators have admitted. What negativism there is, is of two kinds: 1) That of an ironic world in which the hero is fallen man; 2) That of a pattern which reflects the inevitable rise and fall, attainment and loss of natural cycles. Certainly, if, regardless of the irony, the Fisher King can set his lands in order, he is no longer impotent. And it seems relevant that he asks himself "Shall I." There is no question of "can I"; it is only a matter of will. The destruction of London Bridge repeats the symbol of the destruction of the unreal city, of the material city. If, for him, the city of man is destroyed, he has no alternative but to turn to the other city. Thus, it follows that he, like Arnaut Daniel, will gladly accept the necessary purification to achieve this divine life for which he is still fishing. The reference to the swallow is another image of transformation; but, for the present, he is "The Prince of Aquitaine, of the ruined tower." The fragments that he has to prop up his ruins are the memories of infidelities, death, rebirth, and the Voice of the Thunder. Many are mad like Hieronymo who eagerly accepted the invitation to supply the court with a play ("Why then Ile fit you.") so that he might achieve his goal. The final words of the poem are negative to the extent that the first stage of the purgative way itself is negative—negative, certainly, in respect to other stages of the mystic quest. But even the realization that "Give, Sympathize, Control" result in "the peace which passeth understanding," is a far more positive attitude than "April is the cruellest month." The quester of *The Waste Land* seems to have reached a stage of acceptance and of resignation not too much different than that of Eliot's Simeon:

> Not for me the martyrdom, the ecstasy of thought
> and prayer,
> Not for me the ultimate vision.
> Grant me thy peace.

Editor's Note: "The Goal of the Quest in The Waste Land" is a slightly revised version of "The Goal of the Waste Land Quest,"

Renascence, XIII (1961), pp. 171–179. Printed by permission of William T. Moynihan and *Renascence.*

Professor Moynihan is Head of the English Department at The University of Connecticut. He has published a number of critical essays on modern literature, edited several college texts, and is the author of *The Craft and Art of Dylan Thomas.*

THE SPIRITUAL STATUS OF T. S. ELIOT'S HOLLOW MEN

EVERETT A. GILLIS

There is a noticeable tendency in recent expositions of T. S. Eliot's *The Hollow Men* to read some affirmation into a poem traditionally associated with *The Waste Land* as a work of sterility and desolation, and thus to offer a degree of spiritual hope to Eliot's famous effigies. Yet the orthodox view of the poem is still very tenable, and a thorough examination of the sources and probable origin of the poem suggests that it is in many respects closer to *The Waste Land* in theme, method, and mood than it is to Eliot's later, more affirmative work.

The Hollow Men opens with the familiar picture of a desert landscape in which a chorus declares their spiritual status to be that of hollow men, straw effigies, caught in a stance of frozen immobility: "Shape without form, shade without color, / Paralyzed force, gesture without motion." Except for certain details which will be taken up later, Eliot derives his picture almost entirely from Dante's *Divine Comedy*. As a matter of fact, the first section of the poem is to all effects a direct transcription of the third canto of Dante's *Inferno*— of the dark, desolate plain lying between Hell's portal and the river Acheron, which flows as a formidable barrier between the plain and Hell's abyss. Here Dante and Virgil perceive vast hordes of souls futilely pursuing a great whirling banner. Their cries fill the air, "reverberating in the starless air"; and when Dante asks why they lament so bitterly, Virgil replies that they are those souls who on earth were neither spiritually alive nor spiritually dead, that is, neither good nor evil; and who, consequently, are altogether void of any spiritual meaning. As a result, these creatures may never pass beyond the river into the true realm of death (referred to variously in *The Hollow Men* as "death's other Kingdom," "death's dream kingdom," and "death's twilight kingdom"), where punishments or rewards are meted to the evil and the good, for they have known neither. Indeed, declares Virgil: "Mercy and justice scorn them, both alike." Dante's souls, like the souls in Eliot's poem, are thus *hollow* too—totally empty of any real spiritual validity. The notion of spiritual hollowness, seized upon by Eliot to bring a devastating castigation of his own age, is thus enormously reinforced by its reminiscence of the *Commedia's* gloomy setting.

The salient features of the middle sections of *The Hollow Men* likewise derive from this source. The opening lines of Section II again come straight from Dante, this time from Cantos XXX and XXXI of the *Purgatorio*. In these cantos Dante and Virgil, having climbed the Mountain of Purgatory to the Garden of Eden situated on its summit, witness the triumphal progress of the Church in the form of a chariot drawn by a griffin, whose twofold nature represents simultaneously the human and the divine natures of Christ. In the processional Dante perceives his beloved and fixes his eyes upon hers:

> A myriad desires, that burned like flames,
> Constrained my gaze upon those gleaming eyes;
> But they were looking over on the gryphon.
> And like the sun reflected in a glass,
> Within her eyes that twofold creature glowed,
> Now with one nature's actions, now with the other's.[1]

The group now moves to the Tree of the Knowledge of Good and Evil, which, long barren, at their approach breaks into foliage to the accompaniment of hymns:

> Even as our trees on earth begin to swell . . .
> Just so that tree, which had been stripped so bare,
> Broke into leaf, disclosing lovely things

[1] This and subsequent quotations are from Pantheon Books Edition of *The Divine Comedy*, translated by Lawrence Grant White (New York, 1948).

That ranged between the violet's and the rose's.
I could not understand—nor mortals sing—
The hymn which then was sung by that assembly.

But in the hollow land, as one might expect, Dante's supernal vision is distorted and empty. Here are the opening lines of Section II:

Eyes I dare not meet in dreams
In death's dream kingdom
These do not appear:
There, the eyes are
Sunlight on a broken column
There, is a tree swinging
And voices are
In the wind's singing
More distant and more solemn
Than a fading star.

The hollow-man speaker does not dare to meet the eyes of Beatrice. As a matter of fact, here in the Limbo the eyes do not even appear. They are "there"—far beyond the river-barrier and Hell's abyss, in the Garden of Eden. And the details of Dante's vision, so clearly perceived by him, exist as little more than hallucinatory glimmer. The reality of Christ in Beatrice's eyes is mere "Sunlight on a broken column"—the word "broken" suggesting both an inadequate grasp on the speaker's part and the shifting of Christ's image in Beatrice's eyes like the sun flashing in a mirror. The Tree of the Knowledge of Good and Evil (since the hollow men have never known *either* good or evil), rather than a significant phenomenon, is a "tree swinging"—that is, wavering like an illusion. The hymning hosts which so impressed Dante are to the hollow men as faint and incomprehensible as the voice of the wind: voices "In the wind's singing."

The concluding portion of Section IV of *The Hollow Men* is indebted to the *Paradiso*. In Canto XXXV Dante is carried by Beatrice into the heavens, where he observes the ranks of the redeemed "in the semblance of a snow-white rose," and observes that they fix their attention eternally on God, the "Trinal Light, which in a single star / Gavest them all such rapture." But in *The Hollow Men* the vision of the redeemed exists only as a remote, ironic possibility of hope to the dwellers of the Limbo, who remain, says the speaker—

> Sightless, unless
> The eyes reappear
> As the perpetual star
> Multifoliate rose
> Of death's twilight kingdom.

Section III of *The Hollow Men* owes somewhat to the *Commedia,* since it contains a reference to the compulsive spiritual force of Beatrice's eyes—to their absence in the hollow men's world. But the concluding lines of the section depend more on Dante's *Vita Nuova,* in which he offers an account of his first glimpse of the youthful Beatrice. The account records an experience of immediate, overwhelming love in which sexual desire and spiritual awareness awaken simultaneously and function as part of the total phenomenon of adolescent love. Leonard Unger[2] has traced this experience as a persistent motif in Eliot's poetry, the most typical manifestation of which is in the Rose Garden setting of *Burnt Norton.* It appears also, in distorted fashion, in the Hyacinth Girl passage of the first section of *The Waste Land.* In the latter passage, however, the experience is frustrated of its ultimate result and the narrator cries out: "I was neither / Living nor dead, and I knew nothing." Although Unger does not note the occurrence of the experience in *The Hollow Men,* it also seems to be the source of the rather curious details of the opening lines of Section III, which reveal what seems to be a truncated worship service in which details of an erotic nature occur. Stone images, the hollow-man speaker declares, are raised, but only to receive the supplication of a dead man's hand. Then he asks whether in death's other kingdom the experience of worship is as it is here in the Limbo:

> Is it like this
> In death's other kingdom
> Waking alone
> At the hour when we are
> Trembling with tenderness
> Lips that would kiss
> Form prayers to broken stone.

[2] "T. S. Eliot's Rose Garden: A Persistent Theme," *The Southern Review,* VII (Spring, 1942), 667–689.

Undoubtedly this is another instance, like that in *The Waste Land,* when the valid expectation from this experience fails to materialize.

Before leaving the subject of the direct influence of *The Divine Comedy* on Eliot's poem we should note that the role played by the speaker in the poem is very like that of Dante himself in the earlier work. The "I" of *The Hollow Men,* the hollow men's spokesman, is himself, in effect, a modern Dante. For like Dante he too presents a "dream kingdom" and is part of that kingdom in experiential terms. But unlike his medieval predecessor, who lived in a world in which religious efficacy was possible, the hollow-man spokesman does not. The author of the *Commedia* by means of his fervent vision of Beatrice's eyes is able to traverse both Inferno and Purgatory and to arrive at last in Paradise; the hollow-man Dante is forever immured within his desolate Limbo, barred even from crossing the river immediately into death's kingdom of Hell, into which "lost / Violent souls" may go; and whatever dream visions might conceivably be vouchsafed him must of necessity be meaningless or misleading because of his spiritual incapacity. "In this last of meeting places," he suggests, speaking for himself and his fellows, "We grope together / And avoid speech / Gathered on this beach of the tumid river." Such, Eliot suggests, is the modern Dante in the sterile landscape of contemporary civilization.

Intrinsic likenesses between *The Hollow Men* and *The Waste Land* are many, and readily apparent: the poems have the same desert landscape characterized by images of desiccation and ruin; their spiritual values are similarly distorted and perverted; even the inhabitants who dwell in these two desolate worlds are alike. For the crowds of white-collar workers enroute to their daily office routine in the "Unreal City" passage in the first section of *The Waste Land* are likewise hollow—wraiths going through their daily activities in a dream-like trance; this passage, too, according to Eliot's notes to *The Waste Land,* being derived from Canto III of the *Inferno.* Equally important is the extrinsic evidence of the close link between these two famous poems. From an exchange of letters[3] between Eliot and Ezra Pound relative to Pound's abridgment of the *Waste Land* manuscript to approximately half its length we learn two important facts: (1) from the rejected portions of the manuscript Eliot apparently salvaged certain lines that are closely

[3] *The Letters of Ezra Pound 1907–1941,* ed. D. D. Paige (New York, 1940), pp. 170–171.

associated with the little suite of lyrics called "Doris's Dream Songs"—the first published version of *The Hollow Men*; (2) Eliot originally planned to use as an epigraph to *The Waste Land* a quotation from Conrad's *Heart of Darkness*, but was dissuaded by Pound. It is from Conrad's story that one of the epigraphs for *The Hollow Men* was ultimately drawn.

The three untitled lyrics in "Doris's Dream Songs," published in 1924, begin respectively, "This is the dead land," "Eyes that last I saw in tears," and "The wind sprang up at four o'clock." Only the first was retained for the final version of *The Hollow Men,* the other two being relegated to the "Minor Poems" section of Eliot's *Collected Poems,* where they are readily available. But since they represent an important link with *The Waste Land,* we shall examine them in some detail. "Eyes that last I saw in tears" pictures a dream kingdom like that in *The Hollow Men.* There are eyes here also, but between them and the speaker is an abyss of division, and though a golden vision of the eyes reappears, the tears are now gone and they have become "Eyes of decision." He shall not see them again, the speaker laments, unless "At the door of death's other kingdom," where they remain momentarily: "The eyes outlast a little while / A little while outlast the tears / And hold us in derision." These, in the light of what we already know about *The Hollow Men,* are the eyes of Beatrice, and they are derisive here, presumably, because the speaker cannot comprehend their significance. They are in effect thus turned from symbols of hope into symbols of ridicule and recall Virgil's descriptive line that justice ("Eyes of decision") and mercy ("Eyes that last I saw in tears") both alike scorn hollow men.

"The wind sprang up at four o'clock" is closely connected with its companion lyric by the key image of tears, the latter portion of the poem being concerned with "a face that sweats with tears." It opens as if marking the beginning of a dream vision comparable to Dante's: the wind springs up at four o'clock in the morning, breaking into the sleeper's repose with its bell-like sound:

> The wind sprang up at four o'clock
> The wind sprang up and broke the bells
> Swinging between life and death
> Here, in death's dream kingdom
> The waking echo of confusing strife.

The startled moment of half-waking, half-dreaming, suggested by the lines is vividly evoked by the word "swinging," which intimates the wavering fantasy associated with dreams; but at the same time the moment retains a "waking echo" of reality. The poem thus opens from the standpoint of an individual in the realm of life— e.g., of a Dante, but one faced by a nightmare rather than an authentic vision—but the prevalent point of view is that of a dweller in Limbo. For as the poem proceeds, we are facing, as in the final version of *The Hollow Men,* a blackened river, suffused with miasmic mists, from the other side of which comes the clamor of vigorous vandal hordes of Tartar horsemen:

> Is it a dream or something else
> When the surface of the blackened river
> Is a face that sweats with tears?
> I saw across the blackened river
> The campfire shake with alien spears.
> Here, across death's other river
> The Tartar horsemen shake their spears.

The Tartar horsemen are rather evident prototypes of the lost, violent souls in *The Hollow Men.* The lines containing the nightmarish vision of a river sweating tears seem to be the lines which Eliot had in mind when he wrote Pound concerning the excisions in the *Waste Land* manuscript: "Would advise working sweats with tears etc. into nerves monologue; only place where it can go?" (The "nerves monologue" occurs in the first part of Section II of *The Waste Land.*) Pound's reply was: "I dare say the sweats with tears will wait." The lines consequently never appeared in *The Waste Land* in its final draft, but do form part of the first version of *The Hollow Men.*

The curious title "Doris's Dream Songs" also throws some light on the meaning of the final draft of the poem. The use of "dream" as a designation for Doris's songs implies that Eliot already has the *Commedia* in mind as background for his poem; and Doris becomes in effect the Beatrice of the speaker in the three lyrics, to whom she sends her dream visions. The visions are, however, mere distortions. Furthermore, Beatrice's symbolism as Dante's beloved on earth and spiritual guide beyond is totally lost; for the Beatrice of the Dream Songs has efficacy in neither, being lacking on both counts. For

when speaking to Doris of life's meaning in *Sweeney Agonistes,*
Sweeney declares that life on a cannibal island consists of birth,
copulation, and death, she replies: "Id be bored"; and, as just
shown, the spiritual dreams that she sends the speaker are dreams
of blackened rivers like faces sweating tears, hallucinations rather
than valid insights. The speaker of "Doris's Dream Songs" is no
better off spiritually after the dreams than before.

Although Eliot rejected Joseph Conrad's *Heart of Darkness* as a
source for an epigraph for *The Waste Land,* as a consequence of
Pound's persuasion, he returned to the story for one of the epigraphs of *The Hollow Men.* The phrase "Mistah Kurtz—he dead"
recalls for any reader of Conrad's short novel the virulently evil
ivory trader Kurtz. Kurtz had come to Africa to Christianize and
civilize the natives, but instead had early fallen under the jungle's
sway which awakened in him "forgotten and brutal instincts," and
had remained to "snatch their ivory" and to line the poles of his
stockade with their shrunken heads. The "impenetrable darkness"
that possessed him was revealed even to himself in his last hour
and he died breathing the desolate words, "The horror! The horror!" A moment later his death is announced by a native boy in
the words of the epigraph. Kurtz exists as a vivid contrast to the
degenerate world of British imperialism depicted in the tale. The
sordid picture of company servants sweating their lives away in
grimy jungle stations, their hearts eaten up with greed and frustrated ambitions, is reminiscent both of the deadened crowds of
white-collar workers flowing across London Bridge in *The Waste
Land* and the huddled figures on the beach of the tumid river in
The Hollow Men. They too live in a sort of Dantesque dream.
The environs of the company headquarters remind Captain Marlow,
the narrator, of "the gloomy circle of some Inferno" in which the
black shapes of Negroes ruined by slave labor "crouched, lay, sat
between, the trees leaning against the trunks, clinging to the earth,
half coming out, half effaced within the dim light, in all the attitudes of pain, abandonment, and despair." The mood of this passage closely approximates that of *The Hollow Men,* as does the following. Describing life in one of the up-river stations, Marlow
remarks:

> They wandered here and there with their absurd long staves
> in their hands, like a lot of faithless pilgrims bewitched inside

a rotten fence. The word "ivory" rang in the air, was whispered, was sighed. You would think they were praying to it. A taint of imbecile rapacity blew through it all, like a whiff from some corpse. By Jove! I've never seen anything so unreal in my life.

In contrast to this world Kurtz is, of course, one of the violent evil souls who have crossed beyond the river.

So likewise is Guy Fawkes, whose presence in *The Hollow Men* is evoked by the second epigraph, "A penny for the Old Guy." The virility of the evil of the historical Fawkes, Eliot suggests, has disappeared on the decadent modern scene, which represents him by trivial ceremonies—the cry of English street urchins begging for pennies for fireworks, the burning of straw effigies of the real Guy Fawkes, the selling of firecrackers—themselves, ironically, pale symbols of the explosive violence implicit in the barrels of gunpowder stacked beneath Parliament.

Further details which Eliot owes to *Heart of Darkness* and Guy Fawkes' Day activities are too numerous to list here, but we may mention one or two of the most important. The effigy of the "Old Guy" obviously furnished him with his picture of the hollow men as "stuffed men / Leaning together / Headpieces filled with straw"; and the firecrackers with an appropriate reference in the closing lines of the poem, in which the world ends not with a "bang" but a "whimper." Direct influences of *Heart of Darkness* possibly include the epithet "hollow." Kurtz is on one occasion said to be "hollow to the core," and speaking of one of the agents of an up-river trading post, Captain Marlow remarks: "I let him run on, this papier-mâché mephistopheles, and it seemed to me that if I tried I could poke my fore-finger through him, and would find nothing inside." For the lines "Shape without form, shade without color / Paralyzed force, gesture without emotion," Eliot may be indebted to a sentence in which Marlow, describing an ivory-hungry trading expedition, remarks (italics mine): "This devoted band called itself the Eldorado Exploring Expedition, and I believe they were sworn to secrecy. Their talk, however, was the talk of sordid buccaneers: it was *reckless without hardihood, greedy without audacity, and cruel without courage.*"

One further likeness between *The Waste Land* and *The Hollow Men* should be noted. This is the fact that both poems follow a musical organization. But whereas the former is based on the familiar sonata arrangement of the later *Four Quartets, The Hollow Men* is a musical suite, consisting of choruses and recitatives. It opens with a chorus chanted in unison by the hollow men, then continues in its three middle sections with recitative passages by the hollow-man spokesman, and ends in the last section with a combination of the two modes. Section V opens and closes with a chorus in unison by the hollow men (indicated by italics) enclosing an antiphony in which the spokesman participates as leader and the hollow-man chorus responds. The fact of the analogy of music is further emphasized by the poem's essentially thematic development. The basic theme of spiritual deadness is developed in its larger aspects throughout the poem, each section making its special contribution: the first picturing the nebulous hordes of souls dwelling in a spiritual desert and caught in the grip of a spiritual paralysis; the second, the state of the religious leader in such a Limbo; the third, the ineffectual nature of worship; the fourth, the decadent state of religious vision; and the fifth, the necessarily inchoate form of any worship service in which the hollow men might engage. The general effect of the thematic development is an almost unrelieved concentration on the effects of spiritual unreality. The poem likewise contains elements which are analogous to counterpoint in music: the lost violent souls of Section I who contrast with the spiritual paralysis of the hollow men; the eyes of Beatrice with their spiritual reality in the three middle sections; the vision of the perpetual star and multifoliate rose of Section IV. These faint possibilities of hope—"The hope only / Of empty men"—are shown to be merely ironic, however, by the dismal picture of worship detailed in the last section, which follows them.

Our discussion of *The Hollow Men* may appropriately conclude with a reading of its five movements against the background provided by the preceding pages. Section I, as already suggested, is concerned chiefly with setting the Limbo scene—the desert terrain of wind in dry grass and rats' feet over broken glass—and with establishing the spiritual status of the principals. Souls who have known neither good nor evil on earth are appropriately characterized as hollow, as straw effigies leaning upon one another, fit only to be burned in a trivial holiday celebration on Guy Fawkes' Day. They are shape, yet without shape; shade, without shade; force, without energy; gesture halted in mid-air. In the concluding lines of the section they are sharply contrasted with those who in life did show spiritual energy—"lost / Violent souls"—whose intransigent evil has carried them over the river into death's true kingdom of punishment and reward. Such souls as Kurtz and Fawkes—if they did deign to recognize the hollow men at all, would recognize them, suggests the chorus, for what they truly are: hollow men, stuffed men.

Section II expresses the state of the modern religious leader, or religious poet, like Dante, in the Limbo of contemporary civilization. This Dante, however, is incapable of arriving at any spiritual validity. Indeed, he does not even "dare" to meet in his *Commedia* the eyes that for the earlier poet symbolized spiritual efficacy. As a matter of fact, the eyes do not appear here in the Limbo at all; but only "there"—over beyond in the Garden of Eden, far beyond the speaker's power to achieve. The eyes of Beatrice that mirror the spiritual reality of Christ, the Tree of the Knowledge of Good and Evil, the hymns of praise—are in the hollow land of necessity "more distant and more seldom / Than a fading star." Thus, unable to bear even the reality of an abortive vision, the modern Dante begs in the second portion of the section to be no nearer to it than he is now, and hastens to take upon himself the trappings of his fellow hollow men: "Let me also wear / Such deliberate disguises / Rat's coat, crowskin, crossed staves." Not for him, he suggests, is "that final meeting / In the twilight kingdom" with the commanding symbol of spiritual truth, the eyes of Beatrice.

Section III explores the probable nature of worship in the hollow land. Here we find it to be an abortive phenomenon which can achieve no vestige of the spiritual power one might ordinarily expect of the worship experience. For, complains the spokesman in the opening lines, this is a dead land, a cactus land, and although stone images of worship are raised, they receive only the supplication of a dead man's hand. And though similar stone images might in some primitive religion conceivably be invested with magic or mystery, here they are broken and impotent. The spokesman then asks if worship is like this in death's other kingdom—perhaps in the Garden of Eden where Beatrice may be found. He provides his own answer: in the cactus land the phenomenon of the spiritual ecstasy associated with the awakening of love fails utterly to be realized. At the moment when lips are ready, trembling with tenderness, to kiss, they form prayers only to broken stone, and the hollow men can receive no actual spiritual benefit. It is no wonder, then, that they do not even "dare" to meet Beatrice's eyes, which for Dante were symbols both of transcendent love and transcendent spiritual reality.

The fourth section of *The Hollow Men* presents an example of the failure of spiritual vision in the hollow land. This failure has already been implied in the opening portion of Section II, which presents the modern Dante's illusory vision of the ceremony in the Garden of Eden. The spokesman now repeats his statement that there are no eyes here in Limbo—"In this hollow valley / This broken jaw of our lost kingdoms." The prayers to broken stones have brought no influx of spiritual vision comparable to Beatrice's eyes. The total lack of spiritual reality thus implied is further stressed in the lines that follow by imagery of almost complete lack of energy: images of groping and avoidance of speech on the beach of the swollen, miasmic river:

> In this last of meeting places
> We grope together
> And avoid speech
> Gathered on the beach of the tumid river.

The sense of blind groping here described introduces in turn the idea of sightlessness that is developed in the concluding lines of the passage, which state that the hollow men must remain spiritually "sightless" unless by some utterly unforeseen circumstances the eyes should "reappear." That they should reappear—as those which drew Dante into the empyrean where dwell the saints as a "Multifoliate rose" engaged in perpetual worship of God the Trinal Star—is of such transcendent hope that it can only be taken, in a hollow land, as ironic: as, as already suggested, an element of musical counterpoint used for rhetorical purposes only. For as Virgil has observed, not only justice, but *mercy* also, has rejected the hollow men.

Considering the absolute impotence of any form of worship in the Limbo, then, the grotesque parody of religious rituals presented in the last section of the poem comes as no surprise. Section V opens with a mordant parody of the child's rhyme: "Here we go round the mulberry bush / So early in the morning." If the hollow men should engage in a formal worship service, it is implied, a childish chant would be the most logical choice for their ritual since they have no more apprehension of the meaning of spiritual reality than do young children, who likewise have no experiential knowledge of good or evil. The distortion of the mulberry bush into a prickly pear is both in keeping with the desert landscape and with the prevalent warping of religious values in the poem as a whole: it represents an appropriate altar for hollow men. The ritual of going round the prickly pear likewise recalls the fruitless pursuit of the whirling banner by the souls described by Dante in Canto III of the *Inferno*.

The central portion of this section constitutes an antiphonal passage between the hollow-man spokesman and the hollow-men chorus. The leader's chant consists wholly of statements descriptive of incomplete realization. Its beginning—

> Between the idea
> And the reality
> Between the motion
> And the act
> Falls the Shadow—

is followed by two other segments expressing similar examples of frustration: between the inception and the completion of *any* effort falls the shadow of impotence. The hollow men are indeed form without shape, shade without color, paralyzed force, gesture without motion. The response of the hollow men consists of broken fragments of the worship litany: *"For Thine is the Kingdom," "Life is very long."* The spokesman echoes them in a similar fashion: "For thine is / Life is / For thine is the."

The worship service of the hollow men ends with an ironic benediction, which picks up again the rhetoric of the nursery rhyme opening; but instead of repeating the opening it substitutes a perverse doxology:

> *This is the way the world ends*
> *This is the way the world ends*
> *This is the way the world ends*
> *Not with a bang but a whimper.*

This ending suggests that as the conventional worship service at its climax looks toward union with its source of spiritual strength at the Day of Judgment when God gathers His children to Him, the hollow-men worshipers also grope toward a similar realization. But to no avail. For the Judgment Day trump of the hollow men does not have the power even of a firecracker on Guy Fawkes' Day. It is merely a whimper—the word "whimper" further strengthening the association with children initiated by the opening nursery-rhyme parody, and suggesting—ambivalently—both the moaning cry of young children, and hence less force even than the explosion of a firecracker, and the possible response of street children denied their pennies for fireworks and thus incapable of engaging even in the superficial activities of Guy Fawkes' Day. The conclusion of Section V thus fittingly underscores the spiritual unreality permeating both the section and the poem as a whole. And we should conclude, perhaps, that *The Hollow Men*, rather than embodying any affirmative note, however meager, is to be considered merely as an extension of Eliot's earlier poem—that it is, as it were, a *Waste Land* in little.

Editor's Note: "The Spiritual Status of T. S. Eliot's Hollow Men" by Everett A. Gillis is reprinted by permission of the University of Texas Press from *Texas Studies in Literature and Language,* II (1961), pp. 464–475. Copyright © 1961 by the University of Texas Press.

Professor Gillis is Head of the Department of English at Texas Technological College. In addition to critical and historical essays, he has published numerous volumes of verse, including *Sunrise in Texas* and *Angles of the Wind.*

WALLACE STEVENS

1879-1955

Wallace Stevens was born in Reading, Pennsylvania. He attended Harvard University, and while preparing for law school, contributed to the undergraduate literary publication, *The Harvard Advocate*. He attended New York Law School, was admitted to the Bar, and practiced law in New York City from 1904 to 1916. During this period he had been writing, and in 1914 he published four poems in *Poetry* magazine, winning the recognition of Harriet Monroe, Alfred Kreymborg, and other promoters of new American poetry. His first book of poems, *Harmonium*, was published in 1923.

In 1916 Stevens began his profitable association with the Hartford Accident and Indemnity Company. He had married Elsie Kachel of Reading in 1909, and a daughter, Holly, was born in Hartford in 1924. In 1934 he was promoted to vice president, a capacity he maintained effectively until his retirement. With his professional position secure, his literary output increased: *Ideas of Order* (1935), *Owl's Clover* (1936), *The Man with the Blue Guitar and Other Poems* (1937), *Parts of a World* (1942), *Notes Toward a Supreme Fiction* (1942), *Esthétique du Mal* (1945), *Transport to Summer* (1947), *Three Academic Pieces* (1947), *A Primitive Like an Orb* (1948), and *The Auroras of Autumn* (1950). *Collected Poems* appeared in 1954, and in 1957, S. F. Morse edited *Opus Posthumous. The Necessary Angel*, a book of essays, came out in 1951.

Elected to the National Institute of Arts and Letters in 1946, Stevens was awarded the Bollingen Prize for Poetry (1949), two National Book Awards for Poetry (1951, 1955), and the Pulitzer Prize for Poetry (1955), as well as numerous honors from universities.

WALLACE STEVENS:
THE LIFE OF THE
IMAGINATION

ROY HARVEY PEARCE

> . . . there is a war between the mind
> And sky, between thought and day and night.
> —Coda to "Notes toward a Supreme Fiction"*

One thing we can now surely say of the achievement of Wallace
Stevens: He has written, over some thirty years, a whole and continuing poetry whose subject is the life, the form and function, of
the imagination.[1] In the recently published *Transport to Summer*[2]
that subject receives its broadest, most complex treatment, yet remains essentially as it was in his first volume, *Harmonium:* in his
language, a problem in the relation of the imagined to the real;
in more general language, of the world as known to the world as
outside knowing. From beginning to end what has been basic is
the predicament of the man who would know. If, read in and of

---

* Quotations are from *Harmonium, The Man with the Blue Guitar, Ideas of
Order, Parts of a World,* and *Transport to Summer,* all by Wallace Stevens, by
permission of Alfred A. Knopf, Inc., copyright 1931, 1936, 1937, 1942, 1947 by
Wallace Stevens.

[1] See particularly Marius Bewley, "The Poetry of Wallace Stevens," *Partisan
Review,* XVI (1949), 895–915; Bernard Heringman, "Wallace Stevens: The Use of
Poetry," *ELH,* XVI (1949), 325–336; Louis L. Martz, "The World of Wallace
Stevens," in B. Rajan, ed. *Modern American Poetry: Focus Five* (London, 1950),
pp. 94–109; and William Van O'Connor, *The Shaping Spirit: A Study of Wallace
Stevens* (Chicago, 1950). All of these, however, are most concerned with iteration
and reiteration of subject and theme in Stevens, rather than with continuity and
development, as I am here.

[2] This was written before the publication of Stevens' *Auroras of Autumn* in
Sept. 1950.

themselves, the poems in *Transport to Summer* contrast vividly with those in *Harmonium,* the contrast is as much an aspect of continuity as of difference and opposition. It is a continuity that represents the growth and achievement which, for good and for bad, make the total of Stevens' work greater than the sum of its parts. Viewed thus, the poems in *Transport to Summer* are inevitable precisely as they show Stevens trying to finish what he began in *Harmonium.*

Treating of the relation of the imagined to the real—figured recently as the war between the mind and sky—Stevens is treating of our problem of belief. Unlike an Eliot, he has refused to move out of our culture into another and to seek a solution for the problem in the discovery of a "usable" form of belief. Rather, he has relied entirely on his own sensibility; he has tried to create the object of belief rather than discover it. This has been his strength and his weakness; this has been his risk. Always he has assumed, as he writes in "Esthétique du Mal," that the war between the mind and sky must be fought with what we have "as and where we are." What we have is the imagining self and a reality which is not part of that self, but which for the sake of belief must somehow be made part of it. We can believe only in a reality so known. To sketch a chronology: Stevens began by looking directly at our experience of the reality in which we are bound, continued by examining our predicament in being so bound, and has most recently been exploring the general implications of the predicament. Put another way, in terms of the problem of belief: He began by looking directly at the world which limits belief, continued by examining the possibility of belief and commitment in the face of that possibility, and has most recently been exploring the nature of possible belief. If the movement in the poems has been away from the descriptive and dramatic towards the discursive and dialectical, this is part of an immanent necessity rising out of a fixed subject-matter and the poet's steadily maturing view of it. Essentially, the styles of *Harmonium* and *Transport to Summer* represent two modes of knowing. But the conception of the act of knowing, of the relation of the imagined to the real, remains constant. It is the degree of knowing, the complexity and inclusiveness of the knowledge, which grows. And it comes finally, in the major poems of *Transport to Summer,* to make for the possibility of mature, considered belief in the reality which we have "as and where we are."

I

What is central in the poems of *Harmonium* (1923, 1931) is an awareness of the texture of reality (in Stevens' sense of *Ding an sich*) as a factor at once for the enriching and for the limiting of experience. The driving concern of these poems is with the sensuously flowing aspect of reality as we come to know, to partake of, and thus to inform it and be informed by it. These are specifically poems of the creative imagination. In "Infanta Marina" we are given a picture of the consummately beautiful woman whose very motions become part of the beauty of her surroundings. The poem ends:

> And thus she roamed
> In the roamings of her fan,
> Partaking of the sea,
>
> And of the evening,
> As they flowed around
> And uttered their subsiding sound.

In "Domination of Black" we are moved "At night, by the fire," from a vision of leaves to a vision of peacock tails, so to the sound of peacock cries and to the sound of terror, and so to a knowledge of terror; each flows into the other, each becomes part of the other. And we are told that there are, after all, at least thirteen ways of looking at a blackbird; yet all these ways are perhaps dominated by this one:

> A man and a woman
> Are one.
> A man and a woman and a blackbird
> Are one.

The mode here is descriptive, for Stevens an act of a creative imagination, with the poet (as an implied speaker in a lyric) always bound up in what he would describe.

Thus in these poems, description is equated with perception, and perception with conception. The poet at once differentiates one segment of his reality from another and learns that in the process he has made every segment so differentiated part of himself. The "ancient star" addressed in "Nuances of a Theme by Williams" is admonished to "Lend no part to any humanity that suffuses / you in its own light," asked to "Be not an intelligence, / Like a widow's bird / Or an old horse." The point is that one asks and admonishes in vain, that the star is the *Ding an sich*, that one cannot know it as unsuffused by the light of humanity, that Stevens' own perceptions are so suffused.

Here the great example is "Sea Surface Full of Clouds":

> In that November off Tehuantepec,
> The slopping of the sea grew still one night
> And in the morning summer hued the deck
>
> And made one think of rosy chocolate
> And gilt umbrellas. Paradisal green
> Gave suavity to the perplexed machine
>
> Of ocean, which like limpid water lay.
> Who, then, in that ambrosial latitude
> Out of the light evolved the moving blooms,
>
> Who, then, evolved the sea-blooms from the clouds
> Diffusing balm in that Pacific calm?
> *C'était mon enfant, mon bijou, mon âme.*

In this opening section we are moved from the relatively bare statement which lets us know that the phenomenon of the sea exists, to a description of the sea as perceived, an account of how one comes to conceive of the sea. The green of the summer morning is known literally to have given all the self-sufficiency, quietness, and ease suggested by "suavity" to an ocean which has been known as something "perplexed." From whom does this and what follows rise? The line in French indicates as precisely as possible the specifically human source and the poet's attitude towards that source—*"enfant, bijou, âme."* The rest of the description will follow from the quality of this attitude. And so it goes throughout the poem. The description is rich ("confected" is a word Stevens has recently used) because the very richness of the perceptive act differentiates the clearly from the dimly perceived, the imagined from the real. In being known, the ocean is given body, literally suffused with the light of humanity. The moral, if Stevens would draw it, would be the one toward the end of "Peter Quince at the Clavier" and would come as necessarily:

> Beauty is momentary in the mind—
> The fitful tracing of a portal;
> But in the flesh it is immortal.

Or, in the words of "The Emperor of Ice Cream," "be" must be "finale of seem." We are, for this Stevens, limited, even condemned, to rich perceptions.

For the Stevens of the *Harmonium* poems and those immediately after, the consequences of such limitation can be pathetic or amusing, hardly tragic. He traces such consequences in poems which are in mode essentially dramatic. They amount to portrayals of the interior conflict of men and women discovering that they must cling only to the world which their rich perceptions have given them. This is the imaginatively compounded world of "Sea Surface" and the rest. Here "Sunday Morning" is the received text—probably, since ours is an age which prefers not the poetry of ideas but rather the poetry of human response to ideas, the poem of Stevens which we have let ourselves know best.

The center of consciousness, the perceiving and informing imagination, in "Sunday Morning" is that of a woman intelligent and sensitive enough to be disturbed by her awareness of a "holy hush of ancient sacrifice" in which she cannot participate. She tries to break through the limits of her bright warm world and to achieve realization of that world of received religion, "Dominion of the blood and sepulchre." She tries to conceive of a divinity which is not immediate and palpable, which is entirely of the spirit. Yet "Divinity must live within herself"; for "All pleasures and all pains"—"These are the measures destined for her soul." So she struggles to break through her hard and sweet reality, to conceive of a God, a paradise, an eternity, which might be abstracted from that reality. We are made to follow each of her thoughts and questionings as one flows into another. We are placed at the center of her predicament; yet we know it as she cannot. Like her, we are bound in time, in the reality which is of time; yet seeing her thus, we may know that we must live and believe only in the light of the sun-as-reality, a light which, above all, may make us aware of experience as concrete and immediate and of infinitely delicate gradation:

> We live in an old chaos of the sun,
> Or old dependency of day and night,
> Or island solitude, unsponsored, free,
> Of that wide water, inescapable.
> Deer walk upon our mountains, and the quail
> Whistle about us their spontaneous cries;
> Sweet berries ripen in the wilderness;
> And, in the isolation of the sky,
> At evening, casual flocks of pigeons make
> Ambiguous undulations as they sink,
> Downward to darkness, on extended wings.

This is the way of the world of *Harmonium*. The elderly lover in "Le Monocle de Mon Oncle" says at the end of his meditation:

> ... I pursued,
> And still pursue, the origin and course
> Of love, but until now I never knew
> That fluttering things have so distinct a shade.

And the speaker in "To the One of Fictive Music" finds that the experience of music (thus, metaphorically, of all created beauty) perfects those who make it, involving them deeply in the intensely imaginative experiences from which, as modern men, they would flee. Here the plea is for acceptance of perceived reality as the very source of humanity:

> Unreal, give back to us what once you gave:
> The imagination that we spurned and crave.

The moods of "Sunday Morning," "Le Monocle," and "To the One of Fictive Music" are those of graceful and profound puzzlement, amused but peaceful resignation, and deep pleading. The mode of the poems is always dramatic and descriptive, marked by a richness and density of language and a tendency to let meaning arise from variations worked upon or out of a set of basic metaphors. These metaphors in turn let us know precisely how it is for the protagonist in each poem to feel as he does; for they represent the working of his sensibility on the reality which it must inform. Ultimately, meaning in all the poems stems from the situation of their protagonists, who are involved in a reality which is not theirs but which they yet must make theirs.

Stevens treats the general implications of this situation in the longest, most difficult, and, I think, most inadequate of the larger poems in *Harmonium,* "The Comedian as the Letter C." Here the protagonist, limited, once more, to a life of rich perceptions, is something of a poet, philosopher, and wit. Thus he is in a position to reflect learnedly and at length on his situation and generally to resolve it. As I understand it, the poem involves the protagonist's growth to artistic maturity.[3] The poet progresses from romantic subjectivism, to crude realism, to exotic realism, to a kind of local-colorism, to a disciplined, mature, and imaginative realism. He comes to know the potentialities and the limits of his own imagination. At this point he can face life squarely; he marries, begets children, and grows wiser. Yet at the end he is in a period of cautious skepticism, dubious about any acceptance of reality, however self-conscious and mature that acceptance may be. The point is that he has made a successful "adjustment." One needs expert guidance to gather this much; one needs more than one should need; for the very manner of the poetry will not allow for the release of such meaning; particulars get in the way of implicit generalization—the sense of detail, however much imaginatively informed, in the way of implicit dialectics. Here, for example, is part of the end of the third section—that which concerns the protagonist's sojourn in commonplace reality:

> He came. The poetic hero without palms
> Or jugglery, without regalia.
> And as he came he saw that it was spring,
> A time abhorrent to the nihilist
> Or searcher for the fecund minimum.
> The moonlight fiction disappeared. The spring,
> Although contending featly in its veils,
> Irised in dew and early fragrancies,
> Was gemmy marionette to him that sought
> A sinewy nakedness . . .

The overplus of language—parallels, appositions, repetitions, words unabsorbed into the whole, an overpowering concreteness—gets in the way of the developing analysis of the poet's situation. That

---

[3] Here I follow Hi Simons, " 'The Comedian as the Letter C': Its Sense and Its Significance," *Southern Review,* v (1940), 453–468.

which we like about the poem, the virtuosity and charming self-indulgence of language, can only obscure that which we should like as much—the argument and the meaning. The poet-protagonist himself—with his powerful sensibility—gets between us and the poem. We never know the nature and quality of that final "adjustment" and his doubts about it. We can see here, as Stevens is trying to derive a general meaning from his materials, the emergence of a need for the mode of the later poetry—an expository, dialectical mode—if he is fully to understand and to resolve the predicament of this protagonist and the other perplexed ones who precede him in "Sunday Morning," "Le Monocle," and "To the One of Fictive Music."

II

The poems in *Ideas of Order* (1935, 1936), the volume after the second edition of *Harmonium* (whose texts I have followed), are for the most part written from the point of view of such a one as the protagonist in "The Comedian as the Letter C": that of a man trying to understand his involvement in the war between reality and imagination. In these later pieces Stevens is mainly concerned to demonstrate, largely in poems of situation, the interpenetration of the one by the other. As poet, he is, as he writes in a jacket note, an "exponent of the imagination." But, as human being, he finds that he must hold the imagination to concrete reality. In "Sad Strains of a Gay Waltz" and "Botanist on Alp (No. 1)," for example, he treats the failure of the imagination to come alive. And then in "Farewell to Florida," "Lions in Sweden," and "Mozart, 1935," he treats the need to hold the imagination to reality, and so indicates how it may come alive. Most important, in "The Idea of Order at Key West," he treats the work of the imagination as it gives to our reality whatever order we can be sure resides therein. In this poem he writes of the woman who sings beside the sea:

> It was her voice that made
> The sky acutest at its vanishing.
> She measured to the hour its solitude.
> She was the single artificer of the world
> In which she sang. And when she sang, the sea,
> Whatever self it had, became the self

> That was her song, for she was the maker. Then we,
> As we beheld her striding there alone,
> Knew that there never was a world for her
> Except the one she sang and, singing, made.

This is that "Blessed rage for order" by which we live.

What one misses in the poems in *Ideas of Order,* for all their competencies, is movement towards consideration of the more general implications of this view of man as caught between his imagination and his reality. There is, after all, a marked limitation to such poems of a descriptive-dramatic mode, poems one of whose uses should be to make us face our own special human predicament. It is something to tell us that the predicament exists and to make us aware of its every nuance, but critical hindsight makes us sense that this was and is not enough. Stevens himself comments generally on such a limitation in the poems in *The Man With the Blue Guitar* (1937) and *Parts of a World* (1942). Particularly, he writes in "The Poems of Our Climate" (in *Parts of a World*) a brilliantly descriptive account of "Clear water in a brilliant bowl, / Pink and white carnations"; and then he comments:

> Say even that this complete simplicity
> Stripped one of all one's torments, concealed
> The evilly compounded, vital I
> And made it fresh in a world of white,
> A world of clear water, brilliant-edged,
> Still one would want more, one would need more,
> More than a world of white and snowy scents.
>
> There would still remain the never-resting mind,
> So that one would want to escape, come back
> To what had been so long composed.
> The imperfect is our paradise.
> Note that, in this bitterness, delight,
> Since the imperfect is so hot in us,
> Lies in flawed words and stubborn sounds.

Poetry must be a means of grasping reality; but we must be aware of the process by which we grasp reality, however imperfectly; for in that process—which is the imaginative process—lies our humanity. What we need, in a phrase from "Of Modern Poetry" (also in *Parts of a World*), is "The poem of the act of the mind."

The greater part of the work in *The Man With the Blue Guitar* and *Parts of a World* consists of attempts to write such a poem. In the work in these volumes Stevens is concerned to get at the problem of reality and the imagination directly, not through a dramatic situation. As a result he begins to develop, particularly in *Parts of a World,* a mode adequate to such a direct approach to his problem. This, as I have noted, is the dialectical mode which is to be fully developed in *Transport to Summer* (1947): still and forever mannered, witty, and elegant—yet now discursive, centered on logical (and alogical) analysis; built out of a language which is as often abstract and nativist as it is richly concrete and exotic; with a syntactic and structural freedom which allows him to invent as he will, to explore the most general implications of his themes and still to return when he wishes to his local and particular starting-point, which is, as always, the sensitive individual trying to satisfy simultaneously the claims of reality and the imagination. The poet-protagonist is now explicitly the philosopher, meditating abundantly and easily.

Yet the mode, and consequently the analysis, as developed in the poems in *The Man With the Blue Guitar* and in *Parts of a World,* is not made to do its proper job. It comes too easily, too casually; it represents, perhaps, an attempt to explore, and thus forecasts the later poems. As Stevens indicates—in another jacket-note—the title poem in *The Man With the Blue Guitar* consists simply of a series of notes on "the incessant conjunctioning between things as they are and things imagined." This, for example, is the fifth in the series:

> Do not speak to us of the greatness of poetry,
> Of the torches wisping in the underground,
>
> Of the structure of vaults upon a point of light.
> There are no shadows in the sun,
>
> Day is desire and night is sleep.
> There are no shadows anywhere.
>
> The earth, for us, is flat and bare.
> There are no shadows. Poetry
>
> Exceeding music must take the place
> Of empty heaven and its hymns.

> Ourselves in poetry must take their place,
> Even in the chattering of your guitar.

The last nine lines are simply turned against the first three; discursive statement cancels out concrete realization and demonstrates the need for a poetry of ourselves. This is the role of the man with the guitar, the role of the poet, or (as Stevens makes explicit in his jacket-note), of "any man of imagination."

Likewise, in *Parts of a World* there is everywhere the tendency simply to assert the place of the imagination and to demand of the poet that he do his proper work and conjoin imagination and reality. The themes of the earlier poems are restated and made to point explicitly to such a conclusion: "Sea Surface Full of Clouds," for example, is in "Variations on a Summer Day"; "Sunday Morning" is in "The Blue Buildings in the Summer Air," "Dezembrum," and "Bouquet of Bell Sçavoir"; and "The Idea of Order at Key West" is in "The Woman That Had More Babies Than That." The sameness of so many of the poems, developing at worst into flatness and at best into rich repetition, derives from Stevens' recognition of a situation and of a need, the precise nature and full implications of which he does not explore. "Landscape with Boat" and "Asides on the Oboe" point towards "Notes Toward a Supreme Fiction"; "Extracts from Addresses to the Academy of Fine Ideas" points towards "Esthétique du Mal." But in each case the conjoining of imagination and reality is limited in scope because it results in a poetry of statement, not of analysis. Stevens does not move from recognition of a problem to an attempt to work out a solution. Stevens will say in "Asides on the Oboe" that

> The prologues are over. It is a question, now,
> Of final belief. So, say that final belief
> Must be in a fiction. It is time to choose.

And he will show us clearly that whatever of our beliefs we have destroyed, we have not destroyed our belief in that

> impossible possible philosopher's man,
> The man who has had the time to think enough,
> The central man, the human globe, responsive
> As a mirror with a voice, the man of glass,
> Who in a million diamonds sums us up.

This is the man, ourselves, whom our imagination enables us to discover "without external reference" at the center of the reality which we have made. This is the reality in which we must believe, the point at which the texture of experience is given final form by the imagination. This is the point at which we discover, as Stevens says in a lecture delivered in 1947, "that poetry and reality are one, or should be . . ."[4] But we ask, if in this fragmented world we can finally discover and believe in ourselves, what does this discovery mean to us? What do *we* mean? Final belief demands, in short, complete philosophic and imaginative awareness. And the triumph of the major poems in *Transport to Summer*—to which the earlier poems are now literally a "prologue"—is the triumph of an elegantly individuated sensibility which has at last realized the possibilities of philosophic understanding and the moral imagination.

III

The title page of Stevens' most recent volume itself indicates the direction in which his poetry has moved. "*Transport to Summer, by Wallace Stevens*": a journey on which we are carried to the clear light of the sun, to reality (and sun-as-reality is a favorite metaphor of Stevens) by a poet, "any man of imagination."

The myriad small poems in *Transport to Summer* widen the possibility of a poetry of recognition and statement. Yet they have little existence of their own, being no more than introductions to the master poems in the volume, "Notes Toward a Supreme Fiction" and "Esthétique du Mal." Glancing back towards the poems preceding them, they rush towards Stevens' masterwork. In these small poems, reality and the situation of the man hemmed in by his reality begin to be comprehended as well as accepted; liberation of the spirit seems possible; the mode, potentially complex and inclusive, is tentatively philosophic. Poetry begins to settle into its place in the world. We are told, for example, that "The Motive for Metaphor" is the need for recollection in tranquility; so one must withdraw from reality, from "The weight of primary noon, / The ABC of being," from "The vital, arrogant, fatal dominant X"; and one must seek the pleasures of the imagination under an "obscure moon." Yet the lesson of such a piece as "The Bed of Old John

---

[4] "The Realm of Resemblance," *Partisan Review*, XIV (1947), 248.

Zeller" is that one must learn not to withdraw entirely, that one must learn "to evade / That habit of wishing and to accept the structure / Of things as the structure of ideas." That structure is, in the title of another poem, one of "Men Made Out of Words"; so, simply enough, "Life consists / Of propositions about life." Steadily and easily we move via words from the imagination to reality and back again; steadily and easily we are made to create our world. In "Credences of Summer" the creative process is thus briefly described. The "self," Stevens writes,

> having possessed
> The object, grips it in savage scrutiny,
> Once to make captive, once to subjugate
> Or yield to subjugation, once to proclaim
> The meaning of the capture, this hard prize,
> Fully made, fully apparent, fully found.

Yet such poems as these are merely notes for propositions about life. The propositions themselves, developed fully, are in "Notes Towards a Supreme Fiction" and "Esthétique du Mal."

In these poems, which seem to me at once the most ambitious and the most important in his whole work, Stevens would finally conjoin reality and the imagination and would discover in such a conjoining the possibility of that ultimate belief which was denied to the protagonists of "Sunday Morning," "Le Monocle de Mon Oncle," "To the One of Fictive Music." So doing, he becomes explicitly philosophical—in the sense that he is concerned with realizing in esthetic form certain epistemological, ontological, and moral propositions. The relationship between the propositions and the poetry is this: that esthetic experience is the only means we have of initiating the inquiry by which we arrive at those propositions and is, moreover, the only means we have of realizing and believing in them. Thus Stevens' poetry is at once an expression and an exposition of a philosophical attitude. Since the authenticity of that attitude depends on origin in esthetic experience, it depends on the sensibility of the poet, a sensibility divorced—ideally—from any abstract system which would impose on it order from without; for order, esthetic order, "the structure of things," must be derived from a dynamic relationship between the individual imagination and the reality which it beholds. So the poet-esthete becomes the philosopher-moralist. To him a philosophical proposition fully realized is one realized as a poem. For propositions are statements involving the conjoining of the individual imagination and reality; and such a conjoining is the work of the poet, of "any man of imagination."

"Notes toward a Supreme Fiction" is a poem about belief. Nominally it turns on the nature of our Supreme Fiction, our supreme center of belief. Yet Stevens can describe the form of our Fiction only by indirection, in terms of what it must be, not of what it is. The three sections in the poem are headed "It Must Be Abstract," "It Must Change," and "It Must Give Pleasure." The "Must" in each of these headings is inferred dialectically as the poet describes and evaluates what it is for the man of imagination fully to live in reality and not to be overwhelmed by it. This is the argument:

"It Must Be Abstract." (I). We must begin with perceived reality, and argue from it to the *Ding an sich,* to "this invented world / The inconceivable idea of the sun"; yet we must not suppose that our perception of reality argues for our creation of reality. We must, in fact, dispose of the idea of any creator, even for the reality which exists outside our perception; for "Phoebus was / A name for something that never could be named." The sun, reality, simply was and is. (II). Still, we are driven by the very divisiveness of our lives to seek a unitive source of our idea of reality: ". . . not to have is the beginning of desire." (III). Poetry is our means to this source:

> The poem refreshes life so that we share,
> For a moment, the first idea . . . It satisfies
> Belief in an immaculate beginning
>
> And sends us, winged by an unconscious will,
> To an immaculate end.

(IV). Thus the origin of poetry, of our ideas of the world and of ourselves, is in our concrete past and present:

> From this the poem springs: that we live in a place
> That is not our own and, much more, not ourselves
> And hard it is in spite of blazoned days.

(V). The act of the poetic imagination is the source of human power

over the world. (VI). Perception, knowledge, and feeling are inter-
dependent—in origin, really one:

> Not to be realized because not to
> Be seen, not to be loved nor hated because
> Not to be realized.

And so we live by "An abstraction blooded, as a man by thought."
(VII). Hence we must hold to reality if we are to hold to abstract
truth; for, once more, the source of truth is reality. (VIII–IX). It
follows then that our hero, our "major man," will be man imagining
—discovering a Supreme Fiction in the flux of reality and making
it available to us; it follows, moreover, that his discovery will be
that our Supreme Fiction is, in fact, "major man" (the abstraction)
known through man (the concrete particular man). Analytic reason abstracts man from reality, but it is the creative imagination
which reveals him to us. (X). Finally there is triumphant affirmation.

> The major abstraction is the idea of man
> And major man is its exponent, abler
> In the abstract than in his singular,
>
> More fecund as principle than particle,
> Happy fecundity, flor-abundant force,
> In being more than an exception, part,
>
> Though an heroic part, of the commonal.
> The major abstraction is the commonal,
> The inanimate, difficult visage. Who is it?
>
> What rabbi, grown furious with human wish,
> What chieftain, walking by himself, crying
> Most miserable, most victorious,
>
> Does not see these separate figures one by one,
> And yet see only one, in his old coat,
> His slouching pantaloons, beyond the town,
>
> Looking for what was, where it used to be?
> Cloudless the morning. It is he. The man
> In that old coat, those sagging pantaloons,
>
> It is of him, ephebe, to make, to confect
> The final elegance, not to console
> Nor sanctify, but plainly to propound.

The problem of "Sunday Morning" is faced and solved. Man, the Supreme Fiction, moves us as an abstraction, yet is known as a particular. The "major man" is the poet ("any man of imagination"), he who makes us know as the "final elegance" even that man whom our religionists and rulers see only as a poor bedraggled creature.

"It Must Change." (I). Change is part of the flow of reality; thus the Supreme Fiction must partake of Change. (II). Growth and mortality—these are change and so are real. Immortality, which is not change, is not real:

> Spring vanishes the scraps of winter, why
> Should there be a question of returning or
> Of death in memory's dream? Is spring asleep?
>
> This warmth is for lovers at last accomplishing
> Their love, this beginning, not resuming . . .

(III). Art which does not express the sense of change violates reality. (IV). Change originates, and we come to know it, in the opposites (man-woman, day-night, winter-summer, and so on) of which our world is constituted. (V). It is, in fact, growth and change which make life bearable. Here, in a poem strikingly in the manner and form of "Sunday Morning," Stevens again resolves the problem of *Harmonium*. He writes of his protagonist, a planter who had lived and died on a tropical island:

> An unaffected man in a negative light
> Could not have borne his labor nor have died
> Sighing that he should leave the banjo's twang.

The use of negatives here literally forces the positiveness of the statement on us. The point is that the planter who lived in a green land "baked greener in the greenest sun" took his abundant life from a positive light, in a positive land of growth and death, of change. He was not hemmed in, but was released by reality. (VI–VII). The positive existence of change is evidenced everywhere—in the beauty of sound which will end, in the earthbound quality of emotional experience. (VIII–IX). Our knowledge, which is "never naked," has always a "fictive covering" involved in temporal reality; it is thus poetic knowledge. For the poem itself is of language, "The gibberish of the vulgate," which itself changes; in so being,

the poem is of change and can make us know the Supreme Fiction.
The poet, then:

> tries by a peculiar speech to speak
>
> The peculiar potency of the general,
> To compound the imagination's Latin with
> The lingua franca et jocundissima.

"Peculiar speech" and "peculiar potency"—the particular—make
possible our knowledge of the general. Imagination's formal language finds expression in reality's "lingua franca et jocundissima."
(x). Change thus is part of the movement of reality, movement
which can be perceived everywhere. (This is the flow of reality
celebrated in "Infanta Marina" and the rest.) Simply enough,
"The freshness of transformation is / The freshness of a world."
That which has baffled the poet of "The Idea of Order at Key
West" no longer baffles him, because he accepts it for what it is.
Man comprehends change by conceiving of the idea of order, by
making poems which express that idea. For "The Freshness of
transformation" is "our own, / It is ourselves, the freshness of
ourselves. . . ."

"It Must Give Pleasure." (I). To celebrate our belief regularly
and ceremoniously, according to tradition—this is "a facile exercise."
But the "difficult rigor" is to celebrate our belief from moment to
moment, in the very flux and disorder of reality—"to catch from
that / Irrational moment its unreasoning." (II). What is needed is
the pleasure of things-in-themselves. This is a pleasure in particulars, certainly; but yet we know the general, the Supreme Fiction,
ourselves, in particulars. (This section is, once more, strikingly in
the form of "Sunday Morning"; but the woman who is the protagonist here accepts her pleasurable reality as the woman in "Sunday
Morning" cannot.) (III–VII). We are able to love things—particularized
reality—because we take joy in them for their own sake. This is ex-
emplified in (III) the love of children which gives beauty and life to
the ugly, in (IV) the love of two persons for the portion of reality in
one another, and negatively in (V–VII) the tale of the canon who
would impose an alien order on reality and so drive delight from it,
who does not know that "to impose is not to discover." (VIII). The

poet affirms that he cannot believe in the abstract in and of itself; he can believe in it only as it is given delightful embodiment in informed reality: "I have not but I am and as I am, I am." (IX). Things-in-themselves, repeated, reexamined, perceived again and again—these are a final good. For through repetitions of things-in-themselves, we approach our Supreme Fiction:

> Perhaps
> The man-hero is not the exceptional monster,
> But he that of repetition is most master.

And it is "the vast repetitions final in / Themselves" which make for the Supreme Fiction. (X). The essential problem is to name one's world, to poetize it, to see it as a general structure of pleasurable particulars, and so to possess it. And inevitably, distortion is characteristic of this structure of particulars:

> That's it: the more than rational distortion,
> The fiction that results from feeling. Yes, that.
>
> They will get it straight one day at the Sorbonne.
> We shall return at twilight from the lecture
> Pleased that the irrational is rational,
>
> Until flicked by feeling, in a gildered street,
> I call you by name, my green, my fluent mundo.
> You will have stopped revolving except in crystal.

Here the poem ends, the possibilities of the reasoned abstract having been realized in the imagination which, as it works, adjusts itself to the distortions of reality, to change, and so adjusting, discovers the rich pleasure of existence. Belief in the world of "Sunday Morning" is not only possible but necessary. It is the exercise of the creative imagination, working out a set of epistemological and ontological propositions, which has made for that possibility and that necessity. After such knowledge there can come only belief.

So it is not so much the act of belief which concerns Stevens as it is preparation for that act—knowing the world which is to be faced, locating abstraction, change, and pleasure in the reality of that world. Stevens is Socratic enough to believe that full knowledge will call forth compulsive belief. When he comes further to examine imaginative experience of the world and finds pain and terror in that experience, he must posit evil as their source in reality. The Supreme Fiction must now also give pain. It is evil, thus, which Stevens studies in "Esthétique du Mal," a poem in which the lesson of the poet's life (the life of "any man of imagination") is most fully drawn. The final condition for belief in the Supreme Fiction is the acceptance of reality. The final condition for the acceptance of reality is the acceptance of the evil in reality. Epistemological and ontological understanding, having made for belief, now make for morality. Good and evil, pleasure and pain, are now comprehended, one with another.

The very title, "Esthétique du Mal," indicates clearly the location of positive evil in the texture of reality, the texture which is the stuff of esthetic experience. As a constituent of reality, however, evil cannot be known directly in itself, but rather must be known as it is shaped by the imagination: This is the source of pain. In Part I, the protagonist, another of Stevens' poets, is in Naples, "writing letters home / And, between his letters, reading paragraphs / On the sublime." As he reads, Vesuvius groans; there is for him in this groaning a knowledge of pain and terror, because he can conceive of such sound only as pain and terror imaginatively informed; the sound is his means of knowing pain and terror. And he sees that, for us, whatever of pain there is in the world is pain only as we know it imaginatively and, knowing it, are in part responsible for it. "This is a part of the sublime / From which we shrink." In Part II, the deep night and its sounds "At a town in which acacias grew," communicate to him "The intelligence of his despair, express / What meditation never quite achieved." He learns that pain is "indifferent" to reality, that reality is not painful except as the imagination is conjoined to it and makes it so. Nor does the imagination alone produce pain. Yet pain "never sees / How that which rejects it saves it in the end." This last contains a central paradox for man: Pain is "saved" in the end, in its human uniqueness, because it is not part of the imagination through which we come to feel it nor of the reality in which we feel it. This is a continuation of the paradox of the Supreme Fiction, which is independent of reality and the imagination, taken singly, but which comes into existence through that conjoining of both which marks the predicament of Stevens' man who would know. Another deceivingly simple way to put it is to say, as Stevens does in the middle of Part I, "Pain is human."

From Part III on, the propositions which give structure to the poem center less and less on the poet-protagonist and become more and more general. The truth ascertained in Part III is that "heaven and hell / are one," that even an "over-human god" discovered this, that "the health of the world," "the honey of common summer," the simple and direct experiencing of pleasurable reality, are not enough for us; paradoxically, we are continually pained to think that they might be, to long for a simpler life which we cannot have. The need is that we understand reality as we make (or re-make) it for ourselves, with its portion of evil—here, in Part IV—even in the purity of music and painting. We cannot be sentimentalists. We must know ourselves as we know our world; and evil is of ourselves as much as of our world:

> The genius of misfortune
> Is not a sentimentalist. He is
> That evil, that evil in the self, from which
> In desperate hallow, rugged gesture, fault
> Falls out on everything: the genius of
> The mind, which is our being, wrong and wrong,
> The genius of the body, which is our world,
> Spent in the false engagements of the mind.

The rest of the poem develops in considerations of the "false engagements of the mind" towards which our genius directs us. In love for our kind in our world we can sustain ourselves against the evil in ourselves and in our world. This is the burden of Part V. Yet as Stevens makes clear, in Part VI, in a characteristically wild fable of a bird insatiably pecking at the sun, even love can never be fully satisfied, for our imperfections always characterize our desires. Then in a lyric of great tenderness, which is Part VII, he writes of evil and death:

> How red the rose that is the soldier's wound,
> The wounds of many soldiers, the wounds of all
> The soldiers that have fallen, red in blood,
> The soldier of time grown deathless in great size.

The soldier's wound is a metaphor for the suffering involved in living in this world; the metaphor is developed as the soldier is shown to be loved and sustained by his fellows in the very world which wounds him. So

> his wound is good because life was.
> No part of him was ever part of death.
> A woman smoothes her forehead with her hand
> And the soldier of time lies calm beneath that stroke.

So far as he is wounded by living in and of the world, he is not dead; living with evil-in-reality is not death, but the highest life. Part VIII is a meditation on the death of Satan, killed by disbelief. In denying and so losing him, however, we lost a means of grasping evil formally. We are left only with ourselves and our acceptance of our reality, and so of evil—with

> the yes of the realist spoken because he must
> Say yes, spoken because under every no
> Lay a passion for yes that had never been broken.

Part IX is a further exploration of the struggle of the "realist" to face evil imaginatively, without Satan. Part X is concerned with the vain nostalgia for escape from evil in the world, the hope to find escape in woman as a mother-wife. Part XI contrasts a reality truly known with one falsely known. It is the bitter reality which we need to know beyond any pleasure-principle:

> The tongue caresses these exacerbations.
> They press it as epicure, distinguishing
> Themselves from its essential savor,
> Like hunger that feeds on its own hungriness.

Parts XII-XIV, with logical analyses, meditations, and seeming-casual commentary, renew the richly informed view of a world of reality, with evil felt fully as "action moving in the blood." And Part XV forces this view of man in his world to its inevitable conclusion:

> The greatest poverty is not to live
> In a physical world, to feel that one's desire
> Is too difficult to tell from despair. Perhaps,
> After death, the non-physical people, in paradise,
> Itself non-physical, may, by chance, observe

The green corn gleaming and experience
The minor of what we feel. The adventurer
In humanity has not conceived of a race
Completely physical in a physical world.
The green corn gleams and the metaphysicals
Lie sprawling in majors of the August heat,
The rotund emotions, paradise unknown.

This is the thesis scrivened in delight,
The reverberating psalm, the right chorale.

One might have thought of sight, but who could think
Of what it sees, for all the ill it sees?
Speech found the ear, for all the evil sound,
But the dark italics it could not propound.
And out of what one sees and hears and out
Of what one feels, who could have thought to make
So many selves, so many sensuous worlds,
As if the air, the mid-day air, was swarming
With the metaphysical changes that occur
Merely in living as and where we live.

This is the morality of the major man: the need for living in an imaginatively known reality; the need, moreover, to endure without despair the pain of having to live so. We can endure because we know that the "non-physical people, in paradise, / Itself non-physical" can know but weakly what we, the physical people, know strongly. Yet even we are not so completely limited by physicality as not to know of metaphysicals, the great abstractions, our fictions; these we know in terms of our physical reality—green, sprawling, and rotund. This had been Stevens' thesis in "Notes toward a Supreme Fiction." Here he discovers its final moral implications for us: This reality which we know imaginatively contains evil inseparably. Since our joy is to live in reality, we needs must live in evil and know it fully. The final statement is quiet, direct, deriving its strength from the emphasis on simple verbs of being. Being, in fact, is "living as and where we live."

"Esthétique du Mal," following on "Notes Towards a Supreme Fiction," makes for a richly secular version of *felix culpa*, the Paradox of the Fortunate Fall. Richness and secularity are the essential qualities. But an outline such as this can only indicate propositions, lines of argument, and conclusions—and so moves too far away from these essential qualities. What makes the argument stick, the poetry, is perhaps lost; but this is a chance that we must take. I think it is worth taking. For such a (temporary) cutting-down of the poems to the critic's size allows one to see them in all their richness and secularity, as growing inevitably out of the earlier poems and the earlier manner. It is indeed the development of a freely inventive, discursive mode that allows (or should one say, that forces?) Stevens fully to explore the general implications of "Infanta Marina," "Sunday Morning," and others like them. What emerges in "Notes towards a Supreme Fiction" and "Esthétique du Mal" is the possibility of belief in a world in which the conditions and forms of belief are themselves products of the interaction of the believer and his world, of the conjoining of the imagination and reality. It is a matter of created and recreated belief, not of belief given from the outside.

If such creativeness runs the danger of romantic irresponsibility, Stevens would avoid that danger of recognizing the strength and recalcitrance, even the evil, of the materials—the reality—on which creativeness must operate. Facing such a reality, all creation must be an act of violence. (In 1941, concluding that poetry was a means of self-preservation, Stevens could find in it "a violence within that protects us from a violence without."[5]) In the poetry it is a paradoxical violence; for it is a quality deriving from the very control which the poet exercises over his world. It is a violence which makes Stevens' dialectic not reasoned but hortatory; a violence which is at the heart of his special elegance, his fantasy, his invention, his exoticism, and his wit; a violence which makes for his tendency to move as often as not merely by association; a violence which allows him at his best to write only a long series of varyingly formed meditations, not a single thoroughly integrated poem. Such violence Stevens can never escape; for inevitably it too is a product of the conjoining of his imagination and his reality.

Such are the strengths and the weaknesses, results of a risk taken, which must rise naturally when a world without a received principle of order is considered by a man who refuses to accept any principle of order he cannot find authorized in the only thing he really

[5] "The Noble Rider and the Sound of Words," in Allen Tate, ed. *The Language of Poetry* (Princeton, 1942), p. 125.

knows, himself. If he is a man of rich sensibility, he will see his world as a green, fluent mundo, not as something out of Aquinas, Locke, Marx, or whoever currently dwells in the Apocalypse. He will improvise a principle of order out of the self. His strength will be his weakness; he will have taken his risk. He will be inadequate, paradoxically enough, when he sees, feels, and writes too much. But he will achieve form and wholeness, however amorphous, and maturity, however disaffected.

A recent poem, "The Lack of Repose," furnishes the proper gloss:

> A young man seated at his table
> Holds in his hand a book you have never written
> Staring at the secretions of the words as
> They reveal themselves.
>
> It is not midnight. It is mid-day,
> The young man is well-disclosed, one of the gang,
> Andrew Jackson Something. But this book
> Is a cloud in which a voice mumbles.
>
> It is a ghost that inhabits a cloud,
> But a ghost for Andrew, not lean, catarrhal
> And pallid. It is the grandfather he liked,
> With an understanding compounded by death
>
> And the associations beyond death, even if only
> Time. What a thing it is to believe that
> One understands, in the intense disclosures
> Of a parent in the French sense.
>
> And not yet to have written a book in which
> One is already a grandfather and to have put there
> A few sounds of meaning, a momentary end
> To the complication, is good, is a good.

This is Stevens on received forms of belief, on forms which are not related to what he takes to be our immediate condition of belief. We know in whom Andrew Jackson Something believes; we have recently been told a great deal about his ghost and his grandfather. Yet we can move from him and the southern traditionalists whom he represents to all those who hold to forms of belief which are not primarily of our time, of our place, and of ourselves; and we can turn to what in Stevens comes to be a strongly individualistic anti-traditionalism. Our problem, certainly, is to find a middle way between a too passive traditionalism and a too active contemporaneity, between a dead reality and one super-charged. With Stevens, at least, we can return to an overpoweringly present reality and see how he tries to control it. Even if we cannot go along with him, we can know fully the possibilities, the strengths and weaknesses, and the risks, of *his* way. And we may pause at the last stanza of "The Lack of Repose." It is indeed, a good—a great good —the service of a major man to men whom he would have live "as and where [they] are."

IV

In the end, what issues from the poems is indeed a kind of estheticism, but as Stevens defiantly insists, the highest estheticism. So it is more than a coincidence that the later Stevens should herein resemble the later James—locating, by means of the elegantly creative act, moral order in the world that men must make and suffer to make. We should remember, for example, the fate of Lambert Strether and of John Marcher. We should remember the end of James's preface to *The Golden Bowl:*

> We are condemned, . . . whether we will or no, to abandon
> and outlive, to forget and disown and hand over to desolation,
> many vital or social performances—if only because the traces,
> records, connexions, and the very memorials we would fain
> preserve, are practically impossible to rescue for that purpose
> from the general mixture. We give them up even when we
> wouldn't—it is not a question of choice. Not so on the other
> hand our really "done" things of this superior and more appre-
> ciable order—which leave us indeed all licence of disconnexion
> and disavowal, but positively impose on us no such necessity.
> Our relation to them is essentially traceable, and in that fact
> abides, we feel, the incomparable luxury of the artist.

Artist=poet="any man of imagination." The price paid for the "really 'done' things" is suffering and pain. The reward, for Stevens as for James, is knowledge and individuality—and a measure of freedom. This is the meaning of the war between the mind and sky; this is, for Stevens, the full life of the imagination.

Editor's Note: "Wallace Stevens: The Life of the Imagination" by Roy Harvey Pearce. From *PMLA,* LXVI (1951), pp. 561–582. This essay appears in different form as part of a study of the whole of Stevens' poetry (Chapter 9) in *The Continuity of American Poetry* by Roy Harvey Pearce, Princeton University Press, 1961. Copyright © 1961 by Princeton University Press. Reprinted by permission of the author, Princeton University Press, and The Modern Language Association of America.

Professor Pearce, who is presently teaching at the University of California, San Diego, has published on a great variety of subjects in American literature. His best known book is *The Continuity of American Poetry.* He has also edited the Whitman volume of the *Twentieth Century Views* series and *Nathaniel Hawthorne: Centenary Essays,* and has co-edited *The Act of the Mind: Essays on the Poetry of Wallace Stevens.* He is one of the general editors of the Centenary Edition of *The Works of Nathaniel Hawthorne.*

REALISM AND NATURALISM

The following essays concern important developments in the history of American fiction after the Civil War which are best reflected in the writing of a number of authors rather than in the works of a single major author.

Attempts to define literary periods or artistic trends differ widely in assumption and methodology. Some definitions tend to be based upon a criterion of *form,* such as style, structure, or technique, while others stress different aspects of *content,* such as moral attitudes, philosophical or scientific beliefs, or characteristic incidents and themes. As indicated by their titles, the essays by Salomon and Figg differ considerably in their critical approaches.

REALISM AS DISINHERITANCE:
TWAIN, HOWELLS AND JAMES

ROGER B. SALOMON

Nowhere else is the mood of the later nineteenth century better described than in the *Autobiography* of William Butler Yeats. One important aspect of this mood was the feeling of psychic and spiritual disinheritance—the sense widely shared by some of the most sensitive minds of an entire generation that they had been "deprived" of the past by an empirically and technologically oriented present. In one passage Yeats describes the varying ways the process of disinheritance affected his father and himself; he also implies a relationship between the problem of the past and the development of realistic schools of painting:

> It was a perpetual bewilderment that when my father, moved perhaps by some memory of his youth, chose some theme from poetic tradition, he would soon weary and leave it unfinished. I had seen the change coming bit by bit and its defense elaborated by young men fresh from the Paris art schools. "We must paint what is in front of us," or "A man must be of his own time," they would say . . . they were very ignorant men; they read nothing, for nothing mattered but "knowing how to paint," being in reaction against a generation that seemed to have wasted its time upon so many things. I thought myself alone in hating these young men, their contempt for the past, their monopoly of the future, but in a few months I was to discover others of my own age, who thought as I did.

Three points are of special significance here: first, the ambivalence of Yeats' father, unable to bridge the gap between his memories and his artistic principles; secondly, the belligerent insistence of the realists that their subject-matter be both tangible and contemporary; and finally, the unwillingness of Yeats and certain of his immediate contemporaries to accept the cultural situation in which they found themselves. One way of looking at Yeats' own literary development is to say that it represents a continuing and increasingly successful effort to bring past and present into a viable relationship through a style supple enough to accommodate the claims of both.

Ambivalence, acceptance, constructive and creative rebellion—these are possible responses to the problem of disinheritance. My concern on the following pages is to show these responses at work in three writers of the first American generation to feel the full impact of realism and, at the same time, to shed further light on a literary movement whose assumptions and implications are still far from adequately defined.

Critics of American realism have been unduly preoccupied with the question of its national origin. For some it reflects the triumph after 1860 of science and patriotism—of the new empirical vision mingled with a heightened national consciousness. It has been described as the product of a society shaken by war, transformed by technology, and discovering the sound and look of its own regions, especially the West. A less nationalistic version of our literary history minimizes the influence of native elements and describes American realism as largely the local response to literary currents already widespread in Europe.

Fortunately it is unnecessary for our purposes to referee the eternal battle between redskins and palefaces. Rather we must examine an assumption common to the entire realistic movement here and abroad: that past and present are discontinuous, that the past can and should be rejected as without serious relevance to the present. Realism denies the continuum of time as meaningful dimension of experience because time cannot be seen or touched—the ultimate empirical criteria. This point is made abundantly clear in the work of French critics of realism during the formative years of the movement from 1840 to 1870. The final aim of literature, says one (I quote at random from their work), "is a thing real, existing, comprehensible, visible, palpable: the scrupulous imitation of nature." Another affirms even more explicitly the existential aspects of realism: "Realism forbids the historic in painting, in the novel, and in the theatre so that it will not find itself lying, and so that the artist can not borrow his intelligence from others. . . . Realism wishes from artists only the study of their epoch." A third critic makes the crucial distinction between "strong intelligences" and what he calls the personal romancer, "who has only to look within to, at a certain age, rediscover in a bottom drawer the dried bouquets of his youth."[1] This last critic might well have been making specific reference to the work of Mark Twain. It is important to observe that Twain gave his intellectual allegiance to a movement which tended to denigrate the memorial and associative qualities of the mind as devices for recapturing the past. To the "strong intelligence"—the sober and tough-minded individual—the remembrance of things past must be alien. The best fiction, Howells noted pointedly in *Criticism and Fiction,* approaches *contemporaneous* history, and he quoted with approval Emerson's wonderful phrase: "today is a king in disguise."

Realism was welcomed by major writers, of course, because it came in response to cultural needs. Everywhere in the nineteenth century the writer felt what Henry James called "the dreadful chill of change." The Boss in the *Connecticut Yankee* is only the prototype of all the wreckers of the century who were uprooting, pulling down, blasting and carting away the past for decent or indecent burial. In *The American Scene* Henry James describes a visit he made in the autumn of 1904 to his early home at Ashburton Place, Boston. He found the building closed and shuttered; a month later when he revisited the spot it had been torn down and the ground cleared. This incident should be compared to one described in a late notebook entry of Twain's entitled "Huck & Tom 50 Years After." The entry is thinly disguised autobiography—an obvious reference to a visit Twain made to Hannibal late in life. It reads: "The Cold Spring—Jim has gone home—they can't find it—all railway tracks. No levee & no steamboats."[2] James analyzed the psychological effect of such experiences: "It was as if the bottom had fallen out of one's own biography, and one plunged backward

---

[1] These and similar quotations are collected in Bernard Weinberg, *French Realism: The Critical Reaction, 1830–1870* (Oxford, 1937), pp. 122–23. Translations are my own.

[2] Quotation © copyright 1964 by the Mark Twain Co. The author gratefully acknowledges the permission of Professor Henry Nash Smith and the Mark Twain Co. to make use of unpublished materials.

into space without meeting anything . . . the sense of the rupture . . . seemed to leave me with my early impression of the place on my hands, inapt, as might be for use; so that I could only try, rather vainly, to fit it to present conditions, among which it tended to shrink and stray." Two or three more visits to the reconstructed Beacon Hill area and James felt his "small cluster of early associations shrivel to a scarcely discernible point."

In short, what our French critic would have called the "dried bouquets" of James' youth seemed without serious relevance to his maturity; indeed the facts of maturity all but obliterated them. The writers of James' generation had the continual feeling, as he said elsewhere, of being "cut in half." Realism was the aesthetic of disinheritance; it solved the problem of the torn thread of time by offering scissors for cutting it into even tinier shreds. In a world of change a kind of stasis could be achieved by, so to speak, "atomizing" time as Twain does in a notebook entry of 1897: "There is in life only one moment & in eternity only one. It is so brief that it is represented by the flitting of a luminous mote through a ray of sunlight—it is visible but a fraction of a second. The moments that preceded it have been lived, are forgotten & are without value; the moments that have not been lived have no existence & will have no value except in the moment that each shall be lived." This note should be compared with the familiar passage in Eliot's *Burnt Norton:* "Time present and time past/ Are both perhaps present in time future,/ And time future contained in time past/ . . . all time is eternally present." A passage from *Ulysses* is also particularly relevant here—Stephen's advice to "hold to the now, the here, through which all future plunges to the past." All these writers in their own way celebrate "time present," but this enduring tenet of realism has been significantly modified in the quarter-century from Twain to Joyce and Eliot. The present of the more recent writers has a temporal dimension; Twain's is discrete, particular, isolated. We might note further in passing that stasis is available to the modern writer only when it is predicated on continuity and transcends it.

If one's personal past seemed increasingly irrelevant to the later-nineteenth-century writer, what was one to make of the *historical* past? In this case, as modern criticism has noted time and time again, the American commitment has *always* been to discontinuity. From the beginning, the American has thought of himself as a new

Adam in a new Eden free forever from the moral horror of Europe—which in American writing has always been the major symbol of the rich but tainted past. The generation of Longfellow and Lowell, however, made important concessions to the past because the national consciousness was not yet clearly defined and because the dominant aesthetic of the period—the so-called psychological picturesque—was predicated on the assumption that the past alone could furnish the feelings, memories and associations necessary for valid imaginative experience. In a recent book David Levin has described the divided commitment of our early great historians, Bancroft, Prescott, Motley and Parkman. Thanks to a careful choice of subject, they were able to trace the rise of liberty against a picturesque background of European institutions. According to Lowell, the role of the past was to provide "hereditary and accumulated culture"; whatever the moral status of America (that is, however "new" or unfallen we were) we shared, at least, in a *cultural continuum*.

For the next generation realism was a direct response to a widespread feeling that "hereditary and accumulated culture" was no longer seriously relevant to a rapidly emerging industrial order. Even an English review of 1846 could write that "in these busy times of ours, when the intellects of men are sorely tasked to keep pace with the advancing spirit of the age . . . the past can never be supposed worthy to absorb attention." Forty years later in a letter to Thomas Sargeant Perry, Howells precisely echoed these sentiments: "I have been turning over a good many books, and putting myself in rapport with Italy again. But I'm not sure that it pays. After all, *we* have the country of the present and the future." In Europe realism was used as an instrument of rebellion against official art. In America rebellion came slower, but by the 1870s Howells and Twain were making perfectly clear that concessions were no longer necessary. For a generation fascinated with change and what it hoped was moral and material progress the picturesque canon seemed hopelessly compromised by its involvement with the past, yet the picturesque canon was still the dominant aesthetic. Accommodation no longer seemed possible; aesthetic experience must be renounced or transformed. Renunciation was a brave possibility; for young men buoyancy and hope carried the day. "I assure you," Howells wrote in an early letter from Europe, "that our American freedom, social, intellectual, and political, is better than all the past and present slavery of Europe, however glorious in art and history that may be." In *The Innocents Abroad* Twain reported with equal complacency that "the popes have long been the patrons and preservers of art, just as our new, practical Republic is the encourager and upholder of mechanics. In their Vatican is stored up all that is curious and beautiful in art; in our Patent Office is hoarded all that is curious or useful in mechanics." The book as a whole makes it clear that this division of labor is complete and irrevocable.

Howells' early novel, *A Foregone Conclusion,* emphasizes the meaning for the artist of Twain's parable of the Vatican and the Patent Office. The narrow Ferris, American consul in Venice and amateur painter (he is modeled roughly, of course, on Howells himself), leads a party of three others one day on a trip to some old villas near Venice. "These haunts of old-time splendor and idleness," says Howells, ". . . belonged as far as the Americans were concerned, to a world as strange as any to which they should go in another life—the world of a faded fashion and an alien history." They are, in other words, prime candidates for a quick dismissal. But Ferris, the artist, lingers; he senses that the villas have imaginative possibilities. But can these possibilities be imported to America? He tells the girl who is with him that Americans "wouldn't know what it all meant, and couldn't imagine that we were inspired by this rascally little villa to sigh longingly over the wicked past." His fears find immediate confirmation when the girl answers warmly: "I'm not sighing over it . . . I'm glad that I'm American and there is no past for me. I can't understand how you and Don Ippolito [he is a priest with the party] can speak so tolerantly of what no one can respect." At this Ferris beats a quick retreat; he is the first to admit that his aesthetic sentiments are grossly anachronistic: "I'm a painter, and the rococo is my weakness. I wish I could paint it, but I can't. I'm a hundred years too late. I couldn't even paint myself in the act of sentimentalizing it." Parody and sentimentality: these are the only possible responses to aestheic feelings which can no longer be legitimized. They suggest Howell's predicament, and they precisely describe the poles between which Twain's sensibility vacillates in *The Innocents Abroad.*

A word must be added about the priest, Don Ippolito, who has aspirations to become an inventor and go to America and who also falls hopelessly in love with the American girl—all this while losing his faith. On all counts, I need hardly add, he fails; his failure is, indeed, a "foregone conclusion" because he is as completely a creature of the past as Ferris is of the present. We can say of him as Ferris says of a Corpus Christi procession: "It's phantasmal. It's the spectral resurrection of the old dead forms into the present . . . it's the corpse of other ages that's haunting Venice." Appropriately enough, it is death that waits for Don Ippolito at the end of the book. His attempt to become an inventor—to somehow establish a bridgehead between past and present—is as doomed as Ferris' abortive attempt at aesthetic experience.

All attempts to adapt certain strategies of the picturesque to the needs of the realistic spirit proved in the long run equally disastrous. In *Tuscan Cities*, for example, one of Howells' later travel books, the imagination paradoxically "realizes" the past only to the degree that it succeeds in muffling or destroying the temporal sense. Howells was abetted in this task by the artifacts of the past everywhere scattered over the Italian landscape. He describes his methodology in the first chapter: "At home, in the closet, one may read history, but one can realize it, as if it were something personally experienced, only on the spot where it was lived." In its manifestation as an empirical phenomenon, history strikes a responsive note, as Howells goes on to explain with something like amazement in his tone. "In this pursuit of the past, the inquirer will often surprise himself in the possession of a genuine emotion; at moments the illustrious or pathetic figures of other days will seem to walk before him . . . it would take little to persuade me that I had vanishing glimpses of many of these figures in Florence. One of the advantages of this method is that you have your historical personages in a sort of picturesque contemporaneity with one another and with yourself and you imbue them with all the sensibilities of our own time. Perhaps this is not an advantage, but it shows what may be done by the imaginative faculty; and if we do not judge men by ourselves, how are we to judge them at all?" Howells precisely labels his own strategy as "picturesque contemporaneity." In other words, the stimulus of the artifact can produce a meaningful imaginative experience provided that this experience is carefully denied any temporal dimension. The color of the past is preserved while empirical reality remains apparently unviolated.

Unfortunately for Howells his clever design concealed a chamber of horrors. He joins the heroes in pursuing the villains all over

Italy only to find the heroes time and again losing the crucial battle or joining up with the villains to pillage some city. In short, to treat the past in contemporary terms was, for the believer in moral progress, to make it ultimately more remote than ever. Howells is only too ready to admit after a harrowing description of the times of Savonarola and Lorenzo de'Medici that "in all things the change is such that if not a new heaven there is a new earth since their day." He ends a long chapter on Florence with a paean to the city of 1884: "contemporary, real, busy in its fashion, and wholesomely and every-daily beautiful." He explains that his "heart still warms to the town," not because of its "wrong-headed and bloody and pitiless" past, but "because of the present, safe, free, kindly, full of possibilities of prosperity and fraternity, like that of Boston or Denver." Such a comment is, of course, reminiscent of Twain's very similar remarks about the Mississippi River towns in *Life on the Mississippi*. As for art, Howells dislikes the "immorality" of the Old Masters, but his ultimate reaction again is their remoteness and irrelevance to the serious concerns of the present. After a long description of certain Italian paintings he adds: "that is what I recall, with a conviction of the idleness and absurdity of recalling anything." Twain in *The Innocents Abroad* makes the implications here even more explicit: "To me there is nothing tangible about these imaginary portraits, nothing I can grasp and take a living interest in." It is no wonder that the middle-aged hero of Howells' novel *Indian Summer* (1886) abandons his plan to live in the "outworn Old World" and decides to return to "the vast, tumultuous American life." Significantly, he also decides not to marry a young woman who romantically wants to help him recoup an early love affair—to help him, in other words, recapture his personal past. Just in time he awakes to his sentimental folly; he becomes aware, like his author, of "the idleness and absurdity of recalling anything."

Realism, in short, was both a response and a solution to the problem of the past. The picturesque tradition was unable to deal with the present, and so realism made a religion of newness and contemporaneity. It dismissed the problem of artistic form (associated with the past) by refusing to acknowledge any distinction between art and life; the writer was not, in fact, a creative artist at all, but rather a reporter, a social commentator, or a psychologist. The recent edition of the Twain-Howells letters emphasizes anew the utter absence of any stylistic tradition with which either writer was willing to identify himself. For both men the only acknowledged alternatives seemed to be, on the one hand, parody or burlesque of past styles that fades off into farce comedy and, on the other, what was confidently referred to as "simple and stately facts." Howells, for example, praises William Allen White's book "In Our Town" as "a series of photographs taken with Roentgen rays." The only form possible was the actual form taken by life itself. Both men yearned at various times for what Twain, in a notebook passage, called the "narrative novel" and defined as one "where you follow the fortunes of two or three people & have no plot more than real life has."[3] Not surprisingly, the work of Howells and Twain moves back and forth across the thin line that separates their reportorial and travel experience from fiction. In a curious fashion realism tended to reinforce what has always been an important strand of the American imagination: the image of the journey, the conception of life as movement and process that finds its central expression in *Moby-Dick* and *Leaves of Grass*—and, of course, a generation later, *Huckleberry Finn*. In any case, realism was the natural and perhaps inevitable response of the new empirical spirit to the noise of collapsing institutions that was everywhere heard in the nineteenth century. For Americans in particular, it offered new opportunities for a Declaration of Literary Independence—for the creation of a truly national literature by a society whose central distinction was its newness. Certainly realism precisely fitted the limits of Howells' individual talent and helped him discover and develop it.

At the same time, every literary movement constitutes, at least by implication, a point of view toward human experience; it makes a set of assumptions about the nature of that wonderfully elusive thing called "reality." These assumptions may "contain multitudes" but they cannot contain everything; if I seem to have stressed the *limitations* of realism, it is because I want to trace the effect of these limitations on the work of two writers far greater than Howells. What was the effect of a theory that denied or dismissed the past on the work of men for whom the time sense was perhaps the most deeply felt dimension of experience?

We can not begin to understand Twain until we acknowledge

---

[3] Quotation © copyright 1964 by the Mark Twain Co.

the fact that *intellectually* he was a convinced realist, a militant foe of romance in all its manifestations. *The Innocents Abroad* sets the pattern of his later books; it is a private Declaration of Independence—his first attempt to define his role as an honest American reporter who "knows" only what he *sees*. In the second part of *Life on the Mississippi* he spends page after page extolling the "genuine and wholesome civilization" of the modern industrial South as opposed to "the absurd past that is dead." In *A Connecticut Yankee* he makes a convulsive effort to destroy the past in one stroke, to sweep the scene clear for his practical, unsentimental man of affairs. And regarding his personal past, we must keep in mind a vigorous comment made to a childhood friend in the 1870s: "I told him to stop being 16 at 40; told him to stop drooling about the sweet yet melancholy past and take a pill. I said there was but one solitary thing about the past worth remembering and that was the fact that it *is* the past—can't be restored."

This, of course, is not the entire story. In the *Connecticut Yankee,* for example, the very violence of the attack suggests an obsessive concern with the past; the Yankee is a modern Merlin who will exorcise the ghosts from the premises. But the fact is the Yankee ultimately fails; instead of destroying the past he is somehow destroyed by it. On the one hand, the tragic conclusion of the book reflects Twain's growing sense of the moral continuity of history, a gradual loss of belief in progress that led him late in life to develop a cyclical theory of history. Here, of course, we are face to face with one of the paradoxes of realism. What was thrown out the front door tended to creep in the back. By its very process of reducing the past from heroics to sordid facts which might be safely rejected, realism opened the way for the re-establishment of one kind of meaningful relationship between past and present. To strip the past of its romance was—if one's belief in moral progress was not strong—simply to come face to face with the enduring spectacle of human nature. Everywhere in his work Howells pulls himself up short of this conclusion only by the most heroic act of faith. Twain eventually gave up trying and Henry James, by and large, never made the attempt.

But there is one other curious and significant aspect of the *Connecticut Yankee* that we must keep in mind. Henry Nash Smith and others have pointed out that Twain tentatively entitled the book "The Lost Land" and described it in the following way in his note-

207

book: "He [i.e., the Yankee] mourns his lost land—has come to England & revisited it, but it is all changed & become old, so old!—& it was so fresh & new, so virgin before . . . Has lost all interest in life—is found dead next morning—suicide."[4] Twain carries over much of this mournful note into the opening chapter of the finished work, which takes place in time long after the main action has been completed. Where we would expect unmitigated rejoicing on the Yankee's part that the changes he fought for have finally come about, we find instead melancholy and longing. In other words, the Yankee's primary identification is ultimately with a past which he had considered it his whole duty to violate. From one point of view, as Twain's note suggests, the book describes an extended act of spiritual suicide.

Twain's comment on the *Connecticut Yankee* is strikingly similar to one he made regarding Howells' *Indian Summer*. "It is a beautiful story," he wrote Howells in a letter, "& makes a body laugh all the time, & cry inside, & feel so old & so forlorn; & gives him gracious glimpses of his lost youth that fill him with a measureless regret, & build up in him a cloudy sense of his having been a prince, once, in some enchanted far-off land, & of being in exile now, & desolate—& lord, no chance to ever get back there again! That is the thing that hurts." Again Twain's particular interpretation is an inversion of the official theme. The whole point of the story for Howells is that the past of Italy and the personal past of the main character must be rejected and that any attempt to recapture them constitutes the most irresponsible kind of sentimental folly. For Twain the exorcism will not work; the ghosts will not fade away in the glaring light of the nineteenth century. His commitment to the past, like that of Henry James, was far too deep and fundamental. Perhaps in some ways it was *more* fundamental than James'. He could not even obey the elementary injunction of realism that James chastized Sarah Orne Jewett for violating after she wrote her historical novel, *The Tory Lover*. "Go back to the dear country of the Pointed Firs," James begged her, *"come* back to the palpable present *intimate* that throbs responsive, and that wants, needs you. . . ."

We are face to face, of course, with Twain's *nostalgia,* his "homesickness"for the home that had been destroyed, his sense of wander-

[4] Quotations © copyright 1964 by the Mark Twain Co.

ing in exile from a "lost country." The sentiment is common to the century and is the product of the same forces that were to produce realism: change, disorientation, the "hateful" sense, as James put it, of "personal antiquity," of being able to trace in one's lifetime where "an age has come out." But nostalgia is also predicated on memory—or perhaps it would be better to say on the refusal to forget. It insists, irrationally, on clinging to the thread of time that realism is busy cutting up; nostalgia is a recessive, indeed, an illegitimate sentiment during this period. Yet it is felt all the more poignantly simply because it is illegitimate, because it is denied the dignity of recognition and rational expression. The crucial fact to remember about Twain is that he was intellectually committed to realism and emotionally committed to a nostalgic sense of the past. As a result he could find nothing but sentimental justification for something of vast psychological importance to him. His reason was constantly nibbling away at his imaginative life. Most important, the very sources of his art rested on foundations that could not be rationally defended. His consciousness was (to use James' phrase) "cut in half" into two different and eternally hostile modes of experience: the tangible world of observation and fact; the intangible world of imagination and memory. Twain alternately fondled and violated the past depending on the mode that was uppermost at any given time. Only occasionally—the great example is, of course, *Huckleberry Finn*—did the modes come into any kind of fruitful equilibrium. Certainly an important reason for the development of so-called "regional" writing in America after the Civil War was that it offered the only legitimate meeting place for "facts" and memory.

It can not be emphasized enough that the nostalgic vision accepts the principle of discontinuity central to the realistic point of view. The nostalgic writer has his own Eden in the past—the place where value resides, where time has not yet begun or is somehow suspended. It is the clear counterpart to the atomistic present of realism. Like the realist also, the nostalgic writer cannot conceive of "youth" turning into "maturity." Twain's young people are "stuck" in the past, denied the possibility of an organic maturation in which innocence, imagination, memory and rational experience unite in a socially integrated personality. Much as he tried—and he tried often—he could never turn one of his young people into an adult. The realistic Twain labeled memory (in so far as it is our central means of preserving and interpreting the past) an "illusion" and violently attacked it; the nostalgic Twain accepted the label but felt very differently about the *value* of illusion. Later in life he wrote in an aphorism: "Don't part with your illusions: when they are gone you may still exist but you have ceased to live." He might have added that for the *artist* of illusions such a loss would have particularly tragic consequences. Where Howells abandoned the past and worked toward an art that made a temple of reflecting the surface of contemporary American life, Twain is most completely the "split" personality who seldom achieved a workable relation between his emotional ties to the past and an intellectual commitment to the present. It was left to James to open up avenues of reconciliation—avenues down which many writers of a more recent generation have walked.

To the task of reconciliation James brought an abiding conviction of the need for continuity; for Americans it was the most pressing national problem left unsolved. We are, he said, dedicated to the "expensively provisional"; "we have nothing to do with continuity, responsibility, transmission." This is the heart of his complaint against America as he developed it late in life in *The American Scene*. European life offered a sharp contrast. Of a thirteenth-century abbey in England which had been turned into a private home, James wrote approvingly: "The new life and the old have melted together; there is no dividing-line." He noted that the townspeople of Arles in France used the Roman arena there as a passageway from one part of town to another and commented that "this familiarity does not kill the place again; it makes it, on the contrary, live a little—makes the present and the past touch each other." The island of Capri, James called "antiquity in solution"—"the old story," he said, "of the deep interfusion of the present with the past." The images here are significant: melting together, touching, deep interfusion. Though he had moments of being swept away by nostalgia, James' most profound vision is not of escape to an ideal past of dreams and fantasy but of the preservation of a real past as a dimension of the living and active present. For James the present could literally *incorporate* the past: make it, that is, one in body. Without a past, an individual or a society had no identity—no "tone" to use James' favorite word.

Such incorporation was seriously conceivable to James because he was willing to accept the *whole* of the past—its cost in human suffering as well as its ingrained beauty of form and color. He senses, for example, what he calls the "horror" of Capri and characteristically goes on to analyze his feelings: "The beauty and the poetry . . . were clear enough, and the extraordinary uplifted distinction; but where, in all this, it may be asked, was the element of 'horror' that I have spoken of as sensible. . . . I'm afraid I'm driven to plead that these evils were exactly in one's imagination, a predestined victim always of the cruel, the fatal historic sense. To make so much distinction, how much history had been needed! . . . the whole air still throbbed and ached with it." To accept fusion was to acknowledge and finally accept the horror; it was, in other words, to deny the absolute moral distinction between past and present which was a cornerstone of American realism. The essence of history, James said elsewhere, is "the sense of human relations"; in this one phrase he rejected both the idealization and the exclusion of the past. To the realist's steady vision James added a new awareness of the variety and complexity of human experience.

But even if one granted the *need* for continuity, how was it to be maintained in a time of change? James' answer, given with many doubts and qualifications, was a testimonial to the value of memory and imagination. Memory was the supreme preserver: "the faculty," as he defined it, "of putting together in an order the sharp minutes and hours that the wave of time has been as ready to pass over as the salt sea to wipe out the letters and words your stick has traced in the sand." The imagination was actively re-creative; from the hints of the past it could reconstruct the total picture. Together with memory it supplied the perceptions and impressions which—to again quote James—"became, not a waste, but a positive gain of consciousness, an intensification . . . of experience." Here James most radically parts company with traditional realism, which made a sharp distinction between tangible and intangible experience. Intangible experience was to be rejected by the strong-minded; the function of the realistic artist was to report the observed facts. Objectivity—the great rallying cry of critical realists—demanded the separation of the author and his consciousness from the book in favor of description, analysis and dialogue. James supported the principle of objectivity just as he believed that the novel should deal with contemporary life; his blunt advice to Sara Orne Jewett shows his awareness that the historical novel was simply a colorful way of perpetrating discontinuity. Yet in arguing that the sense of the past was "not a waste, but a positive gain," he was defending consciousness, the only medium in which this sense could thrive. James' great compromise was to bring to realism the principle of point of view—the device of using centers of consciousness built around various characters to give a sense of the coherence and fusion of all experience without the author himself abandoning his objectivity or his use of "present" time as the primary setting of the novel. For James, as the English critic Dorothea Krook has noted, "the world of art . . . is a beautiful presentation of the appearances present to a particular consciousness under particular conditions." Among these so-called "appearances" the sense of the past played a prominent role, although the past was only meaningful as it manifested itself in immediate experience. In commenting upon his short story the "Altar of the Dead," James reminded his readers that a "sense of the state of the dead is but part of the sense of the state of the living."

The nostalgic mood was by no means foreign to James, but it is not of central importance to his life and work except in so far as it represents the psychic problem whose solution was most pressing for him. Like Yeats and others of a later generation, he refused to accept his disinheritance. Far from being impotent, memory was a vital and valid dimension of the living and creating mind. Indeed, in the creative process the principle of continuity found ultimate expression; this conviction is the central rationale for the revisions included in the New York Edition. In the Preface to *Roderick Hudson* James describes how an artist "cleans up" and looks over an old work until the "strange charm" of subject and treatment rekindles his imagination and helps him "to live back into a forgotten state." He goes on to say how this charm "breathes upon the dead reasons of things buried as they are in the texture of the work, and makes them revive, so that the actual appearances and the old motives fall together once more, and a lesson and a moral and a consecrating light are somehow disengaged." The artist's consciousness, in other words—standing outside each individual work but ultimately the greatest "character" in one supreme fiction—achieves a final order and coherence by giving to the temporal manifestations of this consciousness a "living" immediacy and relevance. The New York Edition constitutes his supreme attempt to bind together the broken threads of time—his testament to what he called the "joy" of "that constructive, that creative passion . . . the great extension, great beyond all others of experience and of consciousness."

Editor's Note: "Realism as Disinheritance: Twain, Howells, and James" is reprinted, by permission of Roger B. Salomon and *American Quarterly,* from *American Quarterly,* XVI (1964), pp. 531–544.

Professor Salomon, a Morse fellow in 1960–1961, is the author of *Twain and the Image of History.*

NATURALISM
AS A
LITERARY FORM

ROBERT M. FIGG

Ever since Vernon L. Parrington defined literary naturalism as "pessimistic realism," American critics, among them such figures as Alfred Kazin, Richard Chase, and Philip Rahv, have by and large followed suit. Naturalism has appeared to them as identical in *kind* with realism, though different in *degree*. It has been interpreted as an extension of realism, as realism intensified, as a "harsher realism," or as realism carried to the *nth* degree. This tendency persists even today, as can be seen in two recent collections of realist documents—*Realism and Romanticism in Fiction: An Approach to the Novel* (1962), whose editors call naturalism "a new type of realism," and *Documents of Modern Literary Realism* (1963), whose editor, George J. Becker, tells us that "in essence and in origin naturalism is no more than an emphatic and explicit philosophical position taken by some realists. . . ."

One readily understands this tendency to classify naturalism under the general heading of realism, for most of these commentators have been mainly concerned with treating the matter from the point of view of literary history, and from that viewpoint naturalism perhaps does appear to be an extension or intensification of realism. But from a strictly literary point of view, it seems to me, the difference between these modes is more than a matter of degree. A few commentators have been aware of this further difference. In *The Responsibilities of the Novelist* Frank Norris tells us that romance—and we know that for Norris naturalism is a form of romance—is "the kind of fiction that takes cognizance of variations from the type of normal life," whereas realism is "the kind of fiction that confines itself to the type of normal life." In his 1915 essay on

Dreiser's barbaric naturalism, the humanist Stuart P. Sherman took as his purpose the finding of "a working distinction between the realistic novel and the naturalistic novel of the present day." He decided that the two literary modes differed essentially, in that a realistic work was based on "a theory of human conduct" whereas a naturalistic work was based on "a theory of animal behavior." In 1931, Russell Blankenship held that the usual definition of naturalism as "pessimistic realism" was false because "the essence of realism is an objective presentation of facts with absolutely no personal or philosophical interpretation," while the naturalist is very much concerned with philosophical interpretation. And finally, most recently, Charles Child Walcutt, in *American Literary Naturalism, A Divided Stream* (1956), has treated naturalism as though he conceived of it as a distinctive and unique literary mode. It is with these voices of dissent that I here wish to identify myself, in the belief that a better understanding of just what sort of thing American literary naturalism is will be gained by viewing it as differing from realism not only in *degree* but also in *kind* than may be gained from adopting the prevailing view.

The distinction in *kind*, it seems to me, is implied in the very definition of naturalism which the majority of commentators have adopted: that it is realism with a philosophy of materialistic determinism added. No matter how one defines "realism," the "addition" of such a philosophy will alter what one is thinking of to something essentially different, for the idea of materialistic determinism is a rigidly prescriptive idea, carrying with it a narrow set of necessary implications concerning how the materials of the work will be treated. Since in the novel meaning is a function of form, the deterministic idea, seriously entertained, *prescribes* a particular structural pattern, a certain type of characterization, and a definite amoral orientation. In addition, the idea also *implies* the presence of a certain type of imagery. We cannot imagine adding the impress of so powerful a governing idea to a novel we have hitherto called "realistic" without admitting that the main fictional elements of that novel would have to be radically and essentially redisposed. From the standpoint of literary form, what would result would bear but a superficial resemblance to what existed before. This would be the case, then, regardless of how we defined "realism."

But let us now look at two specific types of American realism,

realism of the commonplace and critical realism. The former, according to its chief proponent, William Dean Howells, takes as its subject matter the common, the familiar, the ordinary in American life, and proposes to treat this matter with something approaching faithfulness to the given actualities of life. Its matter is gleaned through empirical observation; its manner of treatment is inspired by a desire for scientific objectivity. It has, too, a social aim, to knit men together in the spirit of sympathy and brotherhood through a recognition of the commonality of their experience. All this is not to imply that realism of the commonplace is a mere photographic treatment of observed actuality. It has its selective criterion: the belief that a proportioned, "average" representation of actuality is closer to the truth than a representation of extremes. It has, too, its faith in value—in a sort of relativistic, pragmatic truth which cannot be determined in an *a priori* manner but must be sought in the observable consequences of human actions. Everett Carter has given us an admirable survey of this aspect of the realism of the commonplace:

> To expose the 'bad *a priori*' that the savage and the untutored were necessarily noble was the motive behind Eggleston's realistic portraits in *The Hoosier Schoolmaster* and *The Circuit Rider*. The falsity of the assumption that the agrarian life of the West was inevitably the good life was the subject of Hamlin Garland's, *Main-Travelled Roads* and *Jason Edwards*. The 'pretended absolutes' of the South's chivalric ideals were the targets for John DeForest's criticism in *Miss Ravenel's Conversion* . . . for Mark Twain in *Huckleberry Finn*. . . . A criticism of unexamined 'fixed principles' and closed systems of morality was the motivation for Howells' fiction.

In exposing the bad *a priori* and turning instead to the world of actuality for their reading of truth, these men anticipated what William James was later to call the pragmatic method, that is, "The attitude of looking away from first things, principles, 'categories,' supposed necessities; and of looking towards last things, fruits, consequences, facts." For the dual purposes of bodying forth its proportioned view of actuality and its pragmatic vision of truth, then, commonplace realism necessarily employs selection and arrangement of observed data and hence does not become mere photography. The manipulation of data is solely in the interest of focusing the truth that the author finds operative within the world of actuality. Finally, there is in commonplace realism a sort of optimistic faith that man, through the application of reason to the world of fact, may improve his existence, a faith which was based on the pragmatic assumption that the world of things was full of meaning. The aforementioned principles constitute, of course, a theoretical statement of what realism of the commonplace is, a sort of ideal model of what such realists sought. We would not expect to find a perfect embodiment of this model, the difference between intention and realization in human life being what it is. The closest approximation to an incarnation of these principles is, perhaps, Howells' *The Rise of Silas Lapham*.

The second type of realism we want to look at is what has come to be known as critical realism. As with commonplace realism, its chief theoretician was William Dean Howells, who defined critical realism as an attempt at "dispersing the conventional acceptances by which men live on easy terms with themselves, and obliging them to examine the grounds of their social and moral opinions." Yet in proclaiming this new concept of realism, Howells did not, as Everett Carter reminds us, "discard any of the elements of his former philosophy of fiction. . . ." Critical realism was essentially realism of the commonplace operating on wider and more inclusive grounds, in keeping with Howells' growing awareness that, in the America of the late 1880's, the "smiling aspects" no longer best represented the truth of the American actuality and that the problems of Americans were not so much individual in nature as social. But in shifting grounds Howells kept to "his previous beliefs, with their good-sense and moderation," as Everett Carter has put it, and thus "saved himself from falling into the trap of propaganda." The basis for the socially critical attitude in *A Hazard of New Fortunes*, for instance, is pragmatic rather than doctrinaire: that *laissez-faire* capitalism is reprehensible because of its ruinous and destructive effects upon individuals and upon society as a whole. In his selection and arrangement of the data he has gleaned from observation, Howells still has as his main aim a focused presentation of the truth of the world of actuality. He operates in the faith that, should he manage to capture the essentials of that world in his fictional image, the sensitive reader will necessarily feel his "conventional acceptances" challenged. Thus he leaves the critical inferences largely up to the reader and does not impose them upon him in a direct form, as do the authors of those novels of social criticism which are oriented around a highly prescriptive socio-economic thesis or formula.

In both realism of the commonplace and critical realism, then, there is manipulation of observed data—a selection and arrangement of fictional materials in the interest of embodying the author's view of reality; but the assumptions governing the selection and disposal of these materials are relatively mild and the image of life presented is relatively close to the actual. No highly prescriptive ideas are imposed on the novel, more or less wrenching its materials into shapes and patterns that strike us as distortions of what has been observed in the world of actuality. The "addition" of an unqualified materialistic determinism to a novel based on either of the aforementioned codes of realism—if we can at all imagine such a thing—would have precisely this effect. The incidents of the work would have to be redisposed so as to present the illusion of man as inescapably the creature of forces beyond his control, and the characters would have to be fashioned into relatively "flat" types, representing various examples of passivity, ineffectuality, and futility. Gone would be all pretense that the work presented something approximating observable and verifiable experience, since the idea of the absolute determination of man is but an unproven, and perhaps unprovable, hypothesis. Gone, too, would be the critical purpose and optimistic faith that lie at the heart of both types of Howellsian realism, the idea that man may amend his condition through the application of reason to individual and social problems. The result would be something essentially different from what was before, in respect to both form and significance.

This distinction in *kind* between realism and naturalism was something that Emile Zola, the fountainhead of naturalistic theory, insisted upon in his manifesto, *Le Roman expérimental*. The naturalistic novelist, he tells us, is not simply an observer, but is rather an observer *and* experimenter:

> The observer in him presents data as he has observed them, determines the point of departure, establishes the solid ground on which his characters will stand and his phenomena take place. Then the experimenter appears and institutes the experiment, that is, sets the characters of a particular story in motion, in order to show that the series of events therein will be those demanded by the determinism of the phenomena under study.

218

In other words, as an observer, the naturalistic novelist gleans "facts" from the world of actuality, just as does the realist. As an experimentalist, however, he rearranges or modifies them in accord with the deterministic hypotheses of science. Zola admits that the idea of man being governed by an absolute hereditary and environmental determinism is but an *hypothesis,* that science has not yet proven this to be true, though he tells us that physiology and social science will no doubt someday explain such mechanisms. In the meanwhile, the naturalist is to write of man in the spirit of one "who accepts only facts in conformity with the determinism of phenomena," trusting that what he writes is the truth about man. His product thus involves the imposition upon observed fact of a rigid *assumption* about the nature of reality. The result is an "experiment" that takes the following form: Given character *x,* with his peculiar hereditary or physiological makeup, in the context of environment *y,* what inevitably follows? The author marks the resulting determination in his novel. The action of his characters is but the demonstration of an *a priori* idea.

Such is the scientific hypothesis which the naturalist attempts to apply to the novel. But in the novel meaning is a function of form. He must therefore render the deterministic idea in terms of the basic constituent elements of the novel before we are justified in calling his work a naturalistic novel. Now as has been said before, the philosophy of determinism, by its very nature, *prescribes* a particular structural pattern, a certain type of characterization, and a definite non-moral or amoral orientation, and it *implies* the presence of a certain type of imagery. To the extent, then, that a novel *does* reveal the control of naturalistic assumptions over these essential features, to that extent will it reveal a distinctive aesthetic form and to that extent will it be a naturalistic novel, rather than a novel containing naturalistic elements. This is not to say, of course, that the naturalistic novel must *absolutely* embody the philosophy of materialistic determinism, for, as Charles Walcutt has put it, "A work that was perfectly controlled by the theory of materialistic determinism would not be a novel but a report." All that is required, it seems to me, is that the novel reflect a relatively strong *illusion* of determinism.

The naturalistic picture of life as "a struggle for existence" in which the "unfit" are overwhelmed while the "fittest" manage to adapt to environmental conditions offers the novelist two basic formal patterns: the career of a passive protagonist and the career of a superman protagonist. In both patterns the career of the protagonist is determined by uncontrollable inner or outer forces, or, more usually, by their combination. But the passive protagonist pattern places a far greater emphasis on environmental force and on the incapacity and weakness of human nature. The protagonist may be presented as intellectually or physically deficient; as dominated by untoward instincts, moods, impulses, or compulsions; as given to fantasies and illusions; or as lacking in some fundamental adaptive characteristics. Whatever the cause of his inefficiency, he is portrayed as utterly incapable of coping with the external circumstances confronting him. Specific examples of this pattern are Stephen Crane's *Maggie* and *The Red Badge of Courage;* Frank Norris' *McTeague;* and Theodore Dreiser's *Sister Carrie, Jennie Gerhardt* and *An American Tragedy.* Such novels reflect, in Malcolm Cowley's words, a "magnification of forces and minification of persons." In the superman pattern, on the other hand, the protagonist, because of his strong adaptive characteristics (his heredity), is able to put himself into alignment with external forces and thus becomes something of a force himself. Hence the appearance of "will" in such a character. As long as this state of affairs holds, he will be able to cope with whatever circumstances may beset him. But if the forces confronting him ever exceed his adaptive capabilities, if the alignment is thrown out of balance, he will be quickly overwhelmed. Actually then, the superman protagonist, operating as he must within a framework of natural law, is, from the point of view of naturalistic theory, every bit as passive as the "weak" protagonist; but in the novel the emphasis is on his strength rather than his passivity. This pattern underlies such works as Jack London's *Call of the Wild, The Sea Wolf, Burning Daylight,* and *The Mutiny of the Elsinore;* Norris' *The Octopus* and *The Pit;* and Dreiser's *The Financier* and *The Titan.* In both patterns, of course, the author must adopt an amoral attitude toward his materials, since his ruling thesis holds that men are not free to shape their lives and hence cannot be viewed as subject to moral judgments.

The preceding account of the two main naturalistic patterns presents us, of course, with ideal models, in which there is a strict consistency between philosophy and form. None of the examples given reflect such a rigid consistency, but they all more or less approximate these models. They certainly come close enough to enable one to say that they reveal a distinctive form. In all of them the structure of events is arranged in accordance with a narrow preconceived idea. In all of them, too, characterization is clearly shaped in accordance with scientific assumptions about the nature of man. The result is that the characters of these novels strike us as "distortions" of man as we generally know him, the degree of distortion ranging all the way from a comparatively slight amount in such a figure as Dreiser's Clyde Griffiths, to the radical distortion of human nature present in Crane's Maggie, in Norris' McTeague and Trina, and in all of the supermen characters. Finally, these novels all reveal a strong content of what we may call naturalistic images—images which stress such typical naturalistic themes as the idea of determinism, the animal and mechanical nature of man, the struggle for survival, or the indifference or (from the human point of view) malignancy of nature. These images function to reinforce the meaning that emerges on the levels of structure and characterization.

Like the realist, then, the naturalist draws his fictional materials from the world of observed actuality; but, unlike the realist, he does not regard a well-proportioned representation of what occurs in that world as significant enough in itself. He feels it necessary to give authority and significance to observed events through interpreting them in terms of scientific assumptions about the nature of reality. In his novel he therefore imposes upon these materials a narrow and rigid scientific hypothesis, with the result being a distortion of observed data into certain prescribed patterns and forms. Thus we may say that, though the realist and the naturalist draw their material from a common source—the world of actuality—, they use this material in radically different ways, with radically different consequences for the form that embodies their art.

Editor's Note: "Naturalism as a Literary Form" by Robert M. Figg is reprinted by permission of the *Georgia Review* from *Georgia Review*, XVIII (1964), pp. 308–316.

Robert M. Figg is an Assistant Professor of English at the University of South Florida. He is presently at work on a study of literary naturalism.

SAMUEL LANGHORNE CLEMENS

1835-1910

Samuel L. Clemens lived most of his childhood in Hannibal, Missouri, on the Mississippi River. He learned the printing trade, and when his father died in 1847, began his affiliation with the newspaper business as a printer, first in Hannibal and then in St. Louis, New York City, Philadelphia, Washington, Keokuk, and Cincinnati. His writing career began at this early stage, and he contributed many humorous sketches to periodicals. From 1857–1861 he held the romantic occupation of Mississippi River pilot, until the Civil War ended that profession. He returned to newspaper work in 1862, this time with the pen-name "Mark Twain." He received national attention for "Jim Smiley and His Jumping Frog," New York *Saturday Press,* 1865. He began a lecturing career that was to be enduringly profitable. His first book was published in 1867, *The Celebrated Jumping Frog of Calaveras County and Other Sketches,* and was followed two years later by *The Innocents Abroad,* based upon his trip to Europe and the Holy Land.

In 1870 he married Olivia Langdon and settled into his writing career, publishing over the next nineteen years *Roughing It* (1872), *The Gilded Age* (1873), *The Adventures of Tom Sawyer* (1876), *A Tramp Abroad* (1880), *The Prince and the Pauper* (1882), *Life on the*

Mississippi (1883), *The Adventures of Huckleberry Finn* (1884), and *A Connecticut Yankee in King Arthur's Court* (1889). During these years, however, Clemens sustained serious financial losses as a result of business speculations, including a publishing company and a typesetting machine. His later private life was also strewn with unhappiness. His favorite daughter, Suzy, died at age twenty-four. His daughter Jean suffered from increasingly severe epilepsy. Olivia died in 1904, and Twain, driven into a bitterness that is reflected in his later works, died in 1910.

His important works after *Connecticut Yankee* include *The Tragedy of Pudd'nhead Wilson* (1894), *The Man That Corrupted Hadleyburg and Other Stories and Essays* (1900), and *The Mysterious Stranger* (1916).

MR. ELIOT,
MR. TRILLING, AND
HUCKLEBERRY FINN

LEO MARX

In the losing battle that the plot fights with the characters, it often takes a cowardly revenge. Nearly all novels are feeble at the end. This is because the plot requires to be wound up. Why is this necessary? Why is there not a convention which allows a novelist to stop as soon as he feels muddled or bored? Alas, he has to round things off, and usually the characters go dead while he is at work, and our final impression of them is through deadness.

—E. M. FORSTER

The Adventures of Huckleberry Finn has not always occupied its present high place in the canon of American literature. When it was first published in 1885, the book disturbed and offended many reviewers, particularly spokesmen for the genteel tradition.[1] In fact, a fairly accurate inventory of the narrow standards of such critics might be made simply by listing epithets they applied to Clemens' novel. They called it vulgar, rough, inelegant, irreverent, coarse, semi-obscene, trashy and vicious.[2] So much for them. Today (we

[1] I use the term "genteel tradition" as George Santayana characterized it in his famous address "The Genteel Tradition in American Philosophy," first delivered in 1911 and published the following year in his *Winds of Doctrine.* Santayana described the genteel tradition as an "old mentality" inherited from Europe. It consists of the various dilutions of Christian theology and morality, as in transcendentalism—a fastidious and stale philosophy of life no longer relevant to the thought and activities of the United States. "America," he said, "is a young country with an old mentality." (Later references to Santayana also refer to this essay.)

[2] For an account of the first reviews, see A. L. Vogelback, "The Publication and Reception of *Huckleberry Finn* in America," *American Literature,* XI (November, 1939), 260–272.

like to think) we know the true worth of the book. Everyone now agrees that *Huckleberry Finn* is a masterpiece: it is probably the one book in our literature about which highbrows and lowbrows can agree. Our most serious critics praise it. Nevertheless, a close look at what two of the best among them have recently written will likewise reveal, I believe, serious weaknesses in current criticism. Today the problem of evaluating the book is as much obscured by unqualified praise as it once was by parochial hostility.

I have in mind essays by Lionel Trilling and T. S. Eliot.[3] Both praise the book, but in praising it both feel obligated to say something in justification of what so many readers have felt to be its great flaw: the disappointing "ending," the episode which begins when Huck arrives at the Phelps place and Tom Sawyer reappears. There are good reasons why Mr. Trilling and Mr. Eliot should feel the need to face this issue. From the point of view of scope alone, more is involved than the mere "ending"; the episode comprises almost one-fifth of the text. The problem, in any case, is unavoidable. I have discussed *Huckleberry Finn* in courses with hundreds of college students, and I have found only a handful who did not confess their dissatisfaction with the extravagant mock rescue of Nigger Jim and the denouement itself. The same question always comes up: "What went wrong with Twain's novel?" Even Bernard DeVoto, whose wholehearted commitment to Clemens' genius is well known, has said of the ending that "in the whole reach of the English novel there is no more abrupt or more chilling descent."[4] Mr. Trilling and Mr. Eliot do not agree. They both attempt, and on similar grounds, to explain and defend the conclusion.

Of the two, Mr. Trilling makes the more moderate claim for Clemens' novel. He does admit that there is a "falling off" at the end; nevertheless he supports the episode as having "a certain formal aptness." Mr. Eliot's approval is without serious qualification. He allows no objections, asserts that "it is right that the mood of the end of the book should bring us back to the beginning." I mean later to discuss their views in some detail, but here it is only necessary to note that both critics see the problem as one of form.

[3] Mr. Eliot's essay is the introduction to the edition of *Huckleberry Finn* published by Chanticleer Press, New York, 1950. Mr. Trilling's is the introduction to an edition of the novel published by Rinehart, New York, 1948, and later reprinted in his *The Liberal Imagination*, Viking, New York, 1950.

[4] *Mark Twain At Work* (Cambridge, 1942), p. 92.

And so it is. Like many questions of form in literature, however, this one is not finally separable from a question of "content" of value, or, if you will, of moral insight. To bring *Huckleberry Finn* to a satisfactory close, Clemens had to do more than find a neat device for ending a story. His problem, though it may never have occurred to him, was to invent an action capable of placing in focus the meaning of the journey down the Mississippi.

I believe that the ending of *Huckleberry Finn* makes so many readers uneasy because they rightly sense that it jeopardizes the significance of the entire novel. To take seriously what happens at the Phelps farm is to take lightly the entire downstream journey. What is the meaning of the journey? With this question all discussion of *Huckleberry Finn* must begin. It is true that the voyage down the river has many aspects of a boy's idyl. We owe much of its hold upon our imagination to the enchanting image of the raft's unhurried drift with the current. The leisure, the absence of constraint, the beauty of the river—all these things delight us. "It's lovely to live on a raft." And the multitudinous life of the great valley we see through Huck's eyes has a fascination of its own. Then, of course, there is humor—laughter so spontaneous, so free of the bitterness present almost everywhere in American humor that readers often forget how grim a spectacle of human existence Huck contemplates. Humor in this novel flows from a bright joy of life as remote from our world as living on a raft.

Yet along with the idyllic and the epical and the funny in *Huckleberry Finn,* there is a coil of meaning which does for the disparate elements of the novel what a spring does for a watch. The meaning is not in the least obscure. It is made explicit again and again. The very words with which Clemens launches Huck and Jim upon their voyage indicate that theirs is not a boy's lark but a quest for freedom. From the electrifying moment when Huck comes back to Jackson's Island and rouses Jim with the news that a search party is on the way, we are meant to believe that Huck is enlisted in the cause of freedom. "Git up and hump yourself, Jim!" he cries. "There ain't a minute to lose. They're after us!" What particularly counts here is the *us.* No one is after Huck; no one but Jim knows he is alive. In that small word Clemens compresses the exhilarating power of Huck's instinctive humanity. His unpremeditated identification with Jim's flight from slavery is an unforgettable moment in American experience, and it may be said at once that any culmination of the journey which detracts from the urgency and dignity with which it begins will necessarily be unsatisfactory. Huck realizes this himself, and says so when, much later, he comes back to the raft after discovering that the Duke and the King have sold Jim:

> After all this long journey . . . here it was all come to nothing, everything all busted up and ruined, because they could have the heart to serve Jim such a trick as that, and make him a slave again all his life, and amongst strangers, too, for forty dirty dollars.

Huck knows that the journey will have been a failure unless it takes Jim to freedom. It is true that we do discover, in the end, that Jim is free, but we also find out that the journey was not the means by which he finally reached freedom.

The most obvious thing wrong with the ending, then, is the flimsy contrivance by which Clemens frees Jim. In the end we not only discover that Jim has been a free man for two months, but that his freedom has been granted by old Miss Watson. If this were only a mechanical device for terminating the action, it might not call for much comment. But it is more than that: it is a significant clue to the import of the last ten chapters. Remember who Miss Watson is. She is the Widow's sister whom Huck introduces in the first pages of the novel. It is she who keeps "pecking" at Huck, who tries to teach him to spell and to pray and to keep his feet off the furniture. She is an ardent proselytizer for piety and good manners, and her greed provides the occasion for the journey in the first place. She is Jim's owner, and he decides to flee only when he realizes that she is about to break her word (she cannot resist a slave trader's offer of eight hundred dollars) and sell him down the river away from his family.

Miss Watson, in short, is the Enemy. If we except a predilection for physical violence, she exhibits all the outstanding traits of the valley society. She pronounces the polite lies of civilization that suffocate Huck's spirit. The freedom which Jim seeks, and which Huck and Jim temporarily enjoy aboard the raft, is accordingly freedom *from* everything for which Miss Watson stands. Indeed, the very intensity of the novel derives from the discordance between the aspirations of the fugitives and the respectable code for which she is a spokesman. Therefore, her regeneration, of which the death-bed freeing of Jim is the unconvincing sign, hints a resolution of the novel's essential conflict. Perhaps because this device most transparently reveals that shift in point of view which he could not avoid, and which is less easily discerned elsewhere in the concluding chapters, Clemens plays it down. He makes little attempt to account for Miss Watson's change of heart, a change particularly surprising in view of Jim's brazen escape. Had Clemens given this episode dramatic emphasis appropriate to its function, Miss Watson's bestowal of freedom upon Jim would have proclaimed what the rest of the ending actually accomplishes—a vindication of persons and attitudes Huck and Jim had symbolically repudiated when they set forth downstream.

It may be said, and with some justice, that a reading of the ending as a virtual reversal of meanings implicit in the rest of the novel misses the point—that I have taken the final episode too seriously. I agree that Clemens certainly did not intend us to read it so solemnly. The ending, one might content, is simply a burlesque upon Tom's taste for literary romance. Surely the tone of the episode is familiar to readers of Mark Twain. The preposterous monkey business attendant upon Jim's "rescue," the careless improvisation, the nonchalant disregard for common-sense plausibility—all these things should not surprise readers of Twain or any low comedy in the tradition of "Western humor." However, the trouble is, first, that the ending hardly comes off as burlesque: it is *too* fanciful, *too* extravagant; and it is tedious. For example, to provide a "gaudy" atmosphere for the escape, Huck and Tom catch a couple of dozen snakes. Then the snakes escape.

> No, there warn't no real scarcity of snakes about the house for
> a considerable spell. You'd see them dripping from the rafters
> and places every now and then; and they generly landed in
> your plate, or down the back of your neck. . . .

Even if this were *good* burlesque, which it is not, what is it doing here? It is out of keeping; the slapstick tone jars with the underlying seriousness of the voyage.

Huckleberry Finn is a masterpiece because it brings Western humor to perfection and yet transcends the narrow limits of its conventions. But the ending does not. During the final extravaganza we are forced to put aside many of the mature emotions evoked earlier by the vivid rendering of Jim's fear of capture, the tenderness of Huck's and Jim's regard for each other, and Huck's excruciating moments of wavering between honesty and respectability. None of these emotions are called forth by the anticlimactic final sequence. I do not mean to suggest that the inclusion of low comedy per se is a flaw in *Huckleberry Finn*. One does not object to the shenanigans of the rogues; there is ample precedent for the place of extravagant humor even in works of high seriousness. But here the case differs from most which come to mind: the major characters themselves are forced to play low comedy roles. Moreover, the most serious motive in the novel, Jim's yearning for freedom, is made the object of nonsense. The conclusion, in short, is farce, but the rest of the novel is not.

That Clemens reverts in the end to the conventional manner of Western low comedy is most evident in what happens to the principals. Huck and Jim become comic characters; that is a much more serious ground for dissatisfaction than the unexplained regeneration of Miss Watson. Remember that Huck has grown in stature throughout the journey. By the time he arrives at the Phelps place, he is not the boy who had been playing robbers with Tom's gang in St. Petersburg the summer before. All he has seen and felt since he parted from Tom has deepened his knowledge of human nature and of himself. Clemens makes a point of Huck's development in two scenes which occur just before he meets Tom again. The first describes Huck's final capitulation to his own sense of right and wrong: "All right, then, I'll *go* to Hell." This is the climactic moment in the ripening of his self-knowledge. Shortly afterward, when he comes upon a mob riding the Duke and the King out of town on a rail, we are given his most memorable insight into the nature of man. Although these rogues had subjected Huck to every indignity, what he sees provokes this celebrated comment:

> Well, it made me sick to see it; and I was sorry for them poor pitiful rascals, it seemed like I couldn't ever feel any hardness against them any more in the world. It was a dreadful thing to see. Human beings can be awful cruel to one another.

The sign of Huck's maturity here is neither the compassion nor the skepticism, for both had been marks of his personality from the first. Rather, the special quality of these reflections is the extraordinary combination of the two, a mature blending of his instinctive suspicion of human motives with his capacity for pity.

But at this point Tom reappears. Soon Huck has fallen almost completely under his sway once more, and we are asked to believe that the boy who felt pity for the rogues is now capable of making Jim's capture the occasion for a game. He becomes Tom's helpless accomplice, submissive and gullible. No wonder that Clemens has Huck remark, when Huck first realizes Aunt Sally has mistaken him for Tom, that "it was like being born again." Exactly. In the end, Huck regresses to the subordinate role in which he had first appeared in *The Adventures of Tom Sawyer*. Most of those traits which made him so appealing a hero now disappear. He had never, for example, found pain or misfortune amusing. At the circus, when a clown disguised as a drunk took a precarious ride on a prancing horse, the crowd loved the excitement and danger; "it warn't funny to me, though," said Huck. But now, in the end, he submits in awe to Tom's notion of what is amusing. To satisfy Tom's hunger for adventure he makes himself a party to sport which aggravates Jim's misery.

It should be added at once that Jim doesn't mind too much. The fact is that he has undergone a similar transformation. On the raft he was an individual, man enough to denounce Huck when Huck made him the victim of a practical joke. In the closing episide, however, we lose sight of Jim in the maze of farcical invention. He ceases to be a man. He allows Huck and "Mars Tom" to fill his hut with rats and snakes, "and every time a rat bit Jim he would get up and write a line in his journal whilst the ink was fresh." This creature who bleeds ink and feels no pain is something less than human. He has been made over in the image of a flat stereotype: the submissive stage-Negro. These antics divest Jim, as well as Huck, of much of his dignity and individuality.[5]

What I have been saying is that the flimsy devices of plot, the discordant farcical tone, and the disintegration of the major characters all betray the failure of the ending. These are not aspects merely of form in a technical sense, but of meaning. For that matter, I would maintain that this book has little or no formal unity independent of the joint purpose of Huck and Jim. What compo-

[5] For these observations on the transformation of Jim in the closing episodes, I am indebted to the excellent unpublished essay by Mr. Chadwick Hansen on the subject of Clemens and Western humor.

nents of the novel, we may ask, provide the continuity which links one adventure with another? The most important is the unifying consciousness of Huck, the narrator, and the fact that we follow the same principals through the entire string of adventures. Events, moreover, occur in a temporal sequence. Then there is the river; after each adventure Huck and Jim return to the raft and the river. Both Mr. Trilling and Mr. Eliot speak eloquently of the river as a source of unity, and they refer to the river as a god. Mr. Trilling says that Huck is "the servant of the river-god." Mr. Eliot puts it this way: "The River gives the book its form. But for the River, the book might be only a sequence of adventures with a happy ending." This seems to me an extravagant view of the function of the neutral agency of the river. Clemens had a knowledgeable respect for the Mississippi, and, without sanctifying it, was able to provide excellent reasons for Huck's and Jim's intense relation with it. It is a source of food and beauty and terror and serenity of mind. But above all, it provides motion; it is the means by which Huck and Jim move away from a menacing civilization. They return to the river to continue their journey. The river cannot, does not, supply purpose. That purpose is a facet of their consciousness, and without the motive of escape from society, *Huckleberry Finn* would indeed "be only a sequence of adventures." Mr. Eliot's remark indicates how lightly he takes the quest for freedom. His somewhat fanciful exaggeration of the river's role is of a piece with his neglect of the theme at the novel's center.

That theme is heightened by the juxtaposition of sharp images of contrasting social orders: the microcosmic community Huck and Jim establish aboard the raft and the actual society which exists along the Mississippi's banks. The two are separated by the river, the road to freedom upon which Huck and Jim must travel. Huck tells us what the river means to them when, after the Wilks episode, he and Jim once again shove their raft into the current: "It *did* seem so good to be free again and all by ourselves on the big river, and nobody to bother us." The river is indifferent. But its sphere is relatively uncontaminated by the civilization they flee, and so the river allows Huck and Jim some measure of freedom at once, the moment they set foot on Jackson's Island or the raft. Only on the island and the raft do they have a chance to practice that idea of brotherhood to which they are devoted. "Other places do seem so cramped and smothery," Huck explains, "but a raft don't. You feel mighty free and easy and comfortable on a raft." The main thing is freedom.

On the raft the escaped slave and the white boy try to practice their code: "What you want, above all things, on a raft, is for everybody to be satisfied, and feel right and kind towards the others." This human credo constitutes the paramount affirmation of *The Adventures of Huckleberry Finn,* and it obliquely aims a devastating criticism at the existing social order. It is a creed which Huck and Jim bring to the river. It neither emanates from nature nor is it addressed to nature. Therefore I do not see that it means much to talk about the river as a god in this novel. The river's connection with this high aspiration for man is that it provides a means of escape, a place where the code can be tested. The truly profound meanings of the novel are generated by the impingement of the actual world of slavery, feuds, lynching, murder, and a spurious Christian morality upon the ideal of the raft. The result is a tension which somehow demands release in the novel's ending.

But Clemens was unable to effect this release and at the same time control the central theme. The unhappy truth about the ending of *Huckleberry Finn* is that the author, having revealed the tawdry nature of the culture of the great valley, yielded to its essential complacency. The general tenor of the closing scenes, to which the token regeneration of Miss Watson is merely one superficial clue, amounts to just that. In fact, this entire reading of *Huckleberry Finn* merely confirms the brilliant insight of George Santayana, who many years ago spoke of American humorists, of whom he considered Mark Twain an outstanding representative, as having only "half escaped" the genteel tradition. Santayana meant that men like Clemens were able to "point to what contradicts it in the facts; but not in order to abandon the genteel tradition, for they have nothing solid to put in its place." This seems to me the real key to the failure of *Huckleberry Finn.* Clemens had presented the contrast between the two social orders but could not, or would not, accept the tragic fact that the one he had rejected was an image of solid reality and the other an ecstatic dream. Instead he gives us the cozy reunion with Aunt Polly in a scene fairly bursting with approbation of the entire family, the Phelpses included.

Like Miss Watson, the Phelpses are almost perfect specimens of the dominant culture. They are kind to their friends and relatives; they have no taste for violence; they are people capable of devoting themselves to their spectacular dinners while they keep Jim locked in the little hut down by the ash hopper, with its lone window boarded up. (Of course Aunt Sally visits Jim to see if he is "comfortable," and Uncle Silas comes in "to pray with him.") These people, with their comfortable Sunday-dinner conviviality and the runaway slave padlocked nearby, are reminiscent of those solid German citizens we have heard about in our time who tried to maintain a similarly *gemütlich* way of life within virtual earshot of Buchenwald. I do not mean to imply that Clemens was unaware of the shabby morality of such people. After the abortive escape of Jim, when Tom asks about him, Aunt Sally replies: "Him? . . . the runaway nigger? . . . They've got him back, safe and sound, and he's in the cabin again, on bread and water, and loaded down with chains, till he's claimed or sold!" Clemens understood people like the Phelpses, but nevertheless he was forced to rely upon them to provide his happy ending. The satisfactory outcome of Jim's quest for freedom must be attributed to the benevolence of the very people whose inhumanity first made it necessary.

But to return to the contention of Mr. Trilling and Mr. Eliot that the ending is more or less satisfactory after all. As I have said, Mr. Trilling approves of the "formal aptness" of the conclusion. He says that "some device is needed to permit Huck to return to his anonymity, to give up the role of hero," and that therefore "nothing could serve better than the mind of Tom Sawyer with its literary furnishings, its conscious romantic desire for experience and the hero's part, and its ingenious schematization of life. . . ." Though more detailed, this is essentially akin to Mr. Eliot's blunt assertion that "it is right that the mood at the end of the book should bring us back to that of the beginning." I submit that it is wrong for the end of the book to bring us back to that mood. The mood of the beginning of *Huckleberry Finn* is the mood of Huck's attempt to accommodate himself to the ways of St. Petersburg. It is the mood of the end of *The Adventures of Tom Sawyer,* when the boys had been acclaimed heroes, and when Huck was accepted as a candidate for respectability. That is the state in which we find him at the beginning of *Huckleberry Finn.* But Huck cannot stand the new way of life, and his mood gradually shifts to the mood of rebellion which dominates the novel until he meets Tom again. At first, in the second chapter, we see him still eager to be accepted by the nice boys of the town. Tom leads the gang in re-enacting adventures he has culled from books, but gradually Huck's pragmatic turn of mind gets him in trouble. He has little tolerance for Tom's brand of make-believe. He irritates Tom. Tom calls him a "numbskull," and finally Huck throws up the whole business:

> So then I judged that all that stuff was only just one of Tom Sawyer's lies. I reckoned he believed in the A-rabs and the elephants, but as for me I think different. It had all the marks of a Sunday-school.

With this statement, which ends the third chapter, Huck parts company with Tom. The fact is that Huck has rejected Tom's romanticizing of experience; moreover, he has rejected it as part of the larger pattern of society's make-believe, typified by Sunday school. But if he cannot accept Tom's harmless fantasies about the A-rabs, how are we to believe that a year later Huck is capable of awe-struck submission to the far more extravagant fantasies with which Tom invests the mock rescue of Jim?

After Huck's escape from his "pap," the drift of the action, like that of the Mississippi's current, is *away* from St. Petersburg. Huck leaves Tom and the A-rabs behind, along with the Widow, Miss Watson, and all the pseudo-religious ritual in which nice boys must partake. The return, in the end, to the mood of the beginning therefore means defeat—Huck's defeat; to return to that mood *joyously* is to portray defeat in the guise of victory.

Mr. Eliot and Mr. Trilling deny this. The overriding consideration for them is form—form which seems largely to mean symmetry of structure. It is fitting, Mr. Eliot maintains, that the book should come full circle and bring Huck once more under Tom's sway. Why? Because it begins that way. But it seems to me that such structural unity is *imposed* upon the novel, and therefore is meretricious. It is a jerry-built structure, achieved only by sacrifice of characters and theme. Here the controlling principle of form apparently is unity, but unfortunately a unity much too superficially conceived. Structure, after all, is only one element—indeed, one of the more mechanical elements—of unity. A unified work must surely manifest coherence of meaning and clear development of theme, yet the ending of *Huckleberry Finn* blurs both. The eagerness of Mr. Eliot and Mr. Trilling to justify the ending is symptomatic of that absolutist impulse of our critics to find reasons, once a work has been admitted to the highest canon of literary reputability, for admiring every bit of it.

What is perhaps most striking about these judgments of Mr. Eliot's and Mr. Trilling's is that they are so patently out of harmony with the basic standards of both critics. For one thing, both men hold far more complex ideas of the nature of literary unity than their comments upon *Huckleberry Finn* would suggest. For another, both critics are essentially moralists, yet here we find them turning away from a moral issue in order to praise a dubious structural unity. Their efforts to explain away the flaw in Clemens' novel suffer from a certain narrowness surprising to anyone who knows their work. These facts suggest that we may be in the presence of a tendency in contemporary criticism which the critics themselves do not fully recognize.

Is there an explanation? How does it happen that two of our most respected critics should seem to treat so lightly the glaring lapse of moral imagination in *Huckleberry Finn?* Perhaps—and I stress the conjectural nature of what I am saying—perhaps the kind of moral issue raised by *Huckleberry Finn* is not the kind of moral issue to which today's criticism readily addresses itself. Today our critics, no less than our novelists and poets, are most sensitively attuned to moral problems which arise in the sphere of individual behavior. They are deeply aware of sin, of individual infractions of our culture's Christian ethic. But my impression is that they are, possibly because of the strength of the reaction against the mechanical sociological criticism of the thirties, less sensitive to questions of what might be called social or political morality.

By social or political morality I refer to the values implicit in a social system, values which may be quite distinct from the personal morality of any given individual within the society. Now *The Adventures of Huckleberry Finn,* like all novels, deals with the behavior of individuals. But one mark of Clemens' greatness is his deft presentation of the disparity between what people do when they behave as individuals and what they do when forced into roles imposed upon them by society. Take, for example, Aunt Sally and Uncle Silas Phelps, who consider themselves Christians, who are by impulse generous and humane, but who happen also to be staunch upholders of certain degrading and inhuman social institutions. When they are confronted with an escaped slave, the imperatives of social morality outweigh all pious professions.

The conflict between what people think they stand for and what social pressure forces them to do is central to the novel. It is present to the mind of Huck and, indeed, accounts for his most serious inner conflicts. He knows how he feels about Jim, but he also knows what he is expected to do about Jim. This division within his mind corresponds to the division of the novel's moral terrain into the areas represented by the raft on the one hand and society on the other. His victory over his "yaller dog" conscience therefore assumes heroic size: it is a victory over the prevailing morality. But the last fifth of the novel has the effect of diminishing the importance and uniqueness of Huck's victory. We are asked to assume that somehow freedom can be achieved in spite of the crippling power of what I have called the social morality. Consequently the less importance we attach to that force as it operates in the novel, the more acceptable the ending becomes.

Moreover, the idea of freedom, which Mr. Eliot and Mr. Trilling seem to slight, takes on its full significance only when we acknowledge the power which society exerts over the minds of men in the world of *Huckleberry Finn*. For freedom in this book specifically means freedom from society and its imperatives. This is not the traditional Christian conception of freedom. Huck and Jim seek freedom not from a burden of individual guilt and sin, but from social constraint. That is to say, evil in *Huckleberry Finn* is the product of civilization, and if this is indicative of Clemens' rather too simple view of human nature, nevertheless the fact is that Huck, when he can divest himself of the taint of social conditioning (as in the incantatory account of sunrise on the river), is entirely free of anxiety and guilt. The only guilt he actually knows arises from infractions of a social code. (The guilt he feels after playing the prank on Jim stems from his betrayal of the law of the raft.) Huck's and Jim's creed is secular. Its object is harmony among men, and so Huck is not much concerned with his own salvation. He repeatedly renounces prayer in favor of pragmatic solutions to his problems. In other words, the central insights of the novel belong to the tradition of the Enlightenment. The meaning of the quest itself is hardly reconcilable with that conception of human nature embodied in the myth of original sin. In view of the current fashion of reaffirming man's innate depravity, it is perhaps not surprising to find the virtues of *Huckleberry Finn* attributed not to its meaning but to its form.

But "if this was not the right ending for the book," Mr. Eliot asks, "what ending would have been right?" Although this question places the critic in an awkward position (he is not always equipped to rewrite what he criticizes), there are some things which may justifiably be said about the "right" ending of *Huckleberry Finn*. It may be legitimate, even if presumptuous, to indicate certain conditions which a hypothetical ending would have to satisfy if it were to be congruent with the rest of the novel. If the conclusion is not to be something merely tacked on to close the action, then its broad outline must be immanent in the body of the work.

It is surely reasonable to ask that the conclusion provide a plausible outcome to the quest. Yet freedom, in the ecstatic sense that Huck and Jim knew it aboard the raft, was hardly to be had in the Mississippi Valley in the 1840's, or, for that matter, in any other known human society. A satisfactory ending would inevitably cause the reader some frustration. That Clemens felt such disappointment to be inevitable is borne out by an examination of the novel's clear, if unconscious, symbolic pattern. Consider, for instance, the inferences to be drawn from the book's geography. The river, to whose current Huck and Jim entrust themselves, actually carries them to the heart of slave territory. Once the raft passes Cairo, the quest is virtually doomed. Until the steamboat smashes the raft, we are kept in a state of anxiety about Jim's escape. (It may be significant that at this point Clemens found himself unable to continue work on the manuscript, and put it aside for several years.) Beyond Cairo, Clemens allows the intensity of that anxiety to diminish, and it is probably no accident that the fainter it becomes, the more he falls back upon the devices of low comedy. Huck and Jim make no serious effort to turn north, and there are times (during the Wilks episode) when Clemens allows Huck to forget all about Jim. It is as if the author, anticipating the dilemma he had finally to face, instinctively dissipated the power of his major theme.

Consider, too, the circumscribed nature of the raft as a means of moving toward freedom. The raft lacks power and maneuverability. It can only move easily with the current—southward into slave country. Nor can it evade the mechanized power of the steamboat. These impotencies of the raft correspond to the innocent helplessness of its occupants. Unresisted, the rogues invade and take over the raft. Though it is the symbolic locus of the novel's central affirmations, the raft provides an uncertain and indeed precarious mode of traveling toward freedom. This seems another confirmation of Santayana's perception. To say that Clemens only half escaped the genteel tradition is not to say that he failed to note any of the creed's inadequacies, but rather that he had "nothing solid" to put in its place. The raft patently was not capable of carrying the burden of hope Clemens placed upon it.[6] (Whether this is to be attributed to the nature of his vision or to the actual state of American society in the nineteenth century is another interesting question.) In any case, the geography of the novel, the raft's powerlessness, the goodness and vulnerability of Huck and Jim, all prefigure a conclusion quite different in tone from that which Clemens gave us. These facts constitute what Hart Crane might have called the novel's "logic of metaphor," and this logic—probably inadvertent—actually takes us to the underlying meaning of *The Adventures of Huckleberry Finn*. Through the symbols we reach a truth which the ending obscures: the quest cannot succeed.

Fortunately, Clemens broke through to this truth in the novel's last sentences:

> But I reckon I got to light out for the territory ahead of the rest, because Aunt Sally she's going to adopt me and civilize me, and I can't stand it. I been there before.

Mr. Eliot properly praises this as "the only possible concluding sentence." But one sentence can hardly be advanced, as Mr. Eliot advances this one, to support the rightness of ten chapters. Moreover, if this sentence is right, then the rest of the conclusion is wrong, for its meaning clashes with that of the final burlesque. Huck's decision to go west ahead of the inescapable advance of civilization is a confession of defeat. It means that the raft is to be abandoned. On the other hand, the jubilation of the family reunion and the proclaiming of Jim's freedom create a quite different mood. The tone, except for these last words, is one of unclouded

---

[6] Gladys Bellamy (*Mark Twain As a Literary Artist*, Norman, Oklahoma, 1950, p. 221) has noted the insubstantial, dream-like quality of the image of the raft. Clemens thus discusses travel by raft in *A Tramp Abroad*: "The motion of the raft is . . . gentle, and gliding, and smooth, and noiseless; it calms down all feverish activities, it soothes to sleep all nervous . . . impatience; under its restful influence all the troubles and vexations and sorrows that harass the mind vanish away, and existence becomes a dream . . . a deep and tranquil ecstasy."

success. I believe this is the source of the almost universal dissatisfaction with the conclusion. One can hardly forget that a bloody civil war did not resolve the issue.

Should Clemens have made Huck a tragic hero? Both Mr. Eliot and Mr. Trilling argue that that would have been a mistake, and they are very probably correct. But between the ending as we have it and tragedy in the fullest sense, there was vast room for invention. Clemens might have contrived an action which left Jim's fate as much in doubt as Huck's. Such an ending would have allowed us to assume that the principals were defeated but alive, and the quest unsuccessful but not abandoned. This, after all, would have been consonant with the symbols, the characters, and the theme as Clemens had created them—and with history.

Clemens did not acknowledge the truth his novel contained. He had taken hold of a situation in which a partial defeat was inevitable, but he was unable to—or unaware of the need to—give imaginative substance to that fact. If an illusion of success was indispensable, where was it to come from? Obviously Huck and Jim could not succeed by their own efforts. At this point Clemens, having only half escaped the genteel tradition, one of whose pre-eminent characteristics was an optimism undaunted by disheartening truth, returned to it. *Why* he did so is another story, having to do with his parents and his boyhood, with his own personality and his wife's, and especially with the character of his audience. But whatever the explanation, the faint-hearted ending of *The Adventures of Huckleberry Finn* remains an important datum in the record of American thought and imagination. It has been noted before, both by critics and non-professional readers. It should not be forgotten now.

To minimize the seriousness of what must be accounted a major flaw in so great a work is, in a sense, to repeat Clemens' failure of nerve. This is a disservice to criticism. Today we particularly need a criticism alert to lapses of moral vision. A measured appraisal of the failures and successes of our writers, past and present, can show us a great deal about literature and about ourselves. That is the critic's function. But he cannot perform that function if he substitutes considerations of technique for considerations of truth. Not only will such methods lead to errors of literary judgment, but beyond that, they may well encourage comparable evasions in other areas. It seems not unlikely, for instance, that the current preoccupation with matters of form is bound up with a tendency, by no means confined to literary quarters, to shy away from painful answers to complex questions of political morality. The conclusion to *The Adventures of Huckleberry Finn* shielded both Clemens and his audience from such an answer. But we ought not to be as tender-minded. For Huck Finn's besetting problem, the disparity between his best impulses and the behavior the community attempted to impose upon him, is as surely ours as it was Twain's.

Editor's Note: "Mr. Eliot, Mr. Trilling and *Huckleberry Finn*," by Leo Marx is reprinted from *The American Scholar*, Volume XXII (1953), pp. 423–440. Copyright © 1953 by the United Chapters of Phi Beta Kappa. By permission of the publishers.

Currently a Professor of English and American Studies at Amherst College, Professor Marx's publications include *The Machine in the Garden* and (editor of) *Adventures of Huckleberry Finn* (annotated). He was a Fulbright Lecturer in Rennes (France), 1955–56, and in Nottingham, 1956–57, and was a Guggenheim Fellow in 1966.

HUCK'S FINAL TRIUMPH

RAY B. BROWNE

Nearly all readers affirm the greatness of *Huckleberry Finn*. Most critics, with varying emphases, concur on the reasons for this greatness. The book is a bitter criticism of ante-bellum Southern life and its consequent social and religious attitudes; it pictures the growth of a boy to adulthood; and, most deeply, it depicts a quest for freedom. Leo Marx epitomizes critics' feelings in saying: "The truly profound meanings of the novel are generated by the impingement of the actual world of slavery, feuds, lynching, murder, and a spurious Christian morality upon the ideal of the raft."[1]

Agreement on the achievement of the novel splits, however, on the ending. Many critics hold strong reservations about this part. DeVoto, generally a staunch supporter of Twain, called it a "chilling descent."[2] Henry Nash Smith feels the Huck of this section is "inferior" to the great lad who developed during the river voyage, and says that Jim's sacrifice of his freedom in order to assist Tom does not "fully redeem the ending."[3] Smith and Marx censure it for being, in the latter's words, perhaps "simply a burlesque on Tom's taste for literary romance," and Marx further reproves it by saying that the ending "jeopardizes the significance of the entire novel."[4]

Other critics stoutly defend the final chapters. Lionel Trilling, though admitting it is a "falling off," sees the ending as having "a certain formal aptness" which allows Huck to return to his needed former anonymity.[5] T. S. Eliot applauds it without reservation for

[1] "Mr. Eliot, Mr. Trilling and *Huckleberry Finn*," *American Scholar*, XXII (Autumn, 1953), 431.

[2] *Mark Twain at Work* (Cambridge, Mass., 1942), p. 92.

[3] Introduction to *Huckleberry Finn* (Boston: Houghton Mifflin Co., 1958), p. xxii. All subsequent references to the novel are to this edition and are given in the text.

[4] Marx, *op. cit.*, pp. 425, 427.

[5] Introduction to *Huckleberry Finn* (New York: Rinehart, 1958), p. xv.

correctly bringing us "back to the beginning."[6] R. P. Adams perceptively declares that the ending leaves in the reader's mind the feeling that "Huck will continue to develop. He will escape again. . . . The conclusion is deliberately inconclusive."[7] James Cox asserts that the ending is a "stylistic rather than a structural flaw"; "Tom's presence" there is "not only vital but inevitable; it proves that Huck must go west because he knows that to be Huck Finn is to be the outcast beyond the paling fences."[8] Thomas A. Gullason insists that the ending rounds out Twain's objectives of killing off romanticism and of demonstrating "man's inhumanity to man, and Huck's faith in Jim's humanity."[9]

These approvals of the novel *in toto*, as I shall demonstrate, are correct, but for the wrong reasons. The ending, though unnecessarily long, is indispensable for the working out of the real purpose of the book. This purpose, however, has not been properly understood.

The main, overriding theme of the novel is Huck's search for personal liberation, for the freedom which can come only with his growth into the maturity which will allow him to declare once and for all times unequivocally that he is his own master, able to rise above and to be indifferent to the lures to refuge cast out by society. It is this quest—not the Huck-Jim flight from physical slavery, not Huck's attempted escape from society *per se*, not even Huck's victory of heart over conscience—which forms the backbone of the book.

This theme develops in three interwoven strands: Huck's growth away from and above the other main characters—Tom, Jim, and Pap—and what they symbolize. Each strand must be traced through the novel until all coalesce in the climactic last few lines.

I

Throughout the book Huck's attitude toward the life around him is remarkably ambivalent. Though he clearly is rebelling

---

[6] Introduction to *Huckleberry Finn* (New York: Chanticleer, 1950), p. xiv.

[7] "The Unity and Coherence of *Huckleberry Finn*," *Tulane Studies in English*, VI (1956), 102.

[8] "Remarks on the Sad Initiation of Huckleberry Finn," *Sewanee Review*, LXII (Summer, 1954), 401.

[9] "The 'Fatal' Ending of *Huckleberry Finn*," *American Literature*, XXIX (March, 1957), 87.

against respectability and civilization, he rebels mainly because they make him uncomfortable and ill at ease. He fights them by running away. When he can no longer abide the "pecking" of the Widow and Miss Watson, and the privations they force upon him, he flees, but only to the rags and sugar-hogshead of the other side of town. He does not need to go farther. In fact, he must stay within commuting distance of respectable folk. And he quickly and easily returns when a lure is held up to him. The agent who entices Huck back from rags to respectability is, of course, Tom Sawyer. Tom at this time clearly symbolized Huck's ideal.

Tom is a rebel. He battles the world around him. He attacks the *status quo,* and seemingly threatens to overturn it. Yet his battles are all shams. If he ever overthrew his paper dragons, his crusading spirit would collapse. He lives happily in his society. After the lark of playing battler, he always joyously returns to the safety and security of Aunt Polly. This clash of danger and safety appeals to Huck, and it is epitomized in the person of Tom. Huck will therefore make any sacrifice for his hero, even to giving up the comfort and freedom he so immensely enjoys. Tom has saturated and captivated Huck's consciousness. Near or far he is the older boy's evil genius.

But Huck is not satisfied or happy for long in his enslavement. Though he sees the world through Tom's rose colored glasses, and though his spontaneous reaction to any situation is usually Tom's, Huck is restive. He is galled by his fetters and tries to break away. The fact is that he cannot live without Tom—or with him. He seeks a *modus vivendi* with Tom and his world, but cannot find it. Huck's victory over this forced compromise constitutes one of the great achievements in the book.

Demonstration of Huck's ambivalence begins at the outset of the novel. Huck recounts how in *Tom Sawyer* he was adopted by Widow Douglas, could not tolerate her "sivilizing" him and therefore ran away to his rags, where he was "free and satisfied." But Tom lured him back with the promise that he could become a member of the band of robbers. "So I went back," Huck states matter-of-factly. The close bond between the two boys is further revealed when Miss Watson tries to get Huck, who is hell-bent, to reform and thus prepare for the other destination; Huck is content with hell when Miss Watson assures him that Tom will be there too: "I wanted him and me to be together."

But no sooner does Huck join the band of robbers than the two boys' incompatibility manifests itself and he begins to drag his feet. After playing robber for a month, Huck resigns. He can no longer pretend that hogs are "ingots" and turnips are "julery." He wants to see the "di'monds," A-rabs and elephants. For his protests, Tom calls him a "numbskull," and "perfect sap-head." Huck's revulsion overcomes him. "I judged that all that stuff was only one of Tom Sawyer's lies. . . . It had all the marks of a Sunday School." Tom the romantic dreamer, the sham adventurer, thus symbolized everything that frightens Huck: St. Petersburg civilization, religion, romantic literature. From this monster Huck flees.

Yet fly as he will, Huck cannot shake off Tom, who is a ghost that refuses to be laid. When Huck "kills" himself to escape from Pap, he does it on Tom's terms: "I did wish Tom Sawyer was there, I knowed he would take an interest in this kind of business, and throw in the fancy touches" (p. 29). Again, on the night of the storm, when Huck is trying to convince Jim to board the wrecked *Walter Scott,* the force that drives Huck aboard is not the promise of loot—of "seegars" and "solid cash"—but the irresistible urge to imitate Tom. "I can't rest, Jim, till we give her a rummaging. Do you reckon Tom Sawyer would ever go by this thing? Not for pie, he wouldn't. . . . I wish Tom Sawyer *was* here" (p. 57).

Later, in Tennessee while the King and Duke play Peter Wilks' brothers, when Huck has adroitly maneuvered Mary Jane away from the house and has satisfactorily lied to the other girls, he congratulates himself, with his inevitable comparison: "I felt very good; I judged I had done it pretty neat—I reckon Tom Sawyer couldn't a done it no neater himself" (p. 163). Still later, in Pikesville, when Huck discovers that the King has turned in Jim for the sum of $40, he decides to write home and have Jim's owner send for him. But he automatically thinks of writing to Tom and having him tell Miss Watson where Jim is. The point is that in Huck's mind St. Petersburg—that world—and Tom are one and the same, inseparable, with Tom the symbol.

With Tom so constantly—and so heavily—on his mind, Huck naturally—and not surprisingly—acquiesces in the deception when Aunt Sally mistakes him for Tom. Huck's first impulse has always been to give in to Tom. Why should he not be flattered *to be* Tom? Indeed, discovering that he was supposed to be Tom Sawyer "was like being born again," in the sense of being re-born into the world of St. Petersburg and of Tom. "Being Tom Sawyer was easy and comfortable," Huck confesses immediately. Once it is settled that Huck will be Tom and Tom will be Sid, the future looks rosy. Everything will be "easy and comfortable." Huck relaxes completely, suspending his mental processes—becoming again the blind disciple. For example, it is inconceivable that the Huck of the voyage, with his mind alerted for signs of Jim, could see a slave enter an isolated cabin with food—part of it watermelon—and not suspect its purpose.

Yet the somnolent Huck does: "Well, it does beat all, that I never thought about a dog not eating watermelon. It shows how a body can see and don't see at the same time" (p. 195).

But in Huck's acquiescence there immediately becomes manifest the old attraction-revulsion tug-of-war he felt in St. Petersburg. And after the initial joy of being Tom has worn off, Huck begins to protest. In the old environment, the last time the boys shared an adventure, it took Huck a month to break away. Now, however, Huck's new nature shows through quickly. When he and Tom are concocting schemes for the release of Jim, Huck gives his plan first, then sits back waiting for the "superior" one; when Tom springs his, Huck reflects ironically: "I see in a minute it was worth fifteen of mine, for style, and would make Jim just as free a man as mine would, and maybe get us all killed besides" (p. 195).

After this initial resistance, Huck protests each new detail of the plan, as the more mature person realizes the absurdity of Tom's childish pranks. He protests, but he gives in each time. Each protest, in fact, is weaker than its predecessor. In this increasing weakness lies Huck's downfall. His resistance—his maturity—is being abraded. He is coming more and more under the mesmeric influence of Tom. Finally he capitulates completely: "Anyway that suits you suits me," he says when Tom wants him to dress up like a servant-girl to deliver the warning of the release of Jim.

Throughout the remainder of the evasion, Huck protests not at all. During the actual escape he apparently enjoys himself. It is action, of course, instead of romantic theorizing, and therefore appeals to the pragmatic Huck. But—far more significantly—Huck's new self is being subsumed under Tom's. So fast has been the activity since Tom's arrival that Huck has not had a chance to be alone and to reflect, and it is only when he has searched his soul through active thinking that his true self emerges. Now, caught up in activity, he is becoming the old Huck again, so completely under the influence of Tom that he is ready to "slide out" with Tom and Jim and "go for howling adventures amongst the Injuns, over in the Territory, for a couple of weeks or two."

At this point Huck is faced with the greatest crisis of his life. Once before he was confronted with a mighty decision, when he had to choose between being respectable and returning Jim to Miss Watson, and being himself, listening to the voice of his heart, not returning Jim—and going to hell. He chose the latter course, but only after great soul-searching, in solitude and silence: "I . . . set there thinking—thinking. . . . And went on thinking. And got to thinking . . ." (p. 179). In this even greater crisis if the new boy is to prevail over the old, clearly he needs time to think and think. Luckily, time is provided.

II

Jim, while in the environment of St. Petersburg, is far from extraordinary. Like Huck he is completely duped by Tom and thoroughly under his influence. He is lazy and drowsy-headed. For example, on the night that Huck comes out of the Widow's house in answer to Tom's "meow," Jim overhears them and comes out to investigate the noise. He stands between the hiding boys close enough to touch either but does not detect them. Almost immediately he relaxes into his favorite position and occupation: he sits down between them to "listen till I hears [the noise] again," and falls asleep.

He is also haughty and without integrity. After he wakes from this sleep and finds his hat hung on a limb, put there by Tom as a joke, he begins to claim that witches rode him all over the State. Subsequently he enlarges the area over which he was ridden to New Orleans, then to all the world. As proof of this witch-riding, he fraudulently introduces the five-cent piece that Tom had left on the kitchen table in payment for the candles. He swaggers and struts, and charges the other slaves "anything they had" just for a sight of the coin. He "got so stuck up" that he was "almost ruined for a servant."

Furthermore Jim is a con man. When Huck sees his father's boottrack in the snow, he is terrified, and goes to Jim to have his future read. This is clearly no time for humbuggery. Jim gets out his hair-ball, tests it, and discovers that "sometimes it won't talk without money." Huck gives him a counterfeit quarter that has the brass showing through. Jim smells, bites and rubs it, then declares it will suffice, because he can place it in a split potato and leave it overnight and thus make it undetectable, and "anybody in town would take it in a minute, let alone a hair-ball" (p. 16). Obviously the quarter will not remain with the hair-ball.

Jim deceives the distraught boy shamelessly. In answer to Huck's question about his father's future activities, Jim answers that he had not yet made up his mind; two angels are "hovering over him" trying to influence his behavior. But Huck need not worry, for he is "all right." Huck is thus reassured. But when he "lit my candle and went up to my room that night, there sat Pap, his own self!" Jim's hair-ball had not seen very clearly or deeply for the counterfeit quarter.

This Jim is infinitely inferior to the noble man of the raft. The explanation is simple. As long as he is in St. Petersburg, Jim is dominated by his society. In a slave's world he has a slave's mentality and morality; in Tom Sawyer's world Jim behaves as he had been trained: he has the superstitions, prejudices of the white society; he must be a fraud and a con man. Only when he is purged of this civilization and is protected by the dominating influence of Huck does his noble self rise to the surface. If Jim is the catalytic agent that brings out the best in Huck (as he is to a certain extent), so is Huck the means by which Jim achieves his true stature.

Away from St. Petersburg Jim is a moral giant until he arrives at Pikesville. Here he undergoes his second metamorphosis. Like Huck he could say he is re-born when he is turned over to Phelps as a runaway slave. Although he is eleven hundred miles down the river, he is reintroduced into the society of his former home.

Immediately he begins to act like a citizen of St. Petersburg. He reveals the truth about the "Royal Nonesuch," knowing full well the consequences to the Duke and King. This informing is an act of revenge. Jim suffers no heart-rending debate between conscience and heart. He wants to get even. His moral lapse is apparently instantaneous and complete. He is again a full-fledged citizen of the slave world he knew earlier.

This is the creature who passively and unprotestingly submits to all the indignities piled upon him by Tom. Then after being drubbed through them, he is placated by a gift of $40. More than placated; he is "pleased most to death." There is great significance in the sum of money. Jim was sold into physical slavery for the same amount; he went protestingly, snapping at the man responsible. But now for an equal amount he has sold all claims to dignity: he is thoroughly human, as venal as the whites around him. To gauge the distance he has fallen, one need only remember Huck's effort on the raft to impose on Jim's dignity—and the lacing he received for his efforts. It is inconceivable that Jim on the river would have sold his dignity. (Parenthetically, it should be noted that Tom is much worse than the King. The latter sold a body into physical slavery when he needed money badly. Tom, however, bought human dignity, out of mere whimsy. Likewise, it should not be overlooked how prices in the western world have gone up. Christ was worth only thirty pieces of silver; in Twain's good Christian America, however, bodies and souls came higher.)

Nor does Jim regain his dignity—his true human dignity—when he refuses to continue his flight and abandon the wounded Tom. Jim's impulse is completely unselfish but his reasoning is soft-headed. He says he cannot leave because under similar circumstances Tom would not abandon him. But the fact is that unless Tom could look upon staying as an adventure, he surely would leave: if he stayed it would be for self-aggrandizement. Jim says he will not leave until a doctor comes, "not if it's forty years!" There is nothing noble about a man who after being so debased as Jim has been looks upon his debaser as Moses, whom he is willing to suffer for forty years! There could hardly be a more scathing, and more typically Twainian, remark than Huck's editorializing: "I knew he was white inside, and I reckined he'd say what he did say." Huck, as we shall see, is at this time the alter ego of Tom. His voice is Tom's, his point of view is Tom's. Therefore his statements are twisted through all of Tom's ignorance and prejudice. All of this ignorance and prejudice is reflected in Huck's paying Jim the greatest compliment he can: declaring that, though black on the outside, he is white on the inside! This is the voice of the age and place.

This Jim is not sufficiently pure to accompany the real Huck on his search for personal freedom. Jim is now rich and complacent. He will undoubtedly be hoodwinked out of this fortune, as he was out of his first, but he will continue to fit into society. He will toady to St. Petersburg. Perhaps like Tom he will want to go on an adventure for a couple of weeks. But he is no better prepared than Tom is for Huck's odyssey.

There is no more pathetic, no more nearly tragic, figure in Twain's works than Jim. Like Huck he absorbs the traits of the society in which he lives. But there is a difference in the way and in the degree to which they absorb society. Jim is more passive than Huck. He is therefore lost. Legally free, he is condemned to the slavery of Tom's society for the rest of his life and to Tom's heaven after death. He is not capable of rising above what Twain liked to call, with both meanings, the "damned human race."

If we protest that Twain's sentence is too harsh, that Jim never really enjoyed equal opportunity with Huck, we probably echo Twain's feelings. Jim's fate was undoubtedly closely tied in with Twain's compulsion to overcompensate for the Negro in general: the compulsion which caused him to pay two Negroes' way through college and to insist that this was the debt he owed as a *white* person; the complex perhaps best revealed in Livy's advice to Mark, that in dealing with people, so that they be treated fairly, he should consider everybody colored until he was proved white. Unfortunately Jim *was* proved white.

III

The third theme—Huck's escape from Pap—is equal in importance to the first. In many ways this escape requires stronger battle. Huck's attitude toward his father is as ambivalent as that toward St. Petersburg and Tom. Sometimes he prefers Pap's society to that of the town. It allows him to be more comfortable. When, for example, Pap takes him over to the cabin on the Illinois bank, Huck soon finds life "kind of lazy and jolly," there were "pretty good times," and he "didn't want to go back no more" (p. 22).

But generally Huck's revulsion toward Pap is greater than his attraction. Manifestly Pap represents the dregs of society. And Huck's attraction to St. Petersburg causes him to apologize for himself by laying the blame on Pap. Numerous times he excuses some bit of ignorance or some attitude by saying that he was not "brung up" as other folks were.

Far more important than this superficial attitude, however, is what Pap represents: something fundamental and primal; that is, he symbolizes Fatherhood. One aspect of Fatherhood—tyranny and physical restraint and punishment—Huck finds intolerable. To escape Pap's brutality he becomes respectable, allows himself to be adopted, gives up his fortune to Judge Thatcher, even seeks the wisdom of the fortune-telling hairball. When Pap gets "too handy with his hick'ry," at the cabin, Huck resorts to his extreme act, that of "killing" himself. Thus it can hardly be correct to state, as several critics say, that Huck is searching for a father; on the contrary, he is trying to escape the one he has.

It is hardly correct, either, to insist, as Leo Marx insists, that Huck has nothing to run from, that when on Jackson's Island he tells Jim "They're after us!" he unconsciously allies himself with the great stream of (controlled) humanity. On the contrary, Huck is desperately fleeing from Pap, who is very much after him. Only a few days before, the steamboat had come around the island firing the cannon to force Huck's corpse to rise to the surface, and next to the rail was the terrifying figure of Pap. He was sober. The last time Huck had seen him—paddling the canoe back to the cabin the time he "killed" himself—he was sober. Pap sober was a more formidable figure to elude than Pap drunk. If the slave-hunters came to Jackson's Island and discovered Jim, they would find Huck also, and would turn him over either to the town or to Pap. Either way he would live under the threat of Pap, who was determined to claim him by legal means or physical abduction.

As Huck and Jim float down the river, Pap is never far away. There are numerous tangible reminders. When Huck ran away from the cabin, he took everything that "was worth a cent," and all belonged to his father: gun, fishhooks, food, etc. When, because Huck wants to play a joke on his companion, Jim is bitten by a snake, Pap's presence is summoned up frighteningly. Jim drinks Pap's whiskey until "the drunk begun to come," and Huck knows that Jim is "all right." In a sense, then, Pap saves Jim's life, and both Jim and Huck must be aware of it. But earlier associations with Pap's "forty-rod" obtrude on Huck's mind, and he says, "I'd druther been bit with a snake than pap's whisky" (p. 46).

Pap's influence extends long after the physical reminders are gone. Gliding down the river, Huck buys food in the villages they pass. But he *steals* chickens ("Pap always said, take a chicken when you get a chance"), and "borrows" watermelons, "mushmelons, and punkins" ("Pap always said it warn't no harm to borrow things"). Later, when the canoe has been lost, and the two realize their desperate need of one, Huck says that they intended to buy one, not "borrow it when there warn't anybody around, the way pap would do" (p. 80).

Again, when Huck is describing Colonel Grangerford as a gentleman well born, which is "worth as much as in man as it is in a horse," for substantiation of his comparison he cites as one authority Widow Douglas, and "pap he always said it, too" (p. 89). Later, when the King and Duke come aboard the raft, and the need for peace and harmony becomes obvious, Huck philosophizes: "If I never learnt nothing else out of pap, I learnt that the best way to get along with this kind of people is to let them have their own way" (p. 106). Finally, it should be noticed that in nearly every instance when Huck tells one of his lies to explain his presence somewhere he says that his family up-river or down-river has suffered some kind of disaster, and he begins his lament with reference to a father. Clearly his is a patriarchal society.

If Huck is to grow to his full stature as a man, he must realize that the weight of his father no longer bears down on him. This realization comes to him just before he is to make his greatest—and seemingly irrevocable—decision.

The climax of the novel does not extend throughout the last eleven chapters, which serve to carry on and intensify the development, but begins with the entry of Aunt Polly after the failure of the evasion. She reveals that Tom is really Huck, and Sid is really Tom. Her coming at this point—completely gratuitously—means that Twain wants to strip "Tom" of his false identity and thus to re-establish him as his true self. In other words, the masquerade— the past—is over, and the future lies open. Whatever Huck thinks or does from here on will be in his own name: he can no longer hide behind the cloak of anonymity or pseudonymity. He is pushed to the front *as himself*.

All the nonsense of the evasion, however, was carried out under a blanket of false identities. Huck was not himself; he was Tom Sawyer. Huck, therefore, is not personally responsible for the acts he committed while being Tom. The real Tom played the goody-goody-sissy Sid, whom in the past he has so despised. In Sid, Twain gives a picture of the future Tom. Thus, from this masquerade, we get a double or compound picture of the absurd world of Tom: Tom aided and abetted by an alter ego. We see doubly this world in its romantic, stupid, selfish, immoral, inhuman worst—where religion insists that Negroes are not people; where cruelty is practiced out of whimsy; where anybody—Jim included—can be bought for money or pleasure. It is Tom's world—of today and of tomorrow.

This evil world has had its attractions for Huck. He quickly became Tom's shadow, and soon found his role easy and comfortable. This role allowed Huck the luxury of being in rebellion without any of the dangers. Without perhaps fully realizing it, Huck is now faced with the greatest crisis of his life—of greater importance to his future in this world than that which gripped him when he had to decide Jim's fate.

The key to Huck's triumphal emergence into his true self lies in the last twenty-nine lines of the book. In these lines are woven the three strands I have discussed above, inseparable and inextricable.

Tom has just given Jim the forty dollars, and Jim is oozing self-congratulation. Tom then proposes that the three—he, Huck and Jim—"slide out of here, one of these nights, and get an outfit, and go for howling adventures amongst the Injuns, over in the Territory, for a couple of weeks or two." Huck agrees whole-heartedly, then remembers that he has no money to buy supplies. In this memory he brings to the surface one of the great fears that have haunted him for the last year: "It's likely pap's been back before now. . . ." Tom says that Pap has not returned; Jim reveals that it was Pap's corpse that was in the floating house on the river long ago.

Then there is a considerable lapse of time before the last paragraph. This passage of time is of utmost importance to Huck. The whole paragraph must be read closely:

> Tom's most well, *now,* and got his bullet around his neck on a watch-guard for a watch, and is always seeing what time it is, and so there ain't nothing to write about, and I am rotten glad of it, because if I'd a knowed what a trouble it was to make a book I wouldn't a tackled it and ain't agoing to no more. *But* I reckon I got to light out for the Territory *ahead of the rest,* because Aunt Sally she's going to adopt me and sivilize me and I can't stand it. I been there before. [*My* italics]

During the lapse of time between the penultimate and the last paragraphs Huck has had time to think over the situation. Before learning that Pap is dead, he agrees to go off with his fellow-citizens—even wants to go. But after being told that his father is dead, and after realizing his consequent release from the tension he felt while his father was alive, he has had time to think, time for the same kind of soul-searching he wrestled with before finally deciding to go to hell for Jim, and he has realized the absurdity of Tom's plan. Notice the revulsion with which Huck takes leave of the evil genius Tom: he has a bullet around his neck and is always flaunting it. Huck gladly parts with this jackanapes. Since he is parting with him forever, and since this escape was one of the major themes in the book, naturally, "there ain't nothing to write about," and surely Huck is "rotten glad" to be done with Tom. Huck will not write another book, because he has no reason for another: he has found himself; his search for true self is ended.

Critics err in thinking that Huck wants to go west ahead of all other settlers, of all Civilization. Or they err in insisting that this is all Huck wants to escape. True, Twain from the vantage point of his Hartford mansion is becoming more and more soured on civilization in general. But *Huckleberry Finn* centers on the antebellum South, and the sins of this civilization are the immediate objects of Twain's hate. Therefore it is the civilization of St. Petersburg that Huck wants to flee. This civilization extends to the Phelps' farm. Its representative there is Aunt Sally—the soft-headed Aunt Sally who was so thoroughly and so easily duped by the shenanigans of the two Toms, who in her ineffectiveness is much worse than the Widow Douglas ever was. Having her try to civilize Huck would be pathetic beyond words. In fleeing all this world, Huck wants above all to get away from Tom and Jim because they personally symbolize all the Life that he now finds intolerable.

Huck realizes that he is now freed of all the restraints which hitherto have bound him. Tom and Pap have been cast off. Jim, the nearest true companion he ever knew, can journey with him no farther. But, most important, the world of these three holds no attraction for him. Intellectually and spiritually, as well as physically, he is free. Now he can exercise his freedom and continue his growth. He can be true to himself because there is no reason to be false to himself in order to be true to society.

Editor's Note: "Huck's Final Triumph" is reprinted with the permission of Ray B. Browne and *The Ball State University Forum,* VI (winter, 1965), i, pp. 3–12.

Professor Browne, of Purdue University, is the author of *Popular Beliefs and Practices in Alabama, The Burke-Paine Controversy,* and *A Night with the Hants.*

MARK TWAIN AND J. D. SALINGER: A STUDY IN LITERARY CONTINUITY

EDGAR BRANCH

In J. D. Salinger's *The Catcher in the Rye* Holden Caulfield reflects on Mr. Antolini, his former teacher, from whose homosexual pettings he has just fled in panic: "I started thinking that even if he was a flit he certainly'd been very nice to me. I thought how he hadn't minded it when I'd called him up so late, and how he'd told me to come right over . . . And how he went to all that trouble giving me that advice about finding out the size of your mind and all . . ." Huckleberry Finn, in his "close place" a century earlier, muses on his best teacher, Jim: "I . . . got to thinking over our trip down the river; and I see Jim . . . standing my watch on top of his'n, . . . so I could go on sleeping; and see him how glad he was when I come back out of the fog . . . and such-like times; and would always call me honey, and pet me and do everything he could think of for me . . ." Huck can always depend on Jim; their physical relationship is consciously innocent. But Mr. Antolini is Holden's last adult refuge in his disintegrating world. Huck, resolving his inner conflict by a free moral decision, takes immediate bold steps to help Jim. But Holden becomes "more depressed and screwed up" than ever after fleeing Mr. Antolini. Ominously, as he walks down Fifth Avenue, he feels he is disappearing. He retreats to the Museum of Natural History, the "place where the mummies were" and a favorite childhood haunt that he remembers as "so nice and

255

peaceful"—like Huck's raft. But even there life-obscenity intrudes—Huck's raft has its Duke and Dauphin too—and he learns that "You can't ever find a place that's nice and peaceful, because there isn't any." Each of these experienced boys knows all about fraud and violence but retains the charity of an innocent heart. Each is a measure of the need and possibility for human love in his society.

Holden's society differs as dramatically from Huck's as does a Broadway traffic jam from a raft drifting down the Mississippi a long century ago. Yet a flight down the river and a flight through New York streets turn out to be not so different after all. The pattern of Holden's experience is essentially Huck's. Salinger's writing carries familiar rhythms and attitudes. The creative imaginations of these two authors who fuse given fact and boyish consciousness into expressive, dramatized narrative are strikingly similar. *The Catcher in the Rye,* in fact, is a kind of *Huckleberry Finn* in modern dress. This paper does not propose to reveal any direct, "real" or conscious "influences"—if these exist at all—that *Huckleberry Finn* had upon Salinger's novel. Nor is its purpose to compare the "then" and "now" of American society through the illustrative use of these books. Rather, it attempts to bare one nerve of cultural continuity in America by dissecting some literary relationships between the two novels.

II

Consider first the narrative patterns and styles.

Huck initially flees conventionalities, constraint and terror. On the river he meets murderous thieves, a treacherous fog, Negro-hunters and a steamboat that rips through the raft and thrusts him among feuding country gentility. He lives with professional crooks who fatten on "greenhorns" and "flatheads." He sees a harmless drunk shot dead and a Southern Colonel almost lynched, observes some theatrical obscenities and at great personal risk saves the inheritance of three innocent girls. Experience teaches Huck that truth is usually weak, trouble best avoided and evil often inevitable. It confirms his love of beauty and peaceful security. But notably in his greatest struggle, over Jim, he acts spontaneously and defiantly for goodness. Huck eventually comes to the Phelps plantation, the homelike place where Jim finds freedom and where Huck will take leave of "sivilization" by going West.

Holden Caulfield, intensely troubled, escapes initially from the stupid constraints and violence of his prep school life. Like Huck, he enters a jungle world, New York City, where he knows his way around but from which he is alienated. There for two hectic days and nights he steers his course through battering adventures with fearsome "dopes," "fakers," "morons" and sluggers. On this journey Holden's Jim is primarily the recurring image of Jane Gallagher, an old friend who needs love and whom he loves with strange unawareness. Holden's Jim is also all little children, whom he would save from adult sexuality. Like Huck, Holden has a conflict. His adolescent sexual urges are somehow entangled with what is predatory in the "mean guys" he hates. They befoul his sense of the fine and good. Although not as self-sufficient as Huck, Holden is usually as realistic, and he too loves beauty and peace. Yet he values goodness above know-how, sophistication, style, success. After a secret visit home, he plans to lead a hermit's life in the West, but is reconciled to the city by the love of his little sister Phoebe. Physically weakened and psychically wounded, he is last seen recuperating in a sanitarium. Clearly Mark Twain and Salinger present parallel myths of American youth confronting his world—Huck Finn over many months, when time was expendable; Holden over two days when, Salinger seems to imply, time is rapidly running out.

Each novel employs an appropriate first person vernacular. Holden has the more "educated" vocabulary, he speaks with a modern schoolboy's idiom and slang and he can spell. Also he can swear. Both boys observe accurately and swiftly. Both are artists of deadpan, yet can subtly convey the interplay of feeling and scene. Huck arrives at the Phelps farm: "When I got there it was all still and Sunday-like, and hot and sunshiny—the hands was gone to the fields; and there was them kind of faint dronings of bugs and flies in the air that makes it seem so lonesome and like everybody's dead and gone; and if a breeze fans along and quivers the leaves, it makes you feel mournful, because you feel like it's spirits whispering—spirits that's been dead ever so many years—and you always think they're talking about *you*. As a general thing it makes a body wish *he* was dead, too, and done with it all." Holden observes New York's streets from a taxicab: "What made it worse, it was so quiet and lonesome out, even though it was Saturday night. I didn't see hardly anybody on the street. Now and then you just saw a man and a girl crossing a street, with their arms around each other's

257

waists and all, or a bunch of hoodlumy-looking guys and their dates, all of them laughing like hyenas at something you could just bet wasn't funny. New York's terrible when somebody laughs on the street very late at night. You can hear it for miles. It makes you feel so lonesome and depressed. I kept wishing I could go home."

Huck's speech, usually dispassionate and matter-of-fact, is relaxed and flexibly rhythmical. Holden, frequently conscious of the smothering omnipresence of sex, draws most things taut. Nervous, jerky reiteration often points up his emotional tensions. His speech is sometimes raucous and jarring. He tends to rail and condemn. Huck's direct apprehension gives us an objective recording rich in implication. His vision etches an open world, clear, solid, real, with living characters moving autonomously in it. Holden's tense outpouring is a convincing expression of his psychological unrest and of the release he is finding in psychiatric treatment. His speech carries hints of the frantic overtones of a Poe character speaking from a madhouse (humanized by delightful comedy), and his world and its people, though violently alive, revolve in the whirlpool of his egocentricity. Both styles are effectively ironic and humorous.

Perhaps Huck's profoundest relation to life is an animal faith, an acceptance of reality that assimilates the irrational and cruel even while it condemns them through exposure. That acceptance promotes a classic simplicity of style, the more dignified for the dark undertones present. But Holden's rejection and disgust create a feverish modern dissonance. Alienation is expressed by obsessive revelation, sometimes more suggestive of Theodor Fischer in Mark Twain's *The Mysterious Stranger* than of Huck Finn. Holden's speech is indeed suited to his neurotic experience of the all-engulfing modern city. Huck's speech is equally well suited to his personality and to what Mark Twain had to say about a vanished era, a time permitting Huck's hard won victory over self and circumstance. Salinger's adaptation of the language to his hero's speech habits, character and times points up the stylistic continuity between the two books.

III

What experience brings Holden to the sanitarium? A brief answer to this question is required at this stage of the discussion.

Holden's parents are wealthy, seemingly happily married people.

The father is a prominent corporation lawyer, the mother an able, tasteful woman. Phoebe, Holden's ten-year-old sister, is a staunch, wise little girl. Holden's younger brother, Allie, the "wizard" of the family, died of leukemia three years ago, and Holden is still guilt-stricken for the way he used to treat him. Allie used to write Emily Dickinson's poems on his fielder's mitt to have something to read when nobody was at bat. The night Allie died Holden "broke all the windows in the garage . . . with my fists, just for the hell of it." Huck also knew death at first hand, and when he looked down on Buck Grangerford's body, he felt guilty and sickened by life.

Holden himself is a rangy sixteen-year-old who is prematurely gray and has grown too fast. He is creative and intelligent but bewildered by strange impulses, a "madman." Girls are on his mind. "Sex," he admits, "is something I really don't understand too hot." If girls "like a boy, no matter how big a bastard he is, they'll say he has an inferiority complex, and if they *don't* like him, no matter how nice a guy he is, or how big an inferiority complex he has, they'll say he's conceited." Still, whenever girls "do something pretty," even if they're ugly or stupid, "you fall half in love with them." Whereas Huck is the sexless pre-adolescent, Holden is the sex-conscious boy who yearns for the uncomplicated state of Huck.

Pencey Prep is the third school Holden has flunked out of. All of them cater to pocketbook snobs. At Pencey "they had this goddam secret fraternity that I was too yellow not to join." At Elkton Hills School Holden had seen James Castle, an independent, stubborn, "skinny little weak-looking guy, with wrists about as big as pencils," lying dead, a gory mess on the sidewalk, after jumping out the window to escape the hazing of seven superior bullies.

Saturday evening Holden spends his last hours at Pencey with two dorm-mates. Unpopular Ackley, sullen and mean-minded, is an obvious slob—always squeezing his pimples and cutting his dirty fingernails where Holden will walk on them in his bare feet. Stradlater, Holden's roommate, is the handsome sexy egotist and *secret* slob. "He always *looked* all right, Stradlater, but for instance you should've seen the razor he shaved himself with. It was always rusty as hell and full of lather and hairs and crap . . ." To Holden's anguish it is Stradlater, with one idea in mind, who dates the visiting Jane Gallagher that very evening. After Stradlater is provoked into slugging him heavily, Holden packs up and clears out for New York.

There he seeks companionship in bar and night club, but feels only more depressed. Back at his hotel, a place "lousy with perverts," he pays Sunny, a prostitute, five dollars to talk with him and is then slugged by the tough pimp and shakedown artist, Maurice the elevator boy. He wants to jump out the window. "I probably would've done it, too, if I'd been sure somebody'd cover me up as soon as I landed. I didn't want a bunch of stupid rubbernecks looking at me when I was all gory"—the way they crowded around Boggs in Huck's story. But the next day Holden is off to a play and to the Radio City ice skating rink with his friend Sally Hayes, culture-hound and cute little "butt-twitcher." Then hours of desperate, lonely wandering through New York movies, bars and freezing streets leave Holden shivering and sick in body and spirit. He sneaks into his family's apartment after midnight to see Phoebe.

Phoebe gives Holden all her love and trust, but tells him: "You don't like *any*thing that's happening," and she challenges him to name one thing he would like to *be*. He recalls the joyful little kid he had heard that morning singing "Comin' Thro' the Rye," but he wrongly remembers the words as "If a body catch a body . . ." Holden answers: "I keep picturing all these little kids playing some game in this big field of rye and all. . . . and nobody's around—nobody big, I mean—except me. And I'm standing on the edge of some crazy cliff. What I have to do, I have to catch everybody if they start to go over the cliff—I mean if they're running and they don't look where they're going I have to come out from somewhere and *catch* them. That's all I'd do all day. I'd just be the catcher in the rye and all. I know it's crazy, but that's the only thing I'd really like to be." No comment from Phoebe.

In the early morning hours Holden visits Mr. Antolini, his Elkton Hills teacher. Mr. Antolini compassionately assures Holden that others also have been troubled morally and spiritually by human behavior, but warns him that he is heading for the kind of crack-up "designed for men who . . . were looking for something their own environment couldn't supply them with." Having fallen asleep on the couch, Holden wakes up minutes later to feel Mr. Antolini, next to him in the blackness, stroking his head. "Boy, I was shaking like a madman. I was sweating too. . . . That kind of stuff's happened to me about twenty times since I was a kid. I can't stand it." For the rest of the night he finds privacy in Grand Central Station.

Hardly able to walk the next morning, Holden plans to hitchhike west and live alone, but first says goodbye to Phoebe. Her sturdy refusal to let him go alone saves him from himself, and as the book ends he elatedly watches her ride the zoo merry-go-round. "I was damn near bawling. I felt so damn happy, if you want to know the truth. I don't know why. It was just that she looked so damn *nice,* the way she kept going around and around, in her blue coat and all."

The carrousel, bearing the beautiful child and playing the songs of Holden's childhood, goes round and round, going nowhere—a dynamic moment of happy, static immaturity eternalized in his mind. "Certain things," believes Holden, "they should stay the way they are." But he is unwilling to put this belief to the test for fear things will be different. He will not enter the Museum on his first trip there. And does he really want to talk with Jane Gallagher, whom he's always going to ring but never quite does? Will she be the same, or changed—like all the rest? Mr. Antolini sees Holden as a potential martyr, an idealist capable of "dying nobly . . . for some highly unworthy cause." Holden is imaginatively capable of feeling Maurice's horny fist bruising his flesh ("my old heart was damn near beating me out of the room"), yet he won't pay five measly shakedown dollars to escape the slugging. But he easily gives ten dollars to two nuns eating their breakfast of toast and coffee, because "I hate it if I'm eating bacon and eggs or something and somebody else is only eating toast and coffee." Holden lived and Allie died; life itself is a bacon-and-eggs injustice. Death is the rain beating down on Allie's grave, "on the grass on his stomach." Life smirks its grief, puts its flowers on Allie's stomach and runs for its plush sedans when the rain starts, to "go somewhere nice for dinner." Confused and sickened by human conduct, Holden fears what is new, including the life within. His compulsive wanderings lead him back to New York, to old scenes, to his childhood and to Phoebe. He sees himself as the preserver of innocence, the catcher in the rye.

IV

Especially in its characterization of the hero, *The Catcher in the Rye* is a haunting reminder of *Huckleberry Finn.*

Holden wants to shepherd the young, to be the only big person around; but Huck is the youthful liberator of a grown man, and whether he knows it or not his effort is directed toward making maturity possible. Holden is a conscious idealist who yet says, "I kept wishing I could go home." Huck lives humbly and prudently to get what he wants, but for *his* future home he chooses hell. Mr. Antolini is warning Holden when he says that the immature man wants to die nobly for a cause, while the mature man wants to live humbly for one—but he might have been approving Huck. The hope in Mark Twain's novel is that a ragamuffin pre-adolescent acts maturely for what is good in an open society. The underlying despair of Salinger's book is that a privileged adolescent wants to act immaturely for what he believes is good in a society thickened into vulgarity.

Yet Holden is truly a kind of latter-day, urbanized Huck. He is acutely sensitive to places and times, whether groping through a dark foyer in the early morning hours or relaxing in the cozy auditorium of the Museum of Natural History, where it "always smelled like it was raining outside, even if it wasn't . . ." He knows the uniqueness of things: the feel of a roller-skate key is unforgettable, everlasting, shimmering with human meaning. With every nerve he feels the moral character of others. He sharply registers the unguarded phrase or facial expression—the prostitute Sunny's childish "Like fun you are," or the beauty of Phoebe's open-mouthed sleep. Although Huck can easily spot "phonies"—witness the Widow Douglas, who approved of taking snuff "because she done it herself"—Holden is violently allergic to them: Carl Luce, a specialist in extracting intimate sex confessions from young boys but a sorehead "if you start asking *him* questions about *himself*"; or the popular entertainer Ernie who, when playing the piano, *"sounds like the kind of guy that won't talk to you unless you're a big shot."* But the kettle drummer in the Radio City orchestra, whom Holden had observed closely for years, never looked bored even though he might bang the drums only twice during a piece. "Then when he does bang them, he does it so nice and sweet, with this nervous expression on his face." The drummer is what "Jesus *really* would've liked" in all the lavish Radio City Christmas pageant.

Holden has Huck's judicious mind and his respect for fact and knowledge. Huck "studies," Holden "analyzes." Both will generously grant any person his particular points. Harris Macklin, for instance, is the biggest bore Holden knows, but Harris is an inimitable whistler—"So I don't know about bores. . . . They don't hurt anybody, most of them, and maybe they're secretly all terrific whistlers or something." But Holden is not equally generous with himself. He is the "only really dumb one" in his family, "very yellow" and a "sacrilegious atheist." His relentless self-criticism is alerted by the slightest stirring of "phoniness" within. As with Huck, his humility ironically reveals his goodness and integrity.

This realist Holden is as skeptical of men and as wary of circumstances as is Huck. He cultivates the timely maneuver and the saving lie to get out of tight spots, although he is not the slippery character Huck is. Dr. Thurmer, Headmaster at Pencey, does not admit the inevitability of tight spots. He preaches that Life is a rewarding game if played "according to the rules," and Pencey teaches the rules. "Some game," Holden thinks. "If you get on the side where all the hot-shots are, then it's a game, all right." In this game "people always clap for the wrong things," "people never believe you" and "people are always ruining things for you." It's a game that favors money-grubbers and callous egotists. Holden observes that a sentimental movie-goer weeping over the "putrid" movie characters is "as kindhearted as a goddam wolf" to her child. Here, as in the Grangerford episode, sentimentality reinforces inhumanity. Human kindness sometimes shines forth unexpectedly, but Holden's attitude is that "the sun only comes out when it feels like coming out," and you can't count on it.

In this corrupt world Holden miraculously keeps the uncorrupted heart that most reminds us of Huckleberry Finn. He genuinely loves natural beauty and the socially unspoiled. Freer than Huck from conventional responses, he is an instinctive moralistic democrat whose feelings recall Whitman's "By God! I will accept nothing which all cannot have their counterpart of on the same terms." He sympathizes with the kindhearted, the suffering and the helpless. He lies outrageously to protect a mother from the knowledge that her son's basic character is displayed in his passion for snapping, with his soggy knotted towel, the backsides of boys emerging from the shower. In a touching flashback he comforts unhappy Jane Gallagher, whom he values for her human eccentricities and her real quality—her "muckle-mouthed" way of talking, her curious way of playing checkers and her love of poetry. He best conceives peace and virtue in the imagery of physical and mental cripples—the Bible "lunatic . . . that lived in the tombs and kept cutting himself with stones," and the "poor deaf-mute bastard" Holden himself would like to be. He is haunted by the peace of two nuns he meets, and in several of his actions he unconsciously imitates the compassion of Jesus.

Holden, in short, like Huck, respects human personality and hates whatever demeans it. He knows that snobbery is aggression, and that subordinating people to ideas and things destroys fruitful human intercourse. A self-styled pacifist, he strives to create relationships with others through discussion, a kind of decent and creative give-and-take. "That's the way you can always tell a moron. They never want to discuss anything . . ." He likes books chiefly for the quality that makes "you wish the author that wrote it was a terrific friend of yours and you could call him up on the phone whenever you felt like it." But Ring Lardner and "old Thomas Hardy," two favorites, can't be reached by telephone; something nearly always prevents human intimacy. Possessions, "Goddam money" and creeds get in the way. Holden remembers that his budding friendship with Louis Shaney, a Catholic boy, was tainted because "you could tell he would've enjoyed [our conversation] *more* if I was a Catholic and all." Also Holden defends Richard Kinsella, his very nervous classmate who was academically hazed, by order of the Oral Expression instructor, for digressing in his class speeches. "It's nice when somebody tells you about their . . . father's farm and then all of a sudden get[s] more interested in their uncle. I mean it's dirty to keep yelling 'Digression!' at him when he's all nice and excited."

Unselfish love and spontaneous joy—Holden values these expressions of the uncontaminated spirit above all. So rarely are they found and so often thwarted in adult life that their slightest appearance saddens him. As he prepares to leave Pencey and packs the brand-new ice skates his mother had just bought him, he can see her "going in Spaulding's and asking the salesman a million dopey questions—and here I was getting the ax again. It made me feel pretty sad." Later on, Sunny, who sells her love at so much a throw, wants Holden to hang up her new dress to prevent wrinkles. Again he feels sad as he thinks of her buying it and "nobody in the store knowing she was a prostitute and all. The salesman probably just thought she was a regular girl when she bought it." But the little boy singing "Comin' Thro' the Rye" is a regular kid, happy, fulfilled, innocently insulated from the disagreeable. "He had a pretty little voice, too. . . . The cars zoomed by, brakes screeched all over the place, his parents paid no attention to him, and he kept on walking next to the curb and singing 'If a body catch a body coming through the rye.' It made me feel better." Holden is happy in the world of innocence that creates its own conditions. Desperately lonesome, he reveals his need for human intimacy by using the word "catch."

Clearly Holden and Huck, who so often shape their experience in similar patterns, have similar qualities. Holden's acute self-consciousness and his evident neuroticism do not diminish the reality or worth of what he is and feels. Nor do they invalidate the comparison between the two boys. Rather, by appropriately distinguishing a typically modern personality from Huck Finn, still predominantly one of the "Divine Inert" but already, in his extreme and sensitive youth, bearing the scars of harsh experience, they help define the direct descent of Holden from Huck.

V

Huckleberry Finn and *The Catcher in the Rye* are akin also in ethical-social import. Each book is a devastating criticism of American society and voices a morality of love and humanity.

In many important matters, as we have just seen, Huck and Holden—not to speak of others like Jim and Phoebe—affirm goodness, honesty and loyalty. Huck does so almost unconsciously, backhandedly, often against his conventional conscience, and Holden does so with an agonizing self-consciousness and a bitter spirit. In each the perception of innocence is radical: from their mouths come pessimistic judgments damning the social forms that help make men less than fully human. "Human beings *can* be awful cruel to one another," observes Huck after seeing the Duke and Dauphin tarred and feathered. And Huck assumes his share of the guilt. Holden, with searingly honest insight that gets to the root of sadistic practices and class jealousies, remarks: "I can even get to hate somebody, just *looking* at them, if they have cheap suitcases with them. . . . It's really hard to be roommates with people if your suitcases are much better than theirs . . . You think if they're intelligent . . . they don't give a damn whose suitcases are better, but they do. They really do." To Aunt Sally's question whether anybody was hurt in the steamboat accident, Huck replies, "No'm. Killed a nigger," and the blindness of a civilization is bared with terrible casualness. The same ironic exposure comes in Holden's apology for having to like a girl before he can get sexy—"I mean *really* sexy"—with her. So he remarks, "My sex life stinks." And Carl Luce, the modern expert on love, answers: "Naturally it does, for God's sake."

Such examples might easily be multiplied: the vision is often identical. Yet we must grant that the reliability and quality of Holden's vision are complicated, far beyond Huck's straightforward objectivity, by the loss he has sustained. As Holden recognizes, he is mentally ill. "I don't get hardly anything out of anything. I'm in bad shape. I'm in *lousy* shape." Bad as the modern world is, his view of it adds a distortion not found in Huck's picture. Almost everyone in Holden's world is "phony"—headmasters, students, alumni, bar-tenders, movie actors, movie goers, people who say "Glad to've met you" or "Good luck!" or "Grand!," virile hand-shakers, Holy Joe ministers, even partially bald men who hopefully comb their hair over the bald spot. The book reeks with Holden's revulsion and nausea. He experiences things in an aura of disgusting physical details. The park is "lousy" with "dog crap, globs of spit and cigar butts." A chair is "vomity" looking. A cab smells as though someone had "tossed his cookies in it." Moreover, although Holden keeps his innocent heart, his adolescence has riddled the innocence of mind, that naiveté, which Huck in good measure still possesses. What Holden's heart seeks and responds to, his mind sees is violated everywhere by the mere fact of human maturity. Adult activities become expressive masks for adult sexuality. The four-letter word he reads with horror—and erases—on the wall of Phoebe's school, follows him wherever he goes. In the quiet tomb of Pharaoh in the Museum, he feels at peace for the first time—until suddenly he sees the same word in red crayon on the wall. Despairingly, hysterically, he thinks that even in death he will not escape that word which someone surely will write on his tombstone. A great difference between the two boys is measured by Huck's sensitive but reserved opinion of the obscene words on the wall of the abandoned house floating down the June rise: "the ignorantest kind of words . . ."

Certainly if Huck's vision reveals both the limitations and promises of democracy—the hope and despair—Holden's, in direct descent from Huck's, focuses upon the despair. In the predatory wasteland of the city, Holden can foresee no future refuge or good. (Is it by accident that some lines of weary futility from "The Love Song of J. Alfred Prufrock" are echoed in Holden's words to Sally Hayes: "It wouldn't be the same at all. You don't see what I mean at all"?) If he and Sally were married, Holden knows he would be an office worker "making a lot of dough, and riding to work in . . . Madison Avenue buses, and reading newspapers, and playing bridge all the time, and going to the movies and seeing a lot of stupid shorts and coming attractions and newsreels." He accurately describes the commercialized Christmas spirit as something over which "old Jesus probably would've puked if He could see it." He damns the competitive drive for status. Even the cab drivers, primitives of the city, are suspicious, raw-nerved. And nowhere is there peace. Holden's view of modern war concludes: "I'm sort of glad they've got the atomic bomb invented. If there's ever another war, I'm going to sit right the hell on top of it. I'll volunteer for it . . ." Neurotic or not, Holden's criticism often hits home.

Like Holden, Huck knows the meaning of respectable routine, competition and violence, but the difference is that what is organized nightmare in Holden's world is merely nascent in Huck's. Everyone can remember the brutal and degenerate persons Huck encounters and some of the dozen or more corpses that bloody up his story. Holden's society holds far more possibilities for horror and depravity, and on a massive scale. Feverishly, obsessively on the move, it has more irritants and fewer profound satisfactions than does Huck's. Holden's cherished memory of one little duck pond in Central Park replaces Huck's Jackson's Island and lazy days on the Mississippi. The three or four lights Huck sees, "twinkling where there were sick folks, maybe," are not so much, compared to the health, the beauty, the freedom of the river. The sparkling metropolis Holden sees looming over the forlorn duck pond is inescapable, portentous. The life Huck explores, despite its evil and treachery, is still daring and redemptive, not just sodden, mean and self-destructive.

Given such contrasting conditions, what moral destiny confronts the individual in the worlds Salinger and Mark Twain create? Like the Central Park ducks in winter, Holden is essentially homeless, frozen out. But Huck, although an outcast, is a true home-maker wherever he is. Allie's baseball mitt is all that is left to Holden of Allie's love, and unlike Huck, he seems unable to break through the ring of hostility to find new sources of affection. Deprived of real opportunity for the sort of soul-shaking sacrifice Huck makes for Jim, Holden expresses his love for Phoebe by the gift of a phonograph record—which breaks. Of greater significance, Huck has Jim; but Holden, so desperately in need of love, is one of the loneliest characters in fiction. Obviously Huck is not as critically wounded as Holden. He has far more resilience, a stronger power of renewal. Necessity shows him the wisdom of prudence, and his natural environment provides therapeutic primal sanities. Both boys are rebels—with a difference. Huck can often go naked, but Holden can defy convention only by wearing his "corny" red hunting cap. Capable of making a free choice, Huck outwits his enemies and rises above the compulsions within. He is a practical rebel like Thoreau. He runs away to confront and modify reality, and thereby he proves, for his day, the explosive force of individual ethical action. Holden runs off too, but his actions are usually ineffective, and the path of escape leads him deeper into the mire of his personal difficulties.

Huckleberry Finn, in short, recognizes both necessity and freedom, the restrictions limiting moral accomplishment and its possibility. *The Catcher in the Rye* leaves us doubtful that the individual, even assisted by the analyst's best efforts, can ever truly escape the double trap of society and self. How well the two concluding scenes contrast these moral outlooks! Throughout *The Catcher in the Rye* Holden makes, and is, a telling criticism of our civilization: his "madness" in itself is a damning fact of our times; yet, doubly damning, what the "madman" says is often true, what he feels often unimpeachable. Supremely ironical, then, is our last glimpse of Holden making recovery and adjustment in the sanitarium—a prelude to compromise in the outside world—as Father Peter in Mark Twain's *The Mysterious Stranger* can not do. Holden says: "I sort of *miss* everybody I told about. Even old Stradlater and Ackley, for instance. I think I even miss that goddam Maurice. It's funny. Don't ever tell anybody anything. If you do, you start missing everybody." Modern therapy takes over, Holden will return. For Holden's sake we wouldn't have it otherwise, even though it's a return to the big money and dopey newsreels. But we remember Huck with admiration and with confidence in his personal future as, Jim freed and the Duke and Dauphin in limbo, he says: "I reckon I got to light out for the Territory ahead of the rest, because Aunt Sally she's going to adopt me and sivilize me and I can't stand it. I been there before."

No wonder Holden wants to remain forever the catcher in the rye—*his* free Territory—oblivious to the trap that maturity finally springs. His recessive traits suggest that the logical, perhaps desirable, end for him and his civilization is the pure silence of death, the final release from imperfect life. *Huckleberry Finn,* as Philip Young has recently realized, appeals to rescuing death in the series of escapes—gliding, still and dark—made by Huck and Jim as the raft slips into the flowing, mythic river.[1] Huck, too, has guilt-feelings that, if sufficiently intensified, could conceivably lead to self-destruction. But such suggestions are muted in Huck's story, for Huck is committed to life. In Salinger's book death symbols are more pronounced, and death openly fascinates Holden not only for its horror but for the peaceful refuge it offers from the consciousness of life. Beneath the appealing and often hilarious humor, comparable to some of the best of Mark Twain's, life is felt in this book fundamentally as a ceaseless, pushing round of activity that one would be well rid of. Holden carries with him a dim sense of the eternal and transcendental. He is something like a soul unknowingly striving to rise from the muck of this world to the peace of nirvana. Jane Gallagher is always beyond his reach; he must settle for Sally Hayes, the "queen of the Phonies." Like Teddy McArdle in Salinger's story "Teddy," Holden might have called his contemporaries a "bunch of apple-eaters." Like Jean in Salinger's "De Daumier—Smith's Blue Period," Holden might have felt that in this life he "would always at best be a visitor in a garden of enamel urinals and bedpans, with a sightless, wooden dummy-deity standing by . . ." But for Jean, "the sun came up." Sudden spiritual insight transforms that garden into a "shimmering field of exquisite, twice-blessed, enamel flowers." Nirvana is here and now. Holden, of course, has hardly begun to find the peace and illumination inherent in a full understanding of the Zen koan inscribed in Salinger's second book, *Nine Stories:*

> We know the sound of two hands clapping.
> But what is the sound of one hand clapping?

but the urge to find them works deeply within him. Salinger's social criticism, it would seem, has a mystical base, a support more pro-

---

[1] Philip Young, *Ernest Hemingway* (New York: Rinehart and Company, 1952), p. 181 ff.

found than mere belief in Holden's Christian virtues, though that belief is present too. It constantly implies a religious feeling, possibly a conviction, that dimly hints a way out of the life-trap. Mark Twain's social criticism in *Huckleberry Finn* is more simply that of the rational democrat and humanitarian who has not lost faith in the practical effectiveness of the good heart on this earth.

We have seen that *Huckleberry Finn* and *The Catcher in the Rye* share certain ethical and social attitudes. Yet Salinger's critical view assumes a cultural determinism that in *Huckleberry Finn,* although always present, permits freedom through self-guidance. Salinger's viewpoint also draws upon a mystical sense merely inchoate in Mark Twain's imagination. We have seen too that Holden's neuroticism is both literary cause and social effect. It is Salinger's means of etching the modern picture the more deeply, and a product of the culture it so sweepingly condemns on moral grounds. But Mark Twain's moral vision is projected through the prevailing normality of Huck's temperament. It is eminently central; fundamentally there is nothing rigged about Huck's experience or eccentric in his responses. So Huck on a raft, as profoundly symbolic today as Thoreau in his cabin, is ever more meaningful as our national experience hurtles us along routes more menacing than the Mississippi. *The Catcher in the Rye,* always cautionary, often horrifying in moral tone, creates an overwhelming sense of that hurtling. The point is not that Salinger's moral vision is therefore defective. Rather, because his vision is lit by the sick lamps of civilization, *The Catcher in the Rye* is as appropriate to our age as *Huckleberry Finn* is to an earlier America. Salinger's novel, in fact, suggests great truths about our times, as Whitman's *Democratic Vistas* did, in polemic form, about an earlier age that was cankered, crude, materialistic, depraved. *The Catcher in the Rye* has the same awesome relevance to our collective civilized fate that more subtly pervades Mark Twain's masterpiece. Nowhere is its literary descent from *Huckleberry Finn* more clearly seen than in its critical modern dramatization of moral and social themes.

VI

To conclude, the two novels are clearly related in narrative pattern and style, characterization of the hero and critical import—the three areas discussed in this paper. The relationship argues the continuing vitality of Huck's archetypal story, absorbed by generations and still creatively at work in contemporary thought and art. *The Catcher in the Rye* takes its place in that literary tradition—spreading beyond Anderson, Lardner, Hemingway, Faulkner—that has one of its great sources in *Huckleberry Finn*.[2] But the literary kinship of these two novels presupposes a type of cultural continuity more basic than the dynamics of literary tradition or than the persistence of Huck's story in the popular imagination. We have seen that each author responds sensitively to the times he depicts, appropriately choosing his facts and shaping his language and meaning to portray the social and moral realities clustered in and about his hero. Yet the resulting differences do not obscure the similarity in the conformations of character and social relationships that emerge. Fundamentally these books are brothers under the skin because they reflect a slowly developing but always recognizable pattern of moral and social meaning that is part of the active experience of young Americans let loose in the world, in this century and the last. Independently and in his own right, each author has probed beneath surface facts—so dramatically contrasted in Huck's and Holden's environments—to the experiential continuity of American life.

Editor's Note: "Mark Twain and J. D. Salinger: A Study in Literary Continuity" is reprinted, by permission of Edgar Branch and *American Quarterly*, from *American Quarterly*, IX (1957), pp. 144–159.

Professor Branch, of Miami University, Ohio, is the author of *The Literary Apprenticeship of Mark Twain* and *James T. Farrell*.

---

[2] See, for example: Horace Gregory (ed.), *The Portable Sherwood Anderson* (New York: The Viking Press, 1949), pp. 8–9; Irving Howe, *Sherwood Anderson* (New York: William Sloane Associates, 1951), pp. 94, 124–27; Gilbert Seldes (ed.), *The Portable Ring Lardner* (New York: The Viking Press, 1946), pp. 1–2, 13–15; Carlos Baker, *Hemingway the Writer as Artist* (Princeton, N. J.: Princeton University Press, 1952), pp. 180–81; Philip Young, *Ernest Hemingway* (New York: Rinehart and Company, 1952), pp. 159–61, 181–212; Malcolm Cowley (ed.), *The Portable Faulkner* (New York: The Viking Press, 1946), p. 22; Randall Stewart and Dorothy Bethurum (eds.), *Modern American Narration, Mark Twain, Ernest Hemingway, William Faulkner* (Chicago: Scott Foresman and Company, 1954), "Foreword."

HENRY JAMES

1843-1916

Henry James had inherited wealth and devoted his consequent liberty to philosophy and theology. His older brother was William James, the philosopher and psychologist. Besides providing the fruitful cultural atmosphere of New York City for his family, Henry's father took the boys to Europe. There, from the age of twelve to seventeen, Henry was exposed to the influence of London, Geneva, and Paris. In 1860, the family returned to Newport. An injury, probably to his back, prevented James from serving in the Civil War. He went to Harvard Law School in 1862. Two years later he began to contribute stories and reviews to magazines. His first important publications were *A Passionate Pilgrim and Other Tales* (1875) and *Roderick Hudson* (1876), a novel in serial form. In the years leading up to these works, James had been devoting himself increasingly to writing and to absorbing the best of literary influences in America and Europe, including particularly Hawthorne, Lowell, Howells, George Eliot, Flaubert, and Turgenev. In 1876, after periodic stays in Cambridge, New York, and the major cities of Europe, he made London his home, and in 1915 he declared himself an English citizen, partly in objection to American reticence in World War I.

The fruits of James's early maturity include *The American* (1877), *Daisy Miller* (1879), *The Portrait of a Lady* (1881), and *The Princess Casamassima* (1886). His later masterpieces, reflecting his development of an increas-

273

ingly complex, involuted style, include *The Wings of the Dove,* (1902), *The Ambassadors* (1903), and *The Golden Bowl* (1904). In addition to his prolific fictional ouput, James has bestowed upon us a body of important literary criticism, particularly in his *Hawthorne* (1879), *Partial Portraits* (1888), *Notes on Novelists* (1914), and the Prefaces to his own novels (1907). Also of interest are his autobiographical works, *A Small Boy and Others* (1913) *Notes of a Son and Brother* (1914), and *The Middle Years* (1917, unfinished).

'DAISY MILLER':
AN ABORTIVE QUEST FOR
INNOCENCE

JAMES W. GARGANO

When John Foster Kirk rejected *Daisy Miller* as "an outrage on American girlhood," he unhappily misled critics of Henry James's novel into an obsessive preoccupation with its heroine. In his preface to the New York edition, James himself, perhaps still smarting from his rebuff, waives consideration of other aspects of the novel in his excessive concern with justifying his portrait of the maligned Daisy. Howells, too, because of the nature of his subject in *Heroines of Fiction,* focuses discussion of the novel on the appealing heroine.

Critical preoccupation with Daisy has fostered the view that the theme of the novel is the peril of a good but naïve American girl in a stiffly conventional society. This simplification ignores the fact that Frederick Winterbourne, as the central intelligence, represents the consciousness upon which the events and characters of the novel have the greatest impact. Since he is always on the scene, observing, discriminating, and seeking to unravel the mystery of the enigmatic Daisy, the drama must, if James' art can be said to have any intention, structurally center in him. He, I believe, is the subject of the novel and not merely the lens through which Daisy's career is seen. His story has a richness that makes *Daisy Miller* more than a thin commentary on the lawless innocence of the American girl.

Winterbourne's visit to Vevey begins an experience which can be described, in one of James' favorite words, as an "initiation." In other words, Winterbourne leaves a world of fixed values, and adventures into a foreign one where only innate sensibility and large sympathy can guide him and where commitment to a restrictive code will surely hurt him. His attraction to Daisy, by wrenching him out of his moral and social insularity, offers him an opportunity to enlarge his consciousness and gain the psychic fulfilment that James' characters constantly seek and very rarely find in love. Thus, for all her independent charm, Daisy exists to test Winterbourne's ability to grow beyond his hitherto narrow and one-sided state into a fully realized human being.

Considered as Winterbourne's story, *Daisy Miller* is essentially the study of a young man's quest for innocence, a virtue from which his society has alienated itself. It is by no means accidental that Winterbourne meets Daisy in a garden—commonly associated with innocence—or that the severe Mrs. Costello describes the girl as romping "on from day to day, from hour to hour, as they did in the Golden Age." Indeed, the *mise-en-scène* of the first section of the novel cleverly foreshadows the later conflict between innocence (here related to freedom) and the dark assumptions with which Winterbourne faces life. Winterbourne is visiting Vevey, which, because it resembles "an American watering-place," exhibits a more relaxed social life than is to be found elsewhere in Europe. Vevey is further identified with freedom by its proximity to the Castle of Chillon, unmistakably associated with Bonivard, a famous foe of tyranny. With typical finesse, James immediately emphasizes the spiritual distance between Vevey and Winterbourne, who "had an old attachment for the little capital of Calvinism." Certainly Geneva, later referred to "as the dark old city at the other end of the lake," symbolizes a rigidly conventional way of life whose forms mask a Puritan distrust of spontaneous and natural behavior. Winterbourne, who significantly attended school in Geneva and has many friends there, constantly assess his new experiences by the standards of his spiritual home.

Vevey is the appropriate scene for Winterbourne's reencounter with a bewildering girl who "looked extremely innocent." But since innocence is the very thing in which Geneva has lost faith, Winterbourne consistently misreads Daisy's character and seeks to ferret out the *arrière-pensée,* the dubious motive behind her artless conversation. Still, his admiration of her constitutes a self-betrayal, a persistent belief in innocence perhaps rooted in his American origin and fortified by the romantic idealism of youth. Lacking as yet a fatal rigidity, he is offered an opportunity to discover innocence and escape the propriety that menaces the full flowering of his nature.

Winterbourne's initiation begins in a comic manner calculated to show his inability to appreciate instinctively the innocence of Daisy's character. When, contrary to the code of Geneva, he speaks to the unmarried Daisy, he wonders whether "he has gone too far." He risks "an observation on the beauty of the scene" and wrongly assumes that an excursion to Chillon with the girl must perforce include her mother as chaperone. When he attempts to classify her, she undermines all of his stuffy and inapplicable generalizations. He decides that she may be "cold," "austere," and "prim" only to find her spontaneous and as "decently limpid as the very cleanest water."

Winterbourne's perplexity in the presence of innocence indicates the extent to which he is "morally muddled." Unable to believe in natural goodness, which usurps freedoms of speech and action, he must analyze it with the suspicious rationalism of Geneva and thus miss its essential luster. Distrusting the authority of his feeling for Daisy's "natural elegance," he complacently pronounces her a flirt:

> Winterbourne was almost grateful for having found the formula that applied to Miss Daisy Miller. He leaned back in his seat; . . . he wondered what were the regular conditions and limitations of one's intercourse with a pretty American flirt.

Winterbourne's comic ineptness demonstrates how poorly Geneva's formulas have prepared him to understand innocence.

His self-assurance is so halfhearted, however, that he takes his problem to his aunt, Mrs. Costello, the most reliable social authority he knows. Going to her with "a desire for trustworthy information," he suddenly betrays an inchoate perception of Daisy's nature. Though he uncritically allows Mrs. Costello's reference to the girl's "intimacy" with Eugenio to "make up his mind about Miss Daisy," he generously declares, "Ah you're cruel! . . . She's a very innocent girl!" In spite of his aunt's innuendoes, he holds to his purpose of taking Daisy to Chillon. Indeed, his momentary defection from Geneva appears so extreme that Mrs. Costello is confirmed in her refusal to be presented to his new acquaintance.

Winterbourne's recognition of Daisy's innocence may represent impatience with the stringent code of Geneva, but it can by no means be interpreted as thoroughgoing disillusionment. He sees only enough to be less blind than Mrs. Costello; if he departs from the dictates of propriety, he does so with customary prudence. Lacking the ardor and recklessness of a rebel, he is temperamentally doomed to swing in permanent vacillation between opposing claims. He has sensibility enough to be "touched, mortified, shocked" when he perceives Daisy's hurt at Mrs. Costello's refusal to see her; yet he is too tepid to do anything more than think of sacrificing "his aunt—conversationally." Even his trip to Chillon—perhaps his most daring action—is followed by his symbolical return to the bleak city of conformity. In his paralyzing introspection and most of his behavior, he is a morbid, though superficially cultivated, latter-day Puritan.

Nevertheless, before his visit to Rome, Winterbourne has found Daisy's innocence appealing enough to defend. On the free soil of Vevey, he has even dared to take an unchaperoned young lady on an excursion. He may cut a comic figure in his attempts to reduce Daisy's ingenuous license to formula, but his mind is open to impressions that the bigoted Mrs. Costello refuses to receive. Since Rome, however, is the city where one behaves as the Romans do, Winterbourne's capacity for freedom and conversely the extent of his commitment to Geneva are tested there.

The Roman phase of the novel ironically dramatizes the disintegration of Winterbourne's somewhat nebulous faith in innocence. In the presence of Daisy's critics, he defends her in a manner which reveals a desire to strengthen his own faltering belief in her. To Mrs. Costello's indictment of the Millers, he timidly responds: "They are very ignorant—very innocent only, and utterly uncivilized." When Mrs. Walker's carriage appears in the Pincian Gardens to rescue Daisy from her "tryst" with Giovanelli, Winterbourne again insists upon the girl's innocence, but as he does so he "reasoned in his own troubled interest." Indeed, before Mrs. Walker's intrusion, he had himself explored all manner of doubts about the "fineness" of Daisy's character. Obviously, then, in his debates with the girl's critics he is confronting, and only temporarily triumphing over, his own sinister suspicions. Basically, he never triumphs at all, for after his colloquy with Mrs. Costello he "checked his impulse to go straightway" to visit Daisy and after his bout with Mrs. Walker he confesses, "I suspect, Mrs. Walker, that you and I have lived too long at Geneva." His evaluation of himself is so accurate that when Mrs. Walker affords him a chance to return to Daisy, and thus to conquer his doubts, he permits mere appearance, "the couple united beneath the parasol," to undermine his insecure faith in innocence.

Winterbourne's desertion of Daisy in the Pincian Gardens (again the garden suggests innocence) characterizes him as incapable of embracing values larger than those of his parochial society. His acuteness in recognizing the cruelties of Mrs. Costello and Mrs. Walker is not vision, and his persistent defense of Daisy is hardly courage. With a finicky, formal taste, he wants his innocence well-bred and prudent, not realizing that innocence is by nature averse to calculation. When Daisy asks him if he thinks she should desert Giovanelli and enter Mrs. Walker's carriage, he advises her to "listen to the voice of civilized society." Sententiously, stiffly— Daisy describes him as having no more "give than a ramrod,"—he lectures her about the "custom of the country" and the "ineptitude of innocence."

His final incapacity to champion innocence is shown when, Mrs. Walker having turned her back on Daisy, he is "greatly touched" by the girl's "blighted grace" but characteristically does nothing more than accuse Mrs. Walker of cruelty. It is no wonder that he soon feels "that holding fast to a belief in [Daisy's] 'innocence' was more and more but a matter of gallantry too fine-spun for use." He admits that "he had helplessly missed her, and now it was too late." Yet, he cannot completely abandon his belief in an innocence that once charmed as well as bewildered him until he discovers Daisy and Giovanelli together in the Colosseum at night. Then, with "final horror" as well as "final relief," he capitulates to Geneva:

> It was as if a sudden clearance had taken place in the ambiguity of the poor girl's appearances and the whole riddle of her contradictions had grown easy to read. She was a young lady about the shades of whose perversity a foolish puzzled gentleman need no longer trouble his head or his heart. That once questionable quantity *had* no shades—it was a mere black little blot.

Winterbourne's quest has thus ended in a typically Puritan repudiation of innocence. Now, giving greater faith to his new discovery of Daisy's "evil nature" than he had ever given to his timid belief in her goodness, he spurns her with a severity as inhumane as Mrs. Costello's and Mrs. Walker's. His last conversation with the girl is a caustic revelation that his nature has shriveled rather than expanded. He counters her assurance that she is not engaged to Giovanelli with a confession of indifference made "with infinite point." "It was a wonder," says James, "how she didn't wince for it." Essentially the slave of a society that worships form and ignores humane considerations, he lifts his hat and leaves her while Daisy cries out, "I don't care . . . whether I have the Roman fever or not!" Even Daisy's death-bed message, reminding him of their trip to Chillon (freedom) and disavowing the rumors concerning Giovanelli and herself, leaves him intransigent and unaffected.

Winterbourne's harsh certainty about Daisy's character convicts him of a fatal coldness of heart fostered by the sin-obsessed society of Geneva. Having failed to respond to Daisy's need for affection, he can gain enlightenment only from without, never from within. Ultimately, he must be convinced of Daisy's purity by the impressionable fortune hunter, Giovanelli. Their short conversation after Daisy's burial brings home to Winterbourne how irremediably the dark old city has played him false. He has seen innocence—the only kind of innocence this complex world affords—and has conspired with Mrs. Costello and Mrs. Walker to kill it. Listening to Giovanelli's elegy to Daisy, he is made to face his own incredible error:

> "She was the most beautiful young lady I ever saw, and the most amiable." To which he added in a moment: "Also— naturally!—the most innocent."
>
> Winterbourne sounded him with hard dry eyes, but presently repeated his words, "The most innocent?"
>
> It came somehow so much too late that our friend could only glare at its having come at all.

Months later Winterbourne reveals to Mrs. Costello that he has brooded over and measured the depth of his mistake. Nevertheless, though he locates the cause of his failure in his "foreign" education, his wisdom culminates in a retreat to Geneva. The quest for innocence has thus merely brought him experience of his own lugubrious inadequacy to transcend—even with the advantage of knowledge—the sham and cruel proprieties of the dark old city.

Editor's Note: " 'Daisy Miller,' an Abortive Quest for Innocence" is reprinted by permission of James W. Gargano and the Duke University Press from *South Atlantic Quarterly*, LIX (1960), pp. 114–120.

Professor Gargano is Chairman of the Department of English at Washington and Jefferson College. He was Fulbright lecturer, 1963–64, at the University of Caen, France. His numerous publications have been primarily on Poe and Henry James, but also on Whitman, Melville, Hawthorne, Howells, Stephen Crane, and others.

THE FIRST PARAGRAPH OF
THE AMBASSADORS:
AN EXPLICATION[1]

IAN WATT

I

Strether's first question, when he reached the hotel, was about his friend; yet on his learning that Waymarsh was apparently not to arrive till evening he was not wholly disconcerted. A telegram from him bespeaking a room 'only 5 if not noisy', reply paid, was produced for the inquirer at the office, so that the understanding they should meet at Chester rather than at Liverpool remained to that extent sound. The same secret principle, however, that had prompted Strether not absolutely to desire Waymarsh's 10 presence at the dock, that had led him thus to postpone for a few hours his enjoyment of it, now operated to make him feel he could still wait without disappointment. They would dine together at the worst, and, with all respect to dear old Waymarsh—if not even, for the matter, to him- 15 self—there was little fear that in the sequel they shouldn't see enough of each other. The principle I have just mentioned as operating had been, with the most newly disembarked of the two men, wholly instinctive—the fruit of a

---

[1] A paper given at the Ninth Annual Conference of Non-Professorial University Teachers of English, at Oxford on April 5th, 1959. I am very grateful for the many criticisms and suggestions made in the course of the subsequent discussion; in preparing the paper for publication I have taken as much account of them as was possible, short of drastic expansion or alteration. I also acknowledge my debt to Dorothea Krook, Frederick C. Crews, and Henry Nash Smith. **Editor's Note:** Professor Watt's original essay began with a prefatory summary, here omitted, of the historical meaning and techniques of "explication." Consequently, the essay as reprinted here begins rather abruptly.

sharp sense that, delightful as it would be to find himself
20 looking, after so much separation, into his comrade's face,
his business would be a trifle bungled should he simply
arrange for this countenance to present itself to the nearing steamer as the first "note" of Europe. Mixed with everything was the apprehension, already, on Strether's part,
25 that it would, at best, throughout, prove the note of Europe
in quite a sufficient degree.[2]

. . . It seems a fairly ordinary sort of prose, but for its faint air of
elaborate portent; and on second reading its general quality reminds one of what Strether is later to observe—approvingly—in
Maria Gostrey: an effect of 'expensive, subdued suitability'. There's
certainly nothing particularly striking in the diction or syntax;
none of the immediate drama or rich description that we often get
at the beginning of novels; and certainly none of the sensuous concreteness that, until recently, was regarded as a chief criterion of
good prose in our long post-imagistic phase: if anything, the pas-

---

[2] Henry James, *The Ambassadors* (Revised Collected Edition, Macmillan:
London, 1923). Since there are a few variants that have a bearing on the argument, it seems desirable to give a collation of the main editions; P is the
periodical publication (*The North American Review*, CLXXVI, 1903); 1A the first
American editon (Harper and Brothers, New York, 1903); 1E the first English
edition (Methuen and Co., London, 1903); N.Y., the 'New York Edition,' New
York and London, 1907–9 (the London Macmillan edition used the sheets of
the American edition); CR the 'Collected Revised Edition,' London and New
York, 1921–31 (which uses the text of the New York Edition). It should perhaps
be explained that the most widely used editions in England and America make
misleading claims about their text: the 'Everyman' edition claims to use the
text 'of the revised Collected Edition', but actually follows the 1st English edition
in the last variant; while the 'Anchor' edition, claiming to be 'a faithful copy
of the text of the Methuen first edition', actually follows the first American
edition, including the famous misplaced chapters.

   1.5.   *reply paid* NY, CR; *with the answer paid* P, 1A, 1E.

   1.5.   *inquirer* P, 1A, 1E, CR; *enquirer* NY.

   1.6.   *Understanding they* NY, CR; *understanding that they*, P, 1A, 1E,

   1.12.   *feel he* NY, CR; *feel that he* P, 1A, 1E.

   1.15.   *Shouldn't* CR; *shouldn't* NY; *should not* P, 1A, 1E.

11.17–18.   *Newly disembarked,* all eds. except P: *Newly-disembarked.*

   1.22.   *arrange that this countenance to present* NY, CR; *arrange that this
         countenance should present* P, 1A, 1E.

   1.23.   *"note" of Europe* CR; *"note", for him, of Europe,* P, 1A, 1E; *"note",
         of Europe,* NY.

   1.25.   *that it would* P, 1A, NY, CR; *that he would,* 1E.

sage is conspicuously un-sensuous and un-concrete, a little dull perhaps, and certainly not easy reading.

The difficulty isn't one of particularly long or complicated sentences: actually they're of fairly usual length: I make it an average of 41 words; a little, but not very much, longer than James' average of 35 (in Book 2, ch. 2. of *The Ambassadors,* according to R. W. Short's count, in his very useful article 'The Sentence Structure of Henry James' (*American Literature,* XVIII [March 1946], 71–88.[3] The main cause of difficulty seems rather to come from what may be called the delayed specification of referents: 'Strether' and 'the hotel' and 'his friend' are mentioned before we are told who or where they are. But this difficulty is so intimately connected with James's general narrative technique that it may be better to begin with purely verbal idiosyncrasies, which are more easily isolated. The most distinctive ones in the passage seem to be these: a preference for non-transitive verbs; many abstract nouns; much use of 'that'; a certain amount of elegant variation to avoid piling up personal pronouns and adjectives such as 'he', 'his' and 'him'; and the presence of a great many negatives and near-negatives.

By the preference for non-transitive verbs I mean three related habits: a great reliance on copulatives—'Strether's first question *was* about his friend'; '*was* apparently not to arrive': a frequent use of the passive voice—'*was* not wholly *disconcerted';* 'a telegram . . . *was produced';* 'his business *would be* a trifle *bungled'*: and the employment of many intransitive verbs—'the understanding . . . remained . . . sound'; 'the . . . principle . . . operated to'. My count of all the verbs in the indicative would give a total of 14 passive, copulative or intransitive uses as opposed to only 6 transitive ones: and there are in addition frequent infinitive, participial, or gerundial uses of transitive verbs, in all of which the active nature of the subject-verb-and-object sequence is considerably abated—'on his learning'; 'bespeaking a room'; 'not absolutely to desire'; 'led him thus to postpone'.

This relative infrequency of transitive verbal usages in the passage is associated with the even more pronounced tendency towards using abstract nouns as subjects of main or subordinate clauses: 'question'; 'understanding'; 'the same secret principle'; 'the prin-

[3] I am also indebted to the same author's 'Henry James's World of Images', *PMLA,* LXVIII (Dec., 1953), 943–960.

ciple'; 'his business'. If one takes only the main clauses, there are four such abstract nouns as subjects, while only three main clauses have concrete and particular subjects ('he', or 'they').[4]

I detail these features only to establish that in this passage, at least, there is a clear quantitative basis for the common enough view that James's late prose style is characteristically abstract; more explicitly, that the main grammatical subjects are very often nouns for mental ideas, 'question', 'principle', etc.; and that the verbs—because they are mainly used either non-transitively, or in infinitive, participial and gerundial forms,—tend to express states of being rather than particular finite actions affecting objects.

The main use of abstractions is to deal at the same time with many objects or events rather than single and particular ones: and we use verbs that denote states of being rather than actions for exactly the same reason—their much more general applicability. But in this passage, of course, James isn't in the ordinary sense making abstract or general statements; it's narrative, not expository prose; what needs exploring, therefore, are the particular literary imperatives which impose on his style so many of the verbal and syntactical qualities of abstract and general discourse; of expository rather than narrative prose.

Consider the first sentence. The obvious narrative way of making things particular and concrete would presumably be 'When Strether reached the hotel, he first asked "Has Mr. Waymarsh arrived yet?"' Why does James say it the way he does? One effect is surely that, instead of a sheer stated event, we get a very special view of it; the mere fact that actuality has been digested into reported speech—the question 'was about his friend'—involves a narrator to do the job, to interpret the action, and also a presumed audience that he does it for: and by implication, the heat of the action itself must have cooled off somewhat for the translation and analysis of the events into this form of statement to have had time to occur. Lastly, making the subject of the sentence 'question' rather than 'he', has the effect of subordinating the particular actor, and therefore the particular act, to a much more general perspective: mental rather than physical, and subjective rather than objective; 'question' is a word which involves analysis of a physical event into terms of meaning

---

[4] Sentences one and four are compound or multiple, but in my count I haven't included the second clause in the latter—'there was little fear': though if we can talk of the clause having a subject it's an abstract one—'fear'.

and intention: it involves, in fact, both Strether's mind and the narrator's. The narrator's, because he interprets Strether's act: if James had sought the most concrete method of taking us into Strether's mind—' "Has Mr. Waymarsh come yet?" I at once asked'— he would have obviated the need for the implied external categoriser of Strether's action. But James disliked the 'mere platitude of statement' involved in first-person narrative; partly, presumably, because it would merge Strether's consciousness into the narrative, and not isolate it for the reader's inspection. For such isolation, a more expository method is needed: no confusion of subject and object, as in first-person narration, but a narrator forcing the reader to pay attention to James's primary objective—Strether's mental and subjective state.

The 'multidimensional' quality of the narrative, with its continual implication of a community of three minds—Strether's, James's, and the reader's—isn't signalled very obviously until the fourth sentence—'The principle I have just mentioned as operating . . .'; but it's already been established tacitly in every detail of diction and structure, and it remains pervasive. One reason for the special demand James's fictional prose makes on our attention is surely that there are always at least three levels of development— all of them subjective: the characters' awareness of events: the narrator's seeing of them; and our own trailing perception of the relation between these two.

The primary location of the narrative in a mental rather than a physical continuum gives the narrative a great freedom from the restrictions of particular time and place. Materially, we are, of course, in Chester, at the hotel—characteristically 'the hotel' because a fully particularised specification—'The Pied Bull Inn' say— would be an irrelevant brute fact which would distract attention from the mental train of thought we are invited to partake in. But actually we don't have any pressing sense of time and place: we feel ourselves to be spectators, rather specifically, of Strether's thought processes, which easily and imperceptibly range forwards and backwards both in time and space. Sentence three, for example, begins in the past, at the Liverpool dock; sentence four looks forward to the reunion later that day, and to its many sequels: such transitions of time and place are much easier to effect when the main subjects of the sentences are abstract: a 'principle' exists independently of its context.

The multiplicity of relations—between narrator and object, and between the ideas in Strether's mind—held in even suspension throughout the narrative, is presumably the main explanation for the number of 'thats' in the passage, as well as of the several examples of elegant variation. There are 9 'thats'—only two of them demonstrative and the rest relative pronouns (or conjunctions or particles if you prefer those terms); actually there were no less than three more of them in the first edition, which James removed from the somewhat more colloquial and informal New York edition; while there are several other 'thats' implied—in 'the principle [that] I have just mentioned', for instance.

The number of 'thats' follows from two habits already noted in the passage. 'That' characteristically introduces relative clauses dealing not with persons but with objects, including abstractions; and it is also used to introduce reported speech—'on his learning that Waymarsh'—not 'Mr. Waymarsh isn't here'. Both functions are combined in the third sentence where we get a triple definition of a timeless idea based on the report of three chronologically separate events 'the same secret principle that had prompted Strether not absolutely to desire Waymarsh's presence at the dock, that had led him thus to postpone for a few hours his enjoyment of it, now operated to make him feel that he could still wait without disappointment'.

Reported rather than direct speech also increases the pressure towards elegant variation: the use, for example, in sentence 1 of his friend,' where in direct speech it would be 'Mr. Waymarsh' (and the reply—'*He* hasn't come yet'). In the second sentence—'a telegram . . . was produced for the inquirer'—'inquirer' is needed because 'him' has already been used for Waymarsh just above; of course, 'the inquirer' is logical enough after the subject of the first sentence has been an abstract noun—'question'; and the epithet also gives James an opportunity for underlining the ironic distance and detachment with which we are invited to view his dedicated 'inquirer', Strether. Later, when Strether is 'the most newly disembarked of the two men', we see how both elegant variation and the grammatical subordination of physical events are related to the general Jamesian tendency to present characters and actions on a plane of abstract categorisation; the mere statement, 'Mr. Waymarsh had already been in England for [so many] months', would itself go far to destroy the primarily mental continuum in which the paragraph as a whole exists.

The last general stylistic feature of the passage listed above was the use of negative forms. There are 6 'noes' or 'nots' in the first 4 sentences; four implied negatives—'postpone'; 'without disappointment'; 'at the worst'; 'there was little fear': and two qualifications that modify positiveness of affirmation—'not wholly', and 'to that extent'. This abundance of negatives has no doubt several functions: it enacts Strether's tendency to hesitation and qualification; it puts the reader into the right judicial frame of mind; and it has the further effect of subordinating concrete events to their mental reflection; 'Waymarsh was not to arrive', for example, is not a concrete statement of a physical event: it is subjective—because it implies an expectation in Strether's mind (which was not fulfilled); and it has an abstract quality—because while Waymarsh's arriving would be particular and physical, his *not* arriving is an idea, a non-action. More generally, James's great use of negatives or near-negatives may also, perhaps, be regarded as part of his subjective and abstractive tendency: there are no negatives in nature but only in the human consciousness.

II

The most obvious grammatical features of what Richard Chase has called Henry James's 'infinitely syntactical language' (*The American Novel and its Tradition,* New York, 1957), can, then, be shown to reflect the essential imperatives of his narrative point of view; and they could therefore lead into a discussion of the philosophical qualities of his mind, as they are discussed, for example, by Dorothea Krook in her notable article 'The Method of the Later Works of Henry James' (*London Magazine,* I [1954], 55–70); our passage surely exemplifies James's power 'to generalise to the limit the particulars of experience', and with it the characteristic way in which both his 'perceptions of the world itself, and his perceptions of the logic of the world . . . happen simultaneously, are part of a single comprehensive experience'. Another aspect of the connection between James's metaphysic and his method as a novelist has inspired a stimulating stylistic study—Carlo Izzo's 'Henry James, Scrittore Sintattico' (*Studi Americani,* II [1956], 127–142). The connection between thought and style finds its historical perspective in John Henry Raleigh's illuminating study 'Henry James: The Poetics of Empiricism' (*PMLA,* LXVI [1951], 107–123), which establishes connections between Lockean epistemology and James's extreme, almost anarchic, individualism; while this epistemological preoccupation, which is central to Quentin Anderson's view of how James worked out his father's cosmology in fictional terms (*The American Henry James,* New Brunswick, 1957), also leads towards another large general question, the concern with 'point of view', which became a crucial problem in the history and criticism of fiction under the influence of the sceptical relativism of the late nineteenth-century.

In James's case, the problem is fairly complicated. He may be classed as an 'Impressionist', concerned, that is, to show not as much the events themselves, but the impressions which they make on the characters. But James's continual need to generalize and place and order, combined with his absolute demand for a point of view that would be plastic enough to allow him freedom for the formal 'architectonics' of the novelists' craft, eventually involved him in a very idiosyncratic kind of multiple Impressionism: idiosyncratic because the dual presence of Strether's consciousness and of that of the narrator, who translates what he sees there into more general terms, makes the narrative point of view both intensely individual and yet ultimately social.

Another possible direction of investigation would be to show that the abstractness and indirection of James's style are essentially the result of this characteristic multiplicity of his vision. There is, for example, the story reported by Edith Wharton that after his first stroke James told Lady Prothero that 'in the very act of falling . . . he heard in the room a voice which was distinctly, it seemed, not his own, saying: "So here it is at last, the distinguished thing".' James, apparently, could not but see even his own most fateful personal experience, except as evoked by some other observer's voice in terms of the long historical and literary tradition of death. Carlo Izzo regards this tendency as typical of the Alexandrian style, where there is a marked disparity between the rich inheritance of the means of literary expression, and the meaner creative world which it is used to express; but the defence of the Jamesian habit of mind must surely be that what the human vision shares with that of animals is presumably the perception of concrete images, not the power to conceive universals: such was Aristotle's notion of man's distinguishing capacity. The universals in the present context are presumably the awareness that behind every petty individual circumstance there ramifies an endless network of general moral, social and historical relations. Henry James's style can therefore be seen as supremely civilized effort to relate every event and every moment of life to the full complexity of its circumambient conditions.

Obviously James's multiple awareness can go too far; and in the later novels it often poses the special problem that we do not quite know whether the awareness implied in a given passage is the narrator's or that of his character. Most simply, a pronoun referring to the subject of a preceding clause is always liable to give trouble if one hasn't been very much aware of what the grammatical subject of that preceding clause was; in the last sentence of the paragraph, for example, 'the apprehension, already, on Strether's part, that . . . it would, at best, . . . prove the "note" of Europe,' 'it' refers to Waymarsh's countenance: but this isn't at first obvious; which is no doubt why, in his revision of the periodical version for the English edition James replaced 'it' by 'he'—simpler, grammatically, but losing some of the ironic visual precision of the original. More seriously, because the narrator's consciousness and Strether's are both present, we often don't know whose mental operations and evaluative judgments are involved in particular cases. We pass, for instance, from the objective analysis of sentence 3 where the analytic terminology of 'the same secret principle' must be the responsibility of the narrator, to what must be a verbatim quotation of Strether's mind in sentence 4: 'with all respect to dear old Waymarsh' is obviously Strether's licensed familiarity.

But although the various difficulties of tense, voice, and reference require a vigilance of attention in the reader which some have found too much to give, they are not in themselves very considerable: and what perhaps is much more in need of attention is how the difficulties arising from the multiplicity of points of view don't by any means prevent James from ordering all the elements of his narrative style into an amazingly precise means of expression: and it is this positive, and in the present case, as it seems to me, triumphant, mastery of the difficulties which I want next to consider.

Our passage is not, I think, James either at his most memorable or at his most idiosyncratic: *The Ambassadors* is written with considerable sobriety and has, for example, little of the vivid and direct style of the early part of *The Wings of the Dove,* or of the happy symbolic complexities of *The Golden Bowl.* Still, the passage is fairly typical of the later James; and I think it can be proved that all or at least nearly all the idiosyncrasies of diction or syntax in the present passage are fully justified by the particular emphases they create.

The most flagrant eccentricity of diction is presumably that where James writes 'the most newly disembarked of the two men' (lines 16-17). 'Most' may very well be a mere slip; and it must certainly seem indefensible to any one who takes it as an absolute rule that the comparative must always be used when only two items are involved.[5] But a defence is at least possible. 'Most newly disembarked' means something rather different from 'more newly disembarked.' James, it may be surmised, did not want to compare the recency of the two men's arrival, but to inform us that Strether's arrival was 'very' or as we might say, 'most' recent; the use of the superlative also had the advantage of suggesting the long and fateful tradition of transatlantic disembarcations in general.

The reasons for the other main syntactical idiosyncrasies in the passage are much clearer. In the first part of the opening sentence, for example, the separation of subject—'question'—from verb—'was' —by the longish temporal clause 'when he reached the hotel', is no doubt a dislocation of normal sentence structure; but, of course, 'Strether' must be the first word of the novel: while, even more important, the delayed placing of the temporal clause, forces a pause after 'question' and thus gives it a very significant resonance. Similarly with the last sentence; it has several peculiarities, of which the placing of 'throughout' seems the most obvious. The sentence has three parts: the first and last are comparatively straightforward, but the middle is a massed block of portentous qualifications: 'Mixed with everything was the apprehension—already, on Strether's part, that he would, at best, throughout,—prove the note of Europe in quite a sufficient degree.' The echoing doom started by the connotation of 'apprehension'—reverberates through 'already', ('much more to come later') 'on Strether's part' ('even he knows') and 'at best' ('the worst has been envisaged, too'); but it is the final collapse of the terse rhythm of the parenthesis that isolates the rather awkwardly placed 'throughout', and thus enables James to sound the fine full fatal note; there is no limit to the poignant eloquence of 'throughout'. It was this effect, of course,

---

[5] Though consider *Rasselas*, ch. XXVIII: 'Both conditions may be bad, but they cannot both be worst'.

which dictated the preceding inversion which places 'apprehension' not at the start of the sentence, but in the middle where, largely freed from its syntactical nexus, it may be directly exposed to its salvos of qualification.

The mockingly fateful emphasis on 'throughout' tells us, if nothing had before, that James's tone is in the last analysis ironic, comic, or better, as I shall try to suggest, humorous. The general reasons for this have already been suggested. To use Maynard Mack's distinction (in his Preface to *Joseph Andrews,* Rinehart Editions, New York, 1948), 'the comic artist subordinates the presentation of life as experience, where the relationship between ourselves and the characters experiencing it is a primary one, to the presentation of life as a spectacle, where the primary relation is between himself and us as on-lookers'. In the James passage, the primacy of the relation between the narrator and the reader has already been noted, as has its connection with the abstraction of the diction, which brings home the distance between the narrator and Strether. Of course, the application of abstract diction to particular persons always tends towards irony,[6] because it imposes a dual way of looking at them: few of us can survive being presented as general representatives of humanity.

The paragraph, of course, is based on one of the classic contradictions in psychological comedy—Strether's reluctance to admit to himself that he has very mixed feelings about his friend: and James develops this with the narrative equivalent of *commedia dell'arte* technique: virtuoso feats of ironic balance, comic exaggeration, and deceptive hesitation conduct us on a complicated progress towards the foreordained illumination.

In structure, to begin with, the six sentences form three groups of two: each pair of them gives one aspect of Strether's delay; and they are arranged in an ascending order of complication so that the fifth sentence—72 words—is almost twice as long as any other, and is succeeded by the final sentence, the punch line, which is noticeably the shortest—26 words. The development of the ideas is as controlled as the sentence structure. Strether is obviously a man with an enormous sense of responsibility about personal relationships; so his first question is about his friend. That loyal *empressement,*

<hr>

[6] As I have argued in 'The Ironic Tradition in Augustan Prose from Swift to Johnson,' *Restoration and Augustan Prose* (Los Angeles, 1957).

however, is immediately checked by the balanced twin negatives that follow: 'on his learning that Waymarsh *was not* to arrive till evening, he *was not* wholly disconcerted': one of the diagnostic elements of irony, surely, is hyperbole qualified with mock-scrupulousness, such as we get in 'not wholly disconcerted'. Why there are limits to Lambert Strether's consternation is to transpire in the next sentence; Waymarsh's telegram bespeaking a room 'only if not noisy' is a laconic suggestion of that inarticulate worthy's habitually gloomy expectations—from his past experiences of the indignities of European hotel noise we adumbrate the notion that the cost of their friendly *rencontre* may be his sleeping in the street. In the second part of the sentence we have another similar, though more muted, hint: 'the understanding that they should meet in Chester rather than at Liverpool remained to that extent sound'; 'to that extent', no doubt, but to *any other?*—echo seems to answer 'No.'

In the second group of sentences we are getting into Strether's mind, and we have been prepared to relish the irony of its ambivalences. The negatived hyperbole of 'not absolutely to desire', turns out to mean 'postpone'; and, of course, a voluntarily postponed 'enjoyment' itself denotes a very modified rapture, although Strether's own consciousness of the problem is apparently no further advanced than that 'he could still wait without disappointment.' Comically loyal to what he would like to feel, therefore, we have him putting in the consoling reflection that 'they would dine together at the worst'; and the ambiguity of 'at the worst' is followed by the equally dubious thought: 'there was little fear that in the sequel they shouldn't see enough of each other.' That they should, in fact, see too much of each other; but social decorum and Strether's own loyalties demand that the outrage of the open statement be veiled in the obscurity of formal negation.

By the time we arrive at the climactic pair of sentences, we have been told enough for more ambitious effects to be possible. The twice-mentioned 'secret principle', it appears, is actually wholly 'instinctive' (line 18); but in other ways Strether is almost ludicrously self-conscious. The qualified hyperbole of 'his business would be a trifle bungled', underlined as it is by the alliteration, prepares us for a half-realized image which amusingly defines Strether's sense of his role: he sees himself, it appears, as the stage-manager of an enterprise in which his solemn obligations as an implicated friend are counterbalanced by his equally ceremonious sense that due decorums must also be attended to when he comes face to face with another friend of long ago—no less a person than Europe. It is, of course, silly of him, as James makes him acknowledge in the characteristic italicizing of 'the "note" of Europe';[7] but still, he does have a comically ponderous sense of protocol which leads him to feel that 'his business would be a trifle bungled' should he simply arrange for this countenance to present itself to the nearing steamer as the first 'note' of Europe. The steamer, one imagines, would not have turned hard astern at the proximity of Waymarsh's sacred rage; but Strether's fitness for ambassadorial functions is defined by his thinking in terms of 'arranging' for a certain countenance at the docks to give just the right symbolic greeting.

Strether's notion of what Europe demands also shows us the force of his aesthetic sense. But in the last sentence the metaphor, though it remains equally self-conscious, changes its mode of operation from the dramatic, aesthetic, and diplomatic, to something more scientific: for, although ten years ago I should not have failed to point out, and my readers would not, I suppose, have failed to applaud, the ambiguity of 'prove', it now seems to me that we must choose between its two possible meanings. James may be using 'prove' to mean that Waymarsh's face will 'turn out to be' the 'note of Europe' for Strether. But 'prove' in this sense is intransitive, and 'to be' would have to be supplied; it therefore seems more likely that James is using 'prove' in the older sense of 'to test': Waymarsh is indeed suited to the role of being the sourly acid test of the siren songs of Europe 'in quite a sufficient degree', as Strether puts it with solemn but arch understanding.

The basic development structure of the passage, then, is one of progressive and yet artfully delayed clarification; and this pattern is also typical of James's general novelistic method. The reasons for this are suggested in the Preface to *The Princess Casamassima*, where James deals with the problem of maintaining a balance between the intelligence a character must have to be interesting, and the bewilderment which is nevertheless an essential condition of the novel's having surprise, development, and tension: 'It seems probable that if we were never bewildered there would never be a story to tell about us.'

[7] See George Knox, 'James's Rhetoric Quotes,' *College English*, XVII (1956), 293–297.

In the first paragraph of *The Ambassadors* James apprises us both of his hero's supreme qualities and of his associated limitations. Strether's delicate critical intelligence is often blinkered by a highly vulnerable mixture of moral generosity towards others combined with an obsessive sense of personal inadequacy; we see the tension in relation to Waymarsh, as later we are to see it in relation to all his other friends; and we understand, long before Strether, how deeply it bewilders him; most poignantly about the true nature of Chad, Madame de Vionnet—and himself.

This counterpoint of intelligence and bewilderment is, of course, another reason for the split narrative point of view we've already noted: we and the narrator are inside Strether's mind, and yet we are also outside it, knowing more about Strether than he knows about himself. This is the classic posture of irony. Yet I think that to insist too exclusively on the ironic function of James's narrative point of view would be mistaken.

Irony has lately been enshrined as the supreme deity in the critical pantheon: but, I wonder, is there really anything so wonderful about being distant and objective? Who wants to see life only or mainly in intellectual terms? In art as in life we no doubt can have need of intellectual distance as well as of emotional commitment; but the uninvolvement of the artist surely doesn't go very far without the total involvement of the person; or, at least, without a deeper human involvement than irony customarily establishes. One could, I suppose, call the aesthetically perfect balance between distance and involvement, open or positive irony: but I'm not sure that humour isn't a better word, especially when the final balance is tipped in favour of involvement, of ultimate commitment to the characters; and I hope that our next critical movement will be the New Gelastics.

At all events, although the first paragraph alone doesn't allow the point to be established fully here, it seems to me that James's attitude to Strether is better described as humorous than ironical; we must learn like Maria Gostrey, to see him 'at last all comically, all tragically'. James's later novels in general are his most intellectual; but they are also, surely, his most compassionate: and in this particular paragraph Strether's dilemma is developed in such a way that we feel for him even more than we smile at him. This balance of intention, I think, probably explains why James keeps his irony in such a low key: we must be aware of Strether's 'secret' ambiv-

alence towards Waymarsh, but not to the point that his unawareness of it would verge on fatuity; and our controlling sympathy for
the causes of Strether's ambivalance turns what might have been
irony into something closer to what Constance Rourke characterizes
as James's typical 'low-keyed humor of defeat' (*American Humor*,
1931).

That James's final attitude is humorous rather than ironic is further suggested by the likeness of the basic structural technique of
the paragraph to that of the funny story—the incremental involvement in an endemic human perplexity which can only be resolved
by laughter's final acceptance of contradiction and absurdity. We
don't, in the end, see Strether's probing hesitations mainly as an
ironic indication by James of mankind's general muddlement; we
find it, increasingly, a touching example of how, despite all their
inevitable incongruities and shortcomings, human ties remain only,
but still, human.

Here it is perhaps James's very slowness and deliberation throughout the narrative which gives us our best supporting evidence:
greater love hath no man than hearing his friend out patiently.

III

The function of an introductory paragraph in a novel is presumably to introduce: and this paragraph surely has the distinction of being a supremely complex and inclusive introduction to a
novel. It introduces the hero, of course, and one of his companions;
also the time; the place; something of what's gone before. But
James has carefully avoided giving us the usual retrospective beginning, that pile of details which he scornfully termed a 'mere seated
mass of information'. All the details are scrupulously presented as
reflections from the novel's essential centre—the narrator's patterning of the ideas going forwards and backwards in Strether's mind.
Of course, this initially makes the novel more difficult, because what
we probably think of as primary—event and its setting—is subordi-
nated to what James thinks is—the mental drama of the hero's consciousness, which, of course, is not told but shown: scenically dramatized. At the same time, by selecting thoughts and events which
are representative of the book as a whole, and narrating them with
an abstractness which suggests their larger import, James introduces
the most general themes of the novel.

James, we saw, carefully arranged to make 'Strether's first question', the first three words; and, of course, throughout the novel, Strether is to go on asking questions—and getting increasingly dusty answers. This, it may be added, is stressed by the apparent aposiopesis: for a 'first' question when no second is mentioned, is surely an intimation that more are—in a way unknown to us or to Strether—yet to come. The later dislocations of normal word-order already noted above emphasize other major themes; the 'secret principle' in Strether's mind, and the antithesis Waymarsh-Europe, for instance.

The extent to which these processes were conscious on James's part cannot, of course, be resolved; but it is significant that the meeting with Maria Gostrey was interposed before the meeting with Waymarsh, which James had originally planned as his beginning in the long (20,000) word scenario of the plot which he prepared for *Harper's*. The unexpected meeting had many advantages; not least that James could repeat the first paragraph's pattern of delayed clarification in the structure of the first chapter as a whole. On Strether's mind we get a momentously clear judgment at the end of the second paragraph: 'there was detachment in his zeal, and curiosity in his indifference'; but then the meeting with Maria Gostrey, and its gay opportunities for a much fuller presentation of Strether's mind, intervene before Waymarsh himself finally appears at the end of the chapter; only then is the joke behind Strether's uneasy hesitations in the first paragraph brought to its hilariously blunt climax: 'It was already upon him even at that distance—Mr. Waymarsh was for *his* part joyless'.

One way of evaluating James's achievement in this paragraph, I suppose, would be to compare the opening of James's other novels, and with those of previous writers: but it would take too long to do more than sketch the possibilities of this approach. James's early openings certainly have some of the banality of the 'mere seated mass of information': in *Roderick Hudson* (1876), for example: 'Rowland Mallet had made his arrangements to sail for Europe on the 5th of September, and having in the interval a fortnight to spare, he determined to spend it with his cousin Cecilia, the widow of a nephew of his father. . . .' Later, James showed a much more comprehensive notion of what the introductory paragraph should attempt: even in the relatively simple and concrete opening of *The Wings of the Dove* (1902): 'She waited,

Kate Croy, for her father to come in, but he kept her unconscionably, and there were moments at which she showed herself, in the glass over the mantle, a face positively pale with irritation that had brought her to the point of going away without sight of him. . . .'
'She waited, Kate Croy'—an odd parenthetic apposition artfully contrived to prefigure her role throughout the novel—to wait.

One could, I suppose, find this sort of symbolic prefiguring in the work of earlier novelists; but never, I imagine, in association with all the other levels of introductory function that James manages to combine in a single paragraph. Jane Austen has her famous thematic irony in the opening of *Pride and Prejudice* (1813) : 'It is a truth universally acknowledged, that a single man in possession of a good fortune must be in want of a wife'; but pride and prejudice must come later. Dickens can hurl us overpoweringly into *Bleak House* (1852–3), into its time and place and general theme; but characters and opening action have to wait:

> London. Michaelmas Term lately over, and the Lord Chancellor sitting in Lincoln's Inn Hall. Implacable November weather. As much mud in the streets, as if the waters had but newly retired from the face of the earth, and it would not be wonderful to meet a Megalosaurus, forty feet long or so, waddling like an elephantine lizard up Holborn-Hill. Smoke lowering down from chimney-pots. . . .

In Dickens, characteristically, we get a loud note that sets the tone, rather than a polyphonic series of chords that contain all the later melodic developments, as in James. And either the Dickens method, or the 'mere seated mass of information', seem to be commonest kinds of opening in nineteenth-century novels. For openings that suggest something of James's ambitious attempt to achieve a prologue that is a synchronic introduction of all the main aspects of the narrative, I think that Conrad is his closest rival. But Conrad, whether in expository or dramatic vein, tends to an arresting initial vigour that has dangers which James's more muted tones avoid. In *An Outcast of the Islands* (1896), for example:

> When he stepped off the straight and narrow path of his peculiar honesty, it was with an inward assertion of unflinching resolve to fall back again into the monotonous but safe stride of virtue as soon as his little excursion into the wayside

quagmires had produced the desired effect. It was going to be a short episode—a sentence in brackets, so to speak, in the flowing tale of his life. . . .

Conrad's sardonic force has enormous immediate impact; but it surely gives too much away: the character, Willems, has been dissected so vigorously that it takes great effort for Conrad—and the reader—to revivify him later. The danger lurks even in the masterly combination of physical notation and symbolic evaluation at the beginning of *Lord Jim* (1900): 'He was an inch, perhaps two, under six feet . . .': the heroic proportion is for ever missed, by an inch, perhaps two; which is perhaps too much, to begin with.

It is not for me to assess how far I have succeeded in carrying out the general intentions with which I began, or how far similar methods of analysis would be applicable to other kinds of prose. As regards the explication of the passage itself, the main argument must by now be sufficiently clear, although a full demonstration would require a much wider sampling both of other novels and of other passages in *The Ambassadors*.[8] The most obvious and demonstrable features of James's prose style, its vocabulary and syntax, are direct reflections of his attitude to life and his conception of the novel; and these features, like the relation of the paragraph to the rest of the novel, and to other novels, make clear that the notorious idiosyncrasies of Jamesian prose are directly related to the imperatives which led him to develop a narrative texture as richly complicated and as highly organized as that of poetry.

No wonder James scorned translation and rejoiced, as he so engagingly confessed to his French translator, Auguste Monod, that his later works were 'locked fast in the golden cage of the *intraduisible*'. Translation could hardly do justice to a paragraph in which so many levels of meaning and implication are kept in continuous operation; in which the usual introductory exposition of time, place, character, and previous action, are rendered through an immediate immersion in the processes of the hero's mind as he's

---

[8] A similar analysis of eight other paragraphs selected at fifty page intervals revealed that, as would be expected, there is much variation: the tendency to use non-transitive verbs, and abstract nouns as subjects, for instance, seems to be strong throughout the novel, though especially so in analytic rather than narrative passages; but the frequent use of 'that' and of negative forms of statement does not recur significantly.

involved in perplexities which are characteristic of the novel as a whole and which are articulated in a mode of comic development which is essentially that, not only of the following chapter, but of the total structure. To have done all that is to have gone far towards demonstrating the contention which James announced at the end of the Preface to *The Ambassadors,* that 'the Novel remains still, under the right persuasion, the most independent, most elastic, most prodigious of literary forms'; and the variety and complexity of the functions carried out in the book's quite short first paragraph also suggest that, contrary to some notions, the demonstration is, as James claimed, made with 'a splendid particular economy'.

Editor's Note: "The First Paragraph of *The Ambassadors:* An Explication" is reprinted in a slightly revised form from *Essays in Criticism,* X (1960), pp. 250–274. Permission by Ian Watt.

A Professor of English at Stanford University, Ian Watt is best known for his work in the eighteenth century: *The Rise of the Novel: Studies in Defoe, Richardson and Fielding;* an edition of *Tristram Shandy;* and numerous articles and reviews; but he has also published a good deal on modern literature, especially fiction.

STEPHEN CRANE

1871-1900

Stephen Crane was the fourteenth child of the Reverend Jonathan Townley Crane, a Methodist minister. Born in Newark, New Jersey, his education was at Pennington Seminary, Hudson River Institute at Claverack, a semester at Lafayette College, where he conveyed to his English class the bomb-shell opinion that Tennyson's poetry was "swill," and a semester at Syracuse University, where he wrote the first draft of *Maggie: A Girl of the Streets*. Three years later, without benefit of first-hand battle experience, Crane wrote *The Red Badge of Courage*. It was first serialized for the papers, then appeared in book form in 1895, and with this, Crane's literary reputation blossomed on both sides of the Atlantic. He was twenty-four.

Even as early as his college years Crane had been writing articles for the newspapers. His thirst for experience naturally led him into a career as journalist and war correspondent. In order to cover the brewing trouble in Cuba in 1896, he joined a filibustering expedition. The shipwreck he survived en route provided the basis for his famous story, *The Open Boat*. He covered the Greco-Turkish War for several months in 1897, and the next year he was in Cuba covering the Spanish-American War. In debt, his health broken by malaria and tuberculosis, he collapsed in April, 1900. Two months later, in a sanatarium in Badenweiler, Germany, he died at the age of twenty-eight.

STRUCTURE AND THEME IN STEPHEN CRANE'S FICTION

JAMES B. COLVERT

In a passage in Stephen Crane's "The Open Boat" the narrator describes the predicament of the men in the ten-foot dinghy as they precariously navigate the heavy seas.

> As each slaty wall of water approached, it shut all else from the view of the men in the boat, and it was not difficult to imagine that this particular wave was the final outburst of the ocean, the last effort of the grim water. There was a terrible grace in the move of the waves, and they came in silence, save for the snarling of the crests. . . . Viewed from a balcony, the whole thing would doubtless have been picturesque.

To the men in the boat the horizon of jagged waves at which their eyes glance level marks the extreme limit of the universe. "None of them knew the colour of the sky." The waves shut all else from view, and as they sweep down upon the dinghy they seem to threaten the very nucleus of all visible creation, the men in the open boat. But suddenly the perspective changes. The narrator intrudes to suggest that the plight of the men might seem from a different point of view something less than cosmic in its significance. "Viewed from a balcony" their situation might seem simply "weirdly picturesque."

A brilliant passage in "The Blue Hotel" shows clearly how the distancing effect of the speaker's point of view is achieved through metaphor and imagery. The Swede, crazy with rage and terror after a ferocious fight with old Scully's son at the blue hotel, is making his way through town in a howling blizzard.

> He might have been in a deserted village. We picture the world as thick with conquering and elate humanity, but here, with the bugles of the tempest pealing, it was hard to imagine a peopled earth. One viewed the existence of man then as a marvel, and conceded a glamour of wonder to these lice which were caused to cling to a whirling, fire-smitten, ice-locked, disease-stricken, space-lost bulb.

The imagery suggests a cosmic distance between the narrator and his subject. The speaker sees the Swede as if from a balcony in space, and both the crazy Swede and his world seem indeed pathetically small and insignificant.

These passages throw light on the characteristic structural pattern of the Crane story. The narrative design of Crane's best fiction is defined by the tension between two ironically divergent points of view: the narrowing and deluding point of view of the actors and the enlarging and ruthlessly revealing point of view of the observer-narrator. To the men in the boat the universe seems to have shrunk to the horizon and to have concentrated within its narrow limits all the malignant powers of creation; but the longer view of the narrator reveals this as a delusion born in the men's egoistic assumption that they occupy a central position in Nature's hostile regard. The correspondent sees the waves as "wrongfully and barbarously abrupt," but in the very act of passing moral judgment upon Nature, he implicitly asserts his superior worth and significance. He errs in the judgment because his perspective, unlike the narrator's, is limited by his acute self-consciousness. And the Swede's point of view, again in contrast to the narrator's, admits no "glamour of wonder" in his clinging to an "ice-locked . . . space-lost bulb," for in the flush of his victory over young Scully, he is "elate and conquering humanity" who can say to the bartender in the saloon, "Yes, I like this weather. I like it. It suits me."

In Crane this handling of point of view is more than a technical expediency for bringing order and clarity into the narrative structure. It is a manner of expression which grows inevitably out of his vision of the world. One sees by means of this double perspective the two polar images of the Crane man. In the narrator's view man is insignificant, blind to his human weakness and the futility of his actions, pathetically incompetent in the large scheme of things. But from the limited point of view originating in his aspiring inner-consciousness, the Crane hero creates a more flattering image of himself and the world. Trapped within the confining circle of his swelling emotions of self, he sees himself as god-like, dauntless, heroic, the master of his circumstances. The two images mark the extreme boundaries of Crane's imaginative scope—define, as it were, the limits of his vision of the world. For the Crane story again and again interprets the human situation in terms of the ironic tensions created in the contrast between man as he idealizes himself in his inner thought and emotion and man as he actualizes himself in the stress of experience. In the meaning evoked by the ironic projection of the deflated man against the inflated man lies Crane's essential theme: the consequence of false pride, vanity, and blinding delusion. The sentence which follows the passage quoted from "The Blue Hotel" goes to the thematic dead center of his fiction: "The conceit of man was explained by this storm to be the very engine of life."

II

This way of seeing the world and ordering his vision in art is evident in Crane's first fiction, the little sketches he wrote in 1892 about his youthful hunting and camping experience in the Sullivan County wilds.[1] The hero of these stories is without even the dignity of a name; he is simply "the little man." Yet his egotism, his outrageous sense of self-importance, the heroic image of the world he creates in the ballooning illusions of his personal vision are wonderful to behold. In the opening scene of "Four Men in a Cave" he is discovered in his favorite stance of orator, declaring to his companions his intent to explore a cave "because its black mouth gaped at him." "We can tell a great tale," he boasts, "when we get back to the city." In "Killing His Bear" he has dreams of himself as a mighty hunter and sees "swift pictures of himself in a thousand attitudes under a thousand combination of circumstances,

---

[1] *The Sullivan County Sketches of Stephen Crane*, ed. Melvin Schoberlin (Syracuse University Press, 1949).

killing a thousand bears. . . ." Another time he imagines that his ego has been mystically challenged by a stolid, imperturbable hill which he vows to conquer. He attacks in a blind fury and at last reaches the top, where, reassured as to his personal prowess, he struts like a proud victor. "Immediately he swaggered with valor to the edge of the cliff. His hands were scornfully in his pockets."

But the movement of the tales is always toward the ironic deflation of "the little man." Despite his delusions of grandeur, he usually ends up in ignoble and humiliating defeat. When the bear lies dead under his gun, shot from the safety of concealment, "the little man" springs forward "waving his hat is if he were leading the cheering of thousands," but the final sentences suggest his true moral position: "He ran up and kicked the ribs of the bear. Upon his face was the smile of the successful lover." The last sentence of "The Mesmeric Mountain," upon which "the little man" is striding like a conqueror, puts him and his puny egotism in true perspective: "The mountain under his feet was motionless." In "The Octopush" a drunken guide leaves him stranded all night on a stump in the middle of a lake, and not even "the little man's" shouted oratory can effect his rescue. In another story he is ignobly beaten by a giant woman who mistakes him for a fly-paper salesman; and in "A Ghoul's Accountant" he is kidnapped by two farmers to settle an argument about the solution to a problem in arithmetic, and since he cannot satisfy both disputants, he is scornfully kicked by the loser for his pains.

Though the 1892 Sullivan County stories are hardly more than crude groping toward a fictional subject and manner, they nevertheless throw valuable light on Crane's mature work. One is struck by the persistent recurrence of themes, motifs, and imagery which appear again and again in his later fiction—images of delusion, vanity, distorted values, of the pettiness of human pursuits. The hero of the tales is the prototype of the Crane Hero. The "very engine" of his life is the conceit which fabricates a private world of swollen heroic illusions. The motives of his every gesture are rooted in this world of perpetual falseness which his overweening ego creates out of the tag-ends of a tawdry romantic idealism; and though experience sometimes forces upon him disquieting glimpses of his inadequacy and insignificance, he is usually able to maintain his false image of the world against every assault of reality.

This same organizing vision underlies Crane's first novel, *Maggie:*

A Girl of the Streets, begun perhaps as early as 1891 when Crane was a student at Syracuse University, but not finished in its final version until the winter of 1892, several months after the Sullivan County sketches were published in the *New York Tribune. Maggie,* a hard, melodramatic account of the seduction, desertion, and suicide of a New York slum girl, is chiefly responsible for Crane's reputation as a literary naturalist and is often cited as an illustration of his "cold-blooded determinism."[2] His intention in the novel, one critic observes, "was probably to show the malevolence of all men and the indifferent and negative attitude of society to the individual, whose ruin was of no consequence to it."[3] Crane himself wrote about the novel in similar terms: "It tries to show that environment is a tremendous thing in the world and frequently shapes lives regardless."[4] Even so, this is only part of what Crane was saying in *Maggie.* He was aware, of course, of the role impersonal forces and the limitations of human nature play in human affairs; but he was aware, too, and more interested in, infirmities and perversities within the reach of the human will—pride and selfishness—and their effects upon moral responsibility. In a passage in "The Men in the Storm," a sketch he wrote in 1894 after standing half a winter evening with a crowd of derelicts waiting for a Bowery flop-house to open, he clearly qualifies his mechanistic "shapes lives regardless" statement.

> There were men of undoubted patience, industry, and temperance, who in time of ill-fortune, do not habitually turn to rail at the state of society, snarling at the arrogance of the rich, and bemoaning the cowardice of the poor, but who at these times are apt to wear a sudden and singular meekness, as if they saw the world's progress marching from them, and were trying to perceive where they had failed, what they had lacked, to be thus vanquished in the race.

And writing to a Miss Catherine Harris, who had evidently inquired

---

[2] *Literary History of the United States,* eds. Robert Spiller and others (New York: Macmillan, 1948), II, 1021.

[3] Lars Ahnebrink, *The Beginnings of Naturalism in American Fiction, 1891–1903,* (Uppsala, 1950), 191.

[4] Stephen Crane, "Letters," in *Stephen Crane: an Omnibus,* ed. Robert W. Stallman (New York: A. Knopf, 1952), pp. 594, 611.

through Mrs. Howells about Crane's view of slum life, he makes his point even clearer.

> Thank you very much for your letter on Maggie. I will try to answer your questions properly and politely. Mrs. Howells was right in telling you that I have spent a great deal of time on the East Side and that I have no opinion of missions. That—to you—may not be a valid answer since perhaps you have been informed that I am not very friendly to Christianity as seen around town. I do not think that much can be done with the Bowery as long as the . . . [blurred] . . . are in their present state of conceit. A person who thinks himself superior to the rest of us because he has no job and no pride and no clean clothes is as badly conceited as Lillian Russell. In a story of mine called "An Experiment in Misery" I tried to make plain that the root of Bowery life is a sort of cowardice. Perhaps I mean a lack of ambition or to willingly be knocked flat and accept the licking.[5]

In *George's Mother,* another novel about slum life published in 1896, Mrs. Kelcey, through courage, humility, and self-sacrifice, makes a decent, happy home in the same tenement house the brutal Johnsons live in. She is destroyed not by her environment, but by her weak, vain, and will-less son George and her own sentimental and self-indulgent delusion that he is a paragon of virtue.

It is necessary to clear away this common misunderstanding about Crane in order to see the close thematic kinship of *Maggie* and the earlier Sullivan sketches. The basic conceptual pattern is the same. *Maggie,* like the sketches, is an ironic study of vanity and conceit, and like the *Tribune* pieces it depends for its structural coherence upon the ironic sense of situation and event. Crane brought to bear upon his slum study essentially the same attitude and the same literary idea and method he applied to his study of "the little man"; the chief difference is that in the dark and grim *Maggie* he elaborated the moral consequences of the human perversities he comically satirized in the earlier pieces.

The girl Maggie is the victim not so much of the blind impersonal force of her environment as of the inadequate morality of the

---

[5] "Letters," in *Stephen Crane: an Omnibus,* ed. Robert W. Stallman (New York: A. Knopf, 1952), p. 655.

unreal world view rooted in perverse pride and vanity. Like "the little man," the people in *Maggie* entertain false images of self which lead them into moral error. Pete, the villainous bartender, sees himself as a *gallant* of the most dazzling excellence; Maggie's brother, the brawling Jimmy, though he can ignobly take to his heels in a fight, is convinced that his courage is of heroic proportions; the yearning Maggie herself hopes that the poor little tinsel world of the music hall can be for her a real world; the brutal Mrs. Johnson believes that she is the most self-sacrificing of mothers. These illusions are the source of the moral outrage which drives Maggie to despair and suicide. As in the Sullivan County stories, the motif of false self-estimate emerges everywhere—in gesture, statement, act, situation—weaves into structural units, and finally fuses into an implict statement of theme: that human incompetency—comic in the Sullivan County sketches, tragic in *Maggie*—finds its source in vanity, delusion, and ignorance of self.

III

This theme Crane developed more maturely and significantly in *The Red Badge of Courage,* begun in the spring of 1893 shortly after the stillbirth of *Maggie* and published in the newspaper version in December, 1894. The hero of the novel, Henry Fleming, is essentially "the little man," the deluded people of *Maggie,* and the Swede, for the "engine of his life," too, is pride, vanity, and conceit, the moral consequences of which *The Red Badge* explores. But like the correspondent in "The Open Boat" Henry is redeemed by a successful adjustment of his point of view, and for the first time Crane admits into his theme the working out of a solution to his hero's dilemma.

The novel treats four stages in Fleming's growth toward moral maturity. In the beginning he is unable to distinguish between his heroic dreams and hopes and the actual condition of war. Then follows a period of confusion and doubt as reality begins to intrude upon his dream world. Next he goes through a period of desperate but futile struggle to preserve, through deceit and rationalization, his pseudo-heroic image of himself and the world. In the end he solves his problem when he learns to see the world in its true light, when he is finally able to bring his subjectivity into harmony with the reality which his experience makes clear to him.

The structure of the novel is characteristically a series of loosely related, ironic episodes built up in the contrast between two points of view toward reality, a subjective interpretation originating in vanity, pride, and illusion juxtaposed against an "objective" reality originating in the superior long view of the narrator. So long as Henry is under the influence of his swelling vision of himself, he is incapable of acting morally and honestly. But in the end the disparate worlds of illusion and reality are brought into meaningful relationship, and in the resolution of the ironic tension between the two, the meaning of Henry's experience is made clear to him.[6] Only then is he morally capable of facing up to war and life.

As the novel opens, Henry is troubled by the conflict he vaguely senses between his heroic image of self and fleeting glimpses of cold reality. He dreams of thrilling conflicts and his own "eagle-eyed prowess"; "his busy mind had drawn for him large pictures extravagant in color, lurid with breathless deeds." But from the first this heroic image is disturbed by dim, fleeting images of reality. His mother could "with no apparent difficulty give him many hundreds of reasons" for not enlisting, and "she had certain ways of expression that told him that her statements of the subject came from a deep conviction." Yet Henry is blinded by conceit: he rebels firmly "against this yellow light thrown upon the color of his ambitions."

The story continues to unfold as a variation on this basic idea. Henry plans a fine speech after his enlistment. He imagines sentences "which . . . could be used with touching effect." Actually, his noble oration turned out as a pathetically inadequate, "Ma, I've enlisted." At the seminary, where he goes to say goodbye to his old school mates, he struts; but one girl makes "vivacious fun at his martial spirit." His illusion that "real war was a series of death struggles with small time in between" is pricked momentarily by the reality of the monotonous camp life. Veterans bolster his romantic

---

[6] Mr. Robert W. Stallman, in his *Stephen Crane: An Omnibus* (see "Notes Toward an Analysis of *The Red Badge of Courage,*" pp. 191–201) makes a similar point about the structure of *The Red Badge*. But by his reading the religious symbolism that "radiates outwards from Jim Conklin" is the key to the structure of the novel. The difference between my reading and Mr. Stallman's is a matter of emphasis at this point, but the implications of Mr. Stallman's claim for religious symbolism leads away, in my opinion, from the core of Crane's true meaning.

conception when they talk much of smoke, fire, and blood and the "bewhiskered hordes" who were the enemy; yet he talks across the river to an enemy picket who says, "Yank, yer a right dum good feller." The real world makes constant inroads upon his innocent and egotistical dreams, until at last these opposing images burst into open conflict in his mind.

> He contemplated the lurking menaces of the future, and failed in an effort to see himself standing stoutly in the midst of them. He recalled his visions of broken-bladed glory, but in the shadow of the impending tumult he suspected them to be impossible pictures.

Henry's problem is the re-discovery of himself, for he now knows that "whatever he had learned of himself was here of no avail. He was an unknown quantity. He saw that he would again be obliged to experiment as he had in early youth."

Deprived abruptly of the security of his false views, he can at first find no meaning in anything. Refracted through the thick prism of his ego, reality appears to him irrational, incoherent, terrible in its nightmarish disorder. The actions of his officers, who have "no appreciation of fine minds," are unreasonable. There is no purpose in the movements of the regiment. Nature appears to him in confusing guises—sometimes placid and friendly, now formidable and menacing, again neutral and indifferent. Determined by the immediate demands of his self-regard, his reading of events is shifting and inconsistent, providing one moment a basis for self-glorification, proving the next the falseness of his private world order. Thus in a moment of despair after he runs from battle, he can see nature's law of self-preservation as the justification of his ignoble flight. He is in perfect harmony with a law of nature. But later, when he experiences the horror of Jim Conklin's death, he sees in nature the power of a menacing fate, of which the baleful red sun, hanging over the carnage, is the hateful symbol.

Next, he desperately seeks solace in bold deceit. Indeed, the pretense that his wound was honorably received forms a basis for the reconstruction of his old vainglorious image of himself. "When he remembered his fortunes of yesterday, and looked at them from a distance he began to see something fine there. He had license to be pompous and veteran-like." But as always, the constructions of his vanity are destroyed. He overhears a more objective estimate of a staff officer, who refers contemptuously to Henry's regiment as "muledrivers."

In the end he is forced to abandon his search for comfortable justifications. When he throws himself into battle, blind with rage and despair, he symbolically accepts the world for what it is and tries to come to terms with it. In the thick of reality, so to speak, he undergoes a change; he experiences for the first time "a sublime absence of selfishness" and emerges a triumphant victor over falseness. Liberated from his imprisoning ego, he can marshal all his acts and from a new point of view "look at them in spectator fashion and criticize them with some correctness. . . ." He sees himself, as it were, from a balcony—from the same point of view, in the same perspective, as the observer-narrator sees him. And his "new condition had already defeated certain sympathies." He sees "that those tempestuous moments were of the wild mistakes and ravings of a novice who did not comprehend." In his new humility he finds that he can "look back upon the brass and bombast of his earlier gospels and see them truly." And he has a truer measure of his personal insignificance. He sees that he is "tiny but not inconsequent to the sun," that "in the space-wide whirl of events no grain like him would be lost."

He can understand now that his experience from the first has been pointing toward these conclusions, even when he was least capable of realizing it. Had he not been blinded by his overweening sense of self, he might have been less surprised, looking up after the ordeal of his first battle, to see that "Nature had gone tranquilly on with her golden process in the midst of so much devilment." Had he been able to see through the screen of his vanity, he might have realized that the flaming red sun which hung so ominously over Conklin's death scene was menacing only in his fancy that nature regarded him and his affairs as important. He comes to realize that the sun—as the symbol of nature, of course—is after all "imperturbable" and shines indifferently upon "insult and worship." Or he might have seen that the tattered man, "who loaned his last of strength and intellect for the tall soldier, who, blind with weariness and pain, had been deserted in the field," was a living reproof of Henry's vanity and selfishness. Or again, he might have noted the change in Wilson, the "loud soldier," after the first battle.

> He [Wilson] seemed no more to be continually regarding the
> proportions of his personal prowess. He was not furious at
> small words that pricked his conceits. He was no more a loud
> young soldier. There was about him now a fine reliance. He
> showed a quiet belief in his purposes and his abilities.

But earlier he could not assimilate these experiences; they appeared
to him as discontinuous fragments in a welter of meaningless events.
Only when he sees them in spectator fashion do events in reality
seem to fit into a comprehensible order.

Crane's fiction from the first progressively treats the same basic
theme. One notes how closely the situation of "the little man" in
"The Mesmeric Mountain," one of the early Sullivan County tales,
curiously parallels Henry Fleming's in *The Red Badge*. Standing
before the lowering challenge of the hill, "the little man" cowers in
terror and frustration and wins its top finally in a mad, blind rush;
in the face of war, Henry Fleming, too, is stricken with doubt and
terror, and like "the little man" he conquers the spectre which
haunts him in a wild, enraged assault. But "the little man," unlike
Henry, does not change; he struts and swaggers atop the mountain,
whereas Henry looks down, so to speak, with a new humility and
understanding. "The little man's" world is still false; Fleming's is
true.

In "The Blue Hotel" and "The Open Boat," Crane's best stories
after *The Red Badge,* the fundamental thematic situation, with all
its moral and ethical implication, is again defined in the tension
between the world as it really is and as it is falsely perceived. Thus
the men in "The Open Boat" can be interpreters only when in the
trial of experience they come to realize their true relation to the
universe and to their fellow men. Like Henry, the correspondent
comes to know that the best experience of his life is the object lesson
in humility and self-sacrifice, that in a cold and indifferent cosmos,
illusions of friendly or hostile Nature notwithstanding, the best
values are realized in humble human performance. In "The Blue
Hotel" the Swede, like Fleming before the self-redeeming correction
of his perspective, is a human failure because he is not equipped to
cope with reality, even on the simplest level of behavior. Blind
egotism—the "very engine of life"—distorts every manifestation of
reality and creates the circumstances of his destruction.

Not many of Crane's heroes escape the predicaments their preposterous emotions of self create for them, for it is upon the absurd and sometimes pathetic world of their illusions that his vision is most narrowly focused. In the reduction of this vision to the forms of art, he was led to irony as a characteristic mode of expression. The effect of the usual Crane story is to place between the narrator and his subject a certain distance from which people and events are observed with the most ruthless detachment. At all times the observer is the master of the meanings of the enacted drama; he knows the sublime egotism and the tragic inadequacies of the actors: the prejudices of their points of view, the limitations of their wisdom, the selfish motives of their imaginations. And in narrow and brilliant ironic vision of them he recreates their shining false worlds and simultaneously destroys their illusions with laconic mockery. Only those few actors who can become interpreters survive.

Editor's Note: "Structure and Theme in Stephen Crane's Fiction" is reprinted, by permission of the Purdue Research Institute, from *Modern Fiction Studies,* V (1959), pp. 209–219.

James B. Colvert is Associate Professor of English at the University of Virginia. He has written several essays on Stephen Crane, and is associated with the production of the new Virginia edition of Crane's work.

ERNEST HEMINGWAY

1898-1961

Ernest Hemingway grew up in Oak Park, Illinois. He
excelled in football and boxing in high school and acquired a deep attachment to hunting and fishing from
the many summer vacations spent in the woods of
Northern Michigan. In 1917 he became a reporter for
the Kansas City *Star,* where his serious training as a
writer began. In 1918 he joined the ambulance corps on
the Italian front in World War I. Two months later
he was seriously wounded and spent three months recuperating in a hospital in Milan. After the war,
Hemingway returned to the Michigan woods and re-
newed his writing career, this time for the Toronto
Daily Star. He devoted his spare time to developing his
artistic ability. In Chicago he met Sherwood Anderson,
who strongly influenced his work. In 1921 he returned
to Europe as roving correspondent for the *Star.* He covered battles in the Near East and then settled in Paris
in 1922 where he met Gertrude Stein, Ezra Pound, James
Joyce, and other artists who provided direction and
incentive to the young expatriot writer. Gertrude Stein
had a particularly strong influence on his prose style.
The fruits of his literary dedication ripened quickly and
resulted in a series of successful novels and short stories:
In Our Time (1925), *The Sun Also Rises* (1926), *Men
Without Women* (1927), and *A Farewell to Arms*
(1929).

Two non-fiction works reflect Hemingway's special interests: *Death in the Afternoon* (1932), a study of bullfighting; and *Green Hills of Africa* (1935), concerned with sporting in general, bullfighting, big-game hunting, and literary matters. Besides the excellent short fiction, the two masterpieces of Hemingway's later career are generally considered to be *For Whom the Bell Tolls* (1940) and *The Old Man and the Sea* (1952). In 1954 he received the Nobel Prize. Debilitated by illnesses in his last years, he took his life in July, 1961.

HEMINGWAY'S AMBIGUITY:
SYMBOLISM AND IRONY

E. M. HALLIDAY

One of the curious things about *The Old Man and the Sea* was the sense of awe that it created in its author, its publisher, and (to judge by many of the reviewers) its readers. "Don't you think it is a strange damn story that it should affect all of us (me especially) the way it does?"[1] wrote Hemingway to one of *Life's* editors. And Scribner's dust jacket responded like a good Greek chorus, "One cannot hope to explain why the reading of this book is so profound an experience."[2]

There has always been a certain mystery about Hemingway's effects in his best writing. From *In Our Time* (1925), with its puzzling "chapters" connecting (or separating) the stories, through *For Whom the Bell Tolls* (1940), with its oddly equivocal interpretation of the Spanish civil war, his best has evoked a somewhat doubtful sound from critics who nevertheless were at pains to recommend. Something, it was felt, was being missed; or if not missed, then sensed too vaguely for critical description. *A Farewell to Arms* (1929), declared Edward Hope in the *New York Herald Tribune*, was "one of those things—like the Grand Canyon—that one doesn't care to talk about."[3] Despite such reverent throwing up of hands by early critics many things were aptly observed; but the emphasis was heavily on Hemingway the realist, whose bright fidelity to the perceptible surfaces of life was accomplished through living dialogue and a prose finely engineered to the accu-

[1] Quoted in *Time*, LX, No. 9, 48 (Sept. 1, 1952).

[2] *The Old Man and the Sea* (New York, 1952).

[3] Quoted on the flyleaf of *A Farewell to Arms*, Bantam Edition (New York, 1954).

rate rendering of sensuous experience. And the brilliance of his reflected surface together with the roughness of the things he preferred to write about—fishing, hunting, skiing, bull-fighting, boxing, horse-racing, and war—perhaps made it difficult to see one of the cardinal facts about Hemingway: that essentially he is a philosophical writer. His main interest, in representing human life through fictional forms, has consistently been to set man against the background of his world and universe, to examine the human situation from various points of view.

Not that he has a "system," for on the final questions Hemingway has always shown himself a skeptic. "It seemed like a fine philosophy," Jake Barnes says to himself at one bitter point in *The Sun Also Rises.* "In five years . . . it will seem just as silly as all the other fine philosophies I've had."[4] Like Jake, Hemingway has been "technically" a Roman Catholic, but the metaphysical doctrines of Christianity seem never to have taken a convincing hold. His most devout characters are only devoutly mystified by the universe: both Anselmo, the good old man of *For Whom the Bell Tolls,* and Santiago, of *The Old Man and the Sea,* disclaim their religiosity, and their Hail-Marys are uttered mechanically enough to evoke a chilly memory of the sleepless waiter in "A Clean, Well-Lighted Place," who prayed, "Hail nothing, full of nothing, nothing is with thee."[5] The parable of the doomed ants on the burning log, in *A Farewell to Arms,*[6] has been thought to represent Hemingway's *Weltanschauung* at its most pessimistic; but there is no reason, actually, to think that there has since been a fundamental change in his view of life. "Everything kills everything else in some way,"[7] reflects the old Cuban fisherman of the latest book; and even the small bird that rests momentarily on his fishing line may fall to the hawks before reaching land, at best must take its chance "like any man or bird or fish."[8] The world, it seems, still breaks everyone, and only the earth and the Gulf Stream abide after the vortex of human vanities has subsided forever.

Given Hemingway's suspicion of ultimate doom and his passionate fondness for being alive, it is no surprise that his philosophical preoccupation is primarily ethical. Extinction may well be

---

[4] *The Sun Also Rises* (New York, 1926), p. 153.
[5] *The Short Stories of Ernest Hemingway* (New York, 1938), p. 481.
[6] *A Farewell to Arms* (New York, 1932), p. 350.
[7] *The Old Man and the Sea,* p. 117.
[8] *Ibid.,* p. 61.

the end of all, as the writer of Ecclesiastes repeatedly remarked, but for Hemingway and his heroes this merely emphasizes the need to live each moment properly and skillfully, to sense judiciously the texture of every fleeting act and perception. The focus is conduct: "Maybe if you found out how to live in it you learned from that what it was all about,"[9] says Jake Barnes. It is not accidental that the French existentialists have shown a strong feeling for Hemingway's work. Like them he has been poised in his hours of despair on the edge of nothingness, the abyss of nonmeaning which confronts most of the characters in the stories of *Winner Take Nothing* (1933); and like them he has looked in his hours of hope to a salvation built out of individual human courage around a code, at once rational and intuitive, of strict, often ritualistic behavior. *"Nous sommes foutus . . . comme toujours,"* says Golz, the Loyalist general commanding the attack with which Jordan's mission is co-ordinated in *For Whom the Bell Tolls*. *". . . Bon. Nous ferons notre petit possible."*[10] As it was for Socrates and Jeremy Taylor, although for quite different reasons, dying well is for Hemingway the crucial corollary to living well. So Robert Jordan fights off an impulse to kill himself to end the anguish of a badly broken leg and avoid possible capture. "You can do nothing for yourself but perhaps you can do something for another,"[11] he tells himself; yet we are to understand that he has died well not just because of his sacrifice, but because he has not abandoned the principle of fortitude. In the image of the crucifixion which has haunted Hemingway from "Today Is Friday" (1926) to *The Old Man and the Sea,* it is the unique courage of the forsaken and crucified man-God that takes his attention. "I'll tell you," says a Roman soldier in the earlier work, "he looked pretty good to me in there today."[12] We are part of a universe offering no assurance beyond the grave, and we are to make what we can of life by a pragmatic ethic spun bravely out of man himself in full and steady cognizance that the end is darkness.

II

Undoubtedly Hemingway's preoccupation with the human predicament and a moral code that might satisfactorily control it, in

---

[9] *The Sun Also Rises,* p. 153.
[10] *For Whom the Bell Tolls* (New York, 1940), pp. 428, 430.
[11] *Ibid.,* p. 466.
[12] *The Short Stories,* p. 457.

itself partly accounts for the sense of hidden significance which many have experienced in reading him. Obscured as this preoccupation has been by his choice of particular fictional materials and by his manner, which has always eschewed explication, it could nevertheless almost always be felt: it was impossible to avoid the impression that this writer was dealing with something of final importance to us all. Like the Elizabethans whom he evidently loves, he never lets us quite forget that death awaits every man at some turn perhaps not far along the way. And like nobody but Hemingway—that is, in his peculiar and distinguished manner as an artist—he continually reminds us that (as he expressed it once to Maxwell Perkins) it is our "performance en route"[13] that counts for good or bad.

But what is the essence of his peculiar manner? It is a manner of implication, clearly, as he himself has said in various notes of self-criticism of which the figure in *Death in the Afternoon* is perhaps the most striking: "The dignity of movement of an ice-berg is due to only one-eighth of it being above water."[14] The question is what mode of narrative technique he exploits in order to make the iceberg principle operative in his work. I do not remember seeing the word "symbolism" in critical writing about Hemingway before 1940, nor have I seen more than one review of *The Old Man and the Sea* that did not lean heavily on the word. The number of exegeses that explain Hemingway as a symbolist has increased geometrically since Malcolm Cowley suggested in 1944 that he should be grouped not among the realists, but "with Poe and Hawthorne and Melville: the haunted and nocturnal writers, the men who dealt in images that were symbols of an inner world."[15] It was a startling and pleasing suggestion. Mr. Cowley advanced it rather tentatively and did not press his discovery very far; but it was taken up with something like a hue and cry by other critics who, it seemed, had been testily waiting for the scent and were eager to get on with the hunt. Literary conversation soon began to reflect the new trend: I recall hearing it asserted on two proximate occasions that the sleeping bag in *For Whom the Bell Tolls* is an "obvious" symbol of the womb; and that a ketchup bottle in "The Killers" patently symbolizes blood. By 1949 it was no great sur-

[13] Quoted by Perkins in *Scribner's Magazine*, LXXXI, 4 (March, 1927).
[14] *Death in the Afternoon* (New York, 1932), p. 192.
[15] Introduction to *The Portable Hemingway* (New York, 1944), p. vii.

prise to open an issue of the *Sewanee Review* to an essay by Caroline Gordon called "Notes on Hemingway and Kafka."[16] It would have been surprising only if the analysis had not hinged on a comparison between the two writers as symbolists.

Is Hemingway genuinely a symbolist? I think he uses certain techniques of symbolism, but I think he does so in a very limited and closely controlled way, and that failure to recognize the controls leads—already has led—to distortions of his meaning and misappreciations of his narrative art. As a sample, Miss Gordon's essay is instructive on this point. Starting calmly, as her title suggests, with the assumption that Hemingway is a symbolist, she proceeds to compare him, not very favorably, with Kafka. And it turns out that Hemingway's trouble is simple—he is not *enough* of a symbolist: "this plane of action is for him a slippery sub-stratum glimpsed intermittently. It does not underlie the Naturalistic plane of action solidly, or over-arch it grandly, as Kafka's Symbolism does."[17]

But this is mistaking an artistic discipline for a fault. Hemingway has not attempted Kafka's kind of symbolism and fallen short: it is something foreign to Hemingway's art. The Kafka story used by Miss Gordon as the basis for her comparison is "The Hunter Gracchus," a carefully elaborated allegory revolving around the life of Christ—that is to say, there are two distinct and parallel narrative lines, the primary, which operates within the confines of a more or less realistic world, and the secondary, which operates within the realm of religious myth and in this case is assumed by the author to be a prior possession on the part of the reader. Incidentally, Miss Gordon forces her comparison from both sides, claiming for Kafka, as something he shares with Hemingway, "a surface which is strictly Naturalistic in detail."[18] But this claim must rest on a curious understanding of the phrase "in detail" since the story on the "Naturalistic" level offers, among other attractions, a corpse that is mysteriously still alive, and a German-speaking dove the size of a rooster.

Hemingway, as far as I know, has never written an allegory—notwithstanding the bright interpretations of *The Old Man and the Sea* that illuminated cocktail parties a few years ago when it was published in *Life*—and for a very good reason. In successful al-

[16] *Sewanee Review*, LVII, 214–226 (Spring, 1949).
[17] *Ibid.*, p. 226.
[18] *Ibid.*, p. 222.

legory, the story on the primary level is dominated by the story on the secondary level, and if the allegorical meaning is to be kept clear, its naturalistic counterpart must pay for it by surrendering realistic probability in one way or another. A strain is imposed on the whole narrative mechanism, for mere connotative symbolism will not do to carry the allegory: there must be a denotative equation, part for part, between symbols and things symbolized in order to identify the actors and action on the allegorical level. The extreme difficulty of satisfactorily conducting the dual action throughout a prolonged narrative is classically illustrated by *The Faerie Queene* and by *The Pilgrim's Progress*. The allegorist who admires realism is constantly pulled in two directions at once, and is very lucky when he can prevent one or the other of his meanings from unbalancing him.

Still, Hemingway has used the symbolism of association to convey by implication his essential meaning from the time of his earliest American publication. It may well be that this was inevitable for a writer starting out with Hemingway's determination to communicate, as he put it (in *Death in the Afternoon*) "what really happened in action; what the actual things were which produced the emotion that you experienced."[19] Nothing could more clearly differentiate Hemingway's kind of realism from Zolaesque naturalistic description than this early statement of intent. Everything is to depend on judicious discrimination of objective details: *what really happened* is not by any means everything that happened; it is only "the actual things . . . which produced the emotion that you experienced." As a matter of fact "produced" is a little too strict, as Hemingway demonstrates again and again in *The Sun Also Rises* and *A Farewell to Arms,* where he depends heavily on the technique of objective epitome—a symbolist technique, if you like—to convey the subjective conditions of his characters. The details selected are not so much those which *produce* the emotion as those which epitomize it; it is the action of the story which has produced the emotion. Thus at the crisis of *The Sun Also Rises*, when Jake Barnes presents Brett to Pedro Romero—a Pandarism for which he is obliged to hate himself—his agonized feelings are not discussed, but are nevertheless most poignantly suggested by the perceptions he reports:

[19] *Death in the Afternoon,* p. 2.

322

> When I came back and looked in the café, twenty minutes
> later, Brett and Pedro Romero were gone. The coffee-glasses
> and our three empty cognac-glasses were on the table. A
> waiter came with a cloth and picked up the glasses and
> mopped off the table.[20]

In *A Farewell to Arms,* Frederic Henry goes dully out for breakfast
from the Swiss maternity hospital where Catherine Barkley is fighting for life in ominously abnormal labor:

> Outside along the street were the refuse cans from the houses
> waiting for the collector. A dog was nosing at one of the cans.
> "What do you want?" I asked and looked in the can to see
> if there was anything I could pull out for him; there was noth-
> ing on top but coffeegrounds, dust and some dead flowers.
> "There isn't anything, dog," I said.[21]

There is, of course, a larger sense, germane to all good fiction, in
which Hemingway may be said to be symbolic in his narrative
method: the sense which indicates his typical creation of key characters who are representative on several levels. We thus find Jake
Barnes's war-wound impotence a kind of metaphor for the whole
atmosphere of sterility and frustration which is the *ambiance* of
The Sun Also Rises; we find Catherine Barkley's naïve simplicity
and warmth the right epitome for the idea and ideal of normal
civilian home life to which Frederic Henry deserts; we find the old
Cuban fisherman in some way representative of the whole human
race in its natural struggle for survival. But the recent criticism of
Hemingway as symbolist goes far beyond such palpable observations
as these, and in considering the fundamental character of his narrative technique I wish to turn attention to more ingenious if not
esoteric explications.

Professor Carlos Baker, in *Hemingway: The Writer as Artist*
(1952), has established himself as the leading oracle of Hemingway's
symbolism. His book is, I think, the most valuable piece of extended Hemingway criticism that we yet have, and to a large extent
its contribution is one of new insights into the symbolist aspect of
his subject's narrative method. He is sweeping: "From the first
Hemingway has been dedicated as a writer to the rendering of

[20] *The Sun Also Rises*, p. 194.
[21] *A Farewell to Arms*, p. 336.

Wahrheit, the precise and at least partly naturalistic rendering of things as they are and were. Yet under all his brilliant surfaces lies the controlling Dichtung, the symbolic underpainting which gives so remarkable a sense of depth and vitality to what otherwise might be flat two-dimensional portraiture."[22] This may fairly be said to represent Mr. Baker's major thesis, and he develops and supports it with remarkable energy and skill. I do not wish to disparage his over-all effort—he is often very enlightening—but I do wish to argue that he has been rather carried away by his thesis, and that therein he eminently typifies the new symbolist criticism of Hemingway which in its enthusiasm slights or ignores other basic aspects of Hemingway's technique.

Mr. Baker's chapter on *A Farewell to Arms* is an original piece of criticism, and it solidly illustrates his approach. He finds that the essential meaning of this novel is conveyed by two master symbols, the Mountain and the Plain, which organize the "Dichtung" around "two poles": "By a process of accrual and coagulation, the images tend to build round the opposed concepts of Home and Not-Home. . . . The Home-concept, for example, is associated with the mountains; with dry-cold weather; with peace and quiet; with love, dignity, health, happiness, and the good life; and with worship or at least the consciousness of God. The Not-Home concept is associated with low-lying plains; with rain and fog; with obscenity, indignity, disease, suffering, nervousness, war and death; and with irreligion."[23] It is in terms of these antipodal concepts that Mr. Baker analyzes the semantic structure of *A Farewell to Arms,* a structure which he finds effective chiefly because of the adroit and subtle development of the correspondingly antipodal symbols, the Mountain and the Plain. He argues that from the first page of the story these are set up in their significant antithesis, that they are the key to the relationships among several of the leading characters, and that the central action—Frederic Henry's desertion from the Italian Army to join Catherine Barkley, the British nurse—can be fully appreciated only on this symbolic basis. *"A Farewell to Arms,"* he concludes, "is entirely and even exclusively acceptable as a naturalistic narrative of what happened. To read it only as such, however, is to miss the controlling symbolism: the deep central antithesis

[22] Carlos Baker, *Hemingway: The Writer as Artist* (Princeton, 1952), p. 289.
[23] *Ibid.,* pp. 101, 102.

between the image of life and home (the mountain) and the image of war and death (the plain)."[24]

Clearly there is some truth in this. The "deep central antithesis" cannot be denied, I would think, by anyone with an acceptable understanding of the book. The question at issue is one of technique; to what extent, and how precisely, is the central antithesis in fact engineered around the Mountain and the Plain as symbols?

One thing is noticeable immediately: as in virtually all of Hemingway, anything that can possibly be construed to operate symbolically does no violence whatsoever to the naturalism (or realism) of the story on the primary level. Nothing could be a more natural—or more traditional—symbol of purity, of escape from the commonplace, in short of elevation, than mountains. If thousands of people have read the passages in *A Farewell to Arms* which associate the mountains "with dry-cold weather; with peace and quiet; with love, dignity, health, happiness and the good life" without taking them to be "symbolic" it is presumably because these associations are almost second nature for all of us. Certainly this seems to be true of Frederic Henry: it is most doubtful that in the course of the novel he is ever to be imagined as consciously regarding the mountains as a symbol. This of course does not prove that Hemingway did not regard them as such, or that the full understanding of this novel as an art structure does not perhaps require the symbolic equation, *mountain* equals *life and home*. It does, however, point differentially to another type of symbolism, where the character in question is shown to be clearly aware of the trope, as when Catherine Barkley says she hates rain because "sometimes I see me dead in it,"[25] or when Frederic Henry says of his plunge into the Tagliamento, "Anger was washed away in the river along with any obligation."[26]

But Mr. Baker has claimed a most exact and detailed use by Hemingway of the Mountain-Plain symbolism, and his ingenious interpretation deserves closer attention. Like many other critics he is an intense admirer of the novel's opening paragraph, which, he says, "does much more than start the book. It helps to establish the dominant mood (which is one of doom), plants a series of important

[24] *Ibid.*, pp. 108, 109.
[25] *A Farewell to Arms,* p. 135.
[26] *Ibid.*, p. 248.

images for future symbolic cultivation, and subtly compels the reader into the position of detached observer."[27] He proceeds to a close analysis of this paragraph:

> The second sentence, which draws attention from the mountainous background to the bed of the river in the middle distance, produces a sense of clearness, dryness, whiteness, and sunniness which is to grow very subtly under the artist's hands until it merges with one of the novel's two dominant symbols, the mountain-image. The other major symbol is the plain. Throughout the sub-structure of the book it is opposed to the mountain-image. Down this plain the river flows. Across it, on the dusty road among the trees, pass the men-at-war, faceless and voiceless and unidentified against the background of the spreading plain.[28]

This is highly specific, and we are entitled to examine it minutely. Mr. Baker says the river is "in the middle distance" in the direction of the mountains with the image of which, as he sees it, the symbolic images of the river are to merge into one great symbol. But is the river really in the middle distance? The narrator tells us he can see not only its boulders but its *pebbles,* "dry and white in the sun." The river must, of course, flow from the mountains, but in the perspective seen from the house occupied by Frederic Henry, it would appear to be very close at hand—closer than the plain, and quite in contrast to the distant mountains. And this raises the question of whether the clearness, dryness, whiteness, and sunniness offered by the river are in fact artfully intended to be associated with the mountain-image and what it is held to symbolize; or, disregarding the question of intent, whether they do in fact so operate in the artistic structure. Why must the river images be dissociated from the images of the plain across which the river, naturally, flows? Because the river images are of a kind which, if they work as symbols, are incongruent with what Mr. Baker has decided the Plain stands for; they must instead be allocated to the Mountain. This is so important to his thesis that the river shifts gracefully, but without textual support, into "the middle distance," closer to the mountains.

[27] Baker, *op. cit.,* p. 94.
[28] *Ibid.,* pp. 94–95.

326

And what of the soldiers on the road? Since they must be firmly associated with the Plain ("war and death"), it is against that background that Mr. Baker sees them in Hemingway's opening paragraph—it would not do to see them against the background of the river, with its Mountain images. But let us look again at the paragraph.

> In the late summer of that year we lived in a house in a village that looked across the river and the plain to the mountains. In the bed of the river there were pebbles and boulders, dry and white in the sun, and the water was clear and swiftly moving and blue in the channels. Troops went by the house and down the road and the dust they raised powdered the leaves of the trees.

Mr. Baker says the road is across the river, as of course it would have to be if we are to see the figures of the soldiers against the background of the plain. Hemingway does not say the road is across the river. Indeed, everything indicates the opposite arrangement: a house on a road running along the near side of the river, across which the plain stretches out to the mountains. "Sometimes in the dark," begins the third paragraph of the novel, "we heard the troops marching under the window. . . ." The truth is that a strong part of Mr. Baker's initially persuasive exegesis of the opening paragraph of *A Farewell to Arms* hangs on a reading that the written words will not support. This is not to deny that the paragraph establishes a mood of doom by its somber tone and the epitomic symbols of dust and falling leaves: what I am questioning is the over-all symbolic organization of the novel's structure in terms of the Mountain and the Plain, which Mr. Baker argues as a prime illustration of his unequivocal judgment of Hemingway as symbolist artist.

As a matter of fact, the plain presented in the opening pages of *A Farewell to Arms* is as troublesome as the river when it comes to supporting Mr. Baker's interpretation. There are plains in many countries that could well serve as symbols of emptiness, desolation, disaster, and death—we have some in the American West. But this does not appear to be that sort of plain: quite the contrary. "The plain," Frederic Henry narrates in the opening words of the second paragraph, "was rich with crops; there were many orchards of fruit trees. . . ." Mr. Baker tells us neither how these images of fertility and fruition are to fit in with "rain and fog; with obscenity, indignity, disease, suffering, nervousness, war and death," nor how we should symbolically interpret the conclusion of the sentence, ". . . and beyond the plain the mountains were brown and bare." One can easily grant that as the novel unfolds the impression of war itself grows steadily more saturated with a sense of doomsday qualities: that was an essential part of Hemingway's theme. But to what degree is this impression heightened by the use of the Plain as symbol? The simple exigencies of history prevent exclusive associations of the war with the plain as opposed to the mountains, as the narrator indicates on the first page: "There was fighting in the mountains and at night we could see flashes from the artillery." Yet if Mr. Baker is right we would expect to find, despite this difficulty, a salient artistic emphasis of the Plain in symbolic association with all those images which his interpretation sets against those coalescing around the Mountain symbol.

Mr. Baker makes much of the fact that Frederic Henry, during his leave, fails to take advantage of the offer of his friend the chaplain and go to the high mountain country of the Abruzzi, "where the roads were frozen and hard as iron, where it was clear cold and dry and the snow was dry and powdery. . . . I had gone to no such place but to the smoke of cafés and nights when the room whirled and you needed to look at the wall to make it stop, nights in bed, drunk, when you knew that that was all there was."[29] Here, Mr. Baker claims, "the mountain-image gets further backing from another low-land contrast."[30] Granting the familar association here of mountain-country with certain delectable and longed-for experiences, one would like to see, in support of the Mountain-Plain explication, a clearer identification of the contrasting, soldier-on-leave experiences, with the lowland or plain. And while wondering about this, one reads on in *A Farewell to Arms* and soon finds Frederic Henry and Catherine Barkley in Milan, where Henry is recuperating from his wound. They are having a wonderful time. They are in love, have frequent opportunities to be alone together in the hospital room, go often to the races, dine at the town's best restaurants, and in general lead an existence that makes the most pleasant contrast imaginable to the dismal life at the front. "We

[29] *A Farewell to Arms*, p. 13.
[30] Baker, *op. cit.*, p. 102.

had a lovely time that summer,"[31] says the hero. What has happened here to the Mountain-Plain machinery? It does not seem to be operating; or perhaps it is operating in reverse, since Milan is definitely in the plain. Mr. Baker passes over these pages of the novel rather quickly, remarking that Catherine here "moves into association with ideas of home, love and happiness."[32] He seems to be aware of the difficulty, although he does not mention it as such: "She does not really [sic] reach the center of the mountain-image until, on the heels of Frederic's harrowing lowland experiences during the retreat from Caporetto, the lovers move to Switzerland. Catherine is the first to go, and Henry follows her there as if she were the genius of the mountains, beckoning him on."[33]

This is romantically pleasant, but inaccurate. Catherine does not go to Switzerland, but to the Italian resort village of Stresa, on Lake Maggiore. Stresa, moreover, although surrounded by mountains, is itself distinctly lowland: you can pedal a bicycle from Milan or Turin without leaving nearly flat country. Still, it can be allowed that the lovers are not free of the contaminating shadow of war until they have escaped up the lake to Switzerland and established themselves in their little chalet above Montreux. Here, again, the associations all of us are likely to make with high-mountain living assert themselves—clear, cold air; magnificent views; white snow; peace and quiet—and the hero and heroine are shown to be happily aware of these. The rain, however, which they have both come to regard as an omen of disaster, grants no immunity to the mountain; it refuses to preserve a unilateral symbolic association with the plain. Mr. Baker knows this, but does not discuss the extent to which it obscures his neat Mountain-Plain antithesis, making the point instead that "the March rains and the approaching need for a good lying-in hospital have driven the young couple down from their magic mountain" to "the lowlands"[34] of Lausanne. Here again observation is fuzzy to the point of distortion: Lausanne happens to stand on a series of steep hills and is an extraordinarily poor specimen of a City of the Plain. This is clear, incidentally, without reference to an atlas, since there are several allusions to the

---

[31] *A Farewell to Arms*, p. 119.
[32] Baker, *op. cit.*, p. 104.
[33] *Ibid.*
[34] *Ibid.*, pp. 104, 108.

hills and steep streets of Lausanne in the novel itself.[35] But Mr. Baker is caught up in his symbolic apparatus, and if one symbol of death (rain) has failed to stay where it belongs in his scheme (on the plain) he still is persuaded to see the topography of Switzerland in a light that will not darken his thesis.

What all this illustrates, it seems to me, is that Mr. Baker has allowed an excellent insight into Hemingway's imagery and acute sense of natural metonymy to turn into an interesting but greatly overelaborated critical gimmick. It is undeniable that in the midst of the darkling plain of struggle and flight which was the war in Italy, Frederic Henry thinks of the Swiss Alps as a neutral refuge of peace and happiness—surely millions must have lifted their eyes to those mountains with like thoughts during both World Wars. But in so far as this is symbolism it belongs to our race and culture; and if it is to be sophisticated into a precise scheme of artistic implication revolving around two distinct polar symbols, the signals transmitted from artist to reader must be more clearly semaphored than anything Mr. Baker has been able to point to accurately. I do not believe this is derogatory to Hemingway. Sensitive as always to those parts of experience that are suggestive and connotative, he used the mountain metaphor which is part of our figurative heritage to deepen the thematic contrast in *A Farewell to Arms,* between war and not-war. But nowhere did he violate realism for the sake of this metaphor; nor did he, as I read the novel, set up the artificially rigid and unrealistic contrast between the Mountain and the Plain which Mr. Baker's analysis requires.

Mr. Baker himself has summed up the sequel to his investigation of *A Farewell to Arms.* "Once the reader has become aware of what Hemingway is doing in those parts of his work which lie below the surface, he is likely to find symbols operating everywhere. . . ."[36] Mr. Baker does find them everywhere, and they not infrequently trip him into strangely vulnerable judgments. Finding an unprecedented display of symbolism in *Across the River and into the Trees* (1950), for instance, he is willing to accord that disappointing novel a richly favorable verdict: "a prose poem, with a remarkable complex emotional structure, on the theme of the three ages of man. . . .

[35] See, for instance, pp. 328, 331, 334.

[36] Baker, *op. cit.,* p. 117.

If *A Farewell to Arms* was his *Romeo and Juliet* . . . this . . . could perhaps be called a lesser kind of *Winter's Tale* or *Tempest*."[37]

III

But we are not interested so much in the narrative technique of Hemingway's weakest work as we are in what happens in his best. To see symbolism as the master device of the earlier novels and short stories tends to obscure another and more characteristic type of ambiguity which makes his best work great fiction in the tacit mode. I mean Hemingway's irony. The extent to which the ironic method has packed his fiction with substrata of meaning has not yet, I think, been adequately appreciated in published criticism. And it needs to be appreciated; for irony as a literary device is singularly suited to the view of life which Hemingway has consistently dramatized now for a quarter of our century in such manner as to distinguish him as a writer.

If you look at Hemingway's earliest American publication in a medium of general circulation you are struck by this irony of view and method, just as it is strikingly there in *The Old Man and the Sea*. "Champs d'Honneur" was the title of one of six short poems printed in *Poetry* for January, 1923:

> Soldiers never do die well;
>   Crosses mark the places—
> Wooden crosses where they fell,
>   Stuck above their faces.
> Soldiers pitch and cough and twitch—
>   All the world roars red and black;
> Soldiers smother in a ditch,
>   Choking through the whole attack.[38]

One of the most interesting things about this is the strong ironic tension set up between the title and the verse itself; the harsh incongruity between the traditional notion of the soldier's heroic death and the grim reality. A tough irony of situation is also the keynote of *In Our Time* (1925), not only as clue to the individual

[37] *Ibid.*, pp. 264, 287.
[38] *Poetry*, XXI, 195 (Jan., 1923).

meanings of most of the stories that make up the book, but as the very principle upon which it was composed. Many readers have tried to puzzle out a nice relationship between each story and the narrative fragment, numbered as a "chapter," which precedes it. But the principle in fact was irrelevance; what Hemingway did was to take the numbered sketches of *in our time* (Paris, 1924) and intersperse them with the longer stories to give a powerfully ironic effect of spurious order supporting the book's subject: modern civil disruption and violence seen against the timeless background of everyday human cross-purposes.

The ironic gap between expectation and fulfilment, pretense and fact, intention and action, the message sent and the message received, the way things are thought or ought to be and the way things are—this has been Hemingway's great theme from the beginning; and it has called for an ironic method to do it artistic justice. All of his work thus far published deserves study with special attention to this method.

I do not think, for example, that a reader must understand the symbolic pattern Mr. Baker claims for *A Farewell to Arms* in order to get the main point of the story; but unless he understands the irony of Catherine Barkley's death he surely has missed it completely. Long before this denouement, however, irony has drawn a chiaroscuro highlighting the meaning of the book. There is from the beginning the curious disproportion between Frederic Henry's lot in the army and his frame of mind. A noncombatant, he lives in comfortable houses, eats and drinks well, makes frequent visits to a brothel maintained exclusively for officers, and has extensive leaves urged on him by a sympathetic commanding officer. Despite such pleasures he is malcontent; and the more this fact emerges the more it becomes evident that his mood is a reflection not of his personal fortune, but of the whole dismal panorama of civilization disjointed by war. His manner of narration is already ironical: "At the start of the winter came the permanent rain and with the rain came the cholera. But it was checked and in the end only seven thousand died of it in the army."[39] Healthy in body, the hero is afflicted by a paralysis of the will, a torpor brought on by too many months of living close to the war; and this is the reason for his paradoxical failure to visit the home of his friend the chaplain

[39] *A Farewell to Arms*, p. 4.

while he is on leave: "I myself felt as badly as he did and could not understand why I had not gone. It was what I had wanted to do. . . ."[40] Even the one constructive effort he has been regularly capable of, the performance of his duty as an ambulance officer, has begun to seem absurdly inconsequential to him: when he returns from leave he finds that his absence apparently has made no difference whatever.

As the war wears on, its grotesqueries receive more attention; it begins to be felt, indeed, that they are perhaps after all indigenous to life itself, and only emphasized by war. Henry is given a protective St. Anthony by the heroine: "After I was wounded I never found him. Some one probably got it at one of the dressing stations."[41] The ambulance unit which he commands makes elaborate preparations to receive wounded soldiers during a forthcoming attack: while they are waiting—and eating cheese and spaghetti—in a dugout, an enemy shell lands squarely on top of them, thus making Lt. Henry himself part of the first load of wounded going to the rear. For this, he learns, he is to receive a bronze medal; his friend Rinaldi hopes it may be silver.

The episode in Milan, so recalcitrant to Mr. Baker's symbolist scheme, has an integral function in the ironic structure of the narrative. Recuperating far behind the lines, the hero becomes part of the incongruously pleasant civilian scene which always—to the incredulous and bitter astonishment of most combat soldiers—goes on while men die at the front. Yet to add a further ironic twist to this, there is Hemingway's satirical portrait of Ettore, the American-Italian who is a "legitimate hero" in the Italian Army. Not only does he see the social life of wartime Milan as perfectly normal, but it is clear that his view of the war as a whole is the reverse of Henry's: "Believe me, they're fine to have," he says, exhibiting his wound stripes. "I'd rather have them than medals. Believe me, boy, when you get three you've got something."[42]

Back at the front for only two days, Henry finds himself mixed up in the nightmarish retreat from Caporetto. Hemingway's famous description of this debacle is a stringent comment on the bewildering stupidity and chaos of war, but he takes the occasion to inject

[40] *Ibid.*, p. 13.
[41] *Ibid.*, p. 47.
[42] *Ibid.*, p. 130.

again a shot of special irony. With one ambulance mired to the hubs on a rainsoaked back road, Lt. Henry shoots a sergeant who, in his anxiety to keep up with the retreat, tries to get away on foot instead of staying to cut brush for the spinning wheels. The sergeant is only wounded, but he is quickly dispatched, with Henry's acquiescence, by Bonello, one of the ambulance drivers. "All my life I've wanted to kill a sergeant,"[43] Bonello says proudly; but a few hours later he too deserts, to let himself be captured by the enemy. The climax of this grim comedy is of course Frederic Henry's own desertion. Threatened with military justice akin to that he so summarily had dealt the sergeant, he dives into the Tagliamento River; and his sarcastic remarks on his would-be executioners ring with hyperironic overtones against the baffle of the earlier incident:

> I saw how their minds worked; if they had minds and if they worked. They were all young men and they were saving their country. . . . The questioners had that beautiful detachment and devotion to stern justice of men dealing in death without being in any danger of it.[44]

There are many other ironic strokes in *A Farewell to Arms,* but it is this series, identifying the activities of war with all that is brutal and meaningless in human life, that gives the novel its predominantly ironic texture. The catastrophe, Catherine Barkley's shocking death, has the ambivalent effect of partly canceling this identification while at the same time violently reinforcing the total effect of irony. It is as if the author had said, "Do not imagine that the kind of cruelty and disruption I have shown you are confined to war: they are the conditions of life itself." It is thus only at the end that the full ironic ambiguity of the title springs into view.

The title of Hemingway's other great war novel is likewise an index of its strongly ironic theme. It was strange how many reviewers and critics underweighed the epigraph from Donne and the meaningful paradox of the whole sentence furnishing the title: "And therefore never send to know for whom the bell tolls: it tolls for thee." Appraisals from both Right and Left accused Hemingway of having gone over to the other side, while certain critics less

---

[43] *Ibid.,* p. 222.
[44] *Ibid.,* pp. 240, 241.

politically biased found that his theme was confused or that it had backfired. "At the center of *For Whom the Bell Tolls*," wrote Maxwell Geismar, "there is a basic confusion of Hemingway's intention. The novel attempts to be a constructive statement on human life. Yet Hemingway's underlying sense of destruction often contradicts this."[45]

But Hemingway was not confused. As always, he wanted to show something true about human life (not necessarily something "constructive") ; and he had come to take a more complex view of humanity at war than he projected in *A Farewell to Arms*. "A plague on both your houses"—the prevailing mood of Frederic Henry—has been replaced by Robert Jordan's unillusioned sense of the community of the human predicament. No man is an island, it turns out; but the storms that sweep the human continent are of such force, and the quakes that rack its surface so disruptive, that none of us can depend on better fortune than that of Jordan, who died making his own small and paradoxical effort to maintain its integrity. His affiliation with the Loyalists is no simple partisan allegiance; and to extend and support the hero's explicit awareness of the inevitable contradictions of his position, Hemingway poses a series of situations pregnant with irony.

Outstanding is Pilar's account of the start of "the movement" in Pablo's home town, with its unflinching report of the steadily mounting sadism which infused the execution of the local Fascists. There is a remarkable tone to this report, as if Pilar were at confession, anxious to tell the whole truth and omitting not even the most shameful details, yet seeking at the same time to make it understood how these grisly acts could have occurred among normally decent Spanish peasants. She tells how, at first, many of the peasants were sickened by Pablo's plan to flail the Fascists down between a double line of men leading to the edge of a steep cliff. But within the ironic frame of the entire episode, in relation to the book, there are lesser ironies: for it is the cowardly behavior of the Fascists themselves that brings these peasants to a pitch of mob hatred and violence equal to Pablo's inveterate cruelty.

Throughout all this the reader is never allowed to forget that it is the Loyalists who are committing the atrocities described, and that the leaders of the massacre are the very people with whom

---

[45] *Writers in Crisis* (Boston, 1942), p. 81.

Jordan is now allied. Robert Penn Warren cites the irony of this, but he suggests that *For Whom the Bell Tolls* is not Hemingway's best novel "primarily because . . . Hemingway does not accept the limitations of his premises . . . the irony . . . runs counter to the ostensible surface direction of the story."[46] So it does—but this is the nature of irony; and this is why it is so valuable to Hemingway in his intense effort to dramatize fully the implications of Donne's epigraph in relation to the ironical self-destruction which is civilized warfare. It is a mistake to think of *For Whom the Bell Tolls* as a document of social optimism in its intent, as opposed to the dark pessimism of Hemingway's earlier books. The darkness is relieved, deliberately, only by a faint existentialist glimmer: the general human enterprise seems very likely to end in failure, but each of us must do what he can—"*Nous ferons notre petit possible.*"

It is to this end that the irony of the Loyalist massacre of the Fascists, which early in the book sets the theme of human sacrifice in a highly critical perspective, is complemented by the irony of the denouement. For the central action—the blowing of the bridge—which is responsible for the deaths of El Sordo, Anselmo, Fernando, and, indeed, Robert Jordan, is rendered a strategic failure by the loose tongues of their comrades behind the lines.

To these two fundamental veins of irony many scenes provide tributary support: three may be cited as exemplary. There is the one in which Jordan reads the letters found in the pockets of a Fascist cavalryman he has just shot, and discovers he is from a Spanish town that Jordan knows well:

> How many is that you have killed? he asked himself. I don't know. Do you think you have a right to kill any one? No. But I have to. . . . But you like the people of Navarra better than those of any other part of Spain. Yes. And you kill them. Yes. . . . Don't you know it is wrong to kill? Yes. But you do it? Yes. And you still believe absolutely that your cause is right? Yes.[47]

This irony of Jordan's self-conscious ambivalence is heightened by juxtapositions of which he knows nothing. In the midst of El Sordo's great last fight, we are suddenly given a decidedly sympathetic

[46] Introduction to *A Farewell to Arms* (New York, 1949), p. xxv.
[47] *For Whom the Bell Tolls*, pp. 303–304.

portrait of Lt. Berrendo, second in command of the Fascist cavalry. Julian, his best friend, has just been killed by Sordo, and Captain Mora, the blustering officer in command, is shouting blasphemies at the hilltop in an effort (which carries its own small irony, in view of his imminent death) to prove that no one is left alive up there. Later, after Mora has become El Sordo's "Comrade Voyager," Berrendo reluctantly has his troopers decapitate the dead guerrillas for "proof and identification," and the Fascists start back towards their headquarters:

> Then he thought of Julian, dead on the hill, dead now, tied
> across a horse there in the first troop, and as he rode down into
> the dark pine forest, leaving the sunlight behind him on the
> hill, riding now in the quiet dark of the forest, he started to
> say a prayer for him again.[48]

At this point Anselmo, watching from a hillside, sees them ride past; and on his way back to the guerrilla cave he crosses El Sordo's hilltop where he finds the headless bodies of his comrades: ". . . as he walked he prayed for the souls of Sordo and of all his band. It was the first time he had prayed since the start of the movement."[49] The episode thus ends in ironic equilibrium, with both sides petitioning Heaven. But we have not yet seen our last of Lt. Berrendo. It is he who looms in the sights of Robert Jordan's machine gun in the last paragraph of the story, lending the finale an ironic depth that protects it from false heroics. For these two young soldiers, preponderant as our sympathy may be for one rather than the other, the same bell tolls. The novel is Hemingway's fullest work so far in scope and artistic realization, and to its fulfilment the ambiguity of irony contributes an essential part.

IV

It would be foolish to argue that the work of any first-rate writer owes its success exclusively or even predominantly to any one narrative artifice. Hemingway has used techniques of symbolism and techniques of irony and used them well; what we want in criticism is an even view of his use of these and other artistic resources that

[48] *Ibid.*, p. 326.
[49] *Ibid.*, p. 327.

does not exaggerate one at the expense of others. A point deserving great attention and emphasis about this writer is his devotion to the implicit rather than the explicit mode: and both symbolism and irony truly serve this artistic purpose. Hemingway, in fact, stirs thought as to the interrelationship of these two kinds of ambiguity. It is remarkable how often they operate together in his stories: an ironic fact, perception, or event on the primary level may epitomize an irony in a broader context, and thus doubly deserve selection and accurate report by the narrator. As an illustration of his early effort to communicate "what really happened in action," Hemingway tells in *Death in the Afternoon* how he worked on the problem of accurately depicting a certain bullfight incident:

> . . . waking in the night I tried to remember what it was that seemed just out of my remembering and that was the thing that I had really seen and, finally, remembering all around it, I got it. When he stood up, his face white and dirty and the silk of his breeches opened from waist to knee, it was the dirtiness of the rented breeches, the dirtiness of his slit underwear and the clean, clean, unbearably clean whiteness of the thigh-bone that I had seen, and it was that which was important.[50]

Clearly, it was the startling irony of the contrast that struck Hemingway here as "important"; but certainly (if not so clearly) there is also the symbolic suggestion of another contrast going far beyond the physical—the ironically pathetic gap, perhaps, between the matador's professional failure and his untouched inner pride which is the subject of "The Undefeated."

In a fictional narrative the double operation, ironic and symbolic, can often be seen more sharply: take *The Old Man and the Sea,* where in effect the same subject is dramatized. The old fisherman's physical triumph in catching the great fish is ironically cut down—or transmuted—into spiritual triumph by the marauding sharks who leave him with only the skeleton of the largest marlin ever seen in Cuba. Without working out the metaphor in precise terms it can be said that the irony of the event itself would hardly be so effective without the broadening and deepening of its implication through symbolic suggestion.

[50] *Death in the Afternoon*, p. 20.

It may be true that all perceptions are reducible finally to perceptions of likeness or perceptions of difference. Perhaps this offers a clue to the effectiveness of both symbolism and irony for a writer who, like Hemingway, makes it his life's business to tell a truth, as he once put it, "truer . . . than anything factual can be."[51] With all his famous skill in writing with his eye upon the object, he understood from the beginning that it was only the object in relationship to other objects and to the observer that really counted: significance is, in short, a matter of likeness and difference. This is to speak broadly; and to apply the generalization to symbolism and irony requires a good deal of qualification. Yet symbolism does depend essentially on likeness, and irony on difference; and as artistic tools both are means of interpreting imaginatively, and with the flexibility of implication, a complex reality. Symbolism signifies through a harmony, irony through a discord; symbolism consolidates, irony complicates; symbolism synthesizes, irony analyzes.

For all of this, I would not like to see Hemingway go down in new literary histories as either "a symbolist" or (less likely, if somewhat more appropriately) "an ironist." Taken at face value the denomination "symbolist" has meanings in the common language of criticism that are quite inapplicable to him. But beyond this, Hemingway uses symbolism, as I have tried to show, with a severe restraint that in his good work always staunchly protects his realism. So likewise does he use irony. It is the ambiguity of life itself that Hemingway has sought to render, and if irony has served him peculiarly well it is because he sees life as inescapably ironic. But if we must classify him let us do him justice: with all his skilful use of artistic ambiguity, he remains the great *realist* of twentieth-century American fiction.

Editor's Note: "Hemingway's Ambiguity: Symbolism and Irony" is reprinted, by permission of E. M. Halliday and the Duke University Press, from *American Literature,* XXVIII (1956), pp. 1–22.

Now an editor of *American Heritage* magazine, E. M. Halliday formerly taught at the Universities of Michigan, Chicago, and North Carolina.

[51] Introduction to *Men at War* (New York, 1952), p. xi.

RITUAL IN HEMINGWAY'S
"BIG TWO-HEARTED RIVER"

WILLIAM BYSSHE STEIN

With the sole exception of "Big Two-Hearted River," the adventures of Hemingway's Nick Adams are a chronicle of sterile egoism. He never learns to adjust the development of his character to the contingent nature of life—to the naturalistic world of unpredictable evil, corruption, suffering, and death. He enacts the role of either the apathetic spectator or, when personally involved in a situation, the self-pitying introvert, unheroic and ethically irresponsible. The only important protagonist in the Hemingway canon (here, for obvious reasons, I have only the novels in mind) who fails to cultivate a code in order to withstand the harrowing dislocations of experience, he finds himself on the threshold of mature adulthood without any self-identity, wholly estranged from the public community of love and fellowship. This radical disengagement from humanity is scrupulously foreshadowed in Hemingway's progressive history of Nick which, of course, recapitulates the fate of the lost generation.

Viewed as an evolving thematic pattern, the gradual dissolution of belief in any individual commitment to the pathos and tragedy of ordinary existence reflects the decay of the ideal of selfless love in Western culture. In the stories concerned with Nick's boyhood and adolescence, this narrative purpose is, I think, clearly in evidence. "Indian Camp" exhibits his callow determination to deny the reality of common suffering, for, after an exposure to an agonizing childbirth and suicide, he loses himself in the fantasy "that he would never die."[1] This unwillingness to relate himself emotionally

[1] *The Short Stories of Ernest Hemingway* (New York, 1953), p. 95; all parenthetical references hereafter are to this edition.

to external distress later precipitates a defection from parental love in "The Doctor and the Doctor's Wife"; from marital love in "The End of Something" and "The Three-Day Blow"; from brotherly love in "The Battler" and "The Killers"; and finally from spiritual love in "The Light of the World," even as the ironic title from the New Testament affirms. These betrayals of man's traditional moral and social roles undermine his own self-esteem; subsequently, during the war, he is ignominiously obsessed by fears of suffering and death ("In Another Country," "Now I Lay Me," and "A Way You'll Never Be"). After the armistice, still without any insight into his egregious selfishness, he immerses himself in irresponsible sensual pleasures ("Hills Like White Elephants" and "Cross-Country Snow").

This retrospect serves to establish the burden of guilt that Nick carries on his conscience in "Big Two-Hearted River." Though he has fully recovered from a wound acquired in battle, he is now afflicted by a graver injury—an acute disunity of sensibility. Without faith in himself, in man, in woman, in civilization, or in God, he is, in one of Melville's phrases, "an *Isolato* living on a separate continent of his own," rootless and lost. Unable to face the terrors and nightmares of this isolation, he desperately turns to nature in order to find some purpose in life. But with his ego disenfranchised of its authority, he is completely at the mercy of his instincts; he is "possessed" by the daemonic-divine powers within and without himself, the supernatural monsters of the eternal waters (the river, the abyss, the underworld, the unconscious). And it is their occult potency that he must assimilate and control, else be destroyed. This has been the perennial task of the redeeming hero—Hercules, Perseus, Theseus, Buddha, and even Christ. Like them, he must bring order out of chaos and re-create a world in the image of human reason and love.

It is in the framework of this conflict that Hemingway executes the form of the story (in the process, like T. S. Eliot, adapting the ancient myth of the Fisher King to his artistic designs). The action unfolds in the pattern of ritual: what is said and done has meaning only in terms of the way it is said and done. Nick, in effect, is the communicant in a primitive magico-religious ceremony of immemorial antecedents. Having throughout his life been terrified by the mystery of death, he now undertakes to penetrate into the heart

341

of darkness, the primordial womb out of which life (and by extension, light and consciousness) first came.

Here the title "Big Two-Hearted River" is a major correlative of the ritual act. Black River is the symbolic center of the unknown, the darkness of "the beyond" in which the secret of all existence lies. It mediates the topographic extremes of the meadow and the swamp, the polarities of life and death in the story. It is the path therefore to either salvation or destruction. It is the route of "the dark night of the soul," of the descent of the spirit into the horrors of individual corruption and sin where, paradoxically, rebirth can be won.

The twofold division of the work integrates with this aspect of Hemingway's narrative strategy. The first part is a ritual of preparation, the second a ritual of initiation. Symbolically, Nick enacts the role of the redeemer in the tradition of all the Waste Land myths. The setting in which he finds himself after he gets off the train is sick, barren, and forsaken: "There was no town, nothing but the rails and the burned-over country." (p. 209) Hemingway does not offer any explanation for this cataclysm. But in the light of Nick's life this region is the blighted world whose spiritual heart has been emptied by unfaith and despair. Its renewal depends upon the hero, for he and the land are under the same curse. And since it is water, in the physical and symbolic sense, that will restore the lost fertility, the river is the controlling image of the thematic conflict. As it can revitalize the earth, so it can rehabilitate Nick. In the course of his ritual ordeal in the stream, he must discover the cause of his own impotence so as to release the healing waters.

In the next phase of the action Hemingway centers on the disposition of the protagonist to engage in the mission of salvation. Striking out toward the area of initiation, Nick evinces a capacity to endure pain (incidentally, a reversal of his attitudes during the war) and to overcome his state of death-in-life: "The road climbed steadily. It was hard work walking up-hill. His muscles ached and the day was hot, but Nick felt happy. He felt he had left everything behind, the need for thinking, the need to write, other needs. It was all back of him." This disavowal of self-gratification is anticipated in an early tableau and reveals the hero's intuition into his redemptive task. Like Santiago in *The Old Man and the Sea*, he associates the act of fishing with some deep, inward fulfillment: "It was a long time since Nick had looked into a stream and seen trout.

They were very satisfactory. As the shadow of the kingfisher moved up the stream, a big trout shot upstream in a long angle . . . Nick's heart tightened as the trout moved. He felt all the old feeling." (p. 210)

And on Nick's journey toward the upper reaches of the river, he carries a heavy pack—the burden of the guilt and shame of his culture. At least so Hemingway's repeated allusions to its weight and discomfort seem to imply. For when, in context, related to the ritual direction of his movement, "Nick kept his direction by the sun," (p. 212) their spiritual import is quite obvious. Likewise part of this pattern is his contemplation of the grasshoppers in this charred, desolate region: "These were just ordinary hoppers, but all a sooty black in color. Nick had wondered about them as he walked, without really thinking about them. Now, as he watched the black hopper that was nibbling at the wool of his sock with its fourway lip, he realized that they had turned black from living in the burned-over land." (pp. 211–12) Conventional symbols of plague and famine, these stigmatized insects herald his conversion of their evil into good when he uses them for bait in his quest for "the big fish."

The preparation for this test climaxes in Hemingway's monotonous and detailed description of Nick's pitching camp on the shores of Black River. Imitating a sacred rite of construction, the hero erects his tent in a manner ordained by custom and tradition, and this ceremonial gesture seems to placate the occult powers hovering in these holy precincts:

> Already there was something mysterious and homelike. Nick was happy as he crawled inside the tent. He had not been unhappy all day. This was different though. Now things were done. There had been this to do. Now it was done. It had been a hard trip. He was very tired. That was done. He had made his camp. He was settled. *Nothing could touch him.* [Italics mine]

Here even the prose style is in keeping with the aura of ritual. Precise, controlled, and prayerfully iterative, it signals Nick's release from self-doubt, his attainment of a new spiritual balance. Appropriately, Hemingway symbolizes this transformation in the image of Nick's ravenous appetite, for on the level of mythic truth it is divine sustenance that he craves: "[He] was hungry. He did not

343

believe he had ever been hungrier." Indeed, he intuitively recognizes that he is under the observation of supernatural agencies. For without even momentary distrust in this perception, he dares to address these invisible presences, almost resentfully defending his hunger for earthly fare: " 'I've got a right to eat this kind of stuff, if I'm willing to carry it' . . . His voice sounded strange in the darkening woods. He did not speak again." (p. 215) Nor is he wrong. The pack that he has shouldered on this journey is the cross of his remorse and penance.

It would seem to follow, then, that this meal is sacramental in character. Even though it serves a biological need, it is still sanctioned by extramundane authority. And a moment later, when Nick procures water from the river for his coffee, a similar impulse controls his action. He bases his conduct on a precedent in the holistic past, a previous interlude in this wilderness when he identified himself with a responsible role in life. In making the coffee in conformity with an exemplary model, he recovers the past. He transforms the remembered into the real, breaking through the barriers of time into the order of mythic timelessness from which all sacred ritual issues. So Part I ends. The hero is on the brink of communion with the daemonic-divine forces that can regenerate the Waste Land.

In Part II Hemingway contains the action in the setting of the impending initiation ordeal. But first he relates the events in immediate time to Nick's spiritual conflict, carefully exhibiting the triadic symbol of its content in the foreground: "There was the meadow, the river and the swamp." Since the dank and slimy recesses of the swamp are the source of the river (and the mysterious origins of human consciousness), Hemingway proceeds to re-create the horror and terror of this confrontment of primordial chaos. This dreadful experience is mutely conveyed in Nick's compulsive infatuation with the view throughout the remainder of the story. From an initial impression of innocent beauty, "There were the birch trees in the green of the swamp on the other side of the river," (p. 221) the prospect slowly constricts into the shape of a loathsome abyss of evil: "Ahead the river narrowed and went into the swamp." (p. 230) This hideous sight (really the outward manifestation of Nick's inward corruption) hints at the peril to the hero's soul; yet, if he can overcome his instinctual fascination with this unlicensed depravity and immorality, he can purge himself of all his doubts and negations. For the spell of the swamp represents the ego's enslavement to infantile pleasures, in the Waste Land myth the recurrent pitfall of the potential redeemer. But as Nick awaits his moment of trial, the signs are auspicious; the rising sun (son) and the vitalizing waters (rebirth) promise a transfiguration of his spiritual inertia: "He was excited by the early morning and the river." (p. 221)

Hemingway signals the advent of this miracle at the outset of Nick's ritual descent into the stream: "He stepped into the stream. It was a shock. His trousers clung tight to his legs. His shoes felt the gravel. The water was a rising cold shock." (p. 224) This sensory trauma is not merely a reaction to coldness; rather it is a symptom of panic, and impulsive recoil from the awesome touch of the holy in the flowing water. But with ceremonial gravity he brings this tremor of fright under control, deliberately executing every detail of baiting, casting, and reeling with meticulous care. When finally a small trout is caught, it is released. On one level of reality, this observance follows the conventional practices of the dedicated fisherman; on another, however, it indicates his desire to hook "the big fish." And so Hemingway contrives the narrative development. Nick's line is suddenly jerked taut by a huge trout which, unaccountably, escapes. At this failure he is visibly upset, on the point of abandoning his studied ritual procedure: "Nick's hand was shaky. He reeled in slowly. The thrill had been too much. He felt, vaguely, a little sick, *as though it would be better to sit down*." And now Hemingway plainly denotes the transcendent quality of this fleeting contact in Nick's intuition that he has achieved communion with the spirit of the river: "He had never seen so big a trout. There was a heaviness, *a power not to be held*." (p. 226, Italics mine)

Since the ritual envisages a complete healing of the communicant, the hero's assimilation of the experience is crucial. He must realize that this occult power cannot be possessed, only used to direct the liberated understanding towards extrahuman apprehension. Precisely this happens. Even while he is disconcerted by the loss of the colossal fish, he impulsively deifies what he has lost: "He had been solidly hooked. Solid as a rock. He felt like a rock, too, before he started off. By God, he was a big one. By God, he was the biggest one I ever heard of." (p. 227) Here the repetition of "rock" and "By God" suggests an immediate association with Christ's pronouncement to Peter: "upon this rock I will build my church." And since Christ was the God revealed in the water (baptism) and in the heavenly fish of the Eucharist (*piscis assus, Christus est passus*), it seems to follow that Nick is under obligation to build his faith on a similar foundation of spiritual security, a belief in the immanence of divine power.

In any event, Hemingway implies that in his struggle with "the big fish" the hero has absorbed some mystic strength; for Nick begins to view his emotional relapse as a sign of inward awareness, not as a symptom of weakness and defeat: "slowly the feeling of disappointment left him. It went away slowly, the feeling of disappointment that came sharply after the thrill that made his shoulders ache. It was all right now." Revived, Nick moves toward the swamp, the symbolic center of the ritual situation: "[He] walked around the shallow shelf near the swamp shore until he came out on the shallow bed of the stream." It was here that "the meadow ended." (p. 227) Now Hemingway works out the pattern of initiation in harmony with the protagonist's recovery of his confidence. Nick nets a small fish under very difficult circumstances in the midst of entangling weeds and rushes; but he nevertheless exhibits a perfect mastery over his will. In sum, he is ready for the decisive test. Hence, a moment later he hooks a much larger trout and skillfully nets it. In contrast with his previous failure, he is pictured in the symbolic position of rapt communion with the river: "He took a cigarette out and struck a match to light it. The match sunk into the gray wood, making a tiny furrow. Nick leaned over the side of the log, found a hard place and lit the match. He sat smoking and watching the river." (p. 230) Now there is no tension, no doubt, no depression—only the serene knowledge that he has come to terms with the spirit of the river. In effect, Hemingway has brought the ritual of healing full turn. The hero is ready to undertake the daring plunge into the swamp, into the heart of darkness in which the light of faith can never be extinguished.

At this juncture the symbol of the swamp is more clearly defined. It evolves into the collective image of the hostile world that Nick has fled. It betokens the actuality of existence—the arena of good and evil in which man enacts his search for selfhood:

> Nick did not want to go in there now. He felt a reaction
> against deep wading with the water deepening up under his

armpits, to hook big trout in places impossible to land them. In the swamp the banks were bare, the big cedars came together overhead, the sun did not come through, except in patches; in the fast deep water, in the half light, *the fishing would be tragic. In the swamp fishing was a tragic adventure.* Nick did not want it. He did not want to go down the stream any further today. [Italics mine]

In the resolution of the action Nick consciously admits the inevitability of defeat, frustration, and death. But at the same time he senses that this knowledge of mortal destiny is in itself the basis of human dignity: "He looked back. The river just showed through the trees. There were plenty of days coming when he could fish in the swamp." (pp. 231–32) Of course, Hemingway does not mean this literally. Healed within and without, Nick can now return to civilization—to life. In the successful performance of an archetypal ritual he has infused human values with divine strength. He now can free the waters that will fertilize the Waste Land. In purging himself of despair he has conquered his sickness of soul. In his communion with "the big fish," the spirit of the river, he has reconciled his mind to the reality of tragic experience. He has learned the truth which the lost generation scorned: only deprivation and suffering can teach man to love man.

In the cycle of exile and return which controls the adventures of Nick Adams, Hemingway lays the foundation for the parable of *The Old Man and the Sea.* In the novel he simply treats explicitly the implicit theme of "Big Two-Hearted River," in the process, however indirectly, affirming the continuity of his moral outlook on the world. Ultimately, then, he writes in a framework of values as traditional as Eliot's in *Four Quartets* or Faulkner's in *The Fable,* yet without their tiring religious nostalgia. Somewhat like Freud, he recognizes that the chaos and violence of external human behavior are expressions of primitive desires which man, throughout time, has used ritual to order and to understand. In his enunciation of the need for a ceremonial adjustment to the dislocations of experience, he attests the sacredness of the cosmic religious consciousness that produced both the Fisher King and Christ.

Editor's Note: "Ritual in Hemingway's 'Big Two-Hearted River' " by William Bysshe Stein is reprinted by permission of the Uni-

A Professor of English at the State University of New York at Binghamton, William Bysshe Stein is the author of *Hawthorne's Faust: A Study of the Devil Archetype, Two Brahman Sources of Thoreau and Emerson,* and numerous essays on Melville, Hawthorne, Whitman, James, Faulkner, and others.

F. SCOTT FITZGERALD

1896-1940

Francis Scott Key Fitzgerald was born in St. Paul, Minnesota, into a family just prosperous enough to involve him in the society of the very rich. Fitzgerald was sent to the Newman School of Hackensack, a fashionable preparatory school, and then to Princeton University, where he cemented his deep ambivalence toward money—and friendships. He carried on an active social life there and contributed stories to *The Nassau Literary Magazine,* but his academic work was unsatisfactory, and he withdrew in 1917 without a degree. He joined the army but was not sent overseas. During this period he worked on what was eventually to be published as *This Side of Paradise* in 1920. His marriage to Zelda Sayre of Montgomery, Alabama followed quickly. The young couple devoted themselves to being living embodiments of the Jazz Age, and Fitzgerald's fiction was bringing in an amount of money unheard of for a writer at that time. His works of the early twenties include *Flappers and Philosophers, The Beautiful and Damned,* and *Tales of the Jazz Age.* In 1925 Fitzgerald published what is usually considered his masterpiece, *The Great Gatsby.*

Crisis increasingly modulated the hilarity of Fitzgerald's exhaustive private life. In 1930 Zelda had the first of a series of nervous breakdowns. Fitzgerald's own deterioration is chronicled in essays collected posthumously by Edmund Wilson under the title, *The Crack-Up* (1945).

Despite the increasing failure of his health and his personal life, he continued to work in a desperate attempt to remove his debts and regain his fame of the early twenties. In addition to script-writing in Hollywood, his literary productions include *All the Sad Young Men* (1926), *Tender Is the Night* (1934), *Taps at Reveille* (1935), and *The Last Tycoon*, which was still unfinished at the time of his death, by heart attack, in 1940.

FITZGERALD'S
BRAVE NEW WORLD

EDWIN FUSSELL

Think of the lost ecstasy of the Elizabethans. "Oh my America,
my new found land," think of what it meant to them and of
what it means to us.

(T. E. Hulme, Speculations)

I

The source of Fitzgerald's excellence is an uncanny ability to
juxtapose the sensibilities implied by the phrase "romantic wonder" with the most conspicuous, as well as the most deeply significant, phenomena of American civilization, and to derive from that
juxtaposition a moral critique of human nature. None of our
major writers is more romantically empathic than this avatar of
Keats in the era of Harding; none draws a steadier bead on the
characteristic shortcomings, not to say disasters, of the most grandiose
social experiment of modern times. Thence the implacable moralist
with stars (Martinis) in his eyes: worshipper, analyst, judge, and
poet. But it is not very illuminating to say that Fitzgerald wrote
the story of his own representative life, unless we are prepared to
read his confessions—and then his evaluation of those confessions—
as American history; and unless we reciprocally learn to read American history as the tale of the romantic imagination in the United
States.

Roughly speaking, Fitzgerald's basic plot is the history of the New
World (ironic *double entendre* here and throughout); more precisely, of the human imagination in the New World. It shows itself
in two predominant patterns, quest and seduction. The quest is
the search for romantic wonder (a kind of febrile secular beatitude),
in the terms proposed by contemporary America; the seduction
represents capitulation to these terms. Obversely, the quest is a

351

flight: from reality, from normality, from time, fate, death, and the conception of *limit*. In the social realm, the pattern of desire may be suggested by such phrases as "the American dream" and "the pursuit of happiness." Fitzgerald begins by exposing the corruption of that dream in industrial America; he ends by discovering that the pursuit is universally seductive and perpetually damned. Driven by inner forces that compel him towards the personal realization of romantic wonder, the Fitzgerald hero is destroyed by the materials which the American experience offers as objects and criteria of passion; or, at best, he is purged of these unholy fires, chastened, and reduced.

In general, this quest has two symptomatic goals. There is, for one, the search for eternal youth and beauty, what might be called the historic myth of Ponce de Leon. ("Historic" because the man was really looking for a fountain; "myth" because no such fountain ever existed).[1] The essence of romantic wonder appears to reside in the illusion of perennial youth and grace and happiness surrounding the leisure class of which Fitzgerald customarily wrote; thus the man of imagination in America, searching for the source of satisfaction of his deepest aesthetic needs, is seduced by the delusion that these qualities are actually to be found in people who, in sober fact, are vacuous and irresponsible. But further, this kind of romantic quest, which implies both escape and destruction, is equated on the level of national ideology with a transcendental and Utopian contempt for time and history, and on the religious level, which Fitzgerald (whose Catholic apostasy was about half genuine and half imagined) persistently but hesitantly approaches, with a blasphemous rejection of the very conditions of human existence.

The second goal is, simply enough, money. The search for wealth is the familiar Anglo-Saxon Protestant ideal of personal material success, most succinctly embodied for our culture in the saga of young Benjamin Franklin. It is the romantic assumption of this aspect of the "American dream" that all the magic of the world can be

---

[1] It is a curious but far from meaningless coincidence that Frederick Jackson Turner used the image of "a magic fountain of youth" to evoke the creative and restorative powers of the unexhausted Western frontier. I am inclined to think Fitzgerald knew what he was about when he called *The Great Gatsby* "a story of the West." Traditionally in American writing "the West" means both the Western part of the United States and the New World, and especially the first as synecdoche of the other.

had for money. Both from a moral, and from a highly personal and idiosyncratic Marxist standpoint, Fitzgerald examines and condemns the plutocratic ambitions of American life and the ruinous price exacted by their lure. But the two dreams are, of course, so intimately related as to be for all practical purposes one: the appearance of eternal youth and beauty centers in a particular social class whose glamor is made possible by social inequality and inequity. Beauty, the presumed object of aesthetic contemplation, is commercialized, love is bought and sold. Money is the means to the violent recovery or specious arrest of an enchanting youth.

In muted contrast, Fitzgerald repeatedly affirms his faith in an older, simpler America, generally identified as pre-Civil War; the emotion is that of pastoral, the social connotations agrarian and democratic. In such areas he continues to find fragments of basic human value, social, moral, and religious. But these affirmations are for the most part subordinate and indirect; Fitzgerald's attention was chiefly directed upon the merchandise of romantic wonder proffered by his own time and place. Like the narrator in *Gatsby,* he was always "within and without, simultaneously enchanted and repelled by the inexhaustible variety of life." Through a delicate and exact imagery, he was able to extend this attitude of simultaneous enchantment and repulsion over the whole of the American civilization he knew. His keenest perception, and the one that told most heavily for his fiction, was the universal quality of the patterns he was tracing, his greatest discovery that there was nothing new about the Lost Generation except its particular toys. The quest for romantic wonder and the inevitable failure were only the latest in a long series.

Fitzgerald approached this major theme slowly and more by intuition than design. Or perhaps he had to live it, and then understand it, before he could write it. In a hazy form it is present in such early stories as "The Offshore Pirate" and "Dalyrimple Goes Wrong." It is allegorized in "The Diamond as Big as the Ritz" and fumbled in *The Beautiful and Damned.*

"May Day," significantly motivated by his first sharp awareness of class cleavages in American society, together with important cleavages of period in American history, is for the reader tracing Fitzgerald's gradual realization of this major theme the most rewarding production of his early career. Its formal construction on social principles ("Mr. In" and "Mr. Out") is obvious enough; what usually goes unnoticed is the way Fitzgerald's symbolic method extends his critique from the manners of drunken undergraduates to the pervasive malaise of an entire civilization. The hubris with which these characters fade from the story in a parody of the Ascension dramatically and comically pinpoints the materialistic hedonism, along with its traditional counterpart, a vulgar idealism, which Fitzgerald is already identifying as his culture's fatal flaw:

> Then they were in an elevator bound skyward.
> "What floor, please?" said the elevator man.
> "Any floor," said Mr. In.
> "Top floor," said Mr. Out.
> "This is the top floor," said the elevator man.
> "Have another floor put on," said Mr. Out.
> "Higher," said Mr. In.
> "Heaven," said Mr. Out.

Set against the story's controlling symbol, the universal significance of this passage frames its particular historical implications. The scene is an all-night restaurant, and the preliminary description emphasizes social and economic inequality, the brutalizations of poverty, the sick insouciance of unmerited riches. As a Yale junior is ejected for throwing hash at the waiters, "the great plate-glass front had turned to a deep creamy blue . . . Dawn had come up in Columbus Circle, magical, breathless dawn, silhouetting the great statue of the immortal Christopher [Christ-bearer], and mingling in a curious and uncanny manner with the fading yellow electric light inside." The final significance of this symbol can only be established after considering the conclusion of *The Great Gatsby* (and perhaps not even then; what, for example, about that oceanic "blue," or the failing efficacy of man-made illumination against the light of day, prior in time to the light it supersedes?). But the general intention is clear enough: Fitzgerald is measuring the behavior and attitudes of the Lost Generation with a symbol of romantic wonder extensive enough to comprehend all American experience, as far back as 1492. The contrast involves the ironic rejection of all that this present generation believes in, the immaturity and triviality of its lust for pleasure. But then, by a further turn of irony, the voyage of Columbus and his discovery of the Western Hemisphere is also the actual event forming the first link in the chain leading to the butt-end of contemporary folly. There is the further implication that some sort of conscious search is at the heart of American experience, but had never before taken so childish a form. What Fitzgerald is almost certainly trying to say with this image is: we are the end of Columbus' dream, and this is our brave new world.

II

With *The Great Gatsby* (1925), Fitzgerald first brought his vision to full and mature realization. Gatsby is essentially the man of imagination in America, given specificity and solidity and precision by the materials American society offers him. "If personality is an unbroken series of successful gestures, then there was something gorgeous about him, some heightened sensitivity to the promises of life, as if he were related to one of those intricate machines that register earthquakes ten thousand miles away." It is Gatsby's capacity for romantic wonder that Fitzgerald is insisting upon in this preliminary exposition, a capacity he goes on to define as "an extraordinary gift for hope, a romantic readiness" (the first phrase suggesting the central theological virtue, the second implying its parodic counterpart). With the simile of the seismograph, a splendid image of the human sensibility in a mechanized age, Fitzgerald has in effect already introduced the vast back-drop of American civilization against which Gatsby's gestures are to be interpreted. The image is as integral as intricate; for if Gatsby is to be taken as the product and manifestation of the seductive and corrupting motivations involved in "the American dream," he is also the instrument by means of which Fitzgerald will register the tremors that point to its self-contained possibilities of destruction, its *fault* (flaw), in the geological sense. "What preyed on Gatsby, what foul dust floated in the wake of his dreams" is the stuff of the novel, the social content of Fitzgerald's fictional world. But it is equally essential to realize that Gatsby, too, has been derailed by values and attitudes held in common with the society that destroys him. How else, indeed, might he be destroyed? Certainly, in such a world, the novel assures us, a dream like Gatsby's cannot possibly remain pristine, given the materials with which the original impulse toward wonder must invest itself. In short, Gatsby is somewhat more than pathetic, a sad figure preyed upon by the American leisure class. The novel is neither melodramatic nor bathetic, but critical. The unreal values of the world of Tom and Daisy Buchanan, to a very considerable degree, are Gatsby's values too, inherent in his dream. Gatsby from the beginning lives in an imaginary world, where "a universe of ineffable gaudiness spun itself out in his brain"; negatively, this quality manifests itself in a dangerous, and frequently vulgar, tendency toward sentimental idealizations: his reveries "were a satisfactory hint of the unreality of reality, a promise that the rock of the world was founded securely on a fairy's wing." (A variety of religious overtones emanates from the word "rock." Gatsby's capacity for wonder is obviously corrupted by the meager and vicious nature of American culture. Potentially, he constitutes a tentative and limited indictment of that culture; actually, he is that culture's thoroughly appropriate scapegoat and victim. "He was a son of God . . . and he must be about His Father's business, the service of a vast, vulgar, and meretricious beauty." God the Father, or the Founding Fathers? In such ambiguity lurk the novel's deepest ironies.

Daisy finally becomes for Gatsby the iconic manifestation of this dubious vision of beauty. Little enough might have been possible for Gatsby at best, but once he "wed his unutterable visions to her perishable breath, his mind would never romp again like the mind of God." (Parody of the Incarnation.) Steadily and surreptitiously, Fitzgerald continues to suggest the idea of blasphemy in connection with Gatsby's Titanic imaginative lusts. But of course the focus of the novel must be sexual and social, for the implication *of* the religious implication is that Gatsby (that is to say American culture) provides mainly secular objects for the religious imagination to feed on, as it also provides tawdry images for the aesthetic imagination. After concentrating Gatsby's wonder on Daisy, Fitzgerald proceeds to an explicit statement of her thematic significance. Gatsby was "overwhelmingly aware of the *youth* and mystery that *wealth* imprisons and *preserves,* of the freshness of many clothes, and of Daisy, gleaming like silver, safe and proud above the hot struggles of the poor" (my italics). Her voice is mysteriously enchanting, the typifying feature of her role as *la belle dame sans merci,* and throughout the action serves to suggest her loveliness and desirability. But only Gatsby, in a rare moment of insight, is able to identify the causes of its subtle and elusive magic, upon which Nick Carraway meditates: "It was full of money—that was the inexhaustible charm that rose and fell in it, the jingle of it, the cymbals' song of it . . . High in a white palace the king's daughter, the golden girl . . ."

Possession of an image like Daisy is all that Gatsby can finally conceive as "success"; and Gatsby is meant to be a very representative American in the intensity of his yearning for success, as well as in the symbols which he equates with it. Gatsby is a contemporary variation on an old American pattern, the rags-to-riches story exalted by American legend as early as Crèvecoeur's *Letters from an American Farmer* (most mawkishly in the "History of Andrew, the Hebridian," significantly appended to the famous Letter III, "What is an American"), and primarily fixed in the popular mind by Benjamin Franklin. Franklin's youthful resolutions are parodied in those that the adolescent Gatsby writes on the back flyleaf of his copy of *Hopalong Cassidy,* a conjunction of documents as eloquently expressive of American continuities as of the progress of civilization in the new world.

The connection between Gatsby's individual tragedy and the tragedy of American civilization is also made, and again through symbol, with respect to historical attitudes. Gatsby's philosophy of history is summed up in his devotion to the green light burning on Daisy's dock. Nick first sees Gatsby in an attitude of supplication, a gesture that pathetically travesties the traditional gestures of worship. He finally discerns that the object of that trembling piety is precisely this green light which, until his disillusion, remains one of Gatsby's "enchanted objects." But only in the novel's concluding passage, toward which all action and symbol relentlessly tend, is the reader given the full implications of the green light as the historically-corrupted religious symbol ("Gatsby believed in the green light, the orgiastic future"). With no historical sense whatever, yet trapped in the detritus of American history, Gatsby is the superbly effective fictional counterpart of that native philistine maxim that "history is bunk." For those interested in such comparisons, he may also recall the more crowing moods of Emerson and Thoreau and the alleged "timelessness" of their idealistic visions and exhortations, now, alas, like Daisy who gleamed like silver, somewhat tarnished. For Fitzgerald, this contemptuous repudiation of tradition, historical necessity, and moral accountability, was deluded and hubristic. When he finally came to see—as he clearly did in *Gatsby*— that in this irresponsibility lay the real meaning behind the obsessive youth-worship of popular culture in his own day, he was able to identify Gatsby as at once the man of his age and the man of the ages, a miserable twentieth-century Ponce de Leon. His fictional world was no longer simply the Jazz Age, the Lost Generation, but the whole of American civilization as it culminated in his own time.

In the final symbol of the novel, Fitzgerald pushes the personal equation to national, even universal scope, in a way that recalls the method of "May Day." Fitzgerald is commenting on Gatsby's state of disillusion immediately before his death:

> He must have felt that he had lost the old warm world, paid a high price for living too long with a single dream. He must have looked up at an unfamiliar sky through frightening leaves and shivered as he found what a grotesque thing a rose is and how raw the sunlight was upon the scarcely created grass. A new world, material without being real, where poor ghosts, breathing dreams like air, drifted fortuitously about. . .

Such was the romantic perception of wonder, when finally stripped of its pleasing and falsifying illusions. Such was Fitzgerald's maturest vision of the United States of America, perhaps the most magnificent statement in all our literature of the cruel modernity of the "new world," its coldness, unreality, and absurdity nourished (if one may use so inappropriate a word) by that great mass neurosis known as "the American Dream." So Fitzgerald, the quintessential outsider-insider, moves to his final critique:

> And as the moon rose higher the inessential houses began to melt away until gradually I became aware of the old island here that flowered once for Dutch sailor's eyes—a fresh, green breast of the new world. Its vanished trees, the trees that had made way for Gatsby's house, had once pandered in whispers to the last and greatest of all human dreams; for a transitory enchanted moment man must have held his breath in the presence of this continent, compelled into an aesthetic contemplation he neither understood nor desired, face to face for the last time in history with something commensurate to his capacity for wonder.

The most obvious point to be made about this passage is its insistence that Gatsby's insatiable capacity for wonder could have, in the modern world, no proper objective. The emotion lingered on, generations of Americans had translated it into one or another set of inadequate terms, but Gatsby, like all his ancestors, though increasingly, was doomed by demanding the impossible. There is also the ironic contrast between the wonder of the New World (to its Old World discoverers) and what Americans (who all came from the Old World in the first place) have made of it; the same point Fitzgerald made in similar fashion with the Columbus image in "May Day." Finally, there is a more universal, an extra-historical meaning implicit in the language of this passage—the hope that the new world could possibly satisfy man's inordinate, secular lusts (displaced religious emotions from the very outset) was "the last and greatest of all human dreams," seductive and unreal. The most impressive associations cluster around the word "pander," which implies the illicit commercial traffic among love, youth, and beauty, and which thus effectually subsumes most of the central meanings of the novel. In a later essay, Fitzgerald repeated with variations the "panders in whispers" phrase: New York City "no longer whispers of fantastic success and eternal youth," a fine instance of how the myths of Benjamin Franklin and Ponce de Leon came to be blended in his mind. The two parallel themes do, of course, meet in *The Great Gatsby*; indeed, they are tangled at the heart of the plot, for the most outrageous irony in Gatsby's tragedy is his belief that he can buy his dream, which is, precisely, to recapture the past. Unfortunately for this all too representative American, his dream "was already behind him, somewhere back in that vast obscurity beyond the city, where the dark fields of the republic rolled on under the night." It hardly needs saying that Fitzgerald chooses his language carefully, and that every word is loaded.

III

Tender Is the Night (1934) restates the essential theme and complicates it. If this novel seems somehow less successful than *Gatsby*, that is perhaps because the greater proliferation of thematic statement is not matched by a corresponding gain in clarity and control. But beneath the additional richness, and apparent confusion, the same general story can be made out. Dick Diver is like Gatsby the American as man of imagination. His chief difference from Gatsby is that he dispenses romantic wonder to others, in addition to living by and for it himself. Gatsby tries to purvey dreams, but doesn't know how. But to Rosemary Hoyt (of whom, more later) Dick's "voice promised that he would . . . open up whole *new worlds* for her, unroll an endless succession of magnificent possibilities" (my italics). Diver is the man with the innate capacity for romantic wonder, temporarily a member of the American leisure class of the 'twenties, an "organizer of private gaiety, curator of richly incrusted happiness." His intellectual and imaginative energies have been diverted from normal creative and functional channels and expended on the effort to prevent, for a handful of the very rich, the American dream from revealing its nightmarish realities.

Although Dick is given a more specific background than Gatsby, he is equally a product of his civilization and shares its characteristic deficiences: "the illusions of eternal strength and health, and of the essential goodness of people; illusions of a nation, the lies of generations of frontier mothers who had to croon falsely that there were no wolves outside the cabin door." (The lies also of generations of American politicians, historians, publicists, fireside poets, and similar confidence-men, who had no such easy excuse.) This inherent romantic has been further weakened, though not quite destroyed, by the particular forms of sentimentality of his own generation: "he must press on toward the Isles of Greece, the cloudy waters of unfamiliar ports, the lost girl on shore, the moon of popular songs. A part of Dick's mind was made up of the tawdry souvenirs of his boyhood. Yet in that somewhat littered Five-and-Ten, he had managed to keep alive the low painful fire of intelligence."

Such is the man, potentially noble like Gatsby, but with the fatal flaw of imagination common to and conditioned by the superficial symbols and motivations of his culture, who is brought against the conditions of temptation represented by Nicole. She is the grand-daughter of a "self-made American capitalist" and of a German Count, and her family is placed in perspective by Fitzgerald's frequent analogies with feudal artistocracy. "Her father would have it on almost any clergyman," such as Dick's father; "they were an American ducal family without a title—the very name . . . caused a psychological metamorphosis in people." Yet behind this facade of glamor and power lies unnatural lust and perversion. Nicole's father, this "fine American type," has committed incest with his daughter—the very incarnation of the American vision of youth, beauty, and wealth—and made of her a psychotic for young Dr. Diver to cure. As Nicole says, " 'I'm a crook by heritage.' "

360

Through Nicole Fitzgerald conveys, as he had with Daisy, all that is sexually and socially desirable in youth and beauty: "there were all the potentialities for romantic love in that lovely body and in the delicate mouth. . . . Nicole had been a beauty as a young girl and she would be a beauty later." Apparently she is eternally youthful, and only at the end of the novel is it discernible that she has aged. Her face, which corresponds in sensuous utility to Daisy's voice, is lovely and hard, "her eyes brave and watchful, looking straight ahead toward nothing." She is an empty child, representative of her social class, of the manners and morals of the 'twenties, and of the world of values for which America, like Diver, was once more selling its soul. But it is chiefly Nicole's semblance of perpetual youth that allows Fitzgerald to exploit her as a central element in the narrative correlative he is constructing for his vision of American life. Occasionally he handles her in a way that goes beyond social criticism, entering, if obliquely and implicitly, the realm of religious apprehension:

> The only physical disparity between Nicole at present and the Nicole of five years before was simply that she was no longer a young girl. But she was enough ridden by the current youth worship, the moving pictures with their myriad faces of girl-children, blandly represented as carrying on the work and wisdom of the world, to feel a jealousy of youth.
>
> She put on the first ankle-length day dress that she had owned for many years, and crossed herself reverently with Chanel Sixteen.

(So Diver, at the end of the novel, but with full consciousness of the blasphemy, "blesses" the Riviera beach "with a papal cross," immediately before returning to the obscurity of small-town America. The malediction may by a later generation of readers be taken as Fitzgerald's also, whose equally obscure end was ironically to come in the most notorious of American small towns, Hollywood.) But while Fitzgerald could upon occasion thus extend the significance of his narrative, he never neglected to keep it firmly grounded in a specific social and economic world, and it is in this realm that most of his correspondences are established:

> Nicole was the product of much ingenuity and toil. For her sake trains began their run at Chicago and traversed the round

belly of the continent to California; chicle factories fumed and
link belts grew link by link in factories; men mixed toothpaste
in vats and drew mouthwash out of copper hogsheads; girls
canned tomatoes quickly in August or worked rudely at the
Five-and-Tens on Christmas Eve; half-breed Indians toiled on
Brazilian coffee plantations and dreamers were muscled out of
patent rights in new tractors—these were some of the people
who gave a tithe to Nicole, and as the whole system swayed
and thundered onward it lent a feverish bloom to such processes of hers as wholesale buying, like the flush of a fireman's
face holding his post before a spreading blaze. She illustrated
very simple principles, containing in herself her own doom,
but illustrated them so accurately that there was grace in the
procedure.[2]

Yet even here religious nuance continues ("Christmas Eve," "tithe");
the simple principles Nicole illustrates are not only Marxian but
also Christian. Still, if her principles are simple, their illustration
is epic in scope and intention. The social ramifications of Fitzgerald's great novels are broad indeed; at their base are criminal
injustice and inhuman waste, on a world-wide scale, and at their
apex the American girl, the king's daughter, beautiful, forever
young, and insane.

In the central scenes of temptation (Book II, chapter V, in the
original form), Fitzgerald quite deliberately allows Nicole to assume her full symbolic significance, thereby revealing unmistakably
that the central action of *Tender Is the Night* must be read against
the broadest background of American life. Throughout this chapter
runs the *leitmotif* of the author's generalizing commentary, beginning with the passage: "the impression of her youth and beauty
grew on Dick until it welled up inside him in a compact paroxysm
of emotion. She smiled, a moving childish smile that was like all
the lost youth in the world." This mood of pathetic nostalgia is
quickly objectified in the talk of Dick and Nicole about American
popular songs; soon Dick feels that "there was that excitement
about her that seemed to reflect all the excitement of the world."
So ends the first of the two scenes that comprise this chapter. The
second meeting opens on a similar key: "Dick wished she had no

[2] Cf. Gatsby as seismograph. Probably it is dangerous to take too literally
Fitzgerald's remark that he was "essentially Marxian"; it seems to me equally
dangerous to ignore it altogether.

background, that she was just a girl lost with no address save the night from which they had come." This time they play the songs they had mentioned the week before: "they were in America now." And Fitzgerald drives the point home in his last sentence: "Now there was this scarcely saved waif of disaster bringing him the essence of a continent. . ."

At first Dick laughs off the notion that Nicole's family has purchased him, but he gradually succumbs, "inundated by a trickling of goods and money." Once again, Nicole is the typifying object of her class and society, especially in the terms she proposes for the destruction of her victim's moral and intellectual integrity: "Naturally Nicole, *wanting to own him, wanting him to stand still forever,* encouraged any slackness on his part" (my italics). Although the pattern is more complex than in *Gatsby,* practically the same controlling lines of theme can be observed. The man of imagination, fed on the emotions of romantic wonder, is tempted and seduced and (in this case, nearly) destroyed by that American dream which customarily takes two forms: the escape from time and the materialistic pursuit of a purely hedonistic happiness. On the historical level, the critique is of the error of American romanticism in attempting to transcend and thus escape historical responsibility. On the economic level, the critique is of the fatal beauty of American capitalism, its destructive charm and recklessness. Thematically, the lines come together when Nicole attempts to own Dick and therefore to escape time—keeping him clear of it, too—as when Gatsby tries to buy back the past. On the religious level, if indeed there is one, the critique must be defined more cautiously: perhaps one can say that Fitzgerald intermittently insinuates the possibility that human kind are inveterately prone to befuddle themselves with the conspicuous similarities between the city of man and the city of God, paying scant attention to their more radical difference.

In Rosemary Hoyt, who brings from Hollywood to Europe the latest American version of the dream of youthful innocence, Fitzgerald has still another important center of consciousness. It is through her eyes, for instance, that Fitzgerald gives us his first elaborate glimpses of the Divers, and their hangers-on, at the Americanized Riviera. Because of Rosemary's acute but undisciplined perceptions, Fitzgerald can insist perpetually on the ironic tensions between the richest texture of social appearance and the hidden reality of moral agony: her "naïveté responded whole-heartedly to the expensive simplicity of the Divers, unaware of its complexity and its lack of innocence, unaware that it was all a selection of quality rather than quantity from the run of the world's bazaar; and that the simplicity of behavior also, the nursery-like peace and good-will, the emphasis on the simpler virtues, was part of a desperate bargain with the gods and had been attained through struggles she could not have guessed at." ("Nursery-like peace and good will" is a good example of how Fitzgerald's subtly paradoxical prose style incessantly supplies the kind of religious-secular befuddlement alluded to above.)

Rosemary manifests the effects of Hollywood sentimentality and meretriciousness on the powers of American perception and imagination. The image-patterns that surround her movements are largely concerned with childhood; she is "as dewy with belief as a child from one of Mrs. Burnett's vicious tracts." Immature and egocentric, she provides one more symbol of the corruption of imagination in American civilization; both deluded and deluding, she is without resources for escape such as are available to Nick Carroway and, to a considerably lesser extent, Dick Diver. It is Diver who sounds the last important note about her: " 'Rosemary didn't grow up.' " That she is intended as a representative figure Fitzgerald makes amply clear in his embittered account of her picture "Daddy's Girl": "There she was—so young and innocent—the product of her mother's loving care . . . embodying all the immaturity of the race, cutting a new cardboard paper doll to pass before its empty harlot's mind."

Nicole and Rosemary are for this novel the objectified images of Fitzgerald's "brave new world." Only occasionally, and only in pathos, does Dick Diver escape the limits of this terrifying world. Once, the three of them are sitting in a restaurant, and Dick notices a group of "gold star mothers": "in their happy faces, the dignity that surrounded and pervaded the party, he perceived all the maturity of an older America. For a while the sobered women who had come to mourn for their dead, for something they could not repair, made the room beautiful. Momentarily, he sat again on his father's knee, riding with Moseby while the old loyalties and devotions fought on around him. Almost with an effort he turned back to his two women at the table and faced the whole new world in which he believed." Only as this illusion fades, to the accompaniment of an almost unbearable "interior laughter," does Dick Diver

achieve a minimal and ambiguous salvation, a few shattered fragments of reality, including the anonymity of professional and social
failure.

IV

For purposes of corroboration, one can add a certain amount of
documentation from Fitzgerald's non-fictional writings, as collected
in the posthumous volume *The Crack-Up* (1945). The point that
most needs buttressing, probably, is that Fitzgerald saw in the quest
for romantic wonder a recurrent pattern of American behavior.
Such an attitude seems strongly implied by the works of fiction, but
of course it is additionally reassuring to find Fitzgerald writing his
daughter: "You speak of how good your generation is, but I think
they share with every generation since the Civil War in America
the sense of being somehow about to inherit the earth. You've
heard me say before that I think the faces of most American women
over thirty are relief maps of petulant and bewildered unhappiness" (p. 306). A brief sketch of a "typical product of our generation" in the *Note-Books* indicates further what qualities were involved in this "sense of being about to inherit the earth": "her
dominant idea and goal is freedom without responsibility, which is
like gold without metal, spring without winter, youth without
age, one of those maddening, coo-coo mirages of wild riches" (p.
166). That this personal attitude, translated into the broader terms
of a whole culture, represented a negation of historical responsibility, is made sufficiently clear in another *Note-Book* passage:
"Americans, he liked to say, should be born with fins, and perhaps
they were—perhaps money was a form of fin. In England, property
begot a strong place sense, but Americans, restless and with shallow
roots, needed fins and wings. There was even a recurrent idea in
America about an education that would leave out history and the
past, that should be a sort of equipment for aerial adventure,
weighed down by none of the stowaways of inheritance or tradition" (p. 109). Still another passage, this time from one of the
"Crack-Up" essays, makes it equally clear that Fitzgerald habitually
saw the universal applicability of all he was saying about the ruling
passions of America: "This is what I think now: that the natural
state of the sentient adult is a qualified unhappiness. I think also
that in an adult the desire to be finer in grain that you are, 'a
constant striving' (as those people say who gain their bread by say-

ing it) only adds to this unhappiness in the end—that end that comes to our youth and hope" (p. 84).

Fortunately, by some kind of unexplained miracle (perhaps nothing more mysterious than his deep-seated integrity as a writer), Fitzgerald did not have it in himself to be a cynic. For all the failure and futility he found in the American experience, his attitude was an attitude of acceptance, remarkably free of that sense of despair which Kierkegaard correctly prophesied as the typical sin of the moderns. There was always in him something of Jimmy Gatz's "extraordinary gift of hope," which enabled him to touch the subjects he touched without being consumed by them. (The tragedies of his personal life are another matter; I am speaking only of his heroism and integrity as an artist.) The exhaustion of the frontier and the rebound of the post-war expatriate movement marked for him the end of a long period in human history, and it was really this entire period, the history of the post-Renaissance man in America, that he made the substance of his works. After exploring his materials to their limits Fitzgerald knew, at his greatest moments, that he had discovered a universal pattern of desire and belief and behavior, and that in it was compounded the imaginative history of modern, especially American, civilization. Thus (again from the *Note-Books*):

> He felt then that if the pilgrimage eastward of the rare poisonous flower of his race was the end of the adventure which had started westward three hundred years ago, if the long serpent of the curiosity had turned too sharp upon itself, cramping its bowels, bursting its shining skin, at least there had been a journey; like to the satisfaction of a man coming to die—one of those human things that one can never understand unless one has made such a journey and heard the man give thanks with the husbanded breath. The frontiers were gone—there were no more barbarians. The short gallop of the last great race, the polyglot, the hated and the despised, the crass and scorned, had gone—at least it was not a meaningless extinction up an alley (p. 199).

There are dozens more such passages, in the non-fictional prose as in the fictional; naturally, for Fitzgerald's subject, however broadly he came to understand it, was in the first instance his own journey. He was by nature almost incredibly sympathetic. He was also more knowledgeable—both morally and intellectually—than he is generally credited with being. To such an extent that his more enthusiastic readers are almost tempted to say: if the polyglot gallop is not a meaningless cancellation of itself, that is chiefly because Fitzgerald—and the few Americans who by virtue of their imaginative grasp of our history can rightly be called his peers—interposed a critical distance between his matter and his expression of it. There is perhaps more difference between an ordinary understanding of America and Fitzgerald's than between the gaudy idealizations of the Elizabethans and the equally comfortable cynicism of twentieth-century London.

Editor's Note: "Fitzgerald's Brave New World," a revision of an article from *English Literary History*, XIX (1952), pp. 291–306, is reprinted by permission of Edwin Fussell and Charles Scribner's Sons.

Poet, critic, editor, and Professor of American Literature at the University of California, San Diego, Edwin Fussell is the author of numerous essays on American fiction and poetry. His books include *Edward Arlington Robinson: The Literary Background of a Traditional Poet* and *Frontier: American Literature and the American West.*

WILLIAM FAULKNER

1897-1962

William Faulkner was born in New Albany, Mississippi and lived most of his life in nearby Oxford, the location of the University of Mississippi. Before finishing high school he enlisted in the Canadian Royal Flying Corps, but returned in about a year to Oxford and spent two years at the University. He was then postmaster at the University and was devoting more and more time to the craft of writing. In 1924 he went to New Orleans, where he met and was influenced by Sherwood Anderson. In New Orleans he wrote *Soldier's Pay,* an undistinguished novel particularly in the light of his later achievements. In 1925 he embarked upon a walking tour of France and Germany. He returned to Oxford and spent a number of years dedicated to reading and the perfection of his literary art. The aftermath of this germinal period was one of the most astonishing bursts of mature productivity in the annals of literature: *Sartoris* (1929), *The Sound and the Fury* (1929), *As I Lay Dying* (1930), *These 13* (1931), *Sanctuary* (1931), and *Light in August* (1932). In 1936 he began doing screenwriting for Hollywood. His prolific literary output continued throughout these years, including among the important works *Doctor Martino and Other Stories* (1934), *Pylon* (1935), *Absalom, Absalom!* (1936), *The Unvanquished* (1938), *The Wild Palms* (1939), *The Hamlet* (1940), *Go Down, Moses* (1942), *Intruder in the Dust* (1948), *Knight's Gambit* (1949), *Requiem for a Nun* (1951), *A Fable* (1954), *Big Woods* (1955), *The Town* (1957), *The Mansion* (1959), and *The Reivers* (1962). He received the Nobel Prize in 1950.

INTRODUCTION TO
WILLIAM FAULKNER

MALCOLM COWLEY

I

When the war was over—the other war—William Faulkner went back to Oxford, Mississippi. He had served in the Royal Air Force in 1918. Now he was home again and not at home, or at least not able to accept the postwar world. He was writing poems, most of them worthless, and dozens of immature but violent and effective stories, while at the same time he was brooding over his own situation and the decline of the South. Slowly the brooding thoughts arranged themselves into the whole interconnected pattern that would form the substance of his later novels.

This pattern, which almost all his critics have overlooked, was based on what he saw in Oxford or remembered from his childhood; on scraps of family tradition (the Falkners, as they spelled the name, had played their part in the history of the state) ; on kitchen dialogues between the black cook and her amiable husband; on Saturday-afternoon gossip in Courthouse Square; on stories told by men in overalls squatting on their heels while they passed around a fruit-jar full of white corn liquor; on all the sources familiar to a small-town Mississippi boy—but the whole of it was elaborated, transformed, given convulsive life by his emotions; until, by the simple intensity of feeling, the figures in it became a little more than human, became heroic or diabolical, became symbols of the old South, of war and reconstruction, of commerce and machinery destroying the standards of the past. There in Oxford, Faulkner performed a labor of imagination that has not been equaled in our time, and a double labor: first, to invent a Mississippi county that was like a mythical kingdom, but was complete and living in all its details; second, to make his story of Yoknapatawpha County stand as a parable or legend of all the Deep South.

For this double task, Faulkner was better equipped by talent and background than he was by schooling. He was born in New Albany, Mississippi, on September 25, 1897; he was the oldest of four brothers. The family soon moved to Oxford, where he attended the public school, but without being graduated from high school. For a year after the war, he was a student at the University of Mississippi, in Oxford, where veterans could then matriculate without a high-school diploma; but he neglected his classroom work and left without taking a degree. He had less of a formal education than any other good writer of his time, except Hart Crane—less even than Hemingway, who never went to college, but who learned to speak three foreign languages and studied writing in Paris from the best masters. Faulkner taught himself, largely, as he says, by "undirected and uncorrelated reading." Among the authors either mentioned or echoed in his early stories and poems are Keats, Balzac, Flaubert, Swinburne, Mallarmé, Wilde, Housman, Joyce, Eliot, Sherwood Anderson, and E. E. Cummings, with fainter suggestions of Hemingway (in a fishing scene), Dos Passos (in the spelling of compound words), and Scott Fitzgerald. The poems he wrote in those days were wholly derivative, but his prose from the beginning was a form of poetry; and in spite of the echoes it was always his own. He traveled less than any of his writing contemporaries. After a succession of odd jobs in Oxford, there was a brief period when he lived in New Orleans with Sherwood Anderson and met the literary crowd—he even satirized them in a very bad early novel, *Mosquitoes;* then he went to New York, where for a few unhappy months he clerked in a bookstore; in 1925 he took a long walking trip in Europe without settling on the Left Bank. Except for recent visits to Hollywood, the rest of his life has been spent in the town where he grew up, less than forty miles from his birthplace.

Although Oxford, Mississippi, is the seat of a university, it is even less of a literary center than was Salem, Massachusetts, during Hawthorne's early years as a writer; and Faulkner himself has shown an even greater dislike than Hawthorne for literary society. His novels are the books of a man who broods about literature but doesn't often discuss it with his friends; there is no ease about them, no feeling that they come from a background of taste refined by argument and of opinions held in common. They make me think of a passage from Henry James's little book on Hawthorne:

The best things come, as a general thing, from the talents that are members of a group; every man works better when he has companions working in the same line, and yielding to the stimulus of suggestion, comparison, emulation. Great things of course have been done by solitary workers; but they have usually been done with double the pains they would have cost if they had been produced in more genial circumstances. The solitary worker loses the profit of example and discussion; he is apt to make awkward experiments; he is in the nature of the case more or less of an empiric. The empiric may, as I say, be treated by the world as an expert; but the drawbacks and discomforts of empiricism remain to him, and are in fact increased by the suspicion that is mingled with his gratitude, of a want in the public taste of a sense of the proportion of things.

Like Hawthorne, Faulkner is a solitary worker by choice, and he has done great things not only with double the pains to himself that they might have cost if produced in more genial circumstances, but sometimes also with double the pains to the reader. Two or three of his books as a whole and many of them in part are awkward experiments. All of them are full of overblown words like "imponderable," "immortal," "immutable," and "immemorial" that he would have used with more discretion, or not at all, if he had followed Hemingway's example and served an apprenticeship to an older writer. He is a most uncertain judge of his own work, and he has no reason to believe that the world's judgment of it is any more to be trusted; indeed, there is no American author who would be justified in feeling more suspicion of "a want in the public taste of a sense of the proportion of things." His early novels were overpraised, usually for the wrong reasons; his later and in many ways better novels have been obstinately condemned or simply neglected; and in 1945 all his seventeen books were out of print, with some of them unobtainable in the second-hand bookshops.

Even his warm admirers, of whom there are many—no author has a higher standing among his fellow novelists—have sometimes shown a rather vague idea of what he is trying to do; and Faulkner himself has never explained. He holds a curious attitude toward the public that appears to be lofty indifference (as in the one preface he wrote, for the Modern Library edition of *Sanctuary*), but really comes closer to being a mixture of skittery distrust and pure unconsciousness that the public exists. He doesn't furnish information or correct misstatements about himself (most of the biographical sketches that deal with him are full of preposterous errors). He doesn't care which way his name is spelled in the records, with or without the "u"—"Either way suits me," he said. Once he has finished a book, he is apparently not concerned with the question how it will be presented, to what sort of audience; and sometimes he doesn't bother to keep a private copy of it. He said in a letter, "I think I have written a lot and sent it off to print before I actually realized strangers might read it." Others might say that Faulkner, at least in those early days, was not so much composing stories for the public as telling them to himself—like a lonely child in his imaginary world, but also like a writer of genius.

II

Faulkner's mythical kingdom is a county in northern Mississippi, on the border between the sand hills covered with scrubby pine and the black earth of the river bottoms. Except for the store keepers, mechanics, and professional men who live in Jefferson, the county seat, all the inhabitants are farmers or woodsmen. Except for a little lumber, their only product is baled cotton for the Memphis market. A few of them live in big plantation houses, the relics of another age, and more of them in substantial wooden farmhouses; but most of them are tenants, no better housed than slaves on good plantations before the Civil War. Yoknapatawpha County—"William Faulkner, sole owner and proprietor," as he inscribed on one of the maps he drew—has a population of 15,611 persons scattered over 2400 square miles. It sometimes seems to me that every house or hovel has been described in one of Faulkner's novels; and that all the people of the imaginary county, black and white, townsmen, farmers, and housewives, have played their parts in one connected story.

He has so far written nine books wholly concerned with Yoknapatawpha County and its people, who also appear in parts of three others and in thirty or more uncollected stories. *Sartoris* was the first of the books to be published, in the spring of 1929; it is a romantic and partly unconvincing novel, but with many fine scenes in it, like the hero's visit to a family of independent pine-hill farmers; and it states most of the themes that the author would later develop at length. *The Sound and the Fury* was written before *Sartoris,* but wasn't published until six months later; it describes the fall of the Compson family, and it was the first of Faulkner's novels to be widely discussed. The books that followed, in the Yoknapatawpha series, are *As I Lay Dying* (1930), about the death and burial of Addie Bundren; *Sanctuary* (1931), always the most popular of his novels; *Light in August* (1932), in many ways the best; *Absalom, Absalom!* (1936), about Colonel Sutpen and his ambition to found a family; *The Unvanquished* (1938), a book of interrelated stories about the Sartoris dynasty; *The Wild Palms* (1939), half of which deals with a convict from back in the pine hills; *The Hamlet* (1940), a novel about the Snopes clan; and *Go Down, Moses* (1942), in which Faulkner's theme is the Negroes. There are also many Yoknapatawpha stories in *These Thirteen* (1931) and *Dr. Martino* (1934), besides other stories privately printed (like "Miss Zilphia Gant") or published in magazines and still to be collected or used as episodes in novels.

Just as Balzac, who seems to have inspired the series, divided his *Comédie Humaine* into "Scenes of Parisian Life," "Scenes of Provincial Life," "Scenes of Private Life," so Faulkner might divide his work into a number of cycles: one about the planters and their descendants, one about the townspeople of Jefferson, one about the poor whites, one about the Indians (consisting of stories already written but never brought together), and one about the Negroes. Or again, if he adopted a division by families, there would be the Compson-Sartoris saga, the still unfinished Snopes saga, the McCaslin saga, dealing with the white and black descendants of Carothers McCaslin, and the Ratliff-Bundren saga, devoted to the backwoods farmers of Frenchman's Bend. All the cycles or sagas are closely interconnected; it is as if each new book was a chord or segment of a total situation always existing in the author's mind. Sometimes a short story is the sequel to an earlier novel. For example, we read in *Sartoris* that Byron Snopes stole a packet of letters from Narcissa Benhow; and in "There Was a Queen," a story published five years later, we learn how Narcissa got the letters back again. Sometimes, on the other hand, a novel contains the sequel to a story; and we discover from an incidental reference in *The Sound and the Fury* that the Negro woman whose terror of death was described in "That Evening Sun" had later been murdered by her husband, who left her body in a ditch for the vultures. Sometimes an episode has a more complicated history. Thus, in the first chapter of *Sanctuary*, we hear about the Old Frenchman place, a ruined mansion near which the people of the neighborhood had been "digging with secret and sporadic optimism for gold which the builder was reputed to have buried somewhere about the place when Grant came through the country on his Vicksburg campaign." Later this digging for gold served as the subject of a story published in the *Saturday Evening Post:* "Lizards in Jamshyd's Courtyard." Still later the story was completely rewritten and became the last chapter of *The Hamlet*.

As one book leads into another, Faulkner sometimes falls into inconsistencies of detail. There is a sewing-machine agent named V. K. Suratt who appears in *Sartoris* and some of the later stories. By the time we reach *The Hamlet*, his name has changed to Ratliff, although his character remains the same (and his age, too, for all the twenty years that separate the backgrounds of the two novels). Henry Armstid is a likable figure in *As I Lay Dying* and *Light in August;* in *The Hamlet* he is mean and half-demented. His wife, whose character remains consistent, is called Lula in one book and Martha in another; in the third she is nameless. There is an Indian chief named Doom who appears in several stories; he starts as the father of Issetibeha and ends as his grandson. The mansion called Sutpen's Hundred was built of brick at the beginning of *Absalom, Absalom!* but at the end of the novel it is all wood and inflammable except for the chimneys. But these errors are comparatively few and inconsequential, considering the scope of Faulkner's series; and I should judge that most of them are afterthoughts rather than oversights.

All his books in the Yoknapatawpha saga are part of the same living pattern. It is this pattern, and not the printed volumes in which part of it is recorded, that is Faulkner's real achievement. Its existence helps to explain one feature of his work: that each novel, each long or short story, seems to reveal more than it states explicitly and to have a subject bigger than itself. All the separate works are like blocks of marble from the same quarry: they show the veins and faults of the mother rock. Or else—to use a rather strained figure—they are like wooden planks that were cut, not from a log, but from a still living tree. The planks are planed and chiseled into their final shapes, but the tree itself heals over the wound and continues to grow. Faulkner is incapable of telling the same story twice without adding new details. In the present volume I wanted to use part of *The Sound and the Fury*, the novel that deals with the fall of the Compson family. I thought that the last part of the book would be most effective as a separate episode, but still it depended too much on what had gone before. Faulkner offered to write a very brief introduction that would explain the relations of the characters. What he finally sent me is the much longer passage here printed as an appendix: a genealogy of the Compsons from their first arrival in this country. Whereas the novel is confined to a period of eighteen years ending in 1928, the genealogy goes back to the battle of Culloden in 1745, and forward to the year 1945, when Jason, last of the Compson males, has sold the family mansion, and Sister Caddy has last been heard of as the mistress of a German general. The novel that Faulkner wrote about the Compsons had long ago been given its final shape; but the pattern or body of legend behind the novel—and behind all his other books—was still developing.

Although the pattern is presented in terms of a single Mississippi county, it can be extended to the Deep South as a whole; and Faulkner always seems conscious of its wider application. He might have been thinking of his own novels when he described the ledgers in the commissary of the McCaslin plantation, in *Go Down, Moses*. They recorded, he said, "that slow trickle of molasses and meal and meat, of shoes and straw hats and overalls, of plowlines and collars and heelbolts and clevises, which returned each fall as cotton"—in a sense they were local and limited; but they were also "the continuation of that record which two hundred years had not been enough to complete and another hundred would not be enough to discharge; that chronicle which was a whole land in miniature, which multiplied and compounded was the entire South."

III

"Tell about the South," says Quentin Compson's roommate at Harvard, a Canadian named Shreve McCannon who is curious about the unknown region beyond the Ohio. "What's it like there?" he asks. "What do they do there? Why do they live there? Why do they live at all?" And Quentin, whose background is a little like that of Faulkner himself and who sometimes seems to speak for him—Quentin answers, "You can't understand it. You would have to be born there." Nevertheless, he tells a long and violent story that he regards as the essence of the Deep South, which is not so much a mere region as it is, in Quentin's mind, an incomplete and frustrated nation trying to relive its legendary past.

The story he tells—I am trying to summarize the plot of *Absalom, Absalom!*—is that of a mountain boy named Thomas Sutpen whose family drifted into the Virginia lowlands, where his father found odd jobs on a plantation. One day the father sent him with a message to the big house, but he was turned away at the door by a black man in livery. Puzzled and humiliated, the mountain boy was seized upon by the lifelong ambition to which he would afterward refer as "the design." He too would own a plantation with slaves and a liveried butler; he would build a mansion as big as any of those in the Tidewater; and he would have a son to inherit his wealth.

A dozen years later, Sutpen appeared in the frontier town of Jefferson, where he managed to obtain a hundred square miles of land from the Chickasaws. With the help of twenty wild Negroes from the jungle and a French architect, he set about building the largest house in northern Mississippi, using timbers from the forest and bricks that his Negroes molded and baked on the spot; it was as if his mansion, Sutpen's Hundred, had been literally torn from the soil. Only one man in Jefferson—he was Quentin's grandfather, General Compson—ever learned how and where Sutpen had acquired his slaves. He had shipped to Haiti from Virginia, worked as overseer on a sugar plantation and married the rich planter's daughter, who had borne him a son. Then, finding that his wife had Negro blood, he had simply put her away, with her child and her fortune, while keeping the twenty slaves as a sort of indemnity.

In Jefferson, Sutpen married again. This time his wife belonged to a pious family of the neighborhood, and she bore him two children, Henry and Judith. He became the biggest cotton planter in Yoknapatawpha County, and it seemed that his "design" had already been fulfilled. At this moment, however, Henry came home from the University of Mississippi with an older and worldlier new friend, Charles Bon, who was in reality Sutpen's son by his first marriage. Charles became engaged to Judith. Sutpen learned his identity and, without making a sign of recognition, ordered him from the house. Henry, who refused to believe that Charles was his half-brother, renounced his birthright and followed him to New Orleans. In 1861, all the male Sutpens went off to war, and all of them survived four years of fighting. Then, in the spring of 1865,

Charles suddenly decided to marry Judith, even though he was certain by now that she was his half-sister. Henry rode beside him all the way back to Sutpen's Hundred, but tried to stop him at the gate, killed him when he insisted on going ahead with his plan, told Judith what he had done, and disappeared.

But Quentin's story of the Deep South does not end with the war. Colonel Sutpen came home, he says, to find his wife dead, his son a fugitive, his slaves dispersed (they had run away even before they were freed by the Union army), and most of his land about to be seized for debt. Still determined to carry out "the design," he did not even pause for breath before undertaking to restore his house and plantation to what they had been. The effort failed and Sutpen was reduced to keeping a crossroads store. Now in his sixties, he tried again to beget a son; but his wife's younger sister, Miss Rosa Coldfield, was outraged by his proposal ("Let's try it," he had said, "and if it's a boy we'll get married"); and later poor Milly Jones, with whom he had an affair, gave birth to a baby girl. At that Sutpen abandoned hope and provoked Milly's grandfather into killing him. Judith survived her father for a time, as did the half-caste son of Charles Bon by a New Orleans octoroon. After the death of these two by yellow fever, the great house was haunted rather than inhabited by an ancient mulatto woman, Sutpen's daughter by one of his slaves. The fugitive Henry Sutpen came home to die; the townspeople heard of his illness and sent an ambulance after him; but old Clytie thought they were arresting him for murder and set fire to Sutpen's Hundred. The only survival of the conflagration was Jim Bond, a half-witted creature who was Charles Bon's grandson.

"Now I want you to tell me just one thing more," Shreve McCannon says after hearing the story. "Why do you hate the South?"—"I don't hate it," Quentin says quickly, at once. "I don't hate it," he repeats, speaking for the author as well as himself. *I don't hate it,* he thinks, panting in the cold air, the iron New England dark; *I don't. I don't hate it! I don't hate it!*

The reader cannot help wondering why this somber and, at moments, plainly incredible story had so seized upon Quentin's mind that he trembled with excitement when telling it and felt that it revealed the essence of the Deep South. It seems to belong in the realm of Gothic romances, with Sutpen's Hundred taking the place of the haunted castle on the Rhine, with Colonel Sutpen as Faust and Charles Bon as Manfred. Then slowly it dawns on you that most of the characters and incidents have a double meaning; that besides their place in the story, they also serve as symbols or metaphors with a general application. Sutpen's great design, the land he stole from the Indians, the French architect who built his house with the help of wild Negroes from the jungle, the woman of mixed blood whom he married and disowned, the unacknowledged son who ruined him, the poor white whom he wronged and who killed him in anger, the final destruction of the mansion like the downfall of a social order: all these might belong to a tragic fable of Southern history. With a little cleverness, the whole novel might be explained as a connected and logical allegory, but this, I think, would be going far beyond the author's intention. First of all he was writing a story, and one that affected him deeply, but he was also brooding over a social situation. More or less unconsciously, the incidents in the story came to represent the forces and elements in the social situation, since the mind naturally works in terms of symbols and parallels. In Faulkner's case, this form of parallelism is not confined to *Absalom, Absalom!* It can be found in the whole fictional framework that he has been elaborating in novel after novel, until his work has become a myth or legend of the South.

I call it a legend because it is obviously no more intended as a historical account of the country south of the Ohio than *The Scarlet Letter* was intended as a history of Massachusetts or *Paradise Lost* as a factual description of the Fall. Briefly stated, the legend might run something like this: The Deep South was settled partly by aristocrats like the Sartoris clan and partly by new men like Colonel Sutpen. Both types of planters were determined to establish a lasting social order on the land they had seized from the Indians (that is, to leave sons behind them). They had the virtue of living single-mindedly by a fixed code; but there was also an inherent guilt in their "design," their way of life; it was slavery that put a curse on the land and brought about the Civil War. After the War was lost, partly as a result of their own mad heroism (for who else but men as brave as Jackson and Stuart could have frightened the Yankees into standing together and fighting back?) they tried to restore "the design" by other methods. But they no longer had the strength to achieve more than a partial success, even after they had freed their land from the carpetbaggers who followed the Northern armies. As time passed, moreover, the men of the old order found that they had Southern enemies too: they had to fight against a new exploiting class descended from the landless whites of slavery days. In this struggle between the clan of Sartoris and the unscrupulous tribe of Snopes, the Sartorises were defeated in advance by a traditional code that kept them from using the weapons of the enemy. As a price of victory, however, the Snopeses had to serve the mechanized civilization of the North, which was morally impotent in itself, but which, with the aid of its Southern retainers, ended by corrupting the Southern nation.

Faulkner's novels of contemporary Southern life continue the legend into a period that he regards as one of moral confusion and social decay. He is continually seeking in them for violent images to convey his sense of despair. *Sanctuary* is the most violent of all his novels; it is also the most popular and by no means the least important (in spite of Faulkner's comment that it was "a cheap idea . . . deliberately conceived to make money"). The story of Popeye and Temple Drake has more meaning than appears on a first hasty reading—the only reading that most of the critics have been willing to grant it. Popeye himself is one of several characters in Faulkner's novels who represent the mechanical civilization that has invaded and partly conquered the South. He is always described in mechanical terms: his eyes "looked like rubber knobs"; his face "just went awry, like the face of a wax doll set too near a hot fire and forgotten"; his tight suit and stiff hat were "all angles, like a modernistic lampshade"; and in general he had "that vicious depthless quality of stamped tin." Popeye was the son of a professional strikebreaker, from whom he had inherited syphilis, and the grandson of a pyromaniac. Like two other villains in Faulkner's novels, Joe Christmas and Januarius Jones, he had spent most of his childhood in an institution. He was the man "who made money and had nothing he could do with it, spend it for, since he knew that alcohol would kill him like poison, who had no friends and had never known a woman"—in other words, he was the compendium of all the hateful qualities that Faulkner assigns to finance capitalism. *Sanctuary* is not a connected allegory, as one critic explained it, but neither is it a mere accumulation of pointless horrors. It is an example of the Freudian method turned backward, being full of sexual nightmares that are in reality social symbols. It is somehow connected in the author's mind with what he regards as the rape and corruption of the South.

In all his novels dealing with the present, Faulkner makes it clear that the descendants of the old ruling caste have the wish but not the courage or the strength to prevent this new disaster. They are defeated by Popeye (like Horace Benbow), or they run away from him (like Gowan Stevens, who had gone to school at Virginia and learned to drink like a gentleman, but not to fight for his principles), or they are robbed and replaced in their positions of influence by the Snopeses (like old Bayard Sartoris, the president of the bank), or they drug themselves with eloquence and alcohol (like Quentin Compson's father), or they retire into the illusion of being inviolable Southern ladies (like Mrs. Compson, who says, "It can't be simply to flout and hurt me. Whoever God is, He would not permit that. I'm a lady."), or they dwell so much on the past that they are incapable of facing the present (like Reverend Hightower of *Light in August*), or they run from danger to danger (like young Bayard Sartoris) frantically seeking their own destruction. Faulkner's novels are full of well-meaning and even admirable persons, not only the grandsons of the cotton aristocracy, but also pine-hill farmers and storekeepers and sewing-machine agents and Negro cooks and sharecroppers; but they are almost all of them defeated by circumstances and they carry with them a sense of their own doom.

They also carry, whether heroes or villians, a curious sense of submission to their fate. "There is not one of Faulkner's characters," says André Gide in his dialogue on "The New American Novelists," "who properly speaking, has a soul"; and I think he means that not one of them exercises the faculty of conscious choice between good and evil. They are haunted, obsessed, driven forward by some inner necessity. Like Miss Rosa Coldfield, in *Absalom, Absalom!* they exist in "that dream state in which you run without moving from a terror in which you cannot believe, toward a safety in which you have no faith." Or, like the slaves freed by General Sherman's army, in the *Unvanquished,* they blindly follow the roads toward any river, believing that it will be their Jordan:

> They were singing, walking along the road singing, not even looking to either side. The dust didn't even settle for two days, because all that night they still passed; we sat up listening to them, and the next morning every few yards along the road would be the old ones who couldn't keep up any more, sitting or lying down and even crawling along, calling to the

others to help them; and the others—the young ones—not stopping, not even looking at them. "Going to Jordan," they told me. "Going to cross Jordan."

All Faulkner's characters, black and white, are a little like that. They dig for gold frenziedly after they have lost their hope of finding it (like Henry Armstid in *The Hamlet* and Lucas Beauchamp in *Go Down, Moses*); or they battle against and survive a Mississippi flood for the one privilege of returning to the state prison farm (like the tall convict in "Old Man"); or, a whole family together, they carry a body through flood and fire and corruption to bury it in the cemetery at Jefferson (like the Bundrens in *As I Lay Dying*); or they tramp the roads week after week in search of men who had promised but never intended to marry them (like Lena Grove, the pregnant woman of *Light in August*); or, pursued by a mob, they turn at the end to meet and accept death (like Joe Christmas in the same novel). Even when they seem to be guided by a conscious purpose, like Colonel Sutpen, it is not something they have chosen by an act of will, but something that has taken possession of them: Sutpen's great design was "not what he wanted to do but what he just had to do, had to do it whether he wanted to or not, because if he did not do it he knew that he could never live with himself for the rest of his life." In the same way, Faulkner himself writes not what he wants to, but what he just has to write whether he wants to or not.

IV

He is not primarily a novelist: that is, his stories do not occur to him in book-length units of 70,000 to 150,000 words. Almost all his novels have some weakness in structure. Some of them combine two or more themes having little relation to each other, like *Light in August,* while others, like *The Hamlet,* tend to resolve themselves into a series of episodes resembling beads on a string. In *The Sound and the Fury,* which is superb as a whole, we can't be sure that the four sections of the novel are presented in the most effective order; at any rate, we can't fully understand and perhaps can't even read the first section until we have read the other three. *Absalom, Absalom!* though pitched in too high a key, is structurally the soundest of all the novels in the Yoknapatawpha series; but even here the author's attention shifts halfway through the book from the principal theme of Colonel Sutpen's ambition to the secondary theme of incest and miscegenation.

Faulkner is best and most nearly himself either in long stories like "The Bear," in *Go Down, Moses,* and "Old Man," which was published as half of *The Wild Palms,* and "Spotted Horses," which was first printed separately, then greatly expanded and fitted into the loose framework of *The Hamlet*—all three stories are included in this volume; or else in the Yoknapatawpha saga as a whole. That is, he is most effective in dealing with the total situation that is always present in his mind as a pattern of the South; or else in shorter units that can be conceived and written in a single burst of creative effort. It is by his best that we should judge him, like every other author; and Faulkner at his best—even sometimes at his worst—has a power, a richness of life, an intensity to be found in no other American novelist of our time. He has—once more I am quoting from Henry James's essay on Hawthorne—"the element of simple genius, the quality of imagination."

Moreover, he has a brooding love for the land where he was born and reared and where, unlike other writers of his generation, he has chosen to spend his life. It is ". . . this land, this South, for which God has done so much, with woods for game and streams for fish and deep rich soil for seed and lush springs to sprout it and long summers to mature it and serene falls to harvest it and short mild winters for men and animals." So far as Faulkner's country includes the Delta, it is also (in the words of old Ike McCaslin)

> . . . this land which man has deswamped and denuded and derivered in two generations so that white men can own plantations and commute every night to Memphis and black men own plantations and ride in jimcrow cars to Chicago and live in millionaires' mansions on Lake Shore Drive, where white men rent farms and live like niggers and niggers crop on shares and live like animals, where cotton is planted and grows man-tall in the very cracks of the sidewalks, and usury and mortgage and bankruptcy and measureless wealth, Chinese and African and Aryan and Jew, all breed and spawn together.

Here are the two sides of Faulkner's feeling for the South: on the one side, an admiring and possessive love; on the other, a compulsive fear lest what he loves should be destroyed by the ignorance of its native serfs and the greed of traders and absentee landlords.

No other American writer takes such delight in the weather. He speaks in various novels of "the hot still pinewiney silence of the August afternoon"; of "the moonless September dust, the trees along the road not rising soaring as trees should but squatting like huge fowl"; of "the tranquil sunset of October mazy with windless wood-smoke"; of the "slow drizzle of November rain just above the ice point"; of "those windless Mississippi December days which are a sort of Indian summer's Indian summer"; of January and February when there is "no movement anywhere save the low constant smoke . . . and no sound save the chopping of axes and the lonely whistle of the daily trains." Spring in Faulkner's country is a hurried season, "all coming at once, pell mell and disordered, fruit and bloom and leaf, pied meadow and blossoming wood and the long fields shearing dark out of winter's slumber, to the shearing plow." Summer is dust-choked and blazing, and it lasts far into what should be autumn. "That's the one trouble with this country," he says in *As I Lay Dying*. "Everything, weather, all, hangs on too long. Like our rivers, our land: opaque, slow, violent; shaping and creating the life of man in its implacable and brooding image."

And Faulkner loves these people created in the image of the land. After a second reading of his novels, you continue to be impressed by his villians, Popeye and Jason and Joe Christmas and Flem Snopes; but this time you find more place in your memory for other figures standing a little in the background yet presented by the author with quiet affection: old ladies like Miss Jenny Du Pre, with their sharp-tongued benevolence; shrewd but kindly bargainers like Ratliff, the sewing-machine agent, and Will Varner, with his cotton gin and general store; long-suffering farm wives like Mrs. Henry Armstid (whether her name is Lula or Martha); and backwoods patriarchs like Pappy MacCullum, with his six middle-aged but unmarried sons named after the generals of Lee's army. You remember the big plantation houses that collapse in flames as if a whole civilization were dying, but you also remember men in patched and faded but quite clean overalls sitting on the gallery— here in the North we should call it the porch—of a crossroads store that is covered with posters advertising soft drinks and patent medicines; and you remember the stories they tell while chewing tobacco until the suption is out of it (everything in their world is reduced to anecdote, and every anecdote is based on character). You remember Quentin Compson, not in his despairing moments, but riding with his father behind the dogs as they quarter a sedge-grown hillside after quail; and not listening to his father's story, but still knowing every word of it, because, as he thought to himself, "You had learned, absorbed it already without the medium of speech somehow from having been born and living beside it, with it, as children will and do: so that what your father was saying did not tell you anything so much as it struck, word by word the reso-nant strings of remembering."

Faulkner's novels have the quality of being lived, absorbed, remem-bered rather than merely observed. And they have what is rare in the novels of our time, a warmth of family affection, brother for brother and sister, the father for his children—a love so warm and proud that it tries to shut out the rest of the world. Compared with that affection, married love is presented as something calculating, and illicit love as a consuming fire. And because the blood relationship is central in his novels, Faulkner finds it hard to create sympathetic characters between the ages of twenty and forty. He is better with children, Negro and white, and incomparably good with older people who preserve the standards that have come down to them "out of the old time, the old days."

In his later books, which have attracted so little attention that they seem to have gone unread, there is a quality not exactly new to Faulkner—it had appeared already in passages of *Sartoris* and *Sanc-tuary*—but now much stronger and no longer overshadowed by violence and horror. It is a sort of homely and sober-sided frontier humor that is seldom achieved in contemporary writing (except by Erskine Caldwell, another Southerner). The horse-trading episodes in *The Hamlet,* and especially the long story of the spotted ponies from Texas, might have been inspired by the Davy Crockett alma-nacs. "Old Man," the story of the convict who surmounted the greatest of all the Mississippi floods, might almost be a continuation of *Huckleberry Finn.* It is as if some older friend of Huck's had taken the raft and drifted on from Aunt Sally Phelps's farm into wilder adventures, described in a wilder style, among Chinese and Cajuns and bayous crawling with alligators. In a curious way, Faulkner combines two of the principal traditions in American let-ters: the tradition of psychological horror, often close to symbolism, that begins with Charles Brockden Brown, our first professional novelist, and extends through Poe, Melville, Henry James (in his later stories), Stephen Crane, and Hemingway; and the other tradition of frontier humor and realism, beginning with Augustus Long-street's *Georgia Scenes* and having Mark Twain as its best example.

But the American author he most resembles is Hawthorne, for all their polar differences. They stand to each other as July to December, as heat to cold, as swamp to mountain, as the luxuriant to the meager but perfect, as planter to Puritan; and yet Hawthorne had much the same attitude toward New England that Faulkner has toward the South, together with a strong sense of regional particularity. The Civil War made Hawthorne feel that "the North and the South were two distinct nations in opinions and habits, and had better not try to live under the same institutions." In the spring of 1861, he wrote to his Bowdoin classmate Horatio Bridge, "We were never one people and never really had a country."—"New England," he said a little later, "is quite as large a lump of earth as my heart can really take in." But it was more than a lump of earth for him; it was a lump of history and a permanent state of consciousness. Like Faulkner in the South, he applied himself to creating its moral fables and elaborating its legends, which existed, as it were, in his solitary heart. Pacing the hillside behind his house in Concord, he listened for a voice; you might say that he lay in wait for it, passively but expectantly, like a hunter behind a rock; then, when it had spoken, he transcribed its words—more slowly and carefully than Faulkner, it is true; with more form and less fire, but with the same essential fidelity. If the voice was silent, he had nothing to write. "I have an instinct that I had better keep quiet," he said in a letter to his publisher. "Perhaps I shall have a new spirit of vigor if I wait quietly for it; perhaps not." Faulkner is another author who has to wait for the spirit and the voice. Essentially he is not a novelist, in the sense of not being a writer who sets out to observe actions and characters, then fits them into the architectural framework of a story. For all the weakness of his own poems, he is an epic or bardic poet in prose, a creator of myths that he weaves together into a legend of the South.

Editor's Note: "Introduction" reprinted from *The Portable Faulkner,* ed., Malcolm Cowley. Copyright © 1946 by The Viking Press, Inc. Reprinted by permission of The Viking Press, Inc.

One of the most influential critics of his generation, Malcolm Cowley has written books on American literature including: *The Portable Faulkner, The Portable Hemingway, Exile's Return, After the Genteel Tradition,* and *The Literary Situation.*

THE EDGE
OF ORDER:
THE PATTERN OF
FAULKNER'S RHETORIC

WALTER J. SLATOFF

In William Faulkner's short story "Delta Autumn," Ike McCaslin says that "the heart dont always have time to bother with thinking up words that fit together."[1] In *Absalom, Absalom!*, when Charles Bon leaves for college, Faulkner describes him as "almost touching the answer, aware of the jig-saw puzzle picture integers of it waiting, almost lurking, just beyond his reach, inextricable, jumbled, and unrecognizable yet on the point of falling into pattern which would reveal to him at once, like a flash of light, the meaning of his whole life" (p. 313). The integers never do fall into place for Charles Bon. Much the same can be said about Benjy and Quentin Compson, Darl Bundren, Gail Hightower, Thomas Sutpen and numerous other characters in Faulkner's novels.

Every Faulkner novel in some way provides the reader with the problem of fitting pieces together, and many readers of Faulkner feel with respect to the meanings of the novels much as Charles

---

[1] William Faulkner, *Go Down, Moses* (Random House, 1942), p. 348; hereafter abbreviated *GDM*. Other abbreviations and editions of Faulkner's works used here are as follows. *AA: Absalom, Absalom!* (New York: Modern Library, 1951); *AILD: As I Lay Dying* (New York: Modern Library, 1946); *CS: Collected Stories* (New York: Random House, 1950); *H: The Hamlet* (New York: Random House, 1940); *ID: Intruder in the Dust* (Random House, 1948); *LIA: Light in August* (New York: Modern Library, 1950); *MCS: Mirrors of Chartres Street* (Minneapolis: Faulkner Studies, 1953); *P: Pylon* (London: Chatto and Windus, 1935); *RN: Requiem for a Nun* (New York: Random House, 1950); *S: Sanctuary* (New York: Modern Library, 1932); *SF: The Sound and the Fury* (New York: Modern Library, 1946); *WP: The Wild Palms* (New York: Random House, 1939).

Bon did about the meaning of his life. Much Faulkner criticism has been devoted to explaining, both in particular novels and in his works in general, how the pieces do fit together, the patterns of meaning they do form. A good many such patterns have been discovered and offered as the essential meanings of the novels and of Faulkner's vision as a whole.

In this paper I wish to suggest that in many ways and on many levels Faulkner seems very anxious to keep pieces from fitting together, and that this is a crucial aspect of his work. It has been generally recognized that the purpose of some of Faulkner's structural complexities is to keep his material in a state of flux or suspension. But it has also generally been thought and argued or assumed that these suspensions are finally resolved, that by the ends of the novels the jig-saw picture puzzle integers do fall into place. There is much evidence, I think, that Faulkner is willing and even anxious to leave most of them in a high degree of suspension, or at least a suspension that cannot be resolved in logical or rational terms. Nor has it been recognized how very much his moment to moment presentation of experience involves a juxtaposition of elements which do not seem to fit together and which to some degree resist synthesis or resolution.

I

A remarkably frequent and persistent phenomenon in Faulkner's writing is his presentation of opposed or contradictory suggestions. In some instances the contradictions are more apparent than real; in others they seem quite real. I shall not try to distinguish between them. My purpose here is simply to suggest something of the number and variety of things which are presented in conflicting terms. Again and again, for example, Faulkner describes objects and events in terms which at once suggest motion and immobility. A large number of wagons, buggies, and engines are described as moving "without progress" or with an effect of "nomotion." The carcasses of hogs hang "immobilized by the heels in attitudes of frantic running" (*ID*, 4). Rosa Coldfield and Clytie face one another: "I motionless in the attitude and action of running, she rigid in that furious immobility" (*AA*, 140). Psychological conditions are often similarly rendered. When the schoolbell rings, Quentin Compson's "insides would move, sitting still. *Moving sit-*

ting still" (*SF*, 107). "Though Joe had not moved since he entered, he was still running" (*LIA*, 187). Frequently the contradictory suggestions are compressed into phrases like "poised and swooping immobility," "terrific immobility," or "dynamic immobility."

Sound and silence, also, are frequently presented as existing simultaneously. Silence often seems not so much the absence of sound as a container for it, a presence even while the sounds are occurring. We read of a "silence filled with the puny sounds of men" (*LIA*, 259) and "a sound . . . which silence itself, seemed to find strange and hard to digest" (*MCS*, 19-20). Very frequently, just as he gives maximum simultaneity and compression to motion and immobility in images like "dynamic immobility," Faulkner compresses the suggestions of sound and silence to the condition of oxymoron. Thus, again and again we find phrases like "crashing silently," "exploded soundlessly," "soundless yelling," and "quiet thunderclap." On at least three occasions Faulkner sets up, in effect, double oxymorons of sound and silence, the most compact being "soundless words in the pattering silence" (*CS*, 899).

Perhaps the most common physical and psychological conditions presented by Faulkner are ones which simultaneously contain elements of quiescence and turbulence. A flood is likely to exhibit a calm, still surface above its raging currents or to suggest "fury in itself quiet with stagnation" (*AILD*, 458). Fights commonly occur in silence or in tranquil surroundings. Characters, even the most violent and tormented, are most apt to possess quiet or calm exteriors, to exhibit furious immobility or quiet rage, or to behave with quiet fury or calm violence. When their tension or torment has become unbearable they may, like a farmer in *The Hamlet*, become "calm and contained and rigidly boiling" (p. 222), or they may like the dietitian in *Light in August* and Wilbourne in *The Wild Palms*, be described as going calmly and quietly mad.

Opposed suggestions are not at all confined to these areas. In every Faulkner novel an astonishing number and variety of characters and events are described in oxymoronic or near oxymoronic terms. Here is a small sampling from two of Faulkner's novels which may give some idea of the pervasiveness of the phenomenon and of the variety of contexts in which it occurs.

In *Light in August*, Doc Hines is "paradoxically rapt and alert at the same time" (p. 323) and has the ability "to flux instantaneously between complete attention that does not seem to hear, and that comalike bemusement in which the stare of his apparently inverted eye is as uncomfortable as though he held them [his companions] with his hand" (p. 334). His wife's face is at the same time "peaceful and terrible" and her attitude is "at once like a rock and like a crouching beast" (p. 348). The face of Hightower, with whom the Hineses are talking, is "at once gaunt and flabby" (p. 77). The Sunday morning service in the church in which he once preached has a "stern and formal fury" (p. 321). He hears singing from the church: "a sound at once austere and rich, abject and proud" (p. 65). When he resigns his pulpit "the town was sorry with being glad" (p. 60). Joe Christmas' feet are capable of moving at "deliberate random" (p. 291). He can "hear without hearing them wails of terror and distress quieter than sighs all about him" (p. 293). Lena Grove gives Armstid, Winterbottom, and Armstid's wagon a glance which is at once "innocent and profound" (p. 7). Later she and the wagon come slowly together "without any semblance of progress" (p. 10). She passes fields and woods "at once static and fluid" (p. 24).

In *The Hamlet* Will Varner is "at once active and lazy" (p. 6). His son Jody wears a costume which is "at once ceremonial and negligee" (p. 11). Tull has a "gentle, almost sad face until you unravelled what were actually two separate expressions—a temporary one of static peace and quiet overlaying a constant one of definite even though faint harriedness" (p. 10). Armstid's eyes are "at once vague and intense" (p. 331). After his illness Ratliff emanates "a sort of delicate robustness" (p. 78). Ab Snopes' homestead is a "cluttered desolation" (p. 54). Eula Varner seems to exist in a "teeming vacuum" (p. 107). At the age of eleven, sitting on the schoolhouse steps eating a cold potato, she "postulated that ungirdled quality of the very goddesses in . . . Homer and Thucydides: of being at once corrupt and immaculate, at once virgins and the mothers of warriors and of grown men" (p. 128). She is "at once supremely unchaste and inviolable" (p. 131). Her admirers depart "seething and decorous" and ride in "furious wordless amity" (p. 150). Houston and the girl he is to marry are "chained irrevocably . . . not by love but by implacable constancy and invincible repudiation" (p. 237). Up to a point their struggle, "for all its deadly seriousness . . . had retained something of childhood, something both illogical and consistent, both reasonable and bizarre" (p. 239).

Some of Faulkner's oxymorons are brilliant and completely justified by their context; others seem mechanical or excessive. I am not here concerned with discriminating between them. What I wish to emphasize is their remarkable frequency and variety, remarkable even in our contemporary literary environment which prizes paradox and linguistic shock. More than anything else, I believe, that baffling figure can help to illuminate Faulkner's work. Not only does its abundance indicate a good deal about Faulkner's general intentions and effects, but the figure, itself, in miniature and extreme form contains or suggests many of the most important qualities of his art and vision.

Like Faulkner's writing in general, the oxymoron involves sharp polarity, extreme tension, a high degree of conceptual and stylistic antithesis, and the simultaneous suggestion of disparate or opposed elements. Moreover, the figure tends to hold these elements in suspension rather than to fuse them. Both terms of an oxymoron are in a sense true. One's recognition that the contradition is apparent rather than real does not eliminate the tension between the terms, for the conflicting elements remain. Neither negates the other. The oxymoron, on the one hand, achieves a kind of order, definiteness, and coherence by virtue of the clear and sharp antithesis it involves. On the other, it moves toward disorder and incoherence by virtue of its qualities of irresolution and self-contradiction. Its validity is usually intuitive and emotional rather than logical or intellectual. It does not so much explore or analyze a condition as render it forcefully. Traditionally it has often been used to reflect desperately divided states of mind.

II

Any oxymoron to some degree defies our customary intellectual desire for logical resolution, for even when we see beyond the contradiction, it still leaves us with the conflicting assertions. But many of Faulkner's oxymorons (e.g., "vague and intense") leave us with especially insoluble suspensions. They involve so complete or balanced a contradiction that they not only oppose our desire for resolution, but remain in opposition to it; no amount of thought and analysis can move us beyond the suspension of opposed elements. In the traditional oxymoron such as "cruel kindness" or "living death" at least a partial resolution is usually possible because one of the opposing elements is given subordinate emphasis either by context or by logical or grammatical subordination. Faulkner, on the other hand, seems especially fond of juxtaposing contradictory terms of equal rank and emphasis, and often further blocks resolution by the prefatory phrase "at once" (e.g., "at once corrupt and immaculate"). That he may be indifferent to the effects even when his oxymorons do involve logical or grammatical subordination is suggested by his apparently synonymous use of "implacable weariness" and "weary implacability" (*H*, 254-255). The essential purpose and effect of most of Faulkner's oxymorons, I believe, is not to force the reader to grasp a reality or unity beneath an apparent contradiction but to leave him with the tension of the contradiction itself. We are to feel and to continue to feel, for example, that the struggle between Houston and his wife had in it "something both illogical and consistent, both reasonable and bizarre."

I have stressed this as much as I have because I wish to show as conclusively as I can that Faulkner frequently seems willing and even anxious to leave his reader with suspensions which are not resolvable in rational terms. This is not to say that he always does so nor does it prove that his novels as wholes are similarly unresolvable, but it does suggest that his novels may be more ambiguous and more resistant to rational analysis than has often been supposed. This possibility is strengthened by the many other aspects of his presentation which resist rational analysis and leave us with an unresolved suspension of varied or opposed suggestions.

A large number of Faulkner's extended metaphors, for example, have these qualities. This partial description of the sermon of the visiting preacher in *The Sound and the Fury* is characteristic.

> He tramped steadily back and forth . . . hunched, his hands clasped behind him. He was like a worn small rock whelmed by the successive waves of his voice. With his body he seemed to feed the voice that, succubus like, had fleshed its teeth in him. And the congregation seemed to watch with its own eyes while the voice consumed him, until he was nothing and they were nothing and there was not even a voice but instead their hearts were speaking to one another in chanting measures beyond the need for words, so that when he came to rest against the reading desk, his monkey face lifted and his whole attitude that of a serene, tortured crucifix that transcended

its shabbiness and insignificance and made it of no moment,
a long moaning expulsion of breath rose from them, and a
woman's single soprano: "Yes, Jesus!" (p. 310).

In context the passage has considerable emotional force and conveys a sense of the minister's power and effect on the congregation.
On the other hand, it is full of opposed and varied suggestions
which resist rational integration. We shift from naturalistic description to a simile in which the preacher is likened to a rock and
his voice to waves. The voice then acquires teeth, and "succubus
like" (i.e., like an *evil* spirit!) consumes him. Is the ugliness of the
image intentional, we wonder. Does Faulkner perhaps add teeth
because they are in antithesis to the "suck" suggestion of "succubus"? The minister and the congregation become "nothing" but
still have hearts. There is no voice, but the hearts "speak" to one
another, although without words. We are then reminded of the
naturalistic monkey face immediately before the preacher's figure
(which was a "rock," fleshly food, "nothing," and a speaking
"heart") becomes suggestive of a crucifix, at once "serene" and
"tortured," "that transcended its [the attitude's? the crucifix's?]
shabbiness and insignificance." Upon close examination even the
general nature of the experience of the congregation is perplexing,
because there is the implication of a peaceful speaking of hearts and
then of release of tension. Faulkner's mixed metaphors of this sort
are not simply occasional accidents, for in general he makes no effort
to keep them consistent and often makes use of the most "mixed"
for his most important communications. And as in the oxymoron,
the irresolvable elements are not accidental but seem an integral
part of structure. Comparable to these mixed metaphors in effect
are Faulkner's frequent synesthetic images which may be considered
psychological oxymorons. Typical examples are "dark cool breeze"
(*SF*, 149), "visibility roaring soundless down about him" (*H*, 195),
and "walked out of their talking" (*LIA*, 9).

Less obvious, perhaps, but equally common are the conflicting
suggestions which often occur in Faulkner's extended presentations
of characters and events. A relatively compact illustration is the
episode in *Light in August* in which McEachern attacks Joe Christmas in the dancehall.

Before this episode, what has been emphasized, above all, about

McEachern is his absolute sense of self-righteousness, and the calm, heavy, methodical quality of all of his actions, even his violent ones. When he realizes that Joe has climbed out of his room and gone off to what he is sure is lechery, he saddles "his big, old, strong white horse" and goes down the road at a "slow and ponderous gallop" (p. 176). So far he is still very much in character. Faulkner then inserts a suggestion of speed by means of metaphor: ". . . the two of them, man and beast, leaning a little stiffly forward as though in some juggernautish simulation of terrific speed though the actual speed itself was absent, as if in that cold and implacable and unde- viating conviction of both omnipotence and clairvoyance of which they both partook known destination and speed were not necessary" (pp. 176–177). When McEachern reaches the dancehall, however, Faulkner has him move with actual speed. He dismounts "almost before the horse had stopped. He did not even tether it. He got down, and in the carpet slippers and the dangling braces and his round head and his short, blunt, outraged beard ran toward the open door" (p. 177). In the next paragraph Faulkner goes on to describe him as thrusting through the dancers, and running toward Joe and the waitress, and then thundering "Away, Jezebel! . . . Away, harlot!" (p. 178)

McEachern's disarray and uncontrolled running and thunderous shouting provide an emotional climax of strong impact and inten- sity; but they may come as rather a shock to the understanding of the reader in view of Faulkner's earlier characterizations of the man as utterly deliberate and controlled.[2] The next paragraph reads:

> Perhaps it did not seem to him that he had been moving fast nor that his voice was loud. Very likely he seemed to him- self to be standing just and rocklike and with neither haste nor anger while on all sides the sluttishness of weak human men seethed in a long sigh of terror about the actual repre- sentative of the wrathful and retributive Throne. Perhaps they were not even his hands which struck at the face of the youth whom he had nurtured and sheltered and clothed from a child, and perhaps when the face ducked the blow and came up again it was not the face of that child. But he could not have been surprised at that, since it was not that child's face which he was concerned with: it was the face of Satan, which he knew

[2] See pp. 124–134.

> as well. And when, staring at the face, he walked steadily toward it with his hand still raised, very likely he walked toward it in the furious and dreamlike exaltation of a martyr who has already been absolved, into the descending chair which Joe swung at his head, and into nothingness. (p. 178)

We begin with what appears not to be the real version of what happened but the way it appeared to McEachern. But the passage slips gradually toward what is presumably a statement of what did happen, and the final picture we have is of the McEachern we knew earlier, who, staring at Joe-Satan, walks "steadily" toward the raised chair "in the furious and dreamlike exaltation of a martyr." In a generally emotive way we are satisfied by the suggestiveness and general movement of the passage. If we stop to reflect, however, we wonder how the event did happen, which image of McEachern to accept: the one of a ponderous and deliberate man whose conviction is such that speed is not necessary; the one suggested by the hanging braces, carpet slippers, the running and thundering rage; or the one of a convinced and peaceful and yet somehow furious martyr? We wonder what McEachern is like. We wonder, also, whether McEachern has been killed. The final description of him offers no resolution: "He looked quite peaceful now. He appeared to sleep: bluntheaded, indomitable even in repose, even the blood on his forehead peaceful and quiet" (p. 178). This final statement is typical of many of Faulkner's endings to situations and even to whole works. It is effective emotionally and dramatically but does not resolve questions which the earlier presentation has raised for the understanding. There is a suggestion of resolution, in this case supplied by the emphasis upon peace and quiescence. At the same time, however, there remain tensions and opposing suggestions, here provided by the unquiet words "bluntheaded," "indomitable," and "blood."

One of the most striking and widely commented upon aspects of Faulkner's writing is his use of marathon sentences whose structure and syntax are often perplexing or obscure. Here is a fragment of a sentence from *Go Down, Moses,* a sentence which runs for over a page and a half. Among sentences and fragments of this type, it is one of the least complex. Contextually, the sentence and fragment would seem to be important, for they presumably communicate a significant part of Ike McCaslin's education and experience.

. . . a boy who wished to learn humility and pride in order to become skillful and worthy in the woods but found himself becoming so skillful so fast that he feared he would never become worthy because he had not learned humility and pride though he had tried, until one day an old man who could not have defined either led him as though by the hand to where an old bear and a little mongrel dog showed him that, by possessing one thing other, he would possess them both; and a little dog, nameless and mongrel and many-fathered, grown yet weighing less than six pounds, who couldn't be dangerous because there was nothing anywhere much smaller, not fierce because that would have been called just noise, not humble because it was already too near the ground to genuflect, and not proud because it would not have been close enough for anyone to discern what was casting that shadow and which didn't even know it was not going to heaven since they had already decided it had no immortal soul, so that all it could be was brave even though they would probably call that too just noise. (pp. 295-296)

We may note first, that all but one of the clauses beginning "because," "since," or "so that," are deliberate non-sequiturs. Moreover, the final statement about the dog's bravery is not consistent with the statement about his fierceness. In one instance the existence of a quality depends upon what people call it; in the other it does not. At the same time, in opposition to the illogicality, there is a promise of clarity, order, and logicality, a frequent characteristic of Faulkner's writing. The description of the dog pretends to be a definition (presumably of "the one thing other") arrived at through careful exclusion and negation. Further promise of clarity and simplicity is made by the cause and effect terminology, antithesis, persistent parallelism, and general division of things into simple pairs. There is also the promise communicated by the suggestion that the mongrel dog showed Ike that *"one* thing" (italics mine) would solve his problem of gaining humility and pride.

The passage quoted is characteristic of many of Faulkner's other structures, also, in its shifts in tone. The context of the description of the dog is serious. Presumably our understanding of the nature of the dog is essential to our understanding of the nature of pride and humility, and to our understanding of Ike. The surrounding passages are serious. The description of the dog's qualities, however, is largely playful.

As in many other passages close scrutiny leads only to further difficulties. There is first the hurdle of the oxymoron "humility and pride." We are then told that the possession of one thing "other" would enable Ike to possess both qualities. If the one thing other is "bravery" (we cannot be sure), we may wonder why Faulkner communicates it so ambiguously, and may wonder about the relationship between bravery, humility, and pride. Our understanding of that relationship is not aided by the fact that the dog, who has the bravery, is described specifically as neither humble nor proud. When we read further we are led to Keats' "Ode on a Grecian Urn" and to the statement that *"Truth is one. It doesn't change. It covers all things which touch the heart—honor and pride and pity and justice and courage and love"* (p. 297), a statement which McCaslin indicates ought to clarify things for Ike. Even if one is not troubled by the meanings of the words "covers" and "touch" and does not wonder whether such qualities as hatred and greed "touch" the heart, one must certainly wonder why humility is missing from the list. A few lines later Faulkner drops this subject and moves to a "discussion" of the curse on the land.

Again Faulkner's presentation has left us with tensions and questions we cannot resolve. I have dwelt upon the difficulties structures of this sort pose for the understanding, and have emphasized their resistance to analysis, because I wish to make clear that they may be organized not merely so as to make intellectual resolution difficult but so as to discourage it and make it impossible, just as synesthetic images make precise sense localization impossible and many of Faulkner's oxymorons make logical resolution impossible. The difficulties in the way of understanding are often not resolvable nor meant to be.

The preceding illustrations show some of the ways by which Faulkner keeps his reader from fitting things together. Instead of moving toward synthesis and resolution, his presentation often provides a suspension of varied or opposed suggestions. Two specific devices which further contribute to this suggestive suspension warrant mention.

The first is the frequent use of "perhaps" and "maybe," and other inconclusive or conjectural terms or phrases in describing motivations, thoughts, and events. The second is that which Warren Beck has labelled "the statement of alternative suggestions":[3] "The

---

[3] Warren Beck, "William Faulkner's Style," in *William Faulkner: Two Decades of Criticism*, ed. F. J. Hoffman and O. W. Vickery (East Lansing: Michigan State College Press, 1950), p. 159.

woman had never seen him but once, but perhaps she remembered him, or perhaps his appearance now was enough."[4] Sometimes the juxtaposed alternatives are so important and so divergent that a choice would be of immense philosophic and practical significance, as in *Go Down, Moses* where McCaslin says that the Bible was written to be read "by the heart, not by the wise of the earth because *maybe they don't need it or maybe the wise no longer have any heart*" (p. 260, italics mine). On occasion the alternatives are diametrically opposed:

> It was as if only half of her had been born, that mentality and body had somehow become either completely separated or hopelessly involved; that either only one of them had ever emerged, or that one had emerged, itself not accompanied by, but rather pregnant with, the other. (*H,* 109)

Note the complete opposition of the alternatives "completely separated" and "hopelessly involved." If we substitute "at once . . . and" where Faulkner has used "either . . . or," the result is an oxymoron. Even as worded in the text, however, the passage is, in effect, an oxymoron, because no real choice is offered. As is true for almost all of Faulkner's "alternative" suggestions, we are to keep in mind both alternatives; no choice or resolution is possible.

III

Faulkner's novels, of course, are far more complex than the structures we have been looking at, and I certainly do not wish to suggest that the kinds of qualities I have been illustrating fully explain or describe them. I do contend, however, that they resemble these structures more closely than has generally been recognized. They have certain kinds of unity and resolution, of course, but in many ways they remain insoluble. Obviously, a thorough or conclusive study of the novels is impossible here. I can do little more than suggest something of the extent to which they are suspensions of the sort I have indicated. Apart from the evidence we have already seen which suggests this possibility, and apart from internal evidence I shall consider later, there is also some external evidence that Faulkner might regard too much coherence as a kind of failure.

[4] *LIA,* 177. Note that the phrasing "had never seen him but once," communicates almost a double suggestion. Compare "had seen him but once," or "had seen him once only."

In a recent interview Faulkner is quoted as saying:

> I was asked the question who were the five best contemporary writers and how did I rate them. And I said Wolfe, Hemingway, Dos Passos, Caldwell and myself. I rated Wolfe first, myself second. I put Hemingway last. I said we were all failures. All of us had failed to match the dream of perfection and I rated the authors on the basis of their splendid failure to do the impossible. I believed Wolfe tried to do the greatest of the impossible, that he tried to reduce all human experience to literature. And I thought after Wolfe I had tried the most. I rated Hemingway last because he stayed within what he knew. He did it fine, but he didn't try for the impossible.

A moment later he adds:

> I rated those authors by the way in which they failed to match the dream of perfection. . . . This had nothing to do with the value of the work, the impact or perfection of its own kind that it had. I was talking only about the magnificence of the failure, the attempt to do the impossible within human experience.[5]

There are ambiguities in Faulkner's statement, but it strongly suggests that he would consider full coherence a sign of weakness and something to be avoided. That is, he not only places a higher value[6] upon the effort to do the *impossible* than upon accepting

[5] The New York Times Book Review, Jan. 30, 1955, p. 4.

[6] I am aware that Faulkner has said that his rating "had nothing to do with the value of the work." The whole tenor of the statement, however, indicates that he does attach high value to the quest for the impossible and to the magnificent failure. His very choice to rate the authors in those terms is an affirmation of the value of those terms. It may be argued that by saying that his rating had nothing to do with value, Faulkner only intends to qualify his earlier statement. But, in fact, the statement about value contradicts his earlier rhetoric and content, both, and involves an unwillingness to commit himself fully to the meanings of that rhetoric and content or to the consequences of his choice to rate the authors in the terms he did. Similar sorts of self contradiction are present in Faulkner's introduction to the Modern Library Edition of *Sanctuary*, in his Foreword to *The Faulkner Reader,* and a bit less obviously, in his Nobel Prize speech and various other public utterances. That this is true suggests that his literary use of ambiguity may be a matter of temperament as well as of conscious artistic intent.

human and artistic limitations, but he also seems to measure the effort by the extent of the failure. His works show, in part, I believe, an active quest for "failure."

It is no accident that every one of Faulkner's experiments with form and style—his rapidly shifting points of view, his use of more or less incoherent narrators such as Benjy, Quentin, Darl, Rosa Coldfield, and Gavin Stevens, his disordered time sequences, his juxtapositions of largely independent stories, his unsyntactical marathon sentences, his whole method, as Conrad Aiken puts it, "of deliberately withheld meaning, of progressive and partial and delayed disclosure"—is a movement away from order and coherence. And it is no accident that every one of Faulkner's novels involves one or more of these experiments and that in most of the novels we find all of them.

It is important to recognize, also, that the effects of Faulkner's fragmentation of material are usually quite different from those produced by others who have used similar techniques. In works like *The Ring and the Book* and the Japanese film *Rashomon* various perspectives are thrown upon the same central event. In *Mrs. Dalloway* and *Ulysses* the seemingly unconnected experiences and events are occurring at the same time or on the same day. That is, either event, time or point of view is held constant. In *The Sound and the Fury, As I Lay Dying,* and *Absalom, Absalom!,* on the other hand, none of these is constant. The various narrators touch upon a few of the same events, but the selection of events seems determined essentially by the particular interests and obsessions of the narrator. In *The Sound and the Fury,* for example, neither Benjy nor Jason throws light on the incest theme which dominates the Quentin section. And Quentin, on the other hand, is dead before many of the events take place which are crucial in the lives of Benjy and Jason. In *Absalom, Absalom!* the various narrators emphasize quite different aspects and periods of Sutpen's history. As a result the reader feels less sense of pattern and equilibrium than in the first named works, is less able to group his thoughts and feelings about a common center.

Particularly indicative of Faulkner's intentions, I think, is the fact that when he does present explicit interpretations of events or analytic commentaries on them he always takes pains to make them either suspect, inconclusive, or incoherent. On many occasions he will narrate or describe an action in perfectly conventional and logical sequence, but his interpretive or philosophic passages are almost invariably disordered. I think we can go so far as to say that the more explanatory or intellectual the content, the less the coherence. The dominant characteristic, in fact, of Faulkner's intellectuals—and it is they, of course, who offer most of the interpretations—is their tendency to be incoherent. The most intellectual character in Faulkner's novels, and probably his favorite commentator, is Gavin Stevens, a Ph.D. from Heidelberg. And, as has been generally recognized, it is his statements which usually provide the greatest resistance to rational understanding. Here, for example, is a part of his final commentary, and the final explicit commentary of any sort, on the meaning of the events in *Intruder in the Dust*. Gavin is talking to his nephew Charles Mallison who has been chiefly responsible for saving the Negro Lucas Beauchamp from being lynched.

> ... what's out yonder in the ground at Caledonia Church was Crawford Gowrie for only a second or two last Saturday and Lucas Beauchamp will be carrying his pigment into ten thousand situations a wiser man would have avoided and a lighter escaped ten thousand times after what was Lucas Beauchamp for a second or so last Saturday is in the ground at his Caledonia church too, because that Yoknapatawpha County which would have stopped you and Aleck Sander and Miss Habersham last Sunday night are right actually, Lucas' life the breathing and eating and sleeping is of no importance just as yours and mine are not but his unchallengeable right to it in peace and security and in fact this earth would be much more comfortable with a good deal fewer Beauchamps and Stevenses and Mallisons of all colors in it if there were only some painless way to efface not the clumsy room-devouring carcasses which can be done but the memory which cannot—that inevictible immortal memory awareness of having once been alive which exists forever still ten thousand years afterward in ten thousand recollections of injustice and suffering, too many of us not because of the room we take up but because we are willing to sell liberty short at any tawdry price for the sake of what we call our own which is a constitutional statutory license to pursue each his private postulate of happiness and contentment regardless of grief and cost even to the crucifixion of someone whose nose or pigment we dont like and even these can be coped with provided that few of others who believe that a human life is valuable simply because it has a right to keep on

breathing no matter what pigment its lungs distend or nose
inhales the air and are willing to defend that right at any
price, it doesn't take many three were enough last Sunday night
even one can be enough and with enough ones willing to be
more than grieved and shamed Lucas will no longer run the
risk of needing without warning to be saved:" (*ID*, 243-244).

Fortunately Faulkner has other voices besides that of Gavin. But
these other voices do not negate or encompass Gavin's so much as
stand in suspension with it.

Probably the most crucial indication of Faulkner's intentions is
the fact that the endings of all his novels not only fail to resolve
many of the tensions and meanings provided in the novels but also
seem carefully designed to prevent such resolution. Above all, they
leave unresolved the question of the meaningfulness of the human
efforts and suffering we have witnessed, whether the sound and the
fury is part of some larger design or whether it has signified nothing
in an essentially meaningless universe.

Consider, for example, the final section of *The Sound and the
Fury*, which is perhaps Faulkner's most unified and tightly woven
novel. By the end of the first three sections we have seen various
parts of the history of the Compson family through the eyes of three
of its members—respectively, the idiot Benjy, the sensitive and romantic but neurotically obsessed Quentin, and the practical, materialistic and self-pitying Jason. And we are groping for some larger
perspective, context, or pattern under which to view and interpret
the unhappy events we have been witnessing. Faulkner has suggested a number of these. The title of the book has suggested
strongly that there is no pattern, and Mr. Compson's nihilistic
philosophy reinforces this, as does the seemingly chaotic order of
events. Opposed to this, however, is our natural disinclination to
accept such a view and our awareness of Faulkner's at least partial
approval of Benjy, Quentin, Caddie, Mr. Compson, and Dilsey and
his disapproval of Mrs. Compson, Herbert, and Jason. And there is
also our recognition of several more or less recurrent motifs which
encourage us to look for pattern and significance. But the search
has sent us in varying directions, none of which has been clearly or
conclusively marked. Some of the events have seemed chiefly in
accord with a socio-economic antithesis between an old and new
culture of the general sort pointed out by the O'Donnell, Cowley,

Warren line of criticism. Some of the events and emphases have suggested interpretation in terms of clinical or even specifically Freudian psychology. We have been strongly encouraged, also, to interpret events in relation to Christian myth and ideology, in relation to concepts of time, and in relation to Shakespearian tragedy.

At the same time we are not sure what attitude we are to take toward the disintegration of the family. In the first two sections Benjy and Quentin have reported events in such a way that we see and feel their pathetic rather than ludicrous or ironic side. We are somewhat aware that Benjy is sub-human and that his suffering is not of an order that requires the highest kind of sympathy, and Quentin's posturing and extreme Romanticism at times seem comic, but essentially we are led to see them both as suffering individuals, to feel considerable compassion for them and to take their predicaments very seriously. In the third section, however, narrated by Jason, the tone has been essentially comic and satiric. Not only does Jason come through as a largely comic character but his narration tends to bathe the whole Compson history in a somewhat comic light which at least temporarily blinds us to the poignancy and pathos of it. We are much more detached than in the earlier sections, less serious. We want to see Jason made a fool of and we are not especially moved by the plight of Quentin. Had the novel ended with this section we would view the Compson history largely with a sense of grim amusement, as a tale of sound and fury signifying that the human condition is essentially hopeless and not worth much thought or compassion.

The final section, narrated from an omniscient and objective point of view, begins with a focus and emphasis that seems to offer a kind of implicit interpretation and resolution, one in accord with the sentiments and mood of Faulkner's Nobel Prize speech. The strong emphasis on Dilsey's fortitude, decency, and Christian humility and on her comprehensive view of time, as numerous critics have pointed out, provides a context for the unhappy events, a perspective from which to view them and a way to feel about them. On the other hand, this episode does not so much offer a synthesis or interpretation as a general vantage point and degree of moral affirmation. It does not help us to understand most of the particulars of the Compson story any better, to illuminate, say, the character and motives of Quentin and Caddie. Nor does it in any but a peripheral way relate to the socio-economic context of the story.

And although it asserts the relevance of Christianity to the story it does not really clarify the nature of that relevance nor make clear how seriously we are to take the Christian context. Still, its tone and general tenor do provide a general way of looking at and feeling about the story and a sense of resolution.

But—and it is a very crucial "but" which most interpreters of the novel have ignored—the emphasis on Dilsey and her trip to church is at the beginning of the final section, and is only one of several emphases in that section. It is followed by the lengthy description of Jason's vain and tormenting pursuit of Quentin which provides a very different perspective, mood, and set of feelings. We are back in a realm of sound and fury, even of melodrama. We do not see Jason from the large perspective we have just shared with Dilsey, but respond to his frustration and defeat with a grim amusement and satisfaction only slightly leavened by pity. Nor does his defeat appear in any way an affirmative thing, for the "heroine" who has eluded him seems equally doomed. Dilsey and her church recede into the landscape and seem barely relevant to Jason's predicament.

The final part of the last section emphasizes Benjy's misery and the callousness and swagger of Dilsey's grandson, Luster, as he torments Benjy, first by taking his bottle, then by shouting Caddie, and finally by driving around the square in the wrong direction. We are reminded for a moment of Dilsey's decency and faith but only to feel its ineffectualness, for neither she nor the church service has touched Luster. The book closes with the carriage ride of Luster and Benjy: with our attention focused on a young Negro whose main desire is to show off, and on an idiot, capable of serenity or anguish but little more than that. Faulkner emphasizes his terrible agony as Luster throws his world into disorder by going around the square in the wrong direction. Jason comes rushing across the square, turns the carriage around and hits both Luster and Benjy. Benjy becomes serene again as the carriage moves in its usual direction and things flow by smoothly from left to right "each in its ordered place."

It is a powerful ending and a fitting one in its focus on Benjy and its application to the general theme of order and disorder which runs through the novel. But it is an ending which provides anything but a synthesis or resolution, and it leaves us with numerous conflicting feelings and ideas.

We are momentarily relieved and pleased by the cessation of Benjy's suffering but we are troubled by the fact that it has been achieved by Jason who cares nothing for Benjy and is concerned only with maintaining an external and superficial decorum. And we can hardly draw any real satisfaction from the serenity and order because the serenity is the "empty" serenity of an idiot and the order that demanded by an idiot. The general tenor of the episode is in accord with Mr. Compson's pessimism rather than Faulkner's Nobel Prize speech, for everything in it suggests the meaninglessness and futility of life.

This final scene does not negate the moderate affirmation of the Dilsey episode, nor does it really qualify it. Rather it stands in suspension with it as a commentary of equal force. We feel and are intended to feel, I think, that the events we have witnessed are at once tragic and futile, significant and meaningless. We cannot move beyond this. Nor does the final section help us to resolve whether the Compsons were defeated essentially by acts of choice or by some kind of doom, or whether the doom was chiefly a matter of fate or of psychological aberration or of socio-economic forces. And it is worth noting that if we do accept as a primary motif the opposition between an older and newer culture we face the impossibility of choosing between them. Our sympathies, like Faulkner's, are with the old, but the best representatives of it in this book are a drunkard, a suicide, and a lost and lonely woman. And between what they are and what Jason is there seems no middle ground offered.

In short, the ending seems designed not to interpret or to integrate but to leave the various elements of the story in much the same suspension in which they were offered, and to leave the reader with a high degree of emotional and intellectual tension.

The endings of Faulkner's other novels are similar. Two brief illustrations will have to suffice. *As I Lay Dying* ends with Pa's acquisition of new teeth and a new wife, a cynical, almost farcical note which suggests that all of the pain and struggle and even heroism of the Bundrens was for nothing, that shiftlessness and ineptitude triumph over all, and that we do not take the story very seriously. At the same time, however, the fact that the family did succeed in its task and the emphasis on the patience and sanity of Cash, as well as the presentation of much of the story suggests that what we have witnessed is significant, even epic, and worthy of the highest seriousness of response. The fate of Darl generates further intellectual and emotional conflict, which Faulkner strengthens in a number of ways. He has Cash speculate inconclusively about the question of Darl's insanity, and neither he nor we can get beyond the feeling that we "ain't so sho that ere a man has the right to say what is crazy and what ain't" (*AILD,* 515). But we are far more disturbed than Cash, for unlike Cash we do not misinterpret Darl's bitter laughter when Cash says he will be better off at the insane asylum at Jackson. Our response is further complicated by Faulkner's emphasis on Darl's humane concern about Cash's bad leg and by the terrible ambiguity of Darl's laughter and reiterated "yes"'s as he is taken away to Jackson. Moreover, these uncertainties reflect back through the novel for Darl has been the dominant narrator of the book and in many respects a sympathetic character. As in *The Sound and the Fury* the ending, far from helping us to order or resolve the suspension of multiple suggestions and points of view presented in the book, seems designed to preserve that suspension in all its complexity and even to make it more complex. There is nothing which points firmly or clearly toward any one way of thinking or feeling about the things we have seen. Above all, the ending suggests that the story we have been told is highly significant and worthy of serious contemplation and emotion and that it signifies nothing and deserves primarily a bitter laugh.

At the very end of *Absalom, Absalom!* there are, in effect, four commentaries on the meaning of the whole Sutpen story. The first is provided by the picture of the last Sutpen, the idiot boy Jim Bond, lurking around the ashes and gutted chimneys that are the remnants of Sutpen's mansion, howling until somone would drive him away (p. 376). The second is provided by the end of Mr. Compsons' letter, the first part of which we have read two hundred odd pages earlier (pp. 173–174), a letter which is obviously and carefully ambiguous and irrelevant so far as any ordering of the story is concerned. The third commentary is that of Shreve, who summarizes the story with brutal and flippant absurdity: " 'So it took Charles Bon and his mother to get rid of old Tom, and Charles Bon and the octoroon to get rid of Judith, and Charles Bon and Clytie to get rid of Henry; and Charles Bon's mother and Charles Bon's grandmother to get rid of Charles Bon. So it takes two niggers to get rid of one Sutpen, dont it?' " (pp. 377–378) He then observes that everything is taken care of except that " 'You've got one nigger left. One nigger Sutpen left,' " and he briefly erects this negro into a symbol of

Southern guilt (p. 378, ll. 11–14). Following this he revels in paradox: The Jim Bonds conquer the western hemisphere and turn white, but still remain Jim Bonds, " 'and so [note the pseudo logic] in a few thousand years, I who regard you will also have sprung from the loins of African kings. Now I want you to tell me just one thing more. Why do you hate the South?' " (p. 378). And the final commentary:

> "I dont hate it," Quentin said, quickly, at once, immediately;
> "I dont hate it." he said. *I dont hate it* he thought, panting
> in the cold air, the iron New England dark; *I dont. I dont! I*
> *dont hate it! I dont hate it!*

It is difficult to conceive of an "ending" which would provide less ordering and resolution. For not only is there no resolution on a cognitive level, but we are also confronted with the differing tones of the four "commentaries," and the terrible emotional ambivalence of Quentin's final outburst. We "end," then, with a psychological oxymoron of simultaneous love and hate, with internal conflict and self-contradiction. It is an intense and powerful ending, and a proper one to seal off and preserve the complex suspension of elements the book has presented. But it is also a pitiful ending. It is pitiful in that Shreve and Quentin seem to have been so little instructed by their immense labor of imagination. It is pitiful (and among many other things, perhaps, Faulkner is saying this, too) in its varied assertions that so much energy, effort, and pain have come to so little: to a lone idiot, an ironic letter, a brutally flippant commentary and act of cruelty to a roommate, and a bewildered cry of pain. It is, above all, pitiful because by it, Faulkner again demonstrates his unwillingness to step beyond the sanctuary of the paradox, to make, himself, as do a number of his characters, the clarifying "gesture," which might enable him and us to move beyond that bewildered cry of pain.

Faulkner's other novels exhibit the same avoidance of resolution, the same intent to present suggestive suspensions rather than comprehensibly integrated wholes. In *The Wild Palms,* where Faulkner alternates the chapters of two completely independent narratives, and in *Requiem for a Nun,* where he juxtaposes sections of broad historical narrative with the acts of a play, and in *Light in August,* where he juxtaposes three largely discrete stories, these suspensions become most amorphous. The greatest degree of resolution is offered, perhaps, by *Intruder in the Dust,* whose plot is relatively uncomplicated, and where there is very little doubt cast upon the propriety or justice of the boy's effort to save Lucas Beauchamp. On the other hand, with respect to the motivation for the effort, and the meaning of it, Faulkner is far from conclusive, and in the final chapter of the novel he complicates the context of the entire event by shifting his focus to the evils of mechanization and standardization. His final re-emphasis upon Beauchamp's almost comic pride and pedantry and his own almost comic treatment of the final scene further complicate our reaction to the story. Works whose ambiguities of content and tone have been especially overlooked in critical discussion are *Pylon,* the tall convict section of *The Wild Palms,* "The Bear," and the play in *Requiem for a Nun.*[7]

IV

As the reader is undoubtedly aware, I have used the terms "suspension" and "resolution" quite loosely and have made no careful effort to distinguish between what is resolved and what is not or between the kinds of elements left in suspension or between effective and ineffective kinds of irresolution. To make these distinctions seems to me a crucial and exceedingly complex problem for future Faulkner criticism. My primary purpose here has been to show that there is a problem, that the irresolution runs both wide and deep. I would like also to suggest some explanations for it.

[7] In discussing the end of *RN,* one critic writes: "Stevens is rightly and necessarily silent as the inarticulate, uneducated Nancy says simply 'Believe.' Nancy is herself the visible sign which Temple had sought, the concrete illustration of what is meant by 'Believe' " (Olga Vickery, "Gavin Stevens: From Rhetoric to Dialectic," *Faulkner Studies* II (Spring, 1953), 4). Mrs. Vickery overlooks the final exchange between Temple and Stevens at the end of the book by which Faulkner, characteristically, avoids resolution. Walking out of the jail Temple speaks: " 'Anyone to save it [reference obscure]. Anyone who wants it. If there is none, I'm sunk. We all are. Doomed. Damned.' " To this Gavin Stevens responds: " 'Of course we are. Hasn't He been telling us that for going on two thousand years?' " (p. 286). If anything, Nancy has believed that man will or can be "saved" (p. 278). Stevens' statement not only qualifies Nancy's by its content and tone but leaves us with what is virtually an oxymoron, for the very use of the "He" contradicts the statement that we are all damned. His statement also suggests that he has not really grown and developed, as Mrs. Vickery has argued.

So far I have written as though Faulkner's ambiguity and irresolution were entirely deliberate, strictly a matter of artistic intent, rather than one of temperament or general irrationalism or mere lack of concern about rational coherence. Up to a point, I think this is actually the case and that we may understand much of the ambiguity and irresolution as serving or reflecting two general intentions.

The first is to achieve powerful emotive and even hypnotic effects. Conrad Aiken has suggested that what Faulkner is after, in part, is a "medium without stops or pauses," an "image stream" toward which the reader "must be powerfully and unremittingly hypnotized," and he suggests that this intent to hypnotize accounts, perhaps, not only for the length and elaborateness of Faulkner's sentence structure but for his repetitiveness as well.[8] It is very likely that Faulkner's frequent resistance to rational analysis also contributes to this hypnotic effect. Some passages from Edward Snyder's *Hypnotic Poetry*[9] strongly suggest this. Professor Snyder notes that in actual hypnosis the stimuli used "are such as to fix the attention while retarding mental activity,"[10] and he concludes that the same retardation of mental activity is helpful in producing the less complete hypnoidal state which he calls "emotional trance," a state in which the subject's emotional susceptibility is highly intensified.[11] In his Foreword to Snyder's book, the psychologist James Leuba writes that Snyder has "demonstrated the existence of a type of poetry which owes its attraction to a method of composition, the effect of which is to limit the intellectual activity, i.e., to induce a state of partial trance, and thereby to free in some measure the emotional life from the trammel of critical thinking."[12]

Whether Faulkner actually induces a state of partial trance is not especially important here. But it does seem likely that the purpose and effect of much of his presentation is to free the emotional life from the "trammel" of critical thinking, so that like the preacher

---

[8] Conrad Aiken, "William Faulkner: The Novel as Form," in Hoffman and Vickery, *Two Decades of Criticism*, pp. 142-143.

[9] *Hypnotic Poetry: A Study of Trance-Inducing Techniques in Certain Poems and its Literary Significance* (Philadelphia: University of Pennsylvania Press, 1930).

[10] Snyder, *Hypnotic Poetry*, p. 25.

[11] Snyder, *Hypnotic Poetry*, pp. 32–33.

[12] Snyder, *Hypnotic Poetry*, p. x.

in *The Sound and the Fury,* who is also in a sense a hypnotist, he might speak directly to the "heart." To some extent, we can say of Faulkner, as McCaslin says was true for God, that he "didn't have His Book written to be read by what must elect and choose, but by the heart" (*GDM,* 260). I do not mean to equate the word "heart" entirely with the words "emotive" or "hypnotic," and Faulkner's own use of the word is ambiguous, but there is no doubt that he sees the heart essentially as an organ of feeling and as antithetic to the head, and that he regards it, and not the head, as the way to truth. "Ideas and facts," he has said in a recent interview, "have very little connection with truth."[13] We give ourselves "mind's reason[s]," says McCaslin, "because the heart dont always have time to bother with thinking up words that fit together" (*GDM,* 348). A generally non-intellectual intention is suggested also by Faulkner's statements that "I must try to express clumsily in words what the pure music would have done better,"[14] and that "I think people try to find more in my work than I've put there. I like to tell stories, to create people, and situations. But that's all. I doubt if an author knows what he puts in a story. All he is trying to do is to tell what he knows about his environment and the people around him in the most moving way possible."[15]

An effort to reach the heart, or to "lift" it, as Faulkner sometimes puts it, by bypassing or retarding mental activity explains certain of Faulkner's obstacles to rational comprehension, but there is much that it does not explain, for Faulkner is not so consistent or complete an irrationalist or even non-intellectual as such an explanation implies. His ambiguity and irresolution must also be understood as asserting and reflecting a view of life. It is a difficult view to define, and the nature of it is such that it is almost impossible to draw a dividing line between the view and temperament. A statement by Warren Beck is helpful toward defining this view of life.

> If Faulkner's sentences sometimes soar and circle involved and prolonged, if his scenes become halls of mirrors repeating tableaux in a progressive magnification, if echoes multiply into

[13] Jean Stein, "The Art of Fiction XII: William Faulkner," *The Paris Review,* No. 12 (Spring, 1956), 49.

[14] Jean Stein, "The Art of Fiction," p. 44.

[15] Cynthia Grenier, "The Art of Fiction: An Interview with William Faulkner," *Accent,* XVI (Summer, 1956), 171.

the dissonance of infinite overtones, it is because the meanings his stories unfold are complex, mysterious, obscure, and incomplete. There is no absolute, no eternal pure white radiance in such presentations, but rather the stain of many colors, refracted and shifting in kaleidoscopic suspension, about the center of man's enigmatic behavior and fate, within the drastic orbit of mortality. Such being Faulkner's view of life, such is his style.[16]

Professor Zink asserts that "at its best, form in Faulkner's art constitutes a living effort to penetrate and to realize in art an ineffable complexity."[17]

Certainly, these critics are right that Faulkner's form often suggests and seeks to communicate a view of life as enigmatic and ineffably complex. To a large extent his shifts in tone and point of view, his avoidance of resolution, and his various obstacles to rational understanding, may be viewed as an effort to present life and experience in such a way as to make facile interpretation impossible. The meaning of the stories of Sutpen and Joe Christmas and others, Faulkner is saying, is largely ambiguous. Whether they are free agents or pawns, heroes or villains, is ambiguous, just as it is uncertain whether the tall convict is a hero or fool, whether Darl Bundren is a seer or madman, and whether the desperate struggles of the convict, the Bundrens, and others are tragic or comic, significant or futile. They are presented as both and neither, just as simpler entities like faces are conceived in the both and neither terms of the oxymoron, and just as Quentin's reaction to the Sutpen story, and to the South, in general, is a both and neither combination of love and hate. Whether there is a God or not is problematical, and if there is, whether he is Jehovah, Christ, Satan, Joker, Umpire, Chess Player, or Life Force. The only certainty that exists, Faulkner sometimes suggests, is that man will "endure," but whether he will endure by virtue of his soul or his folly Faulkner does not make clear, nor is it clear whether enduring means primarily to suffer or to transcend time.

But these descriptions are inadequate, for they leave out impor-

---

[16] Beck, "William Faulkner's Style," p. 162.
[17] Karl E. Zink, "William Faulkner: Form as Experience," *The South Atlantic Quarterly*, LIII (July, 1954), 384.

tant qualities of Faulkner's feeling about life which are inseparable from his view.

> You get born and you try this and you dont know why only you keep on trying it and you are born at the same time with a lot of other people, all mixed up with them, like trying to, having to, move your arms and legs with strings only the same strings are hitched to all the other arms and legs and the others all trying and they dont know why either except that the strings are all in one another's way like five or six people all trying to make a rug on the same loom only each one wants to weave his own pattern into the rug; and it cant matter, you know that, or the Ones that set up the loom would have arranged things a little better, and yet it must matter because you keep on trying. . . . (AA, 127).

The words are Judith Sutpen's but the passage communicates more clearly than any other, I believe, the essence of Faulkner's view of life and feeling toward it. The passage suggests not only the complex and enigmatic qualities of life, but the sense of life as conflict, tension, and frustration, which persistently informs Faulkner's presentation. Above all, it suggests the intense contradictory feelings which, more than anything else, I think, explain Faulkner's attitude toward life and toward his own art: "it can't matter, you know that . . . and yet it must matter." It cannot have meaning and yet it must. The statement does not simply describe a dual perspective—"seems sometimes to matter, sometimes not," nor an uncertainty—"may or may not matter," nor even a paradox—"does and does not matter." The simultaneous "can't and "must" suggests a desperately divided and tormented perspective and condition of mind which tries to move simultaneously and intensely toward both order and chaos, and which understandably seizes upon the figure which most nearly moves in both directions, the oxymoron.

This divided view and feeling about the meaningfulness of life and effort accounts, undoubtedly, for Faulkner's frequent explicit and implicit coupling of terms like "empty" and "profound," "futile" and "tragic," and for statements such as "the substance itself [life] not only not dead, not complete, but in its very insoluble enigma of human folly and blundering possessing a futile and tragic immortality" (P, 82), and "profound and irrevocable if only in the sense of being profoundly and irrevocably unimportant" (P, 109): It helps us to understand Faulkner's seemingly obsessive assertion and denial of immortality and to account for his often perceptive idiots and incoherent intellectuals. It accounts, in part, for his failure to pursue thoroughly many of the ideas and meanings which he has suggested; even more, for his ability to urge certain meanings intensely and then to ignore them or to contradict them with equal intensity, for his use of form both to illuminate and obscure. It is a view and feeling which, in general, makes it necessary for him to try continuously to affirm and deny, to illuminate and obscure, the meaning of his own artistic creations and the significance of the lives and experiences he presents. It accounts, perhaps, for his inability finally to commit himself, and for his ability to treat art both as a plaything and a dedication. Undoubtedly it helps to explain the utterly divergent critical estimates and interpretations of his work. Finally, I believe, it accounts in large measure for the peculiarly compelling and disturbing power of his works, for it reminds us of the similar schizophrenia within ourselves which we have worked hard to bury.

Generally skeptical views of life, or dual perspectives in which life appears in some ways meaningful and in some ways meaningless, are not uncommon, are certainly comprehensible, and have informed much great art, including that of Shakespeare. Metaphysical poetry and Jacobean drama, at times, seem to suggest a division of feeling, as well as of view, about life's meaningfulness which is as intense as Faulkner's. There is still, however, an important difference. Whatever the tensions and opposing suggestions, explicit or implicit, in a poem by Donne or a play by Webster, one feels behind them, I think, a governing mind which never really doubts the validity of its own ideas and perceptions or the possibility if not the existence, of a moral universe in which such ideas and perceptions are relevant, which never abandons the effort to order its thoughts and emotions. Like many modern artists Faulkner has no such certainty.

Unlike any other moderns of comparable stature, however, Faulkner's uncertainty also embraces his art. Joyce, Virginia Woolf, and even Kafka have never really doubted the validity of art and have used it always to resist and to recreate as well as to reflect the dissolving worlds they saw and felt about them. They remain committed to order and reason. There have been some writers and painters, the surrealists and dadaists, who have not resisted, whose uncertainty or despair has led them to deny reason, whose desperation has led them to protest against disorder with disorder. A part of Faulkner remains intensely committed to art and order, and seeks desperately, and of course, paradoxically to find a way by which art can order equally intense convictions that life and art do and do not matter. A part of him is content with disorder.

Faulkner is more of an irrationalist than many of his critics have been willing to accept, but less of one than he, himself, has often suggested by his numerous explicit antitheses of head and heart and by his varied assertions that "ideas and facts have very little connection with truth." It is only partially true that he "didn't have His Book written to be read by what must elect and choose but by the heart" (*GDM*, 260). For the mere act of reading Faulkner requires a large intellectual effort and much of his appeal is clearly intellectual. Like most of the other elements of his work, his irrationalism is not a consistent or systematic thing, not a clearly governing principle of organization; it, too, becomes part of a suspension and will not fall clearly into place. Perhaps the best term for Faulkner is "non-rationlist."

But finally, I do not think we can adequately explain the kinds of tensions and suspensions we find in Faulkner's work except in terms of temperament. For, at bottom, his works seem governed not so much by a view of life, or by a particular gap in his thought and feeling, or by particular principles of organization as by his temperament;[18] that is, by the particular compound of intellectual and emotional inclinations, tendencies, and responses that characterize his mental life and shape his reactions to experience. It is his temperamental responses rather that any theories or ideas or particular torments, which he undoubtedly trusts to produce and to order his art. One fundamental quality of that temperament is its response to tension and opposition. Another is perhaps best described as a tendency toward profusion. It is this which no doubt helps to account for the remarkable scope of his fictional creation, but also for what surely must be criticized as an overabundance of effects and suggestions. Related to his inability or unwillingness to set limits on abundance, but yet to be distinguished from that qual-

---

[18] Any work of art, no doubt, reflects the temperament of its author, and in some ultimate sense is governed by it. In Faulkner's case, however, I am suggesting that the relationship between his art and temperament is a far more immediate, direct, and pervasive one than is true for most novelists.

ity, is his tendency to avoid commitment. It is this, as has no doubt been apparent, which most troubles me, from a human as well as an aesthetic point of view. For, surely, if there are to be any distinctions in art and life between responsibility and irresponsibility, indeed, any distinctions at all, we must insist that man can and must make choices. In both the form and content of Faulkner's works there is often the assertion or implication that man does not need to make choices. "You dont need to choose," says McCaslin. "The heart already knows" (*GDM*, 260). We do need to choose. There is, of course, also, in Faulkner the frequent implication that we do need to choose, and Ike, himself, does seem to make a terribly important choice by relinquishing his land. By suggesting, finally, that Ike both did and did not choose,[19] Faulkner, too, has made a choice, the choice which he can rarely resist, and which, I feel, limits his achievement, the choice not to choose.

Editor's Note: "The Edge of Order: The Pattern of Faulkner's Rhetoric" by Walter J. Slatoff is reprinted, with brief authorial revisions, from *Twentieth Century Literature*, III (1957), pp. 107–127. By permission of Walter J. Slatoff.

Walter J. Slatoff is a Professor of English at Cornell University and Editor of *Epoch* magazine, for which he has written numerous reviews. He is the author of *Quest for Failure: A Study of William Faulkner*.

[19] See *GDM*, 288, 309, 310.

SUTPEN
AND THE SOUTH:
A STUDY OF
ABSALOM, ABSALOM!

MELVIN BACKMAN

Seven years after the publication of *The Sound and the Fury* came *Absalom, Absalom!* (1936). *The Sound and the Fury* dealt with the fall of a family, *Absalom* deals with the fall of a society. The Quentin Compson of *Absalom* is not quite the same as the earlier Quentin: his concern is social rather than personal and his role is identified for the most part with a central quest in the novel—the quest to discover the truth about the rise and fall of his South. In its search for the truth about a whole society, the novel circles and shuttles back and forth in time, its sentences twist and strain, and its narrators attempt to recreate a past on the basis of some fact and much conjecture. Sometimes the narrators mislead unintentionally, sometimes they contradict one another, and often they are carried away by their own bias, preoccupation, or imagination. Yes, it is hard to come by truth, but still one might question whether a novel whose pitch is too shrill, whose approach is emotional and poetic, whose perspective seems unclear and shifting—one might question whether such a work presents the best way of getting at historical truth. The method of narration apparently mirrors not only the difficulty in getting at truth but the struggle to face truth. For all its straining, its complexities and obscurities, *Absalom,* I would conclude, is Faulkner's most historical novel.

Its intention, Ilse Dusoir Lind has said,

> is to create, through the utilization of all the resources of fiction, a grand tragic vision of historic dimension. As in the tragedies of the ancients and in the great myths of the Old

Testament, the action represents issues of timeless moral significance. That Faulkner here links the decline of a social order to an infraction of fundamental morality cannot be doubted. Sutpen falls through innate deficiency of moral insight, but the error which he commits is also socially derived and thus illustrates the flaw which dooms with equal finality the aspirations of a whole culture.[1]

For Mrs. Lind and most other critics, Sutpen is the South.[2] Yet some influential critics have qualified or contradicted this interpretation. Both Malcolm Cowley and Robert Penn Warren have stated in effect that "the Deep South was settled partly by aristocrats like the Sartoris clan and partly by new men like Colonel Sutpen."[3] Whereas they see Sutpen as only partly representative of the Deep South, Cleanth Brooks would question whether Sutpen is a Southerner at all. For Brooks, Sutpen is in many ways a Yankee: he "is a 'planner' who works by blueprint and on a schedule. He is rationalistic and scientific, not traditional, not religious, not even superstitious." "Indeed, Sutpen is at some points more nearly allied to Flem [Snopes] than he is to the Compsons and the Sartorises. Like

---

[1] Ilse Dusoir Lind, "The Design and Meaning of *Absalom, Absalom!*" in Frederick J. Hoffman and Olga W. Vickery (eds.), *William Faulkner: Three Decades of Criticism* (East Lansing: Michigan State Univ. Press, 1960), p. 278; and in *PMLA*, LXX (December 1955), 887.

[2] For example, Mrs. Vickery treats Sutpen as "a mirror image of the South"; O'Connor as "the essence of the history of the South"; Howe regards *Absalom* as the "story of the fall of the homeland"; Sullivan as "the complete statement of Southern ambition, execution and success, guilt, doom and destruction in one novel"; Hoffman as "the vision of the South as a whole (or of human society itself) as a creation of this selfish and impulsive drive"; and Waggoner as both "a lyric evocation of the Southern past" and a "search for the truth about human life as that truth may be discovered by understanding the past." See Olga W. Vickery, *The Novels of William Faulkner* (Baton Rouge: Louisiana State Univ. Press, 1959), pp. 92–95; William Van O'Connor, *The Tangled Fire of William Faulkner* (Minneapolis: Univ. of Minnesota Press, 1954), pp. 94–96; Irving Howe, *William Faulkner: A Critical Study* (New York: Random House, 1952), p. 161; Walter Sullivan, "The Tragic Design of *Absalom, Absalom!*" *South Atlantic Quarterly*, L (Oct. 1951), 560; Frederick J. Hoffman, *William Faulkner* (New York: Twayne, 1961), pp. 74–79; and Hyatt H. Waggoner, *William Faulkner: From Jefferson to the World* (Lexington: Univ. of Kentucky Press, 1959), pp. 149–153.

[3] This is Cowley's statement, which Warren paraphases. See Malcolm Cowley, "Introduction to *The Portable Faulkner*," and Robert Penn Warren, "William Faulkner," in *William Faulkner: Three Decades of Criticism*, pp. 102 and 111 respectively.

Flem, he is a new man with no concern for the past and has a boundless energy with which to carry out his aggressive plans."[4] In seeing Sutpen as basically different from the other Yoknapatawpha planters and in associating him with the Snopeses, Brooks is making use of certain stereotypes that have been best described by George Marion O'Donnell:

> In Mr. Faulkner's mythology there are two kinds of characters; they are Sartorises or Snopeses, whatever the family names may be. [And in the spiritual geography of Mr. Faulkner's work there are two worlds: the Sartoris world and the Snopes world.] In all of his successful books, he is exploring the two worlds in detail, dramatizing the inevitable conflict between them.
>
>   It is a universal conflict. The Sartorises act traditionally; that is to say, they act always with an ethically responsible will. They represent vital morality, humanism. Being antitraditional, the Snopeses are immoral from the Sartoris point of view. But the Snopeses do not recognize this point of view; acting only for self-interest, they acknowledge no ethical duty. Really, then, they are amoral; they represent naturalism or animalism. And the Sartoris-Snopes conflict is fundamentally a struggle between humanism and naturalism.[5]

Such a view—with its simplistic division of the South into Sartorises and Snopeses, its blindness to the guilt and tension and ambivalence which beset its Quentin Compsons—maps the reality neither of the historical South nor of Yoknapatawpha. It would, in fact, shut out reality and substitute legend; it would reduce the complexity of human life and character to a single abstraction. Contrary to the Sartoris-Snopes thesis, the ante-bellum South, though once ruled by the planter class, did not consist only of planter aristocracy and poor whites; the great majority of its people have always been hard-working small farmers,[6] like the Tulls and Bundrens and Houstons and Quicks and Armstids of Yoknapatawpha. Moreover, to attribute the decline of the South to the Snopeses is to compound legend

---

[4] Cleanth Brooks, *William Faulkner: The Yoknapatawpha Country* (New Haven: Yale Univ. Press, 1963), pp. 306, 307.

[5] "Faulkner's Mythology," in *Three Decades of Criticism*, pp. 83–84.

[6] Avery Craven, *The Growth of Southern Nationalism, 1848–1861* (Baton Rouge: Louisiana State Univ. Press, 1953), p. 11; and Herbert Weaver, *Mississippi Farmers, 1850–1860* (Nashville Tenn.: Vanderbilt Univ. Press, 1945), pp. 11–13, 28–29, 41, 48, and 57.

with fantasy, for not only does such a view assume the existence of an aristocratic South based on a benevolent system of slavery and characterized by humanistic values but it finds a ready scapegoat for its ills in a tribe of Southern "Yankees," the Snopeses. It is more logical and just to assign the major responsibility for the fortunes of the South to its rulers—the Thomas Sutpens. And it is essential, if we are to understand *Absalom,* to know (1) the fact and legend of Southern history and (2) how Sutpen's life and career mirror the history and heritage of the South, moral as well as social and political.

Northern Mississippi was settled in the 1830's and 1840's. Mississippi did not become a state until 1817, and the town of Oxford, generally accepted as the prototype for Jefferson, was still an Indian trading post in 1835.[7] Tocqueville, who travelled through America in the 1830's, described Southwestern society as "only an agglomeration of adventurers and speculators,"[8] and Baldwin's *The Flush Times of Alabama and Mississippi* (1853) confirms Tocqueville's appraisal. Historians generally agree that the Deep South, right up to the Civil War, was largely frontier country.[9] W. J. Cash, for example, describes the making of the great or Deep South in this manner:

> 1810 came and went, the battle of New Orleans was fought and won, and it was actually 1820 before the plantation was fully on the march, striding over the hills of Carolina to Mississippi —1820 before the tide of immigration was in full sweep about the base of the Appalachians.
>
> From 1820 to 1860 is but forty years—a little more than the span of a single generation. The whole period from the invention of the cotton gin to the outbreak of the Civil War is less than seventy years—the lifetime of a single man. Yet it was wholly within the longer of these periods, and mainly within

[7] Charles Sackett Sydnor, *Slavery in Mississippi* (New York: Appleton-Century, 1933), pp. 41, 247–248; and Ward L. Miner, *The World of William Faulkner* (Durham, N.C.: Duke Univ. Press, 1952), pp. 18–36.

[8] Alexis de Tocqueville, *Democracy in America,* ed. Phillips Bradley (New York: Knopf, 1946), I, 204.

[9] See, for example, Howard W. Odum, *The Way of the South* (New York: Macmillan. 1947), p. 23; Vernon Lane Wharton, *The Negro in Mississippi, 1865–1890* (Chapel Hill: Univ. of North Carolina Press, 1947), p. 216; and Avery Craven, *The Coming of the Civil War* (New York: Scribners, 1950), pp. 25–27.

the shorter that the development and growth of the great South took place. Men who, as children, had heard the war-whoop of the Cherokee in the Carolina backwoods lived to hear the guns at Vicksburg. And thousands of other men who had looked upon Alabama when it was still a wilderness and upon Mississippi when it was still a stubborn jungle, lived to fight—and to fight well, too—in the ranks of the Confederate armies.

The inference is plain. It is impossible to conceive the great South as being, on the whole, more than a few steps removed from the frontier stage at the beginning of the Civil War. It is imperative, indeed, to conceive it as having remained more or less fully in the frontier stage for a great part—maybe the greater part—of its antebellum history.[10]

If this is so, who were the aristocrats of the Deep South? For the great part, they were "but the natural flower of the backcountry grown prosperous."[11] In Mississippi before 1860 a white man could lay claim to the title of gentry if he acquired the land and the slaves. The importance of the established gentry of the Carolina, Tidewater, and Natchez plantations lay not in their migration to the undeveloped South but in the potency of their influence upon the South's lower classes. Although some planters or their sons did come to the lower South, most of the men pushing into the Mississippi wilderness were from the backwoods. The plantation aristocracy served them as a symbol and goal, as the crown of a Southerner's achievement; it provided the more successful and ambitious with a manner and tradition which they put on, so to speak, like a new cloak. But after the Civil War the South, "beset by the specters of defeat, of shame, of guilt," submerged the fact and romanticized the claim of the planter.[12] Hence was spread the legend of the Old South:

> . . . the legend of which the backbone is, of course, precisely the assumption that every planter was in the most rigid sense of the word a gentleman.
>
> Enabling the South to wrap itself in contemptuous superiority, to sneer down the Yankee as low-bred, crass, and money-grubbing, and even to beget in his bourgeois soul a kind of

[10] *The Mind of the South* (Garden City, N.Y.: Doubleday, 1954), p. 24.

[11] Ibid., p. 33. See also Frank Lawrence Owsley, *Plain Folk of the Old South* (Baton Rouge: Louisiana State Univ. Press, 1949), p. 90.

[12] Cash, p. 73. See also Craven, *The Coming of the Civil War*, pp. 17–18; and Sydnor, *Slavery in Mississippi*, p. 248.

secret and envious awe, it was a nearly perfect defense-mechanism.[13]

Under the spur of the Civil War defeat, the Southerner's need to believe in the aristocracy of his ancestors and in the superiority of his tradition hastened the spread of the Southern legend. The legend affected the whole South, not just the Deep South. The force of its need and conviction submerged the fact that almost no members of the Cavalier aristocracy ever left England for America, that the Southern aristocracy derived from the low and middle classes, and that the aristocracy of the Deep South was made in one generation.[14] Scratch the veneer of the aristocrat of the Deep South and you would find a frontiersman. It was these new planters who took over the leadership of the Old South. The Natchez and Virginia gentry, longer exposed and hence more susceptible to the opinion of the rest of the Western world, were less able to conceive of slavery as a "positive good." But the new men brought to their position the frontier's aggressiveness, the strength and ruthlessness of self-made men, and a fierce faith in the righteousness of their cause and their interests. Nine-tenths of the men who directed the affairs of the Confederate government, like nine-tenths of the men who officered its armies, says Cash, were not Colonial aristocrats but new people.[15]

[13] Cash, p. 73.

[14] Historians have long recognized that the cavalier and planter legends derive from wishful thinking rather than fact. For early research on the subject, see Thomas Jefferson Wertenbaker, *Patrician and Plebeian in Virginia* (Charlottesville, Va.: privately printed, 1910), Preface and pp. 1–21 [recent editions of his works have been published by Russell and Russell]; and G. W. Dyer, *Democracy in the South Before the Civil War* (Nashville: Methodist Episcopal Church, South, 1905), pp. 30–34. Although Wertenbaker established convincingly the non-aristocratic origins of the Virginia gentry, W. J. Cash, writing a generation later, had to explode the myth again. For other historical commentary, see Avery Craven, *The Coming of the Civil War*, pp. 17–34; C. Vann Woodward, *The Burden of Southern History* (Baton Rouge: Louisiana State Univ. Press, 1960), pp. 12–13; and William R. Taylor, *Cavalier and Yankee* (New York: Braziller, 1961), pp. 17–18, 67, 96, 146–148, 203–205, and 334–341. The general acceptance of the Sartoris-Snopes interpretation of Faulkner's works suggests that the myth, in another form, still lives with us.

[15] Cash, p. 71. Avery Craven states: "A careful study of biographical materials and facts revealed in the manuscript census shows that only some 7.73 per cent of the men who represented Virginia, the Carolinas, Alabama, Mississippi, Louisiana, Georgia, and Tennessee in the House and Senate from 1850 to 1860 were plantation owners or had come from families of plantation owners." Craven, *The Growth of Southern Nationalism*, p. 163.

With the possible exception of Sartoris, all the founders of the ruling clans in Yoknapatawpha were new men. Sutpen, McCaslin, and Compson got their land by hook or by crook. Compson acquired his by swapping a mare to the Indians, Sutpen got his with a little Spanish gold, and McCaslin "bought the land, took the land, got the land no matter how."[16] Faulkner has not told us how Sartoris got his land, but Sartoris possessed the "violent and ruthless dictatorialness and will to dominate"[17] which generally characterize the founders of the Yoknapatawpha ruling clans. The getting of the land, the hacking of a plantation out of the wilderness, and the establishment of a family dynasty would naturally promote violence, ruthlessness, and strength of character, and not "vital morality and humanism."

Nevertheless, Faulkner has made a distinction between Sartoris and Sutpen. They are different, not in the sense that Sartoris was an established Yoknapatawpha planter when Sutpen arrived at Jefferson in 1833—Sartoris did not arrive until a few years after Sutpen[18]—but in the sense that Sartoris' origin was "aristocratic" whereas Sutpen's was plebeian. Colonel Sartoris, as we see him in *Sartoris* and later in *The Unvanquished,* is a much more traditionally romantic figure than Sutpen. Sartoris, it is generally acknowledged, has been modelled in part on the character and life of the author's great-grandfather, Colonel William C. Falkner. Yet Falkner's origin more closely approximates that of Sutpen than of Sartoris: Sartoris came to Mississippi "with slaves and gear and money"[19] from a Carolina plantation, but Falkner came out of Tennessee as a poor boy. The inference is plain: Sartoris represents in part a projection of the legend, but Sutpen represents the reality.

To get at the reality, however, would be difficult for Faulkner, difficult because he would not only have to work his way out of the distortions wrought by Southern legend and pride but he would

[16] William Faulkner, *Go Down, Moses, and Other Stories* (New York: Random House, 1942), p. 256.

[17] William Faulkner, *The Unvanquished* (New York: Random House, 1938), p. 258. These words are voiced silently by Colonel Sartoris' son as he broods over his father's character.

[18] William Faulkner, *Requiem for a Nun* (New York: Random House, 1951), p. 44.

[19] Ibid.

have to repudiate the uncritical allegiance and assent demanded by a closed society even though it was still his home and native land. Yet the story, he said, "wouldn't let me alone"; he had to write it.[20] Next to *The Sound and the Fury*, *Absalom* was, admittedly, the novel that gave him the most trouble, the novel that apparently sprang out of compulsion and reluctance, out of pride and guilt, out of love and hate. The character in *Absalom* that expresses these ambivalent feelings is of course Quentin Compson. Without Quentin the story would never be told. He brings together all the facts and conjectures about Sutpen, he is the story's compelled listener and narrator, and he cares most about what Sutpen signifies.[21] "Out of the rag-tag and bob-ends of old tales and talking,"[22] out of Miss Rosa's "demonizing" and his father's speculating, he must reconstruct a past that might have been, a man that apparently was. He must because the man in a sense was his ancestor, the past his past and present too.

The man, like almost all the aristocrats of the Deep South, began his life at the frontier. Most settlers of the South were descended from the English and "the half-wild Scotch and Irish clansmen of the seventeenth and eighteenth centuries,"[23] and some came of course from the house of Old Bailey.[24] Thomas Sutpen was born in the mountains of West Virginia, his mother a Scottish mountain

---

[20] *Faulkner in the University*, ed. by Frederick L. Gwynn and Joseph L. Blotner (Charlottesville: Univ. of Virginia Press, 1959), p. 281.

[21] Many critics have recognized that the Sutpen story is Quentin's story too, that its full meaning does not make itself felt until the story has impacted upon Quentin's brooding, Hamletlike conscience. The very tension between Quentin and what he is hearing and telling gives the novel its peculiar shading and significance. Faulkner himself has said that *Absalom* is both the story of Sutpen and "the story of Quentin Compson's hatred of the bad qualities in the country he loves" (*Faulkner in the University*, p. 71). A good analysis of this aspect of *Absalom* may be found in an essay by Richard B. Sewall, *The Vision of Tragedy* (New Haven: Yale Univ. Press, 1959), pp. 133–147.

[22] *Absalom, Absalom!* (New York: Modern Library, 1951), p. 303. All quotations from *Absalom* are from this edition.

[23] Cash, p. 42. See also Owsley, *Plain Folk of the Old South*, pp. 90–91.

[24] That Faulkner places little stock in the genealogical claims of Southerners may be inferred not only from the origins he assigns to Sutpen but from the words he puts into the mouth of Sartoris himself: "In the nineteenth century . . . genealogy is poppycock. Particularly in America, where only what a man takes and keeps has any significance and where all of us have a common ancestry and the only house from which we can claim descent with any assurance is the Old Bailey." *Sartoris* (New York: Harcourt, Brace, 1929), p. 92.

woman, his father an ex-prisoner of the Old Bailey. In the mountains, "the land belonged to anybody and everybody and so the man who would go to the trouble and work to fence off a piece of it and say 'This is mine' was crazy" (p. 221). At the frontier it was not possessions but physical strength that determined one's worth, the strength "to be measured by lifting anvils or gouging eyes or how much whiskey you could drink then get up and walk out of the room" (p. 226). But at the mother's death the Sutpen family lost its hold upon their mountain home, "slid back down out of the mountains" (p. 223) and "fell" (p. 222) into a "land divided neatly up and actually owned by men who did nothing but ride over it on fine horses or sit in fine clothes on the galleries of big houses while other people worked for them" (p. 221). That the journey from the highland to the lowland, from the democratic way of life of the frontier to the stratified plantation society of the Tidewater region was a fall is confirmed by the disintegration of the Sutpen family and the decline of their pride. The boy Thomas Sutpen saw his mother dead, his father transported in a drunken stupor, his brothers vanishing, his sister giving birth to two nameless bastards, and their home become a rotting cabin. In a futile attempt to salvage something of their frontier pride the father whipped one of Pettibone's "niggers," and the sister sullenly refused to give way to a planter's carriage. But the unhappy transition from frontier independence to sharecropping subservience could not be effaced by violence against the Negro or by an occasional gesture against the planter. Now a man's worth was measured not by his manhood but by his possessions.

It was this humiliating truth that broke abruptly in upon young Sutpen's innocence after the white door of the planter's mansion closed upon him and the "monkey nigger" told him to go around to the back. Retreating to a kind of cave in the woods, he brooded upon the meaning of this rejection. For the first time in his life he saw "his own father and sisters and brothers as the owner, the rich man (not the nigger) must have been seeing them all the time—as cattle, creatures heavy and without grace, brutely evacuated into a world without hope or purpose for them" (p. 235). All that day he looked through his hurt into the face of the world's reality, until he knew that the only way to combat the world was to get for himself the land, the slaves, and the fine house upon which the planter had established his power and glory. He went to the island of Haiti to get what he wanted. He did not know that this "little lost island" (p. 253) had been "manured with black blood" and "torn limbs and outraged hearts" (p. 251). Like the single-minded Ahab, he knew only what he wanted. Crushing a slave rebellion, he rose from overseer to planter's son-in-law, and then to owner of land and house and slaves.

The decision that Sutpen made as a boy becomes the fateful decision of his life: he gave up the values of the frontier for those of a property-caste system. It was a decision full of bitter ironies, for in time it would lead to a war in which the backwoodsman fought by the side of the planter to preserve a system alien to his character and heritage. The planter and backwoodsman were separated by long-standing differences, but in the fierce mounting tension between North and South and in the War and its bitter aftermath, Southerners suppressed their differences. Still the union between planter and backwoodsman, despite its surface solidarity, remained fundamentally uneasy. Faulkner's own sympathies seemed to be on the side of the backwoodsman. Although Faulkner depicted the frontier way of life as crude and often brutal, he presented it as basically more honest and natural and innocent, simply because it was not founded on and sustained by property, by slavery. Ultimately, Sutpen's decision is a moral one: he committed the sin that would visit the iniquity of the father upon the children, and upon the children's children, unto the third and fourth generations. He did not know what he was doing, he would never know.

In 1829 Sutpen got his son. He named him Charles Bon—a name ironically reminiscent of Bonnie Prince Charles, who was heir to a throne he never inherited and prince to a nation that repudiated him. In 1831 Sutpen repudiated his "Negro" wife and son. The repudiation of the Negro was compelled by the planter's "design." Yet the repudiation planted the seed of the system's destruction. Charles Bon represents both the doomed victim and fated undoer of the "design." He incarnates in a sense the tragic history of the American Negro. Running through his veins was the blood of the slavers and planters—the Spanish, French, English, and American—and the blood of the African Negro. But it was the Negro blood that would work like a strange power of fate in the lives of the planters, the slaves, and all their descendants.

Two decades after Columbus' discovery of the New World, Negro slaves were working in the sugar plantations of Haiti. Shortly thereafter Negro slavery spread to the mainland of America. The Renaissance and the Commercial Revolution had unleashed new energies and freedoms; one of them was "the freedom to destroy freedom." The enslaving and trading and working of Negroes were a principal means by which the newly powerful nation-states of Europe exploited the New World and filled their coffers. As Portugal, Spain, Holland, France, and England struggled in the next few centuries to expand their interest in the new hemisphere, the Negro slave became the pawn in the struggle. By the first quarter of the eighteenth century England was taking over most of the world's slave trade, and slavery was becoming a cornerstone in her economic prosperity. The West Indies, whose sugar plantations in the seventeenth century had been Britain's chief source of wealth in the New World, were now yielding their economic primacy to the mainland. In the American colonies, particularly in Virigina and the Carolinas, slavery continued to grow throughout the century. In the decade before the American Revolution, the colonists blamed the British crown for slavery. But, ironically enough, it was the United States, founded on and dedicated to equality and freedom, that became the arena for the greatest expansion of slavery the world had ever seen. Stimulated by a seemingly inexhaustible demand for cotton, which the Industrial Revolution had created, and enabled by Whitney's new invention to separate quickly the seed from the fiber, Southerners moved westward in search for new land to plant cotton. The southwestern lands were rich and ready to be taken. All that was needed was labor. Virginia, its soil exhausted by tobacco, had plenty of slaves and could in time breed more, and there were always the West Indies and Africa from which slaves could be smuggled into the United States. So was born the Cotton Kingdom.[25]

Thomas Sutpen, who transplanted his slaves from Haiti to the Mississippi wilderness and transformed the wilderness to a plantation, was part of a large historical movement. He was part of the movement of slavery from the islands to the mainland and from the Eastern seaboard to the Southwest. Paradoxically, slavery was to find its most aggressive defenders in the Southern democrats of the United States. The very aggressiveness of the defense was related

[25] John Hope Franklin, *From Slavery to Freedom* (New York: Knopf, 1952), pp. 42–183; and W. E. Burghardt Du Bois, *Black Folk: Then and Now* (New York: Holt, 1939), pp. 126–144.

426

to various factors. For the Western world the nineteenth century was a century of industrial progress and intellectual liberalism, but for the South it was a century of resistance to the tide of liberalism and progress. Isolated, feeling itself threatened by a growing and hostile North, and harboring a bad conscience over its peculiar system, the South grew more ready to turn to violence. The Southern historian, C. Vann Woodward, has commented upon the South's state of mind immediately prior to the Civil War:

> The South had been living in a crisis atmosphere for a long time. It was a society in the grip of an insecurity complex, a tension resulting from both rational and irrational fears. One cause of it was the steady, invincible expansion of the free-state system in size and power, after the Southern system had reached the limits of its own expansion. The South, therefore, felt itself to be menaced through encirclement by a power containing elements unfriendly to its interests, elements that were growing strong enough to capture the government. The South's insecurity was heightened by having to defend against constant attack an institution it knew to be discredited throughout the civilized world and of which Southerners had once been among the severest critics. Its reaction was to withdraw increasingly from contact with the offending world, to retreat into an isolationism of spirit, and to attempt by curtailing freedom of speech to avoid criticism.[26]

"Much of the South's intellectual energy," Woodward continues, "went into a desperate effort to convince the world that its peculiar evil was actually a 'positive good,' but it failed even to convince itself. It writhed in the torments of its own conscience until it plunged into catastrophe to escape."[27] According to Woodward, the South, beset by a bad conscience, turned guilt and frustration into aggression and destruction. Woodward may be exaggerating the role played by conscience. We must remember that in the generation preceding the outbreak of the Civil War, the South was expanding: the frontier was being pushed southward and westward, the Cotton Kingdom was growing into the chief economic and social fact of the South's existence, and political power was shifting from

[26] *The Burden of Southern History*, p. 62.
[27] Ibid., pp. 20–21.

Virginia and the Carolinas to the Deep South. The men who were making this expansion were caught up in the grip of their own ambitions and interests. Their proneness to violence was probably due less to bad conscience than to the fact that violence had played an important role in their frontier background and in their making of a plantation. It was a time when the South chose not a Thomas Jefferson but a Jefferson Davis as its leader. It was a time of Thomas Sutpens, not Quentin Compsons.

In the 1830's the men who would later become the leaders of the South during the Civil War were still men on the make, men who had yet to achieve their dream. It was a "dream of grim and castle-like magnificence" (p. 38) that Thomas Sutpen, with the help of his slaves and the captured French architect, built into the great house itself. With an assist from the puritan Goodhue Coldfield, he acquired the appropriate furnishings for his baronial dream: the chandeliers, rugs, mahogany, and "the stainless wife" (p. 51). The marriage of Thomas Sutpen to Ellen Coldfield signifies the union of frontiersman and puritan, a union which would give birth to the very character of the South. Frontier violence would be yoked to fundamentalist religion, frontier individualism would be married to the puritan's conscience. Superimposed on the marriage was the plantation system, with another set of values and with its Peculiar Institution.

In Mississippi the planter-to-be had no time to waste. Out of the virgin land Sutpen "tore violently a plantation" (p. 9), and out of the virgin wife "without gentleness begot" (p. 9) a son and a daughter. He was hurrying his dream into shape. Even the names of his offspring and possessions reflect the dream. Charles and Henry might have come from English and Norman royalty, Judith from the Old Testament, Clytemnestra from the Greeks, and Rob Roy (his thoroughbred stallion) from Sir Walter Scott. By the 1850's Sutpen had become the biggest landowner and planter of Yoknapatawpha. He "acted his role too—a role of arrogant ease and leisure" (p. 72), while his wife "moved, lived, from attitude to attitude against her background of chatelaine to the largest, wife to the wealthiest, mother of the most fortunate" (p. 69). Dream had become actuality. Now he "would take that boy in where he would never again need to stand on the outside of a white door" (p. 261). He had riven himself free from the brutehood of his past, made himself part of the proud and privileged class of the South, and had planted the heir who would perpetuate the achievement. So it seemed—until the Christmas of 1859 when retribution knocked on the white door of Sutpen's great house, and the past he had put away walked back into his life in the person of his first son, Charles Bon.

Charles Bon. Charles Good. In station and manners and breeding he was the elegant New Orleans scion, fortunate member of the planter class and an elite Latin culture. In personality he was "gentle sardonic whimsical and incurably pessimistic" (p. 129). In his heart he was the son whose life had been "enclosed by an unsleeping cabal bent apparently on teaching him that he had never had a father" (p. 313), he was "that mental and spiritual orphan whose fate it apparently was to exist in some limbo" (p. 124), he was that "forlorn nameless and homeless lost child" (p. 267) who came knocking on the white door of Sutpen's house. He wanted no inheritance; he wanted but a word, a sign, a look, a touch from Sutpen which would say you are my son. He got no acknowledgement, he got nothing. Even the love he got from his brother Henry turned into ashes when Henry learned that Bon was *"the nigger that's going to sleep with your sister"* (p. 358). For all his sophistication, Bon remained only the orphan (he never really had a mother since, warped by paranoiac hatred of Sutpen, she had lost the power to love) who never found the father he sought: that was his fate. So it was that he lived as if something had gone out of him, as if he did not really want to live.

The story of Charles Bon is a richly ironic fable of the Old South. Bon embodies both the most favored of whites, a New Orleans scion, and the lowliest of blacks, the white man's bastard. He is the intelligent, cultivated young gentleman who had to be shot by a Mississippi clodhopper because the nigger signified a subhuman threat to white womanhood. Like his father, he could not acknowledge his son by a colored woman. These ironies are part of a system; beneath these ironies rest other parts of the system's foundation. In the Old South the Negro slave had generally no father and little mother. Under a system that made human beings into chattel, the Negro woman, when she did not labor in the fields, served as the breeder of stock and as the instrument for the white man's sexual pleasure. The Negress was a kind of mare, the Negro a stud. The effect was to destroy or warp the institution of the family among a whole people. In removing sex from its familial role, the system did violence to the morality of both whites and blacks.[28] It made sex for the Negro into an irresponsible animal relationship; it made sex for the white man into a guilty, dishonest one. A schism, a kind of unconscious hypocrisy, embedded itself deeply into the soul of the South. For the white man the Negress was the female animalized and his white woman was the female spiritualized. It was as if the planter were trying to make up to his white woman for his faithlessness and duplicity.[29] Reality was two families by the planter, white and black. Reality was a brother who was not a brother, a sister who was not a sister, a wife who was not a wife. Southerners knew of this reality, accepted it, lived with it, even though it violated what they thought they believed in: honor, pride, the family, and the decencies of life. This reality underlies the story of the House of Sutpen.

All the relationships in the Sutpen family are invested with a peculiar irony, doom, and tragedy, as if a curse had been placed on them like the curse on the House of Oedipus. Incest, fratricide, and the fall of a family are all aspects of both curses. Moreover, like several characters in *Oedipus Rex*, the Sutpens, for the most part, did not know the full truth about themselves and could not realize their identity and humanity. Henry and Charles were brothers, yet not brothers; Judith and Charles were sister and brother, yet not sister and brother; Sutpen and Charles were father and son, yet not father and son. They seem compelled by a Greek fate—such is the power of the system—to repudiate or destroy one another; they seem compelled by the Old Testament God to suffer for the sins of their father. It was the father, the nucleus of the culture, who determined the fate and character of the others. He signifies an elemental force, a heroic hybris, in the Southern culture; he is the

---

[28] It is of course difficult to appraise the moral and psychological damage done to the Negro in the process of enslaving him. One can suggest, however, some historians and commentators who provide information and insight: Frederick Bancroft, *Slave Trading in the Old South* (New York: Ungar, 1959); F. Franklin Frazier, *The Negro Family in the United States* (New York: Dryden, 1948); John Hope Franklin, *From Slavery to Freedom;* W. E. Burghardt Du Bois, *Black Folk: Then and Now;* Frank Tannenbaum, *Slave and Citizen: The Negro in the Americas* (New York: Knopf, 1947); Daniel P. Mannix, in collaboration with Malcolm Cowley; *Black Cargoes: A History of the Atlantic Slave Trade* (New York: Viking, 1962); and Frederick Douglass, *Narrative of the Life of Frederick Douglass, An American Slave, Written by Himself,* edited by Benjamin Quarles (Cambridge, Mass.: Belknap, 1960).

[29] See Cash, pp. 97–98.

archetype of the Southern planter. There is a grandeur to the man who hammers out his "design" in the face of God's and nature's opposition. Yet there is a fatal defect too: his Adamic innocence, like that of other American barons on the make, had hardened into moral blindness, and the egoism and energy generated by his rejection and dream of vindication had become ultimately a force for destruction of himself, his family, and his society. In attempting to build a dynasty, he had lost a family; in making himself into the image of the Southern planter, he had lost part of his humanity; in displacing conscience by pride, he had lost the power to see into hmself. Since he was "incapable of that rending of the self and tearing out of pride which forms the tragic element,"[30] his life ended not in tragic affirmation but in gross deterioration and unheroic death.

Ironically, the lowliest of the whites is the instrument of retribution. For Wash Jones the Colonel signified all that was best in the planter: courage, honor, paternalism, and authority. For Wash the Colonel was a god.

> . . . on the week days he would see Sutpen (the fine figure of the man as he called it) on the black stallion, galloping about the plantation, and Father said how for that moment Wash's heart would be quiet and proud both and that maybe it would seem to him that this world where niggers, that the Bible said had been created and cursed by God to be brute and vassal to all men of white skin, were better found and housed and even clothed than he and his granddaughter—that this world where he walked always in mocking and jeering echoes of nigger laughter, was just a dream and an illusion and that the actual world was the one where his own lonely apotheosis (Father said) galloped on the black thoroughbred, thinking maybe, Father said, how the Book said that all men were created in the image of God and so all men were the same in God's eyes anyway, looked the same to God at least, and so he would look at Sutpen and think *A fine proud man. If God Himself was to come down and ride the natural earth, that's what He would aim to look like.* (p. 282)

In spite of the blind contradiction in Wash's belief that the Bible could be used as authority for both the Negro's enslavement and

---

[30] Howe, p. 164.

man's equality, there is something touching about Wash's faith in the planter who had sprung from the same brute origins but who in the span of several decades had become the poor white's apotheosis. By 1869, however, the ravages of the War and Reconstruction had eaten so deeply into the planter and his "design" that his power was being broken and his ruthlessness exposed. The breaking point came when Sutpen, having attended the mare that had just foaled a colt to his stallion, entered Wash's cabin to see whether he had bred a son by Milly, Wash's granddaughter. Bending over the pallet where she lay with her newborn daughter, he said: "Well, Milly; too bad you're not a mare too. Then I could give you a decent stall in the stable" (p. 286). The earth seemed to fall away from beneath Wash's feet. He confronted the planter. Like the Grim Reaper, he raised the rusty scythe; the planter's whip lashed twice across his face, and then the scythe came down.

Although Faulkner made the poor white the instrument of the planter's demise, the deterioration of Sutpen's will and character, wrought by the inroads of the War and Reconstruction, contributed also to his downfall. Nevertheless, though the planter's confidence and power had been deeply shaken by the loss of the War, the Southern people in actuality did not repudiate their planter-leaders immediately afterwards. Toward the end of the nineteenth century they did begin to turn to other leaders, to those who made the Negro the scapegoat for the Lost Cause and current ills. The Negro, who had once been inviolate as the planter's chattel, became fair game for any white. Providing an outlet for the people's frustration and resentment, racism became the official policy of the South. In effect, Faulkner was right; the poor white eventually did turn on the planter.

What survived from Sutpen's "design"? There was the heir apparent, Henry Sutpen, who vanished for a generation, only to reappear at the beginning of the next century like a futile ghost out of a dead but lingering past. And there were the three women: Judith, Clytie, and Rosa Coldfield. Judith had been intended *"by the tradition in which Thomas Sutpen's ruthless will had carved a niche to pass through the soft insulated and unscathed cocoon stages: bud, served prolific queen, then potent and soft-handed matriarch of old age's serene and well-lived content"* (p. 156). Instead, she had become *"the bowed and unwived widow kneeling"* (p. 138) beside her lover's corpse. She lived on in the empty and rotting house, scraping out a meager existence by doing a man's labor. In silent, stoic joylessness she survived the privations of the War and Reconstruction. Her mulatto sister, Clytie, continued long beyond Judith's death as the guardian of her master's house. Clytie represents the Negro family servant so involved with her white folks that she could make no life of her own. Finally there was Miss Rosa. Conceived in her parents' old age, as Gail Hightower had been, she passed from a warped childhood to a spinster's dream world and became a writer of odes to Confederate heroes. But the emotional thrust of her life derived from her hatred of Sutpen, a hatred which stemmed mainly from his matter-of-fact proposal "'that they try it first and if it was a boy and lived, they would be married'" (p. 284). Faulkner's characterization of Miss Rosa has been generally rendered in broad paradox and sly irony. She is both the chaste Southern woman and warped old maid; the romantic defender of the South and paranoiac hater of its supreme representative, Thomas Sutpen; vicarious bride in her dreams to Charles Bon and hater of the Negro. So shielded had she been from the realities of the Old South, Rosa Coldfield never knew she had loved the "nigger" son of Thomas Sutpen.

The true heir of the grand "design" was Charles Etienne Saint-Valery Bon, only child of Thomas Sutpen's elder son. Neither black nor white, living in a much less fortunate time and having less than his father, he became the classic mulatto pariah. He struggled to find his identity by marrying a coal-black woman and living a Negro's life; but he could only express himself by destroying himself, by "treading the thorny and flintpaved path toward the Gethsemane [sic] which he had decreed and created for himself, where he had crucified himself and come down from his cross for a moment and now returned to it" (p. 209). "With a furious and indomitable desperation" (p. 202) he flung the gage of his apparently futile challenge in the white world's face and turned from his "emancipation" to death.

As the nineteenth century yielded to the twentieth, there survived the rotting house, its slave guardian, the death-in-life heir (Henry), and the last Sutpen descendant—the idiot, Jim Bond. It had taken two generations for Bon to become Bond, good to become slave.[31] Not much was left of the planter's baronial dream. Like

[31] I owe this idea to Konrad Hopkins.

the planter's mansion, the dream kept rotting. In December 1909 the house of Sutpen went up in smoke. Only the idiot remained. The others were dead. Dead was the planter with his double family, black and white; dead were the Coldfields, with the shopkeeper's barren puritanism and the spinster's barren gentility; and dead was the poor white family of Wash Jones.

A mood of despair and futility pervades this story of the South. Even the most decent of men, General Compson, could only conclude when touched by the misery and destructiveness of Valery Bon's life, " 'Better that he were dead, better that he had never lived' " (p. 205). Yet the despair has been quickened by a kind of fierce, underground idealism. Valery Bon destroyed himself not only because he would rather be dead but because he felt compelled to make a protest against the system which denies his people their human rights. Even Wash Jones's life ended in protest. From an anguished and outraged heart Faulkner has cried out in *Absalom* against an evil implanted in his South.

Faulkner has presented Sutpen as the source of the evil, but he has presented him too as the only heroic figure in the story. Sutpen is both the pride and shame of the South. For a Quentin Compson the ambivalence of his feelings about his heritage is further complicated by the reality of the present. His heritage is peculiarly compounded of accomplishment and defeat, innocence, and guilt, pride and defensiveness. The ruthless planter-backwoodsman who built his house upon slavery and lived as if the evil were a positive good is dead and gone. For his descendants, accomplishment has often become but a memory, pride has become delusion, and innocence has become unacknowledgeable guilt. As loyalty to the Old South has turned into savage racism, the planter's power to act has deteriorated for his twentieth-century descendants into a stasis of will.

For Quentin, as for his father, Sutpen represented another time when men were "simpler and therefore, integer for integer, larger, more heroic and the figures therefore more heroic too, not dwarfed and involved but distinct, uncomplex who had the gift of loving once or dying once instead of being diffused and scattered creatures drawn blindly limb from limb from a grab bag and assembled" (p. 89). Out of his sense of impotence and alienation, Quentin, like Bon himself, seemed to turn to the godlike Sutpen for the power and virility he lacked, for the father who would solve the son's dilemma. But the giant, rising out of the past like a swiftly growing

djinn from Aladdin's lamp, threatened to consume rather than renew the puny summoner. The vision of the South that Quentin
invoked left him shivering, "panting in the cold air, the iron New
England dark; *I dont. I dont! I dont hate it! I dont hate it!*" (p.
378). Even in the alien air of New England the South was too much
with him. The burden of its history lay heavy upon Quentin
Compson. Torn by loyalty and guilt, by the desire to defend and
the need to expiate, by the desire to suppress and the need to confess, he could only cry out against his burden. And this is how the
novel ends—with the sins of the past unexpiated and the dilemma
of the present apparently irresoluble.

Editor's Note: "Sutpen and the South: A study of *Absalom, Absalom!*" is reprinted by permission of the Modern Language Association from *PMLA,* LXXX (1965), pp. 596–604.

Professor Backman, who teaches at C. W. Post College, Long
Island University, has published numerous articles on Hemingway
and Faulkner. His latest publication is *Faulkner: The Major Years.*

BIBLIOGRAPHY

The following is an introduction to methods and materials for further study of American literature. A Note on American Literary Scholarship discusses the location of scholarship and criticism and provides a selected list of books which contain more thorough bibliographical information. In the Bibliography appears first a list of central thematic studies, critical works and literary histories. Each of the selected reading lists for individual authors, found following each section of the text, contains at least one standard biography, a work of criticism, and a selection of essays indicating the range of existing critical approaches. As in the General Section, our offerings have necessarily been directive rather than complete. The student should also remember that some of the best writing on a certain author may very likely appear in a book listed in the General Section of the Bibliography.

A Note on American Literary Scholarship

PMLA Annual Bibliography

All students of literature should become familiar with *Publications of The Modern Language Association*, abbreviated *PMLA*, our primary and most widely distributed journal in the fields of literary and linguistic scholarship. Each year *PMLA* devotes one issue to an "International Bibliography" of works, criticism and scholarship published in the preceding year, which is comprehensive far beyond the needs of the undergraduate student of American literature. While the regular issues of *PMLA* and other periodicals are usually found in the stacks of college libraries, the *PMLA* Annual Bibliographies are often separated, bound together, and placed in reference rooms, since they are a kind of specialized "card catalogue."

The American literature section of each Annual Bibliography is divided into five sections: I. General; II. Seventeenth and Eighteenth Centuries; III. Nineteenth Century, 1800–1870; IV. Nineteenth Century, 1870–1900; and V. Twentieth Century. Each section is then alphabetically organized according to author, with additional entries such as "Special Bibliographies, Check Lists, and Dictionaries," "Miscellaneous," "Ballad and Folksong," "Fiction," "Transcendentalism," *"Federalist."* Thus it is quite simple to find out, for example, what was published on Melville in any given year.

In the absence of more specific directives, it is generally good strategy to examine recent criticism and scholarship first, for even in the cases when it is not inherently more valuable than earlier material, it still will direct one to earlier works which have proven useful or provocative. Critical articles frequently begin by summarizing the history of a literary controversy; often they contain portmanteau footnotes listing previous works which in the author's opinion are most relevant to his subject (e. g., see the beginning of James Dean Young's "The Nine Gams of the *Pequod*," vol. I, page 387; or that of Melvin Backman's "Sutpen and the South: A Study of *Absalom, Absalom!*" vol. II, page 416.) As the student learns more about a subject, he will soon realize that he cannot rely upon the selected bibliographies of others, but in the early stages of reading, such summaries are often helpful.

Other Bibliographical Aids

In addition to *PMLA,* the student of American literature will want to be aware of at least two other journals: *American Literature,* the main periodical in its field, contains a bibliography at the end of each issue; and *American Quarterly* publishes a bibliography on American studies, including such areas as intellectual and social history in addition to literary subjects.

Also, important bibliographies on special subjects are continually being compiled and published under separate cover. Especially helpful to American literary studies are the following:

Bond, Donald F. *A Reference Guide to English Studies.* Chicago, 1962. (General guide to bibliographies, methods of research, library catalogues, newspapers, periodicals, learned societies, and other topics related to English and American literature. Separate section on American literature. Available in paperback.)

Gohdes, Clarence. *Bibliographical Guide to the Study of the Literature of the U. S. A.* Durham, N. C., 1959. (Lists books relevant to the study of American literature.)

The Golden Tree Bibliographies:
C. Hugh Holman. *The American Novel Through Henry James.* New York, 1966.

E. Hudson Long. *American Drama from its Beginnings to the Present.* New York, 1966.
(Concise and reliable paperback guides to the important scholarship.)

Handlin, Oscar, Arthur M. Schlesinger, and others, eds. *Harvard Guide to American History.* Cambridge, 1954. (Helpful in directing readings in history, the arts, literature, philosophy, and the social sciences. Available in paperback.)

Jones, Howard Mumford, and Richard M. Ludwig. *Guide to American Literature and its Backgrounds Since 1890.* Cambridge, 1964. (In addition to the bibliography, this work contains useful chronologies, lists and descriptions of important historical, literary and cultural events. Available in paperback.)

Leary, Lewis. *Articles on American Literature 1900-1950.* Durham, N. C., 1954. (This work has been supplemented by *Index to Articles on American Literature, 1951–1959, Prepared in the Reference Department of the University of Pennsylvania Library* [Boston, 1960], a compilation from the quarterly bibliographies in *American Literature* for those years.)

Spiller, Robert Ernest, Willard Thorp, Thomas H. Johnson, Henry Seidel Canby, and Richard M. Ludwig, eds. *Literary History of the United States*. New York, 1963. (Volume III is a bibliography.)

Stovall, Floyd, ed. *Eight American Authors: A Review of Research and Criticism*. New York, 1956. (Useful historical surveys of criticism and scholarship on Poe, Emerson, Hawthorne, Thoreau, Melville, Whitman, Mark Twain, and Henry James. Available in paperback.)

GENERAL BIBLIOGRAPHY

Ahnebrink, Lars. *The Beginnings of Naturalism in American Fiction: A Study of the Works of Hamlin Garland, Stephen Crane, and Frank Norris with Special Reference to Some European Influences, 1891–1903.* New York, 1961.

Beach, Joseph W. *American Fiction, 1920–1940.* New York, 1941.

Beard, Charles A. and Mary R. *The Rise of American Civilization.* New York, 1927–1942. (A significant study of American history and civilization.)

Cargill, Oscar. *Intellectual America: Ideas on the March.* New York, 1941. (A study of the influence of European ideas on American literature.)

Chase, Richard. *The American Novel and Its Tradition.* New York, 1957. (Techniques of the Romance in American fiction.)

Cowie, Alexander. *The Rise of the American Novel.* New York, 1948. (Reliable discussion of the important novelists through James.)

Feidelson, Charles, Jr. *Symbolism and American Literature.* Chicago, 1953. (A modern study of artistic techniques in American writing; emphasis on nineteenth century masters.)

Fiedler, Leslie. *Love and Death in the American Novel.* New York, 1960. (A provocative, controversial study diagnosing American life and literature.)

Gregory, Horace and Marya Zaturenska. *A History of American Poetry: 1900–1940.* New York, 1942.

Hart, James D. *The Oxford Companion to American Literature.* New York, 1956. (Alphabetic reference to literary and related subjects. Short biographies, summaries, bibliographies, etc.)

Hoffman, Frederick J. *The Twenties: American Writing in the Postwar Decade.* New York, 1962.

Lewis, R. W. B. *The American Adam: Innocence, Tragedy, and Tradition in the Nineteenth Century.* Chicago, 1955. (An approach to American literature from a mythic point of view.)

Matthiessen, F. O. *American Renaissance: Art and Expression in the Age of Emerson and Whitman.* New York, 1941. (The most important single treatment of Emerson, Thoreau, Hawthorne, Melville and Whitman.)

Miller, Perry. *The New England Mind: The Seventeenth Century.* New York, 1939. *The New England Mind: From Colony to Province.* Cambridge, 1953. (Two standard interpretations of early religious thought in America.)

Parrington, Vernon L. *Main Currents in American Thought.* New York, 1927-1930. (An important reinterpretation of American writers by way of social and political forces.)

Pearce, Roy Harvey. *The Continuity of American Poetry.* Princeton, 1961. (Excellent history of the central developments.)

Pizer, Donald. *Realism and Naturalism in Nineteenth-Century Literature.* Carbondale, Illinois, 1966. (Howells, Mark Twain, James, Norris, Dreiser.)

Schneider, Herbert. *A History of American Philosophy.* New York, 1946. (A survey of American thought from colonial times to the present.)

_____. *The Puritan Mind.* New York, 1930. (Still the best single study of American Puritanism.)

Smith, Henry Nash. *Virgin Land: The American West as Symbol and Myth.* Cambridge, Mass., 1950.

Spiller, Robert Ernest, Willard Thorp, Thomas H. Johnson, Henry Seidel Canby, and Richard M. Ludwig, eds. *Literary History of the United States.* New York, 1963. (The most extensive history of American literature; in three volumes, the third a bibliography.)

Taylor, Walter F. *The Story of American Letters.* Chicago, 1956. (A standard history of literature in the United States, revised from *A History of American Letters,* 1936.)

Tyler, Moses Coit. *A History of American Literature: 1607–1765.* New York, 1878, new printing, 1962.

INDIVIDUAL BIBLIOGRAPHIES

WALT WHITMAN

Allen, Gay W. *The Solitary Singer: Walt Whitman.* New York, 1955, 1959. [Comprehensive critical biography with good bibliographical listings.]

_____. *Walt Whitman Handbook.* Chicago, 1946, 1957.

_____. *Walt Whitman as Man, Poet, and Legend, With a Checklist of Whitman Publications 1945–1966.* Carbondale, Ill., 1961.

Asselineau, Roger. *The Evolution of Walt Whitman,* 2 vols., trans. from French. Cambridge, Mass., 1960, 1962.

Chase, Richard. *Walt Whitman Reconsidered.* New York, 1955.

Miller, James E., Jr. *Walt Whitman.* New York, 1962. [Useful general introduction.]

Adams, Richard P. "Whitman: A Brief Reevaluation," *Tulane Studies in English,* V (1955), 111–149.

Coffman, Stanley K., Jr. "Form and Meaning in Whitman's 'Passage to India,' " *PMLA,* LXX (1955), 337–349.

Fussell, Paul, Jr. "Whitman's Curious Warble: Reminiscence and Reconciliation," in *The Presence of Walt Whitman: Selected Papers from the English Institute.* New York, 1962. pp. 28–51.

Gargano, James W. "Technique in 'Crossing Brooklyn Ferry': The Everlasting Moment," *Journal of English and Germanic Philology,* LXII (1963), 262–269.

Griffin, Robert J. "Notes on Structural Devices in Whitman's Poetry," *Tennessee Studies in Literature,* VI (1961), 15–24.

Jarrell, Randall. "Some Lines from Whitman," in Jarrell's *Poetry and the Age.* New York, 1953, pp, 112–132.

Kinnaird, John. *"Leaves of Grass* and the American Paradox," *Partisan Review,* XXV (1958), 380–405.

Miles, Josephine. "The Poetry of Praise," *Kenyon Review,* XXIII (1961), 104–125.

Miller, Perry. "The Shaping of the American Character," *New England Quarterly,* XXVIII (1955), 435–454.

EMILY DICKINSON

Anderson, Charles R. *Emily Dickinson's Poetry: The Stairway of Surprise.* New York, 1960 [Devoted exclusively to criticism of the poetry.]

Chase, Richard. *Emily Dickinson.* New York, 1951. [A critical study; American Men of Letters Series.]

Griffith, Clark. *The Long Shadow: Emily Dickinson's Tragic Poetry.* Princeton, N.J., 1964. [Argues that Emily Dickinson's best poetry is not reflective of an essentially optimistic mind.]

Johnson, Thomas H. *Emily Dickinson: An Interpretive Biography.* Cambridge, Mass., 1955.

Ward, Theodora. *The Capsule of the Mind: Chapters in the Life of Emily Dickinson.* Cambridge, Mass., 1961. [A sensitive speculation about the relationship between Emily Dickinson's art and life.]

Whicher, George F. *This Was a Poet: A Critical Biography of Emily Dickinson.* New York, 1938.

Aiken, Conrad. "Emily Dickinson," in Aiken's *A Reviewer's ABC.* New York, 1935.

Banzer, Judith. " 'Compound Manner': Emily Dickinson and the Metaphysical Poets," *American Literature,* XXXII (1961), 417–433.

Blackmur, Richard P. "Emily Dickinson's Notation," *Kenyon Review,* XVIII (1956), 224–237.

Bogan, Louise. "A Mystical Poet," in *Emily Dickinson, Three Views: Papers Delivered at Amherst College. . . .* Amherst, Mass., 1959.

MacLeish, Archibald. "The Private World: Poems of Emily Dickinson," in MacLeish's *Poetry and Experience.* Boston, 1960.

Ransom, John Crowe. "Emily Dickinson: A Poet Restored," *Perspectives, USA,* No. 15 (1956), 5–20.

Tate, Allen. "Emily Dickinson," in Tate's *The Man of Letters in the Modern World.* New York, 1956.

Warren, Austin. "Emily Dickinson," *Sewanee Review,* LXV (1957), 565–586.

Wilbur, Richard. "Sumptuous Destitution," in *Emily Dickinson: Three Views: Papers Delivered at Amherst College. . . .* Amherst, Mass., 1959.

Wilson, Suzanne M. "Structural Patterns in the Poetry of Emily Dickinson," *American Literature,* XXXV (1963), 53–59.

ROBERT FROST

Brower, Reuben A. *The Poetry of Robert Frost: Constellations of Intention.* New York, 1963.

Cook, Reginald. L. *The Dimensions of Robert Frost.* New York, 1958.

Cox, Sidney. *A Swinger of Birches: A Portrait of Robert Frost.* New York, 1957.

Lynen, John F. *The Pastoral Art of Robert Frost.* New Haven, Conn., 1960.

Squires, Radcliffe. *The Major Themes of Robert Frost.* Ann Arbor, Mich., 1963.

Thompson, Lawrance. *Fire and Ice: The Art and Thought of Robert Frost.* New York, 1942.

_____. *Robert Frost: The Early Years, 1874–1915.* New York, 1966. [First volume in a definitive life of Frost.]

Beach, Joseph Warren. "Robert Frost," *Yale Review,* XLIII (1954), 204–217.

Coursen, Herbert R., Jr. "A Dramatic Necessity: The Poetry of Robert Frost," *Bucknell Review,* X (1961), 138–147.

Hepburn, James G. "Robert Frost and His Critics," *New England Quarterly,* XXXV (1962), 367–376.

Hopkins, Vivian C. "Robert Frost: Out Far and In Deep," *Western Humanities Review,* XIV (1960), 247–263.

Irwin, W. R. "Robert Frost and the Comic Spirit," *American Literature,* XXXV (1963), 299–310.

Jarrell, Randall. "To the Laodiceans," in Jarrell's *Poetry and the Age.* New York, 1953.

Juhnke, Anna K. "Religion in Robert Frost's Poetry: The Play for Self-Possession," *American Literature,* XXXVI (1964), 153–164.

Montgomery, Marion. "Robert Frost and His Use of Barriers: Man *vs.* Nature Toward God," *South Atlantic Quarterly,* LVII (1958), 339–353.

O'Donnell, W. G. "Robert Frost and New England: A Reevaluation," *Yale Review,* XXXVII (1948), 698–712.

Trilling, Lionel. "A Speech on Robert Frost: A Cultural Episode," *Partisan Review,* XXVI (1959), 445–452.

Watts, Harold H. "Robert Frost and the Interrupted Dialogue," *American Literature,* XXVII (1955), 69–87.

Winters, Yvor. "Robert Frost: or, the Spiritual Drifter as Poet," in Winters' *The Function of Criticism: Problems and Exercises.* Denver, 1957.

T. S. ELIOT

Drew, Elizabeth. *T. S. Eliot: The Design of His Poetry.* New York, 1949. [Good introduction; a Jungian archetypal approach.]

Gardner, Helen. *The Art of T. S. Eliot.* New York, 1959. [Good general introduction.]

Matthiessen, F. O. *The Achievement of T. S. Eliot.* New York, 1959. [An early study which maintains its usefulness.]

Rajan, B., ed. *T. S. Eliot, a Study of his Writings by Several Hands.* New York, 1948.

Smith, Grover, Jr. *T. S. Eliot's Poetry and Plays: A Study in Sources and Meaning.* Chicago, 1956.

Tate, Allen, ed. *T. S. Eliot (1888–1965). Sewanee Review* (special issue), LXXIV (1966). [By various hands, primarily reminiscences both personal and literary.]

Unger, Leonard, ed. *T. S. Eliot: A Selected Critique.* New York, 1948. [A collection of substantial essays.]

Williamson, George. *A Reader's Guide to T. S. Eliot: A Poem-by-poem Analysis.* New York, 1953.

Adams, Robert M. "Donne and Eliot: Metaphysicals," *Kenyon Review,* XVI (1954), 278–291.

Blackmur, Richard P. "T. S. Eliot From '*Ash Wednesday*' to '*Murder in the Cathedral.*'" and "Unappeasable and Peregrine: Behavior and the 'Four Quartets,'" in Blackmur's *Language as Gesture.* New York, 1952.

Boardman, Gwenn R. "*Ash Wednesday:* Eliot's Lenten Mass Sequence," *Renascence,* XV (1962), 28–36.

Brooks, Cleanth. "The Waste Land," in Brooks' *Modern Poetry and the Tradition.* Chapel Hill, N. C., 1939.

McConnell, Daniel J. "*The Heart of Darkness* in T. S. Eliot's 'The Hollow Men,'" *Texas Studies in Literature and Language,* IV (1962), 141–153.

Strothmann, Friedrich W. and Lawrence V. Ryan. "Hope for T. S. Eliot's 'Empty Men,'" *PMLA,* LXXIII (1958), 426–432.

Weatherhead, A. Kingsley. "Four Quartets: Setting Love in Order," *Wisconsin Studies in Contemporary Literature,* III (1962), 32–49.

Wellek, René. "The Criticism of T. S. Eliot," *Sewanee Review,* LXIV (1956), 398–443.

Wilson, Edmund. "T. S. Eliot," in Wilson's *Axel's Castle.* New York, 1931.

WALLACE STEVENS

Doggett, Frank. *Stevens' Poetry of Thought.* Baltimore, 1966. [Influence of contemporaries upon Stevens.]

Enck, John J. *Wallace Stevens: Images and Judgments.* Carbondale, Ill., 1964.

Morse, Samuel F., Jackson R. Bryer, and Joseph N. Riddel. *Wallace Stevens Checklist and Bibliography of Stevens Criticism.* Denver, Colo., 1963.

Pack, Robert. *Wallace Stevens—An Approach to His Poetry and Thought.* New Brunswick, N. J., 1958.

Bewley, Marius. "The Poetry of Wallace Stevens," in Bewley's *The Complex Fate.* London, 1952.

Blackmur, Richard P. "Examples of Wallace Stevens," and "Wallace Stevens: An Abstraction Blooded," in Blackmur's *Language as Gesture.* New York, 1952.

Brown, Merle E. "Concordia Discors in the Poetry of Wallace Stevens," *American Literature,* XXXIV (1962), 246–269.

Frye, Northrop. "The Realistic Oriole: A Study of Wallace Stevens," *Hudson Review,* X (1957), 353–370.

Jarrell, Randall. "The Collected Poems of Wallace Stevens," *Yale Review,* n. s. XLIV (1955), 340–353.

McFadden, George. "Poet, Nature, and Society in Wallace Stevens," *Modern Language Quarterly,* XXIII (1962), 263–271.

McNamara, Peter L. "The Multi-Faceted Blackbird and Wallace Stevens' Poetic Vision," *College English,* XXV (1964), 446–448.

Martz, Louis L. "Wallace Stevens: The World as Meditation," in *Literature and Belief: English Institute Essays, 1957.* New York, 1958.

Mills, Ralph J., Jr. "Wallace Stevens: The Image of the Rock," *Accent,* XVIII (1958), 75-89.

Nemerov, Howard. "Wallace Stevens and the Voices of Imagination," *Carlton Miscellany.* IV (1963), 90–97.

Riddel, Joseph N. "Wallace Stevens' 'Visibility of Thought,'" *PMLA,* LXXVII (1962), 482–498.

SAMUEL CLEMENS

Andrews, Kenneth R. *Nook Farm: Mark Twain's Hartford Circle.* Cambridge, Mass., 1950. [Twain's cultural environment carefully described.]

Brooks, Van Wyck. *The Ordeal of Mark Twain.* New York, 1920. [Diagnoses intellectual and psychological causes for the limitations of Twain's art.]

DeVoto, Bernard. *Mark Twain's America.* Boston, Mass., 1932. [Argument opposed to Brooks's thesis.]

Kaplan, Justin. *Mr. Clemens and Mark Twain: A Biography.* New York, 1966. [Vivid description of Twain's life from age thirty-one (1866).]

Paine, Albert Bigelow. *Mark Twain, A Biography: The Personal and Literary Life of Samuel Langhorne Clemens.* 3 vols. New York, 1912. [Authorized biography by Twain's personal secretary.]

Smith, Henry Nash. *Mark Twain: The Development of a Writer.* Cambridge, Mass., 1962. [Study of Form in the major works.]

Wecter, Dixon. *Sam Clemens of Hannibal.* Boston, 1952. [Carefully detailed study of Twain to age eighteen, with parallels drawn to his works.]

Adams, Richard P. "The Unity and Coherence of *Huckleberry Finn,*" *Tulane Studies in English,* VI (1956), 87–103.

Blair, Walter. "On the Structure of *Tom Sawyer,*" *Modern Philology,* XXXVII (1939), 75–88.

Cox, James M. *"A Connecticut Yankee in King Arthur's Court:* The Machinery of Self-Preservation." *Yale Review,* L (1960), 89–102.

Eliot, T. S. "Introduction," to *The Adventures of Huckleberry Finn,* London, 1950.

Fiedler, Leslie. "Come Back to the Raft Ag'in, Huck Honey!" in Fiedler's *An End to Innocence.* Boston, 1952.

Fussell, E. S. "The Structural Problem in *The Mysterious Stranger.*" *Studies in Philology.* LXIX (1952), 95–104.

Hanson, Chadwick. "The Character of Jim and the Ending of *Huckleberry Finn,*" *Massachusetts Review,* V (1963), 45–66.

Kaplan, Charles. "Holden and Huck: The Odysseys of Youth," *College English,* XVIII (1956), 76–80.

Leavis, F. R. "Mark Twain's Neglected Classic: The Moral Astringency of 'Pudd'nhead Wilson,' " *Commentary,* XXI (1956), 128–136.

Levy, Leo B. "Society and Conscience in *Huckleberry Finn,*" *Nineteenth-Century Fiction,* XVIII (1964), 383–391.

Lynn, Kenneth. "Huck and Jim," *Yale Review,* XLVII (1958), 421–431.

Macdonald, Dwight. "Mark Twain: An Unsentimental Journey," *The New Yorker,* XXXVI (April 9, 1960), 160–196.

Marx, Leo. "The Pilot and the Passenger: Landscape Conventions and the Style of *Huckleberry Finn,*" *American Literature,* XXVIII (1956), 129–146.

Smith, Henry Nash. "Mark Twain's Images of Hannibal: From St. Petersburg to Eseldorf," *The University of Texas Studies in English,* XXXVII (1958), 3–23.

Tanner, Tony. "The Lost America—The Despair of Henry Adams and Mark Twain," *Modern Age,* V (1961), 299–310.

Trilling, Lionel. "Huckleberry Finn," in Trilling's *The Liberal Imagination: Essays on Literature and Society.* New York, 1950.

HENRY JAMES

Bewley, Marius. *The Complex Fate: Hawthorne, Henry James and Some Other American Writers.* London, 1952.

Cargill, Oscar. *The Novels of Henry James.* New York, 1961. [Defines what the issues have been in James criticism.]

Crews, Frederick C. *The Tragedy of Manners: Moral Drama in the Later Novels of Henry James.* New Haven, Conn., 1957.

Edel, Leon. *Henry James: The Untried Years, 1843–1870; The Conquest of London, 1870–1881;* and *The Middle Years,* 1882–1895. Philadelphia, 1953, 1962, and 1962, respectively. [A fourth volume will complete this biography.]

Geismar, Maxwell. *Henry James and the Jacobites.* Boston, 1963.

Matthiessen, F. O. *The James Family: Including Selections from the Writings of Henry James, Senior, William, Henry, and Alice James.* New York, 1947. [Chronology (not comprehensive), illustrations. Good choice of quotations. Not recommended for biographical data.]

Poirer, Richard. *The Comic Sense of Henry James: A Study of the Early Novels.* New York, 1960.

Stone, Edward. *The Battle and the Books: Some Aspects of Henry James.* Athens, Ohio, 1964. [Reviews the critical controversies James has provoked.]

Blackmur, Richard P. "The Loose and Baggy Monsters of Henry James: Notes on the Underlying Classic Form in the Novel," *Accent,* XI (1951), 129–146.

Dove, J. R. "The Tragic Sense in Henry James," *Texas Studies in Literature and Language,* II (1960), 302–314.

Emerson, Donald. "Henry James and the Limitations of Realism," *College English,* XXII (1960), 161–166.

Falk, Robert. *The Victorian Mode in American Fiction,* 1865–1885. East Lansing, Michigan, 1965. [Emphases upon James, Howells, DeForest, Mark Twain.]

Garis, R. E. "The Two Lambert Strethers: A New Reading of *The Ambassadors,*" *Modern Fiction Studies,* VII (1961–62), 305–316.

Hoffman, Frederick J. "Freedom and Conscious Form: Henry James and the American Self," *Virginia Quarterly Review,* XXXVII (1961), 269–285.

Ward, J. A. "The Ineffectual Heroes of James's Middle Period," *Texas Studies in Literature and Language,* II (1960), 315–327.

Warren, Austin. "Symbolic Imagery in the Later Novels," in Warren's *A Rage for Order,* Chicago, 1948. [Emphases upon *The Wings of the Dove, The Golden Bowl, The Sense of the Past, The Ivory Tower.*]

Wellek, Rene. "Henry James's Literary Theory and Criticism," *American Literature,* XXX (1958), 293–321.

STEPHEN CRANE

Berryman, John. *Stephen Crane.* New York, 1950. [A clever, ambitious study of Crane's sensibility.]

Cady, Edwin H. *Stephen Crane.* New York, 1962. [Twayne series.]

Hoffman, Daniel G. *The Poetry of Stephen Crane.* New York, 1957. [Poetry approached via Crane's spiritual and imaginative preoccupations.]

Solomon, Eric. *Stephen Crane, From Parody to Realism.* Cambridge, Mass., 1966.

Dillingham, William B. "Insensibility in *The Red Badge of Courage,*" *College English,* XXV (1963), 194–198.

Greenfield, Stanley B. "The Unmistakable Stephen Crane," *PMLA,* LXXIII (1958), 562–572. [Assessment of irony in *Red Badge.*]

Johnson, George W. "Stephen Crane's Metaphor of Decorum," *PMLA,* LXXVIII (1963), 250–256.

Marcus, Mordecai and Erin. "Animal Imagery in *The Red Badge of Courage,*" *Modern Language Notes,* LXXIV (1959), 108–111.

Rosenfeld, Issac. "Stephen Crane as Symbolist," *Kenyon Review,* XV (1953), 310–314.

Stallmen, Robert W. "Stephen Crane: A Reevaluation," in *Critiques and Essays on Modern Fiction, 1920–1951,* ed. John W. Aldridge, New York, 1952. [A germinal, controversial essay.]

West, Ray B., Jr. "Stephen Crane: Author in Transition," *American Literature,* XXXIV (1962), 213–228. [Illustrates the effects of conflicting aesthetic assumptions upon Crane's art.]

ERNEST HEMINGWAY

Baker, Carlos. *Hemingway: The Writer as Artist.* Princeton, N.J., 1964. [The most comprehensive critical biography; third edition, revised, with new chapter on the last decade of Hemingway's life.]

Hotchner, A. E. *Papa Hemingway, a Personal Memoir.* New York, 1966.

Ross, Lillian. *Portrait of Hemingway.* New York, 1961.

Young, Philip. *Ernest Hemingway, A Reconsideration.* University Park: Penn. State University Press, 1966. [Revision of his *Ernest Hemingway* (1952); new forword and afterword.]

Adams, Richard P. "Sunrise out of the Waste Land," *Tulane Studies in English,* IX (1959), 119–131.

Anderson, Charles. "Hemingway's Other Style," *Modern Language Notes,* LXXVI (1961), 434–442.

Backman, Melvin. "Hemingway: The Matador and the Crucified," *Modern Fiction Studies,* I (1955), 2–11.

Burhans, Clinton S., Jr. "The Old Man and the Sea: Hemingway's Tragic Vision of Man," *American Literature,* XXXI (1960), 446–455.

Clendenning, John. "Hemingway's Gods, Dead and Alive," *Texas Studies in Literature and Language,* III (1963), 489–502.

Cowley, Malcolm. "Nightmare and Ritual in Hemingway," Introduction to *The Portable Hemingway,* ed. Malcolm Cowley. New York, 1945.

D'Agostino, Nemi. "The Later Hemingway," trans. Berbera Arnett Melchiori, *Sewanee Review,* LXVIII (1960), 482–493.

Levin, Harry. "Observations on the Style of Hemingway," *Kenyon Review,* XIII (1951), 581–609. [Hemingway is poet more than novelist; concerned with man in nature rather than in society.]

Lewis, Wyndham. "The Dumb Ox, a Study of Ernest Hemingway," *The American Review,* VI (1934), 289–312. Reprinted in *Men Without Women.* London, 1934, pp. 17–40. [A strongly presented negative evaluation.]

Light, James F. "The Religion of Death in *A Farewell to Arms,*" *Modern Fiction Studies,* VII (1961), 169–173.

Montgomery, Marion. "The Leopard and the Hyena: Symbol and Meaning in 'The Snows of Kilimanjaro,'" *University of Kansas City Review,* XXVII (1961), 277–282.

Oldsey Bern. "The Snows of Ernest Hemingway," *Wisconsin Studies in Contemporary Literature,* IV (1963), 172–198.

Spilka, Mark. "The Death of Love in The Sun Also Rises," in Charles Shapiro, ed. *Twelve Original Essays on Great American Novels,* Detroit, 1958, pp. 238–256.

F. SCOTT FITZGERALD

Cross, K. G. W. *F. Scott Fitzgerald.* New York, 1964.

Lehan, Richard. *F. Scott Fitzgerald and the Craft of Fiction.* Carbondale, Ill., 1966.

Miller, James E., Jr. *F. Scott Fitzgerald: His Art and Technique.* New York, 1964.

Mizener, Arthur. *The Far Side of Paradise.* New York, 1959. [Excellent full-length biographical and critical study.]

Perosa, Sergio. *The Art of F. Scott Fitzgerald.* Ann Arbor, Michigan, 1965.

Piper, Henry D. *F. Scott Fitzgerald, A Critical Portrait.* New York, 1965.

Turnbull, Andrew. *Scott Fitzgerald.* New York, 1963.

Berryman, John. "F. Scott Fitzgerald," *Kenyon Review,* VIII (1946), 103–112.

Bewley, Marius. "Scott Fitzgerald's Criticism of America," in Bewley's *The Eccentric Design Form in the Classic American Novel.* New York, 1959, pp. 259–287.

Burnam, Tom. "The Eyes of Dr. Eckleburg: A Re-examination of *The Great Gatsby*," *College English*, XIV (1952), 7–12.

Fiedler, Leslie. "Some Notes on F. Scott Fitzgerald," in Fiedler's *An End to Innocence*. Boston, 1955. [On Fitzgerald and failure.]

Gross, Seymour L. "Fitzgerald's 'Babylon Revisited,'" *College English*, XXV (1963), 128–135.

Hoffman, Frederick J. *The Twenties*. New York, 1962. [Sections on Fitzgerald as epitome of the epoch.]

Ornstein, Robert. "Scott Fitzgerald's Fable of East and West," *College English*, XVIII (1956), 139–143.

Schorer, Mark. "Fitzgerald's Tragic Sense," in *F. Scott Fitzgerald: The Man and his Work*, ed. Alfred Kazin. New York, 1951.

Taylor, Douglas. "*The Great Gatsby*: Style and Myth," *University of Kansas City Review*, XX (1953), 30–40.

Trilling, Lionel. "F. Scott Fitzgerald," in Trilling's *The Liberal Imagination: Essays on Literature and Society*. New York, 1951.

Troy, William. "F. Scott Fitzgerald: The Authority of Failure," *Accent*, VI (1945), 56–60.

WILLIAM FAULKNER

Beck, Warren. *Man in Motion: Faulkner's Trilogy*. Madison, Wisc., 1961. [On *The Hamlet, The Town,* and *The Mansion*.]

Brooks, Cleanth. *William Faulkner: The Yoknapatawpha Country*. New Haven, Conn., 1963. [Perhaps the best full-length study.]

Gwynn, Frederick L., and Joseph L. Blotner, eds. *Faulkner in the University: Class Conferences at the University of Virginia, 1957–1958*. Charlottesville, Va., 1959. [Transcription of questions and answers.]

Hoffman, Frederick J., and Olga W. Vickery, eds. *William Faulkner: Three Decades of Criticism*. East Lansing, Michigan, 1960.

O'Connor, William Van. *The Tangled Fire of William Faulkner*. Minneapolis, 1954. [Critical study of Faulkner's fiction.]

Sleeth, Irene. *Faulkner: A Bibliography of Criticism*. Denver, 1963. [A 28 pg. pamphlet; American criticism from 1920–1961 and selected foreign criticism.]

Utley, Francis Lee, Lynn Z. Bloom, and Arthur F. Kinney, eds. *Bear, Man, and God: Seven Approaches to William Faulkner's "The Bear."* New York, 1964. [Essays and excerpts by various hands.]

Vickery, Olga W. *The Novels of William Faulkner; A Critical Interpretation*. Baton Rouge, La., 1964.

Warren, Robert Penn, ed. *William Faulkner: A Collection of Critical Essays*. Englewood Cliffs, N.J., 1962. [One of the best of the Prentice-

Hall "Twentieth-Century Views" series. Introductory essay by Warren reviews the development of Faulkner criticism.]

Backman, Melvin. "Sickness and Primitivism: A Dominant Pattern in William Faulkner's World," *Accent*, XIV (1964), 61–73.

Chase, Richard. "The Stone and the Crucifixion: Faulkner's *Light in August*," *Kenyon Review*, X (1948), 539–551.

Howe, Irving. "William Faulkner and the Negroes," *Commentary*, XII (1951), 359–368.

Lewis, R. W. B. "The Hero in the New World," in Lewis's *The Picaresque Saint*. New York, 1959. [On *The Bear*.]

Lyndenberg, John. "Nature Myth in William Faulkner's 'The Bear,'" *American Literature*, XXIV (1952), 62–72.

Morrison, Sister Kristin, IHM. "Faulkner's Joe Christmas: Character Through Voice," *Texas Studies in Literature and Language*, II (1961), 419–443.

O'Connor, William Van. "Hawthorne and Faulkner: Some Common Ground," *Virginia Quarterly Review*, XXXIII (1957), 105–123.

O'Donnell, George Marion. "Faulkner's Mythology," *Kenyon Review*, I (1939), 285–299. [An early, germinal study, interpreting Faulkner's works as a coherent whole.]

Warren, Robert Penn. "Faulkner: The South, the Negro, and Time," *Southern Review*, I (1965), 501–529.

INDEX OF
CONTRIBUTING AUTHORS